The European Union's Broader Neighbourhood

Over the past decade the European Union (EU) has gradually developed the European Neighbourhood Policy (ENP) with its neighbours. At the same time, the 'neighbours of the EU's neighbours' have presented new challenges.

This book addresses issues surrounding the EU's broader neighbourhood, comprising the ENP countries and the neighbours of its neighbours. With specific focus on Saharan Africa, the Middle East and Central Asia, it discusses trans-regional policy issues that arise from the EU's relations with regions beyond the ENP. Based on an interdisciplinary, policy-oriented approach, this volume explores major political, legal, security and socio-economic challenges and identifies opportunities for cooperation across the EU's broader neighbourhood.

This book will be of interest to students, experts and scholars interested in EU affairs and politics, international relations, EU and international law, diplomacy and area studies.

Sieglinde Gstöhl is Director of the Department of EU International Relations and Diplomacy Studies at the College of Europe in Bruges.

Erwan Lannon is Professor in European Law at the Faculty of Law of Ghent University and Visiting Professor at the College of Europe in Bruges and Natolin.

Routledge Series on Global Order Studies
Edited by David Armstrong
University of Exeter, UK
and
Karoline Postel-Vinay
CERI, Sciences-Po, Paris, France

This new series focuses on the major global issues that have surfaced in recent years which will pose significant and complex challenges to global governance in the next few decades. The books will explore challenges to the current global order and relate to these themes:

- The Challenge to Western Dominance
- The Challenge to International Governance
- Religion, Nationalism and Extremism
- Sustainable Growth
- Global Justice and the Poorest Countries
- The Implications of the Global Economic Crisis for Future World Order

Redefining Regional Power in International Relations
Indian and South African perspectives
Miriam Prys

Turkey between Nationalism and Globalization
Riva Kastoryano

Contemporary Political Agency
Theory and practice
Edited by Bice Maiguashca and Raffaele Marchetti

1989 as a Political World Event
Democracy, Europe and the new international system in the age of globalization
Edited by Jacques Rupnik

EU Policies in a Global Perspective
Shaping or taking international regimes?
Edited by Gerda Falkner and Patrick Müller

Immigration Detention
The migration of a policy and its human impact
Edited by Amy Nethery and Stephanie J. Silverman

The European Union's Broader Neighbourhood
Challenges and opportunities for cooperation beyond the European Neighbourhood Policy
Edited by Sieglinde Gstöhl and Erwan Lannon

Nordic Cooperation
A European region in transition
Edited by Johan Strang

Empires of Remorse
Narrative, postcolonialism and
apologies for colonial atrocity
Tom Bentley

The European Union's Broader Neighbourhood

Challenges and opportunities for cooperation beyond the European Neighbourhood Policy

Edited by Sieglinde Gstöhl and Erwan Lannon

Routledge
Taylor & Francis Group

LONDON AND NEW YORK

First published 2015
by Routledge

2 Park Square, Milton Park, Abingdon, Oxon OX14 4RN
711 Third Avenue, New York, NY 10017, USA

*Routledge is an imprint of the Taylor & Francis Group,
an informa business*

First issued in paperback 2017

British Library Cataloguing in Publication Data
A catalogue record for this book is available from the British Library

Library of Congress Cataloging in Publication Data
The European Union's broader neighbourhood : challenges and
opportunities for co-operation beyond the European neighbourhood policy /
edited by Sieglinde Gstöhl and Erwan Lannon.
    pages cm
    1. European Union countries–Foreign relations. 2. European Union
countries–Foreign economic relations. 3. European Union countries–
Foreign relations–Africa, North. 4. Africa, North–Foreign relations–
European Union countries. 5. European Union countries–Foreign
relations–Middle East. 6. Middle East–Foreign relations–European
Union countries. 7. European Union countries–Foreign relations–Asia,
Central. 8. Asia, Central–Foreign relations–European Union countries.
I. Gstöhl, Sieglinde, editor of compilation. II. Lannon, Erwan, editor of
compilation.
    JZ1570.E93347 2015
    341.242′2–dc23   2015002435

ISBN: 978-1-138-77671-5 (hbk)
ISBN: 978-1-138-71680-3 (pbk)

Typeset in Times New Roman
by Wearset Ltd, Boldon, Tyne and Wear

Contents

viii *Contents*

Tables

Contributors

Alyson J.K. Bailes is Adjunct Professor at the University of Iceland in Reykjavik and Visiting Professor at the College of Europe in Bruges, specializing in security studies. She was a British diplomat and from 2002 to 2007 served as Director of the Stockholm International Peace Research Institute (SIPRI). She is a graduate of Oxford University and has published extensively on issues of European security and defence (including EU strategy), regional security governance, arms control, and the role of non-state actors and of small states.

Valeria Bonavita was, at the time of writing, Senior Academic Assistant in the Department of the EU International Relations and Diplomacy Studies at the College of Europe in Bruges (2012–14). She holds a double PhD degree in EU Law from the Università di Bologna and the Université de Strasbourg (2012), an MA in EU International Relations and Diplomacy Studies from the College of Europe (2008) and an MA and a BA in International and Diplomatic Studies from the Università di Bologna. She has *inter alia* been lecturing EU law at the Faculties of Law and of Political Science of the Università di Bologna and at the China-EU School of Law in Beijing. She has also worked at the European Commission in Brussels and at the Italian Representation to the OSCE in Vienna.

Alessandro Carano is Adviser to the Deputy Director General of the European Commission's Economic and Financial Affairs Directorate-General. Previously he was Managerial Adviser and Head of Unit within the Institutional Strategy Department of the European Investment Bank (EIB). He was responsible for the partnership with EU institutions and international financial institutions on policies and activities outside the EU: enlargement, neighbourhood, development and climate action policies. He has worked *inter alia* on the mid-term review of the EIB external mandate, the establishment of the EU Platform for Blending in External Cooperation, the Western Balkans Investment Framework and other loan–grant blending mechanisms. He has also worked in the projects directorate of the EIB as well as for Procter and Gamble. He holds an MBA from Vlerick Business School and an engineering MSc degree from Turin Polytechnic University.

Gilles de Kerchove has been European Union Counter-terrorism Coordinator since September 2007. He coordinates the work of the EU in the field of counter-terrorism, monitors the implementation of the EU counter-terrorism strategy and fosters better communication between the EU and third countries. Before that he was Director for Justice and Home Affairs at the Council Secretariat. He is a professor of European law at the Université Catholique de Louvain, the Free University of Brussels and at the Université Saint Louis Brussels. He was deputy secretary of the convention that drafted the EU Charter of Fundamental Rights (1999–2000).

Pál Dunay has been Director of the OSCE Academy in Bishkek since May 2014. He was senior programme advisor at the Geneva Centre for Security Policy (GCSP), where he was the course director of the International Training Course in Security Policy (1996–2004, 2005–06 and 2007–14). Between 2004 and early 2007 he was senior researcher at the Stockholm International Peace Research Institute (SIPRI). In 2007 he was Director of the Hungarian Institute of International Affairs and member of the advisory board on foreign and security policy of the Prime Minister of Hungary. He was legal advisor of the Hungarian delegation that negotiated the Treaty on Conventional Armed Forces in Europe (1989–90) and the Open Skies Treaty (1991–92). He taught international law at Loránd Eötvös University in Budapest between 1982 and 1997. He is the author of many scholarly publications on Central Asia among other subjects.

Maud Fichet was, at the time of writing, Academic Assistant in the Department of the EU International Relations and Diplomacy Studies at the College of Europe in Bruges (2013–14). She holds an MA in EU International Relations and Diplomacy Studies from the College of Europe (2011) and an MA in International Relations from the University of St Andrews. She worked previously at the European Parliament as Parliamentary Assistant, at the Invest in France Agency at the French Embassy in Stockholm, at a development aid agency in Beirut and in a consultancy in Paris.

Sieglinde Gstöhl is Director of the Department of EU International Relations and Diplomacy Studies at the College of Europe in Bruges. She has been a professor at the College since 2005. From 1999 to 2005 she was Assistant Professor of International Relations at Humboldt University Berlin. She holds a PhD and an MA in International Relations from the Graduate Institute of International and Development Studies in Geneva as well as a degree in Public Affairs from the University of St. Gallen. She has been *inter alia* a research fellow at the Liechtenstein-Institut and at the Center for International Affairs at Harvard University and worked at the EFTA Secretariat. Her research interests include EU trade policy, the European Neighbourhood Policy, EU diplomacy, EU external representation, global governance and international relations theories.

Zuhal Yeşilyurt Gündüz is Associate Professor in the Department of Political Science and International Relations at TED University in Ankara. From 2001 to 2012 she worked in the Department of Political Science and International Relations at Başkent University in Ankara as Assistant Professor and Associate Professor. She studied Political Science (major), American Language and Literature (minor) and Islamic Sciences (minor) at the University of Bonn. She obtained her PhD in Political Science (2000) from the same university. Her areas of interest include Turkey–EU integration, women and gender, EU–Mediterranean relations, economization and securitization of migration, securitization of Islam, and xenophobia and Islamophobia in the EU.

Tressia Hobeika is a Management Consultant at Oliver Wyman in Dubai. At the time of writing, she was an Academic Assistant in the Department of the EU International Relations and Diplomacy Studies at the College of Europe in Bruges (2012–13). She also worked at the European Parliament in Brussels, at Daimler in Berlin and with various development projects in Beirut. She holds an MA in EU International Relations and Diplomacy Studies (2012) from the College of Europe, an MA in Diplomacy and International Relations from the Diplomatic School of Spain and a BE in Mechanical Engineering from the American University of Beirut.

Christiane Höhn is an adviser to the European Union Counter-terrorism Coordinator. She joined the Council of the European Union in 2004. In her previous assignment, she worked on non-proliferation and disarmament. From 2004 to 2009 she was an administrator working on EU–US and EU–Canada relations as well as on issues relating to counter-terrorism and international human rights and humanitarian law. She holds the German State Examinations in law, an LLM from Harvard Law School and a PhD in International law from Heidelberg University. She also studied at the Graduate Institute for International Studies in Geneva and at Passau University. Prior to joining the EU in 2004, she was a researcher at the Max Planck Institute for International Law in Heidelberg and an Affiliate at the Center for Public Leadership, Harvard Kennedy School.

Enrique Ibáñez is Academic Assistant in the Department of the EU International Relations and Diplomacy Studies at the College of Europe in Bruges. He holds an MA in EU International Relations and Diplomacy Studies from the College of Europe (2013) and an MA in International Relations, Diplomacy and Conflict Resolution from the Université Catholique de Louvain. Both of his MA theses dealt with the southern dimension of the European Neighbourhood Policy. He is also a history graduate from the University of Barcelona.

Anders Jägerskog is Counsellor at the Swedish Embassy in Amman. He was until October 2013 Director at the Stockholm International Water Institute (SIWI), where his work focused on international water issues and in particular transboundary waters and water governance. He is also Associate Professor at the School of Global Studies at the University of Gothenburg. Previously he worked at the secretariat of the Expert Group on Development Issues at the Swedish Ministry for Foreign Affairs, as Senior Programme Manager for

Water Resources at the Embassy of Sweden in Nairobi, at the Swedish International Development Cooperation Agency (SIDA) on water resources in southern Africa and at the Stockholm International Peace Research Institute (SIPRI) on Middle East security issues. He obtained his PhD (2003) from the Department of Water and Environmental Studies at the University of Linköping and has published widely on global water issues.

Erwan Lannon is Professor of European Law at Ghent University (since 2002) and Visiting Professor at the College of Europe (since 2004), where he has also worked in the Department of EU International Relations and Diplomacy Studies as part-time professor (2012–14) and in the Department of European Interdisciplinary Studies as Director of Studies (2009–11). He holds an MA in International Politics and Strategic Studies from the Université Libre de Bruxelles and a PhD in European Law from the Université de Rennes I. Erwan Lannon has worked as researcher at Ghent University and as an expert for EU institutions, the EU Institute for Security Studies, Euromed networks, the United Nations Development Programme and the European International Movement. He has published widely on the EU's external relations.

Veronika Orbetsova was, at the time of writing, Research Assistant to the Inbev-Baillet Latour Chair of European Union–China Relations in the Department of EU International Relations and Diplomacy Studies at the College of Europe in Bruges (2012–14). She graduated from the University of Paris 1 Panthéon-Sorbonne with a double-degree Master's in International Relations and European Affairs, her studies including an exchange with the Moscow State Institute of International Relations (MGIMO). She has worked as an intern at the European External Action Service in Brussels, at the Office for Democratic Institutions and Human Rights of the OSCE in Warsaw and at the Bulgarian Ministry of Foreign Affairs in Sofia.

Johannes Theiss is a researcher interested in EU energy and climate policy, currently working as Associate at Steltemeier & Rawe European Affairs in Brussels. He holds an MA in EU International Relations and Diplomacy Studies from the College of Europe in Bruges (2012) and an MA in Political Science from the Otto-Friedrich University of Bamberg. He has *inter alia* worked as Academic Assistant in the Department of EU International Relations and Diplomacy Studies at the College of Europe (2012–13), at the Latin-American Centre for Relations with Europe in Santiago de Chile, at the Press Office of the Federal Government in Berlin, and at Siemens in Erlangen.

Alexander Warkotsch is a Freelance Security Consultant in Berlin. Previously, he worked as a NATO Civilian Consultant at the International Security Assistance Force Headquarters in Kabul. Between 2007 and 2009 he was a Lecturer for European Studies at King's College London and a postdoctoral fellow at the University of Western Australia in Perth. He holds a diploma in economics and an MA and a PhD in Political Science from the University of Würzburg. He has published widely on Europe's relations with Central Asia.

Sarah Wolff is Lecturer in Public Policy at Queen Mary University of London. She holds a PhD in International Relations (2009) and an MSc in European Politics and Governance from the London School of Economics and Political Science and a BA in Public Administration from Sciences Po Grenoble. Sarah Wolff is also a Senior Research Associate Fellow at the Netherlands Institute for International Relations and in 2014 she was a Fulbright-Schuman Fellow at the Transatlantic Academy in Washington, DC. Her research interests focus on EU migration and democratization policies in North Africa, justice and home affairs, and EU–Arab Mediterranean relations. Thanks to a Leverhulme Trust research grant she is currently researching EU engagement with Islamist actors in Morocco and Tunisia.

Richard Youngs is Senior Associate in the Democracy and Rule of Law Programme at the Carnegie Endowment for International Peace in Brussels. He is also Assistant Professor at the University of Warwick. From 2004 to 2013 he was Director General of FRIDE, a think tank in Madrid. He was Senior Fellow at the Transatlantic Academy in Washington, DC (2012–13), EU Marie Curie Research Fellow at the Norwegian Institute for International Relations in Oslo (2001–04), and Senior Research Fellow at the UK Foreign and Commonwealth Office (1995–98). He holds a PhD and an MA in International Studies from the University of Warwick and a BA in Social and Political Science from the University of Cambridge. Richard Young's research focuses mainly on democracy promotion and democratization, European foreign policy, energy security, and the Middle Eastern and North African region.

Preface

The 'broader neighbourhood' of the European Union (EU) refers to the concept of the 'neighbours of the EU's neighbours' which the European Commission introduced in the framework of the European Neighbourhood Policy (ENP). It mainly covers the countries of Saharan Africa, the Middle East and Central Asia: that is, the neighbours of the ENP countries. This book explores some of the major legal, political, security, economic and societal challenges that these regions – and thus also the EU and its Member States – face and identifies opportunities for cooperation and for better connecting Europe with its neighbours and their neighbours in order to find more efficient responses to the various challenges.

This edited volume builds on the presentations and discussions at the international conference 'The Neighbours of the EU's Neighbours: Legal, Political, Security and Socio-Economic Challenges beyond the ENP', which gathered scholars and practitioners to reflect on the European Union's broader neighbourhood at the College of Europe in Bruges, Belgium, in March 2013. The presentations were subsequently revised and updated, while new contributors joined the project. Most contributions were largely completed in the summer of 2014.

We gratefully acknowledge the financial support of the European Commission for this project. This support does not constitute an endorsement of the contents, which reflect the views only of the authors, and the Commission cannot be held responsible for any use which may be made of the information contained therein.

Sieglinde Gstöhl and Erwan Lannon
Bruges, December 2014

With the support of the
Erasmus+ programme

Abbreviations

AA	Association Agreement
AA-DCFTA	Association Agreement – Deep and Comprehensive Free Trade Area
ACP	African, Caribbean and Pacific countries
AFSJ	Area of Freedom, Security and Justice
AMIS	African Union Mission in Sudan
AMISOM	African Union Mission in Somalia
AMU	Arab Maghreb Union
APF	African Peace Facility
AQIM	Al-Qaeda in the Islamic Maghreb
ATP	autonomous trade preferences
AU	African Union
BOMCA	Border Management Programme in Central Asia
BSEC	Black Sea Economic Cooperation
CADAP	Central Asia Drug Action Programme
CAREC	Central Asia Regional Economic Cooperation
CEDAW	Convention on the Elimination of All Forms of Discrimination Against Women
CEFTA	Central European Free Trade Agreement
CFR	Charter of Fundamental Rights
CFSP	Common Foreign and Security Policy
CICA	Conference on Interaction and Confidence Building Measures in Asia
CIS	Commonwealth of Independent States
CJEU	Court of Justice of the European Union
COTER	Council Working Party on Terrorism (International Aspects)
CSDP	Common Security and Defence Policy
CT	counter-terrorism
DAC	Development Assistance Committee
DCAF	Center for the Democratic Control of the Armed Forces
DCFTA	Deep and Comprehensive Free Trade Area
DCI	Development Cooperation Instrument
DG	Directorate General

DG DEVCO	European Commission Directorate General for Development and Cooperation – EuropeAid (previously DG DEV)
DoP	Declaration of Principles
EASO	European Asylum Support Office
EATL	Euro-Asian Transport Links
EBA	Everything-But-Arms initiative
EBC	externalization of border controls
EC	European Community/Communities
ECHO	European Community Humanitarian Office
ECHR	European Convention on Human Rights
ECOWAS	Economic Community of West African States
ECSC	European Coal and Steel Community
ECT	Energy Charter Treaty
ECtHR	European Court of Human Rights
ECU	Eurasian Customs Union
EDF	European Development Fund
EEA	European Economic Area
EEAS	European External Action Service
EEC	European Economic Community
EEU	Eurasian Economic Union
EFTA	European Free Trade Association
EIB	European Investment Bank
EIDHR	European Instrument for Democracy and Human Rights
EMAA	Euro-Mediterranean Association Agreement
EMFTA	Euro-Mediterranean Free Trade Area
EMP	Euro-Mediterranean Partnership
ENC	Energy Community
ENI	European Neighbourhood Instrument
ENP	European Neighbourhood Policy
ENPI	European Neighbourhood and Partnership Instrument
ENRTP	Thematic Programme for Environment and Sustainable Management of Natural Resources
EPA	Economic Partnership Agreement
ESS	European Security Strategy
EU	European Union
EUAVSEC	EU Aviation Security Mission
EUBAM	EU Border Assistance Mission
EUCAP	EU Capacity-building Mission
EUNAVFOR	EU Naval Force
EurAsEC	Eurasian Economic Community
EUSR	EU Special Representative
FDI	foreign direct investment
FoEME	Friends of the Earth Middle East
FRONTEX	European Agency for the Management of Operational Cooperation at the External Borders of the Member States of the European Union

FTA	free trade agreement
GAFTA	Greater Arab Free Trade Area
GCC	Gulf Cooperation Council
GCTF	Global Counter-terrorism Forum
GDP	gross domestic product
GSP	Generalized System of Preferences
HDI	Human Development Index
HDR	Human Development Report
HR/VP	High Representative of the Union for Foreign Affairs and Security Policy/Vice President of the European Commission
IBM	Integrated Border Management
IBPP	Institution Building Partnership Programme
ICI	Financing Instrument for Cooperation with Industrialized and other High-income Countries and Territories
ICT	information and communications technology
IDP	internally displaced people
IFCA	Investment Facility for Central Asia
IFI	international financial institution
IfS	Instrument for Stability
IGAD	Intergovernmental Authority on Development
INOGATE	Interstate Oil and Gas Transportation to Europe Programme
IOM	International Organization for Migration
ISIL	Islamic State in Iraq and the Levant
JAES	Joint Africa–EU Strategy
JAP	Joint Action Programme
JHA	Justice and Home Affairs
JWC	Joint Water Committee
LDCs	least developed countries
MENA	Middle East and North Africa
MFF	Multiannual Financial Framework
MFN	most-favoured nation
MoU	memorandum of understanding
MPC	Mediterranean Partner Countries
NATO	North Atlantic Treaty Organization
NEC	Neighbourhood Economic Community
NGO	non-governmental organization
NSA/LA	non-state actors/local authority
OAU	Organization of African Unity
ODA	Official Development Assistance
OECD	Organization for Economic Cooperation and Development
OPEC	Organization of the Petroleum Exporting Countries
OSCE	Organization for Security and Cooperation in Europe
PCA	Partnership and Cooperation Agreement
PLO	Palestine Liberation Organization
PPP	public–private partnerships

PSGs	Peacebuilding and Statebuilding Goals
SALW	small arms and light weapons
SES	Single Economic Space
SIPRI	Stockholm International Peace Research Institute
SIWI	Stockholm International Water Institute
SPMME	Strategic Partnership with the Mediterranean and the Middle East
SSR	Security Sector Reform
TAIEX	Technical Assistance and Information Exchange
TEN-E	Trans-European Energy Network
TEN-T	Trans-European Transport Network
TEU	Treaty on the European Union
TFEU	Treaty on the Functioning of the European Union
TRACECA	Transport Corridor Europe Caucasus Asia
TRIM	Transit and Irregular Migration Management
UAE	United Arab Emirates
UEA	Unified Economic Agreement
UFL	Unité de Fusion et de Liaison
UfM	Union for the Mediterranean
UK	United Kingdom
UN	United Nations
UNCTAD	United Nations Conference on Trade and Development
UNCTED	UN Counter-terrorism Executive Directorate
UNDP	United Nations Development Programme
UNECE	United Nations Economic Commission for Europe
UNHCR	United Nations High Commissioner for Refugees
UNIFIL	United Nations Interim Force in Lebanon
UNODC	UN Office for Drugs and Crime
UNTSO	United Nations Truce Supervision Organization
US	United States
WBIF	Western Balkan Investment Framework
WMD	Weapons of Mass Destruction
WTO	World Trade Organization

Introduction

Building bridges between the EU's immediate and broader neighbourhood

Sieglinde Gstöhl and Erwan Lannon

Introduction: the European Union's immediate and broader neighbourhood

On the eve of the Eastern enlargement of the European Union (EU), the European Security Strategy adopted by the European Council (2003: 8) stressed the need 'to promote a ring of well governed countries to the East of the European Union and on the borders of the Mediterranean'. The EU has, since then, been developing and implementing the European Neighbourhood Policy (ENP) with most of its eastern and southern neighbours. The first decade of this policy saw several geopolitically important events, among them the Russo-Georgian war of August 2008; the 'Arab Spring' which began in December 2010 and led to the ousting from power of long-time authoritarian rulers in Tunisia, Egypt and Libya and to civil wars in Libya and Syria; the 'Ukrainian Spring' in 2014 and the annexation of the Crimean peninsula by Russia which was followed by a violent conflict involving pro-Russian separatists in eastern Ukraine; and the Israeli military intervention in the Gaza Strip in the summer of 2014.

These events underlined again the interdependence and the vulnerability of the EU's neighbourhood. Spill-over effects from the ENP countries to their neighbours – be it the EU Member States to the north and west or the neighbours further to the east and south – are often unavoidable as a result of the transnational nature of many challenges. Supported by an influx of weaponry from the Libyan civil war, the 2012 Tuareg rebellion in northern Mali led in 2013 to a larger conflict involving several Islamist groups and finally to foreign military interventions and an EU training mission. The advent of the extremely brutal jihadist 'Islamic State of Iraq and the Levant' (ISIL), which in 2013 made rapid military gains in controlling parts of Syria and in 2014 led large-scale offensives in northern Iraq, demonstrated again the inter-connectedness of the EU's (immediate and broader) neighbourhood.

Security in the southern ENP countries also depends on security in the Sahel and the Horn of Africa as well on the roles played by the Arab Gulf countries – and sometimes other regional actors such as Iran, Iraq and Turkey. The development of stability and prosperity for the EU's eastern neighbours also depends on Russia's foreign policy. The EU and its Member States, with their open economies, cannot insulate themselves from the challenges in their neighbour-hood because they are highly dependent on the security of trade and energy flows and because they are primary targets for immigration and all sorts of trafficking.

Although the European Commission (2006: 11) introduced the concept of 'the neighbours of our neighbours' in Central Asia, the Middle East or Africa early in the implementation phase of the ENP, not much has been achieved in this respect (see Lannon 2014). Insights into the importance of the EU's broader neighbourhood have, however, recently been gaining ground among both scholars and practitioners. Before the Vilnius Summit in November 2013, High Representative Catherine Ashton and Commissioner Štefan Füle reassured the Eastern ENP countries about the inclusivity of the Eastern Partnership: 'the cooperation within the Eastern Partnership, including through the Association Agreements, can be beneficial also for the regional cooperation and for the neighbours of the EU's neighbours' (European External Action Service 2013). According to Commissioner Kristalina Georgieva (2014), however, 'Europe's extended neighbourhood is likely to see more instability, and more risk'. Grevi (2014: 16) argues that 'the neighbourhood should be framed as an extended stra-tegic space stretching from West Africa and the Sahel to Central Asia and Russia, via the broader Middle East' because '[t]his is an area where interde-pendencies run deep, geopolitical shifts are resetting power balances, and state fragility threatens regional stability'. And Biscop (2014: 9) claims that

> the EU has come to realise that 'the neighbours of the neighbours' are often as crucial to our interests. Five partially overlapping and strongly inter-related areas are of vital importance to European security: the eastern neigh-bourhood, the Mediterranean, the Sahel, the Horn of Africa, and the Gulf.

This introductory chapter asks why the broader neighbourhood of the European Union, stretching from the Sahel and the Horn of Africa over the Middle East to Central Asia, should be studied and why the EU might want to design a dedicated policy approach to these regions. It first clarifies the concepts of the 'neighbours of the EU's neighbours' and of the EU's 'broader neighbourhood'. The chapter then illustrates some of the main transnational challenges and the potential for building bridges, and introduces the structure of the volume. The chapter argues that ana-lysing and designing a policy towards the broader neighbourhood is in the direct interest of the European Union – as well as in line with its propagated values – in enabling it to better respond to the many challenges emanating from these regions and to fully take advantage of the opportunities for cooperation.

The EU's broader neighbourhood: looking beyond the immediate neighbourhood

The European Neighbourhood Policy was designed to deal with the EU's 'imme-diate neighbourhood' on its southern and eastern borders. The 2002 European

Council Conclusions referred explicitly to Russia, Ukraine, Moldova, Belarus and the southern Mediterranean, while reaffirming at the same time the 'European perspective of the countries of the Western Balkans' (European Council 2002: 6). Russia ultimately refused to participate in the ENP and in 2004 the European Commission proposed to include the three southern Caucasus countries, Armenia, Georgia and Azerbaijan, in the ENP framework (European Commission 2004: 4).

However, more than 10 years after the policy's launching, some of the EU's immediate neighbours were still not fully included in this policy framework. In the southern Mediterranean, Algeria is still negotiating its first ENP Action Plan whereas Libya and Syria for the time being have no contractual relationships with the EU. In the eastern periphery, Belarus is in a similar situation while Armenia, although formally included in the ENP, decided in the run-up to the Vilnius Eastern Partnership Summit 2013 not to sign an Association Agreement including a Deep and Comprehensive Free Trade Area.

When the European Commission (2006: 11) proposed in 2006 to 'look beyond the Union's immediate neighbourhood' and to work with the neighbours of its neighbours, it did not define what it meant by this term although a reference was made to 'Central Asia', the 'Gulf' and 'Africa'. If one adopts a strictly geographical approach, the neighbours of the EU's neighbours comprise:

- Mauritania, Mali, Niger, Chad and Sudan in Africa;
- Iraq, Iran and Saudi Arabia in the Middle East; and
- Kazakhstan and Turkmenistan in Central Asia.

In light of the interconnected challenges, however, it seems more appropriate to take a wider geopolitical approach (Lannon 2014). The EU's 'broader neighbourhood' thus enlarges the scope of the analysis to at least some African countries, especially the Sahel and the Horn of Africa; the Middle Eastern countries not included in the ENP framework – the members of the Gulf Cooperation Council (GCC), Yemen, Iran and Iraq and to a certain extent Afghanistan; and the five Central Asian republics (Kazakhstan, Kyrgyzstan, Tajikistan, Turkmenistan and Uzbekistan).

Challenges of the EU's broader neighbourhood

The ENP faced at its launch many challenges ranging from the management of borders and trade, investment and infrastructure networks to 'threats to mutual security, whether from the trans-border dimension of environmental and nuclear hazards, communicable diseases, illegal immigration, trafficking, organised crime or terrorist networks' (European Commission 2003: 6). In response to these challenges, the 'Wider Europe' strategy (ibid.: 3) declared that

> [t]he EU has a duty, not only towards its citizens and those of the new member states, but *also towards its present and future neighbours* to ensure

continuing social cohesion and economic dynamism. The EU must act to
promote the regional and subregional cooperation and integration that are
preconditions for political stability, economic development and the reduction of poverty and social divisions in our shared environment [emphasis
added].

Yet the neighbours of the EU's neighbours in the Middle East, the Sahel and the
Horn of Africa as well as in Central Asia are often plagued by similar or even
more serious problems and in many cases these challenges are closely interlinked. Compared to the ENP countries, values tend to be less shared with the
EU in the neighbours of its neighbours. In particular the African continent has
been suffering from political instability and state failures, but also from extreme
poverty, food insecurity, humanitarian crises and piracy. Security threats such as
weapon proliferation, terrorism, trafficking and organized crime as well as
regional – open or frozen – conflicts are challenges known in all regions of the
EU's broader neighbourhood.

The EU's Sahel Strategy, for example, acknowledges 'the challenges of
extreme poverty, the effects of climate change, frequent food crises, rapid population growth, fragile governance, corruption, unresolved internal tensions, the
risk of violent extremism and radicalisation, illicit trafficking and terrorist-linked
security threats' (Council of the European Union 2011: 1). The EU's Central
Asia Strategy identifies 'common regional challenges such as organised crime,
human, drugs and arms trafficking, terrorism and non-proliferation issues, inter-
cultural dialogue, energy, environmental pollution, water management, migration as well as border management and transport infrastructure' (Council of the
European Union 2009). The neighbours of the EU's neighbours are also relevant
for shaping the future of the EU's relations with the ENP countries. The EU's
broader neighbourhood 'is an area whose evolution will make a big difference to
Europe and where the EU can have a distinct impact in promoting reform and
stability in cooperation with regional and international partners' (Grevi
2014: 12).

The European Union has – in contrast with its relationships with the ENP
countries – very different policy frameworks of cooperation in place with the
neighbours of its neighbours. This lack of a strategy has led to fragmentation
within the regions as well as to the neglect of explicit linkages between the EU's
direct and broader neighbours in response to common challenges (see Gstöhl
2014). As a result, the EU often fails to leverage regional connections. Whereas
the EU has to some extent developed cooperation with Africa, it punches below
its weight in the Arab world and is at best a marginal player in Central Asia. As
argued elsewhere, the European Union needs a broader strategic vision with
regard to the neighbours of its neighbours (ibid.). This involves a political
assessment of its interests and comparative advantages in a region and of the
coherence of these relationships with its overall foreign policy strategy. If the
EU does not take into account the interconnections between the regions, conflicts may arise between different regional strategies. For instance, the EU's

Sahel Strategy emphasizes security cooperation with Algeria, while the ENP stresses political conditionality with regard to democracy and human rights standards in this country (Mattelaer 2014); and the EU has repeatedly criticized Ethiopia for flawed elections but instead of suspending its budget support to the government, the EU has increased its support despite further democratic setbacks because the country is a strategic regional ally (Vines and Soliman 2014).

Recent events have increasingly challenged the assumption of a gradual convergence of the neighbouring countries to the EU, while other regional powers (such as a more assertive Russia, Turkey or Iran) are seeking to extend their influence across the – at times shared – neighbourhood. If the EU is going to join in the geopolitical game in its broader neighbourhood, it must address the growing expectations regarding the export of stability, peace and prosperity. To be sustainable, the attempt 'to expand the zone of prosperity, stability and security' beyond the borders of the EU (Ferrero-Waldner 2006: 139) cannot stop with the first ring of neighbours. The strategic focus must go beyond the ENP countries to embrace the Sahel and the Horn of Africa, Central Asia and the Gulf countries (Duke 2011: 83). The EU's neighbourhood policy needs to become more geopolitical. The EU's capacity to draft a strategic approach to the neighbouring countries and their neighbours will affect its future influence in these regions and its capacity to act as a global player.

Opportunities for cooperation and building bridges

As the following chapters will show, many challenges such as border controls, irregular migration, and EU return and readmission practices call for closer international cooperation not only for security reasons but *inter alia* also because they raise concerns about fundamental rights. The fight against terrorism in the EU's broader neighbourhood equally requires a holistic vision, in particular a comprehensive development and security approach which includes measures aimed at the prevention of radicalization. The European Union's strategic role with regard to the neighbours of its neighbours is strongest in Saharan Africa but generally speaking its influence, largely based on missions under the Common Security and Defence Policy (CSDP), weapons-related measures and international efforts for more security governance, is still rather limited. Certain CSDP missions in the same region could be linked up to achieve synergy effects, as could the EU Special Representatives. Moreover, EU agencies in the field of operational cooperation on police and justice could reinforce cooperation with their counterparts in the neighbourhood.

Despite the neighbours' economic heterogeneity, the EU has continuously endeavoured to develop trade relations via unilateral, bilateral and regional instruments. There is potential for a more systematic development of linkages between the EU and the different neighbours as well as among them, for instance by connecting (emerging) free trade areas and by supporting sub-regional economic integration. In addition, the EU should promote pro-development policies that include all stakeholders, especially for fragile states. Development cooperation should focus not only on poverty eradication but also on human security, including gender equality and women's empowerment.

Sectoral cooperation in fields such as energy, transboundary waters or infrastructure networks is crucial for many dimensions – socio-economic, political, security and environmental. Here the EU can play a stronger role by supporting cooperation across neighbours, by financing investments connecting the regions and by adopting a clear stance on issues of governance when geopolitical and/or economic interests are at stake. The resource-rich countries in the EU's (broader) neighbourhood tend to be autocratic regimes and the EU needs to find a more credible way to cope with governments where its value-based policies, such as the promotion of democracy and human rights, have little traction. As argued by Keukeleire (2014), a genuine understanding of the EU's broader neighbourhood requires adopting an 'outside-in' perspective which goes beyond a Eurocentric view and attempts to integrate the perspective of the countries or regions concerned.

The EU's current frameworks of cooperation in the broader neighbourhood appear to be looser from west to east: while in Africa multilateralism (with the Cotonou Agreement) prevails in conjunction with an emerging inter-regionalism (the Economic Partnership Agreements), cooperation in the Middle East is characterized by emerging inter-regionalism (EU–GCC free trade agreement) and bilateralism (Iran, Iraq and Yemen) and in Central Asia solely by bilateralism (Gstöhl 2014). Not only do these frameworks lack an overarching strategic approach but also the interconnections between the regions could and should be strengthened. Building sustainable bridges across the regions could, for instance, include the insertion of regional cooperation clauses in the EU financial instruments; a 'neighbours of neighbours' cross-border cooperation programme; the connection of infrastructure (transport, energy, water, etc.) and trade networks across the regions; or a linking of the regional EU strategies and embedding them in an overall strategy for the broader neighbourhood (ibid.). A pragmatic 'EU Strategy on the Neighbours of the Neighbours' which draws on the existing instruments of cooperation and focuses on building bridges across the regions could, in the long run, work towards the aim of transforming the current 'arc of instability' in the EU's broader neighbourhood into a 'second ring of friends' beyond the ENP.

Conclusion

This brief introduction has illustrated why the broader neighbourhood of the European Union, stretching from the Sahel and the Horn of Africa over the Middle East to Central Asia, should be studied and why the EU might want to adopt a specific policy approach. A strategy beyond the immediate neighbourhood is in the interests of the EU in enabling it to better respond to the manifold challenges and to take advantage of the opportunities of cooperation with the ENP countries and their neighbours. These opportunities comprise not only economic, political and security interests but also the promotion of values such as democracy, fundamental rights and gender equality as well as trade liberalization, regional cooperation and integration.

The volume is thus divided into three parts. Part I addresses political, legal and security challenges such as migration and border controls, strategic issues and the fight against terrorism. Part II deals with economic and societal challenges, including EU trade relations and development cooperation with the broader neighbourhood, gender issues and democracy promotion. Part III focuses on the opportunities for better connecting the neighbours of the EU's neighbours with Europe and with the ENP countries. The topics include sub-regional economic integration in the EU's broader neighbourhood and the financing of investments in cross-regional infrastructure as well as cooperation in the fields of energy and trans-boundary waters. Finally, the concluding chapter draws some lessons and formulates policy proposals based on the findings.

References

Biscop, S. (2014) *Game of Zones: The Quest for Influence in Europe's Neighbourhood*, Egmont Paper 67, Brussels: Egmont Royal Institute of International Relations.

Council of the European Union (2009) *The European Union and Central Asia: The New Partnership in Action*, Brussels, June, http://eeas.europa.eu/central_asia/docs/2010_strategy_eu_centralasia_en.pdf (accessed August 2014).

Council of the European Union (2011) *Strategy for Security and Development in the Sahel, Annex to the Council Conclusions on a European Union Strategy for Security and Development in the Sahel*, Brussels, 21 March.

Duke, S. (2011) 'Pax or Pox Europeana after the Lisbon Treaty?', *The International Spectator* 46(1), 83–99.

European Commission (2003) Communication from the Commission to the Council and the European Parliament, *Wider Europe – Neighbourhood: A New Framework for Relations with our Eastern and Southern Neighbours*, COM(2003) 104, 11 March.

European Commission (2004) Communication from the Commission to the Council and the European Parliament, *European Neighbourhood Policy – Strategy Paper*, COM(2004) 373, 12 May.

European Commission (2006) *Communication from the Commission to the Council and the European Parliament on Strengthening the European Neighbourhood Policy*, COM(2006) 726 final, Brussels, 4 December.

European Council (2002) *Revised Version of the Presidency Conclusions of the Copenhagen European Council, 12-13 December*, www.consilium.europa.eu/ueDocs/cms_Data/docs/pressData/en/ec/73842.pdf (accessed August 2014).

European Council (2003) *European Security Strategy, 'A Secure Europe in a Better World'*, Brussels, 12 December.

European External Action Service (2013) 'Eastern Partnership: High Representative Ashton and Commissioner Füle with Foreign Ministers on Preparations for Vilnius', New York, 26 September, http://eeas.europa.eu/statements/docs/2013/130926_01_en.pdf (accessed August 2014).

Ferrero-Waldner, B. (2006) 'The European Neighbourhood Policy: The EU's Newest Foreign Policy Instrument', *European Foreign Affairs Review* 11(2), 139–142.

Georgieva, K. (2014) 'Ready for a More Fragile World? Europe's Role in Responding to Crisis and Conflict', Symposium on Governance in Europe, Hertie School of Governance, Berlin, SPEECH/14/428, 27 May, http://europa.eu/rapid/press-release_SPEECH-14-428_en.htm (accessed August 2014).

Grevi, G. (2014) 'Re-defining the EU's Neighbourhood', in G. Grevi and D. Keohane (eds) *Challenges for European Foreign Policy in 2014: The EU's Extended Neighbourhood*, Madrid: FRIDE, 15–22.

Gstöhl, S. (2014) 'Models of Cooperation with the Neighbours of the EU's Neighbours', in S. Gstöhl and E. Lannon (eds) *The Neighbours of the EU's Neighbours: Diplomatic and Geopolitical Dimensions beyond the European Neighbourhood Policy*, Farnham: Ashgate, 269–289.

Keukeleire, S. (2014) 'Lessons for the Practice and Analysis of EU Diplomacy from an "Outside-in Perspective"', in S. Gstöhl and E. Lannon (eds) *The Neighbours of the EU's Neighbours: Diplomatic and Geopolitical Dimensions beyond the European Neighbourhood Policy*, Farnham: Ashgate, 227–241.

Lannon, E. (2014) 'The "Neighbours of the EU's Neighbours", the "EU's Broader Neighbourhood" and the "Arc of Crisis and Strategic Challenges" from the Sahel to Central Asia', in S. Gstöhl and E. Lannon (eds) *The Neighbours of the EU's Neighbours: Diplomatic and Geopolitical Dimensions beyond the European Neighbourhood Policy*, Farnham: Ashgate, 1–25.

Mattelaer, A. (2014) 'The EU's Growing Engagement in the Sahel: From Development Aid to Military Coordination', in S. Gstöhl and E. Lannon (eds) *The Neighbours of the EU's Neighbours: Diplomatic and Geopolitical Dimensions beyond the European Neighbourhood Policy*, Farnham: Ashgate, 45–65.

Vines, A. and A. Soliman (2014) 'The Horn of Africa: Transnational and Trans-Regional Dynamics in Europe's Broader Neighbourhood', in S. Gstöhl and E. Lannon (eds) *The Neighbours of the EU's Neighbours: Diplomatic and Geopolitical Dimensions beyond the European Neighbourhood Policy*, Farnham: Ashgate, 67–95.

Part I

Political, legal and security challenges

1 The externalization of border controls towards the EU's broader neighbourhood

Challenges of consistency

Valeria Bonavita

Introduction: the externalization of border controls as a challenge to the consistency of the EU's fundamental rights protection regime

In its Communication 'A Strategy on the External Dimension of the Area of Freedom, Security and Justice' (AFSJ), the European Commission (2005b) made geographic prioritization one of the guiding principles for initiatives in this area. While full-spectrum coordination in AFSJ matters should be concentrated on candidate and neighbouring countries of the European Union (EU), targeted cooperation in specific policy domains, such as border management, should be the rule *vis-à-vis* other countries.

Recent statistics show that, unlike in the last decades of the twentieth century, incoming migration flows currently transit through the territory of the EU's neighbouring countries but originate further away (Eurostat 2014: 4–5, 7). When it comes to Africa, for example, the source of such flows lies in the sub-Saharan region.[1] While the observation of such change in migratory trends did not discourage European institutions from carrying on with the pursuit of a policy of active engagement *vis-à-vis* the countries of the European Neighbourhood Policy (ENP) on migration and mobility, it nonetheless imposed a reconsideration of the EU approach towards the 'neighbours of the neighbours' in matters of migration and border controls. Whereas the ENP has been widely dealt with by scholars (see for instance Fargues 2013), little attention has been paid to the EU's engagement towards its broader neighbourhood in this policy area. The purpose of this contribution is to explore those avenues while keeping a watchful eye on issues of consistency and ultimately legitimacy. This study is thus placed at the crossroads of two intertwined debates: on the one hand, it deals with the external dimension of the Area of Freedom, Security and Justice; on the other hand, it strives to assess the consistency – at the horizontal level at least – between the internal and the external aspects of the EU's policies in this field. The main focus is on the quest for consistency between the internal and external dimensions of EU fundamental rights protection and the impact of the EU's

Charter of Fundamental Rights (CFR) on the external dimension of the AFSJ. The concept of horizontal consistency is herein employed according to the definition given by Tietje (1997: 213), who points out that consistency has the negative meaning of absence of contradictions, as opposed to the concept of coherence which entails the existence of positive connections and mechanisms aimed at actively avoiding inconsistencies. Coherence is a matter of degree, and therefore a relative concept, whereas consistency is a static and absolute one: concepts of law can be more or less coherent, but they cannot be more or less consistent – either they are or they are not.

This chapter seeks to assess to what extent and how the EU is currently putting in place mechanisms for the externalization of border management towards its broader neighbourhood as part of the external dimension of the AFSJ and whether such an external policy is consistent with the EU's internal regime of fundamental rights protection. The analysis shows that the question remains open as to whether current forms of cooperation amount to a sufficient critical mass for claiming that border control responsibilities are even partially externalized towards the neighbours of the EU's neighbours; further assessment is needed. However, the current state of affairs does not preclude looking at such forms of cooperation through the lens of policy consistency and, by implication, legitimacy. By building upon the lessons learned from the EU's cooperation in the domain of border management with countries such as Libya, the analysis in this chapter shows that externalizing border controls through either operational arrangements or development cooperation instruments negatively affects the EU's capacity to abide by its internally established regime of fundamental rights protection, including relevant provisions of international law. The chapter does not attempt an analysis of the EU Member States' role in the externalization of border controls. Recent EU practices in this domain remain the sole focus of the research and the findings do not take into account national policies. The conclusions are therefore limited in scope as the Member States continue to be ultimately responsible for the operational management of the EU's external border controls.

This chapter will first provide the reader with a definition of externalization of border controls (EBC) as transfer of responsibility towards third countries, thus leaving aside other forms of EBC such as sub-contracting or burden-shifting. While doing so, the chapter will already give a first glimpse at the impact that different forms of EBC might have on rights related to migration and asylum. Second, the contribution will investigate the EU's cooperation with the neighbours of its neighbours in the field of border management. With this aim, two categories of instruments will be taken into account. On the one hand, the operational arrangements between EU agencies and the neighbours of the EU's neighbours, such as those established between the European Agency for the Management of Operational Cooperation at the External Borders of the Member States of the European Union (FRONTEX) and Mauritania, will be analysed. On the other hand, avenues of capacity-building through the EU's development cooperation instruments will be explored. Finally, in order to limit the speculative nature of the arguments presented, the EU's practice of EBC towards the neighbours of its neighbours will be looked at against the background of the EU's cooperation with Libya in the fight against irregular migration. While Libya is not a neighbour of the EU's neighbours but an ENP country, the analysis of the EU's cooperation with Libya in the fight against irregular migration serves the purpose of this chapter for two reasons: on the one hand, Libya is a country of transit of migratory flows towards the EU's external borders; on the other, EU–Libya bilateral cooperation represents a precedent which unmistakably points towards externalization. Analysing this cooperation allows to establish how the EU puts in place mechanisms of externalization and to point out how such patterns may be duplicated in relation to the neighbours of the European Union's neighbours.

Definition of externalization of border controls

The concept of the externalization of border control management, which is frequently used in the discourse on asylum and migration policy, can be broken down into two main aspects: the EU's practice of outsourcing or relocating border control procedures outside its territory (EBC as sub-contracting), and the EU's policy of making and holding third countries *de facto* accountable, through a transfer of responsibilities (EBC as transfer of responsibilities), for delivering its own preferred policy outcomes concerning border controls, including anti-trafficking and management of migratory flows and ensuing consequences in relation to abidance by applicable international obligations (Slominski 2012: 24–26). This section will introduce some examples of the mechanisms characterizing these two dimensions of EBC and highlight their shortcomings.

Externalization as sub-contracting

Externalization as sub-contracting entails a practice whereby border management is not operated at the EU's external borders but is relocated further away, usually within the territory of third countries with which the EU cooperates. When intended as sub-contracting, extraterritorialization of border management procedures can also take the form of cooperation with private entities such as, for instance, air carriers. While externalization through sub-contracting of entry-related procedures is excluded from the scope of this study due to the scarcity of such EU practice in relation to the neighbours of its neighbours, it will nonetheless be briefly dealt with for the purpose of outlining the main differences and commonalities with externalization as transfer of responsibilities.

As mentioned above, carrier sanctions are an example of cooperation with private entities which results in the sub-contracting of border control procedures. The responsibility for verifying whether or not passengers who intend to enter the EU's territory fulfil all applicable document and visa requirements and are thus legally entitled to cross the Union's external border inbound is delegated to transport companies. A powerful incentive for carriers is represented by the fact that, should the latter perform inadequate controls resulting in unauthorized entries, they will be subject to pecuniary fining and forced to return undocumented passengers.[2] A second avenue of externalization as sub-contracting consists in exporting surveillance and identification techniques and skills to the countries of departure or transit with a view to protecting the Union's borders through a network of Immigration Liaison Officers seconded to those countries (Council of the European Union 2004). Another example of sub-contracting is the establishment of protected entry procedures: this system allows individuals who wish to claim asylum in a EU country to approach an embassy, rather than having to risk the dangerous journey to the country itself. The embassy assesses their claims, and if they are approved the individual can travel safely to the host country.

Despite technical differences, these examples of externalization of border controls via sub-contracting mechanisms all feature a certain degree of institutionalization whereby the EU's counterpart, be it air carriers or third countries' border control authorities, is made formally responsible for ensuring that subjects crossing the EU's external border are legally entitled to do so. The same degree of institutionalization cannot be observed in relation to the mechanisms of externalization as transfer of responsibility that will be analysed below and which are the ones that the European Union operates in relation to the neighbours of its neighbours. However, it is worth noting that the externalization by sub-contracting does not exclude risks in relation to the treatment of potential asylum-seekers to the extent that it is not necessarily accompanied by specific arrangements for safeguarding access to international protection by the subject concerned prior to the physical entry of the latter into the territory of the relevant country.

A recent study on carrier sanctions and Immigration Liaison Officers by McNamara (2013) examines the relations between externalization, judicial competence and effective protection of fundamental rights. State responsibility for externalized migration controls is assessed through the lens of the jurisdiction of the European Court of Human Rights (ECtHR). ECtHR jurisprudence has made it clear that it is the exercise of physical power and control over a person by the state which is pivotal to deciding on its jurisdiction over the claim, that is to say that jurisdiction is engaged only to the extent that the Court finds that physical power and control by the state have been 'effective'. This threshold of 'effective' control which has emerged from the Court's jurisprudence is a demanding hurdle to the extent that only if state control is found to be 'effective' can the state be held responsible for the full range of rights contained within the European Convention on Human Rights (ECHR).

Pending the EU's accession to the Convention, the same considerations appear to be relevant in relation to the Union's possible externalization practices. The question can, however, be raised as to whether the ECtHR can keep abreast of these controls. The difficulty of assessing their extent positively affects the states' capacity to evade jurisdiction and thus avoid fundamental rights responsibilities. One possible interpretation of recent jurisprudence is that the ECtHR is moving toward a broader way of construing jurisdiction. It is in this context that externalized controls have come under renewed scrutiny. A prevailing opinion is that the ECtHR will be able to protect those asylum-seekers who encounter externalized control (McNamara 2013: 3–4). However, an alternative reading of the ECtHR's jurisprudence suggests that the hurdle of extraterritorial jurisdiction is so demanding that states manage to avoid it despite exercising extensive control over migrants. Notwithstanding this considerable control, examination by the ECtHR is likely to result in a failure to satisfy the 'effective' control threshold. Responsibility can thus be avoided while extraterritorial control is retained. The control level held by the state is still capable of guaranteeing a denial of entry to individuals in need of international protection. If jurisdiction is not engaged, then this externalized migration control represents a divergence between state control and state responsibility. Taking the threshold for jurisdiction of the ECtHR as a starting point, McNamara (2013: 13) suggests making a distinction between externalization on the one hand and the external dimension on the other. States, oftentimes with facilitation from the European Union, pursue one of these two alternatives. Externalization affords the state stronger and more direct control over the entry of the migrant into the territory of an EU Member State than the external dimension, where the control is indirect and weaker.

In view of the EU's prospected accession to the ECHR, the shortcomings of externalization in terms of both procedural and substantive protection of migrants' fundamental rights bring about the issue of the consistency between the internal and the external dimensions of the European Union's fundamental rights protection regime.

Externalization as transfer of responsibilities

This contribution focuses on a more nuanced form of externalization, namely making third countries *de facto* partially responsible for the EU's desired outcomes in the domain of border management, particularly in the area of migration and asylum, by providing technical and financial assistance. As far as asylum-seekers are concerned, two options sum up this approach: the sharing of responsibilities *vis-à-vis* the migrant and the idea of affording international protection as close as possible to the regions of origin, also known as 'regional protection'. These two concepts are based on the idea of achieving a more balanced distribution of the burden of asylum claims by requiring third countries' authorities to take responsibility for dealing with those claims. Regional protection in particular refers to the EU's policy of engaging those countries that are situated near the departure areas of migration flows.

Inspired by the principle of solidarity, this approach is not necessarily bad in itself, but because of the way it is implemented by the EU it seems to reflect a desire to cast off rather than share responsibilities, thus engaging in burden-shifting. In this regard, one of the most critical aspects concerning EBC as a transfer of responsibilities is exemplified by the cooperation that can be established by the EU bodies charged with migration and asylum-related issues – FRONTEX and the European Asylum Support Office (EASO) – and third countries. While legally empowered to engage in cooperation with third countries, these agencies are seldom inclined to consider that not all third countries that are strategically relevant in the management of borders and migration flows offer sufficient guarantees in relation to fundamental rights protection, particularly when compared with the standards provided by the regime currently in force within the territory of the European Union, which draws on both the CFR and the ECHR.

As the EU's agency responsible for border management, FRONTEX has concluded multiple working arrangements with third states, including several ENP countries as well as neighbours of the EU's neighbours.[3] With the entry into force of the 2011 FRONTEX Regulation, the agency has acquired even more competences to engage third states in its activities (European Parliament and Council of the European Union 2011: art. 14). For example, the agency is able to place its own liaison officers in third countries and can implement 'assistance projects' there (European Parliament and Council of the European Union 2011). Despite the fact that art. 14 of the FRONTEX Regulation emphasizes the need for the agency to engage in forms of international cooperation which are respectful of migrants' fundamental rights, those third countries with which the agency has a strategic interest in concluding working arrangements are non-EU Member States and are therefore not bound by the CFR nor – in most cases – by the ECHR (Alegre *et al.* 2009: 14, 16–17; Gammeltoft-Hansen 2010: 2–6). This means that those countries are not obliged to abide by the provisions enshrined in the European fundamental rights protection regime. Moreover, even countries that are signatories to international instruments, such as the ECHR or relevant UN Conventions, still deserve a critical scrutiny of the adequacy of their practical implementation of those instruments before FRONTEX cooperates with them.

The risk that FRONTEX engages with national authorities that are not sufficiently committed to and bound by fundamental rights obligations is not to be underestimated. By externalizing border controls to these authorities, even only by exchanging information and providing border control capacity-building, the EU runs the risk of subsidizing practices which do not meet the standards of EU fundamental rights protection. However, as the next section will show with regard to the working arrangements concluded by FRONTEX with Mauritania, the risk is not easy to assess given that the terms of the cooperation are not made public and are therefore not subject to inter-institutional scrutiny, particularly as far as the European Parliament is concerned.

The EASO is in turn mandated to establish relations with third countries on the exchange of information and capacity-building exercises in the areas of asylum and reception conditions. Art. 49(2) of the EASO's founding regulation calls on the office to facilitate operational cooperation between the Member States and third countries within the framework of the EU's external relations policy (European Parliament and Council of the European Union 2010). Given the recent establishment of the office in 2010 and the broad nature of the above provision, it remains to be seen how EASO's capacity-building role, which could touch on aspects sensitive to fundamental rights, will be developed by its Management Board. There is a risk that EASO could be co-opted into EU external policies involving the externalization of border controls. In fact, evidence of such a development can already be observed. For instance, a Communication of the European Commission (2011), which was adopted in response to the migration flows from the Southern Mediterranean in the first half of 2011, calls upon EASO to support capacity-building efforts by North African countries 'for the efficient management of migration' as part of the conditions attached to the creation of Mobility Partnerships with those countries. However, capacity-building on asylum procedures in third countries should not be undertaken with the aim of containing refugees in countries and regions outside the EU. Once again, where third countries are characterized by a weak fundamental rights regime, there is a risk that EASO will implicate the EU in substantially degrading the fundamental rights situation of potential asylum-seekers. Along the same lines, a core component of EASO's relations with third countries being the exchange of information, the question arises as to the nature – including the quality and accuracy – of the information exchanged and the implications for individuals.

The next section will deal with concrete forms of cooperation between the EU and the neighbours of its neighbours in the field of border management. Building on a strictly geographical definition of the neighbours of the EU's neighbours, the following analysis is carried out so as to categorize forms of cooperation as either operational or inspired by a development cooperation rationale.

EU cooperation in border management with the neighbours of its neighbours

While the concept of the neighbours of the EU's neighbours can be interpreted according to different parameters, this chapter relies on a strictly geographical definition thereof.[4] As a result, the question as to whether and to what extent the EU is externalizing border management towards the neighbours of its neighbours will be answered by taking into account instruments put in place *vis-à-vis* countries that share a physical border with one or more ENP countries. From the outset, the analysis has highlighted that various forms of cooperation exist with countries such as Mauritania, Niger, Mali, Chad and Sudan in the Sahel and the Horn of Africa, and with Turkmenistan and Kazakhstan in Central Asia. Concerning the neighbours of the EU's neighbours in the Gulf region, cooperation with the EU in the field of border management has so far been negligible, with the exception of some forms of involvement in Iraq. This is why countries in the Gulf region will not be further dealt with in this analysis.

The EU has put into place two categories of instruments which may qualify as EBC mechanisms and which will be addressed in the following sections. On the one hand, operational arrangements have been established by FRONTEX, such as the ones concluded with Mauritania. On the other hand, capacity-building facilities have been financed through development cooperation instruments. The 'development cooperation' dimension of EBC towards the neighbours of the ENP countries is exemplified by several projects funded, in the Sahel and the Horn of Africa, under the AENEAS programme (2004–06) and more recently under the Thematic Instrument for Migration and Asylum as well as the Border Management Programme in Central Asia (BOMCA).

The analysis will show that the EU's setting of priorities responds to different rationales in the different regions. More specifically, it can be noted that while cooperation in border management seems to be migration-oriented with countries in the Sahel and the Horn of Africa, a trade facilitation and anti-trafficking approach seems to inspire the EU's cooperation in border control with the Central Asian republics.

The operational component: FRONTEX working arrangements with third countries

The EU set out its migration-related priorities for Africa in the first Action Plan for the implementation of the 2007 Africa–EU Partnership on Migration, Mobility and Employment (European Commission 2007). Covering the period 2008–10, the Action Plan aimed at providing a holistic response to development-related issues, in view of the final objective of creating more and better jobs for Africa and of better managing migration flows.

Building on the 2006 Joint AU–EU Tripoli Declaration on Migration and Development[5] and on the African Union's Ouagadougou Declaration and Action Plan on Employment and Poverty Alleviation, the EU–Africa Partnership is intended to ensure that better management of migration and employment issues becomes an essential part of poverty reduction strategies or of other national development and co-development strategies for African countries. Interestingly, the Action Plan puts migration management and employment stimulation on an equal footing for the purpose of promoting sustainable development in the region and underscores the importance of all relevant international agreements and declarations being implemented to this end.

The Sahel in particular seems to have a prominent place on the European Union's political agenda towards the African continent. Besides energy security and the fight against insecurity and organized crime, the containment of and the fight against illegal migration is listed among Europe's key interests in the region. EU fact-finding missions to Mali, Mauritania and Niger conducted prior to the launching of the 2011 EU Strategy for Security and Development in the Sahel identified challenges *inter alia* in security and the rule of law sector (European External Action Service 2011). According to post-mission reports, these states have insufficient operational and strategic capacities in the wider sectors of security, law enforcement and the judiciary (military, police, justice, border management, customs) to control the territory, to ensure human security, to prevent and respond to the various security threats, and to enforce the law (conduct investigations, trials etc.) with due respect to human rights (ibid.: 3). This is notably reflected in the insufficiency of legal frameworks and law enforcement capacity at all levels, including an ineffective border management and insufficient methods of gathering, transmitting and exchanging information, as well as in obsolete or nonexistent equipment and infrastructure. State control of the desert regions in the north of Mali and Niger is qualified as fragile in these reports, and available resources are said to be insufficiently used to target illegal migration towards neighbouring countries to the north.

Against this backdrop and based on art. 14 of the 2011 Regulation, FRONTEX has concluded or is currently engaged in the conclusion of working arrangements with several African countries. Mauritania is one of the countries with which FRONTEX is exploring avenues of operational cooperation. Whereas the methods and extent of this cooperation do not necessarily point towards externalization, caution would nonetheless be advisable for two reasons, the first of which relates to the very reputation of the country. Mauritania does not ensure sufficient fundamental rights standards and is ill-placed to afford international protection to migrants, including potential asylum-seekers.

The second reason concerns the procedures whereby this cooperation is established. Working arrangements concluded by FRONTEX with third countries are similar to administrative *ententes*. They do not qualify as international agreements concluded by the EU and thus do not fall within the scope of art. 218 of the TFEU (Treaty on the Functioning of the European Union). As a result, none of the procedural guarantees which normally bind EU institutions in their negotiations with third countries are applicable here. There are three main consequences of this. First, FRONTEX working arrangements are covered by secrecy to the extent that, unlike international agreements concluded by the EU and ensuing EU decisions, they do not have to be published in the Official Journal of the European Union. As they are not public, nor published, their content remains largely obscure. Second, falling short of the formal requirements which confer legal nature to EU measures, they are not subject to democratic control via EU parliamentary scrutiny (Alegre *et al.* 2009: 23–25; Fink 2012: 25, 29). Third, the non-legal nature of these instruments makes them unsuitable for amenability to justice. The Court of Justice of the EU (CJEU) cannot be called upon to exercise judicial review either on the procedure of conclusion or on the merit of such arrangements. As a result, it is impossible to afford any sort of fundamental rights protection to those affected by these measures, that is, migrants. It is worth noting that McNamara's (2013) argument on the triangular relation between the externalization as sub-contracting, the ECtHR's jurisdiction and fundamental rights protection should be upheld in this context as well. While possible claims of violation of substantive fundamental rights of migrants might or might not be upheld by the Court in the midst of a judicial proceeding, the very inaccessibility of judicial remedies by the migrants who are potential victims of such violations represents a denial of justice, which can be regarded in itself as a violation of fundamental rights.

The above critical aspects are certainly intertwined and nourish a vicious circle. Whereas the issue of insufficient procedural guarantees affects all working arrangements concluded by FRONTEX, regardless of the counterpart, such a lack of transparency and accountability raises even more worries when the third country concerned does not have a clear record of fundamental and human rights protection and does not abide by international standards. At the same time, the classified nature of the content of such *ententes* means that they cannot be used to cast light on the way in which FRONTEX cooperation with third countries may have an impact on their practice in relation to migrants' treatment and they are therefore of no use in defusing concerns over the violation of the latter's rights.

The development cooperation component: capacity-building through development cooperation instruments

During the last decade, the EU has financed initiatives for cooperation with the neighbours of its neighbours in the field of border management via development cooperation programmes. Projects in Africa have notably been financed under the AENEAS programme 2004–06 (European Parliament and Council of the European Union 2004),[6] and under its successor, the Thematic Programme for Migration and Asylum, which covered the period 2007–13 (European Parliament and Council of the European Union 2006).[7] In comparison, the EU's Border Management Programme in Central Asia has been the main financial instrument for attaining capacity-building and the strengthening of border control in the territory between the Southern Caucasus and the Central Asian republics. Looking at some examples of projects financed under the above programmes will help illustrate how the EU has been using its development cooperation policy in order to externalize border control management towards the neighbours of its neighbours. While the lack of transparency characterizing the conclusion of FRONTEX operational arrangements with countries such as Mauritania does not allow an unequivocal identification of the operational component as a means of externalization, border management capacity-building as financed by the four projects analysed below points more clearly in the direction of externalization as burden-shifting.

First, financed by the AENEAS programme (2004–06), 'Across Sahara' was a pilot project of regional cooperation and capacity-building on border and illegal migration management involving relevant central and local services in charge of irregular migration and border management in Libya and Niger (Europe-Aid 2006: 5, 34). This project aimed at enhancing the cooperation between Libya and Niger in border control and the fight against illegal migration, with special reference to irregular migratory flows transiting from sub-Saharan Africa through the two countries and towards the coasts of southern Italy. The project's specific objective was to contribute to the enhancement of policies and practices to prevent and combat illegal migration, trafficking and smuggling of transiting migrants in Libya and Niger.

Activities foreseen under the project encompassed, first of all, the conduction of a survey of illegal migration transiting Niger and Libya, including modalities, routings and main features of criminal groups dealing with migrants' trafficking, as well as the assessment of the performance of the national services in charge of immigration and borders in the two countries. Information sharing represented the second aspect of the project. Based on the result of the survey, technical seminars were planned, with the participation of representatives and experts from Italy, Libya, Niger and the International Organization for Migration (IOM), in order to assess the outcomes of the survey and present an overview of illegal migration in the target region, as well as of specific needs and priorities in terms of capacity-building and training. The final stage of the project aimed at capitalizing on both the survey and the information-sharing with a view to conduct tailor-made training and capacity-building activities focusing in particular on border control techniques and detection of false documents; fight against trafficking in human beings and smuggling of migrants; assistance and protection of victims; illegal migration management; and search and rescue maritime operations, to the extent that the Libyan authorities were concerned.

Second, the 'Law Enforcement Capacity-building Project for West Africa in Preventing and Combating the Smuggling of Migrants' (2007–10; EuropeAid 2006: 31) was funded by the same EU programme and implemented by the United Nations Office on Drugs and Crime (UNODC) and Europol to the benefit of political decision-makers, law enforcement agencies – including border control and customs – and prosecution authorities responsible for combating the smuggling of migrants in West Africa. The project aimed to assist the countries of the Economic Community of West African States (ECOWAS), including Mali and Niger, and Mauritania in building capacities and strengthening cooperation mechanisms among law enforcement and prosecution authorities in order to effectively prevent, investigate and prosecute the smuggling of migrants, and to develop effective cooperation mechanisms with third countries to that end, while at the same time protecting the rights of smuggled migrants. The activities financed by the EU included assessments of the existing anti-smuggling capacities of the criminal justice systems and assistance in national policy development as well as the establishment of coordination frameworks among the different actors on a national level; the development of training curricula and the carrying out of trainings for law enforcement and prosecution; and, finally, the establishment of common anti-smuggling law enforcement units.

Third, under the 'Cooperation with Third Countries' section of the 2010 Action Plan for the Thematic Programme for Migration and Asylum (2007–13) the EU contributed over €36 million to a project of assistance to the Islamic Republic of Mauritania as a follow-up to a previous package of measures to help the country in its efforts to contain the flow of illegal immigrants to the Canary Islands (European Commission 2010: annex 1). As early as 2007, in answering a parliamentary question on the effectiveness of the financial measures from which Mauritania was benefiting, the Justice and Home Affairs (JHA) Commissioner Franco Frattini (2007) was cautious in assessing the overall and long-term impact of the measures mobilized by the Commission in cooperation with the EU Members States and FRONTEX. He underlined, however, that in the short term there had been a major downturn in migrant departures from Mauritania in the summer of 2006, which might be ascribed to the actions of the Mauritanian authorities following the Commission's engagement and to the effectiveness of EU-stimulated joint patrolling operations (ibid.). Moreover, the Commissioner mentioned the rapid enhancement in the capacity of the Mauritanian authorities in managing migratory flows and their full commitment to achieving results and to continuing to cooperate with the Union. The result of this process was the abovementioned mandate for negotiating working arrangements between Mauritania and FRONTEX.

Fourth, in the late 1990s, the then European Community decided to become more active in the area of border management in Central Asia as a result of the dissolution of the Soviet Union. Effective border security – or rather the lack thereof – and the fight against drug trafficking emerged as major challenges for the region and, particularly after the EU's 2004/07 Eastern enlargement, their potential impact on the EU constituted the main driver of the establishment and maintenance of BOMCA. The programme represents the practical expression of the EU's strategic interest in supporting the security and stability of the region via the support to legitimate trade and transit in Central Asia through the introduction of best European practices and the transfer of expertise in the area of integrated border management (IBM). While the overall objective of BOMCA is to secure the gradual adoption of modern border management methods in the region with the purpose of enhancing border security and facilitating legal trade and transit, the programme – which is on-going at the time of writing – specifically aims at strengthening the capacities and infrastructures in countering illicit trafficking.

Initiated in 2002 following the suggestion of the Central Asia Border Security Initiative, BOMCA is one of the largest EU assistance programmes in Central Asia. After several assessment missions and small-scale interventions in 2002–03, the first major multi-annual EU BOMCA phase was launched in early 2004. Implemented for the EU by the United Nations Development Programme (UNDP) with the International Centre for Migration Policy Development (ICMPD) as an implementing partner, the programme is under the direct leadership of the UNDP Country Office in Kyrgyzstan. BOMCA was allocated a budget of over €36 million for 2003–14, of which 95 per cent was financed by the European Commission (Gavrilis 2009: 2).

BOMCA aims at promoting the stability and security of Central Asian states through the introduction of European best practices in IBM while at the same time assisting beneficiary countries in their pursuit of regional economic development and trade facilitation with the EU and its neighbouring countries. From the operational point of view, the programme builds on three components. First of all, it supports policy advice as well as legal and institutional reform: BOMCA has established inter-ministerial commissions and inter-agency working groups in each country to familiarize decision-makers with options for IBM implementation and to initiate the legislative and regulatory reforms necessary to institutionalize the IBM framework. Second, the programme aims at strengthening national training capacities: the programme is renovating and equipping training centres for border agencies in all five Central Asian republics, introducing IBM components to national training curricula, and establishing national training capacities through a training-of-trainers approach that utilizes the best of European expertise. Third, the programme runs pilot site trials in integrated border management: BOMCA is providing infrastructure, equipment and on-the-job training in key skills to border agency staff at selected airports, seaports and stretches of green border in Central Asia, with a view to national governments running trials of IBM in these pilot sites under subsequent phases of the programme.

BOMCA's objectives for the current phase (2011–14), to which the EU is contributing nearly €8 million, are to help increase overall security in Central Asia, to contribute to the facilitation of legitimate trade and transit and to reduce the illicit movement of goods and people. To this end, the programme continues to promote the concept of IBM in different areas of intervention. Yet again, the attention is focused, on the one hand, on the strengthening of training capacities in all the 'stans' and, on the other, on the reinforcement of counter-drug-trafficking capacities across borders with the aim of supporting the interception of drugs and precursor chemicals, notably at airports and railway stations.

By contributing to enhancing border management capacities of the beneficiary countries in the Sahel and Central Asian region, these projects and programmes illustrate clearly the EU's intention to at least partially shift the responsibility of keeping its external borders clear of either irregular migrants or unlawful trafficking. The EU is not new to such courses of action, as epitomized by the EU–Libya bilateral cooperation in matters of migration control. While the quality and quantity of current forms of cooperation with the neighbours of the neighbours does not necessarily amount to a sufficient critical mass for establishing a clear pattern of externalization, the example of Libya provides food for thought as to the developments of such forms of cooperation and the risks they entail with regard to the protection of migrants' fundamental rights.

Externalization towards ENP countries as early warning on the EU's practice *vis-à-vis* the neighbours of its neighbours: the case of Libya

The mechanisms of cooperation in the field of border management which the EU has so far put in place in its relations with the neighbours of its neighbours do not univocally point towards a deliberate attempt at externalizing border control policies. Overall, the current state of affairs features a relatively narrow set of initiatives, whose nature – both in quantitative and qualitative terms – suggests caution in affirming that the EU has been deliberately trying to shift the burden of control towards the beneficiaries of such initiatives. However, this chapter aims to go beyond assessing the present state of the EU's cooperation with the neighbours of its neighbours in the field of border management in order to raise awareness of possible future scenarios. Hence, the need to take a step back and look at the case of EU–Libya cooperation in the fight against irregular migration as an example of how current forms of EU cooperation with the neighbours of its neighbours could develop, focusing in particular on the possible impact on policy consistency and legitimacy.[8]

As early as 2002 the EU had singled out migration, and in particular the tackling of illegal immigration, as an essential field of collaboration with the Libyan authorities. In order to explore the potential for bilateral cooperation, a technical mission on illegal immigration was deployed by the EU between November and December 2004, consisting of Commission staff from Directorates General Relex, JHA and DEV and of experts from interested EU Member States (Council of the European Union 2003).

The mission's findings pointed out two main aspects (Council of the European Union 2005). On the one hand, the Commission found that, particularly with regard to the issue of asylum-seekers and the management of repatriation of illegal migrants, the latter's protection was not guaranteed in Libya on account of reported human rights violations perpetuated in detention centres and collective expulsions indiscriminately operated before even considering the personal situation of potential asylum-seekers. On the other hand, a potential for capacity enhancement was suggested in the form of legislative improvements, institution-building, training and capacity-building, improvement of infrastructures and equipment, improvement of border management and exchange of information. In the context of these orientations, the Commission deemed it necessary to consider how to address the demands of specific equipment that might be needed by the Libyan authorities in order to achieve this progress.

On the ground of those findings, the Council of the European Union (2005) agreed to launch an *ad hoc* dialogue on migration issues between the EU and Libya and to gradually develop concrete cooperation on those issues with the Libyan authorities. The extent and development of such cooperation were made conditional upon Libya's commitment to the respect for asylum and fundamental rights. Fully aware of Libyan practices in relation to the management of migration flows and given Libya's failure to ratify the 1951 Geneva Convention on Refugees and its additional Protocol of 1967 (United Nations 1966),[9] the Council of the European Union (2005) underlined in its conclusions that cooperation between the EU and third countries was to be guided by the full respect for human rights, democratic principles and the rule of law and by the demonstration of a genuine commitment to fulfil their obligations under the Geneva Convention or other relevant international conventions. It also called upon the Libyan authorities to at least demonstrate a commitment to the fulfilment of their obligations under the Convention Governing the Specific Aspects of Refugee Problems in Africa of the Organization of African Unity (OAU) (ibid.). This OAU Convention recognizes that the Geneva Convention on Refugees constitutes the basic and universal instrument relating to the status of refugees and requires effective cooperation with the United Nations High Commissioner for Refugees (UNHCR) and the respect of the principle of *non-refoulement*.[10]

Notwithstanding the concerns caused by the practices of the Gaddafi regime, the Council went on to recommend that the Commission propose measures to intensify cooperation with Libya. In particular, cooperation was recommended between the respective services responsible for the coordination of sea borders management (FRONTEX on the EU side), as well as the training of Libyan services at external borders, including on asylum issues, and the sharing of best practices with regard to the acquisition of travel documents for and removal of illegal migrants. Additional exploratory discussions were foreseen on the prevention of further losses at sea, training on external border control, illegal immigration, asylum and human rights issues and, similarly to what has been shown in relation to the Sahel and the Horn of Africa region, on the association of Libya with concrete operational initiatives such as those covered by the AENEAS programme. Moreover, in the medium term, the EU aimed at strengthening the Libyan legal framework for migration with a view to improve its management; at strengthening the Libyan border control capacity to prevent illegal immigration from Libyan coasts and the smuggling of migrants by sea; and at cooperating in returning illegal migrants to the country.

On a similar note, the 2005 Commission Communication on third countries' policies in the fight against illegal immigration (European Commission 2005a: 13–15) appeared to be even more ambiguous in so far as it seemed to emphasize the limits of the Libyan system while at the same time failing to fine-tune policy proposals. Instead, it reiterated the value of on-going initiatives of cooperation with Libya, such as the projects financed under the AENEAS programme in institution-building, training activities and the establishment of an asylum system. While recognizing that migratory pressure on Libya made the country a top priority for intervention and support in the EU strategy of cooperation with third countries in tackling illegal migration, the Commission mentioned various aspects that in fact should have undermined – or at least questioned – Libya's candidature for a partnership in this domain. The Communication excluded any scope for the negotiation of a readmission agreement in light of the lack of formal bilateral relations. Moreover, it pointed out that Libya had signed neither the 1951 Geneva Convention nor its additional Protocol. The Communication conceded that the Libyan constitution did foresee the protection of refugees, but also highlighted that there was no administrative structure dealing with refugees and asylum-seekers and that no cooperation agreement was in force with the UNHCR, whose local office had no official status (ibid.).[11] Finally, the document considered that migration control measures adopted by the Libyan authorities appeared to be limited to mass expulsions triggered by upsurges in the numbers of undocumented migrants who had managed to enter the country and that the return policy operated in the country amounted to detention in reception centres where living conditions fell short of the most basic hygiene and human dignity requirements. As a matter of fact, the Commission did reiterate the basic conclusion of its 2004 technical mission that neither the international protection of refugees nor the protection of migrants' fundamental rights were assured by the Gaddafi regime (ibid.). Notwithstanding these alarming findings, however, the Commission failed once again to reorient EU relations with Libya towards a more respectful approach *vis-à-vis* migrants' rights and related principles of international law.

Quite to the contrary, the European Union enhanced its cooperation with Libya on migration issues, particularly by strengthening its financial dimension first under the AENEAS programme and later under the Thematic Programme on Migration and Asylum. In the period 2004–06, under the AENEAS programme, the Commission financed 10 projects with Libya among the beneficiary countries, including, for instance, the 'Transit and Irregular Migration Management (TRIM)' and the already mentioned 'Across Sahara' projects (EuropeAid 2006). Run by the IOM, the TRIM project aimed at training staff from the Libyan migration authorities and at providing irregular migrants in custody in Libyan reception centres with more decent living conditions and with assistance to voluntary return. The focus of the project thus appeared to be the migrant as such, whose treatment by the Libyan authorities and living conditions in Libyan centres the Commission acknowledged to be inadequate. The implementation of the 'Across Sahara' project was entrusted to the Italian Ministry of the Interior. The ministry engaged in administering the EU financial support to border surveillance authorities in Libya and Niger along their common border with a view to enhancing their capacities, including through training of staff and equipment supply. It is interesting to note that, differently from the TRIM project, the focus of the 'Across Sahara' was not the protection of migrants in general but rather the management of migration flows across the Libyan southern border, that is to say the gateway to Europe for migrants departing from the African sub-Saharan region. This is arguably the main source of migration towards European southern coasts across countries such as Libya and through the Sicily channel.[12] It is not difficult to detect the Union's hidden purpose of creating an outpost down south in order to prevent migrants in transit to Europe from even entering the Libyan territory. This would have ultimately impeded such migrants from reaching for the Libyan coasts and continuing their journey to the Italian or Maltese shores.

Similarly, other measures were financed under the AENEAS programme for the surveillance of Libya's maritime borders, including in particular the creation of joint European–Libyan patrols to prevent the departure of vessels towards southern European coasts. Also, funds have been allocated to strengthening hosting and protection capacities on the ground, which the Commission considered to be less costly than providing reception in refugee centres set up in the territories of EU Member States. In this light, not even projects such as TRIM seem to be truly migrant-oriented, in that the real aim of enhancing Libyan reception capacities appears to be the mere resettlement of refugees – actual or potential, as they may be – and the creation of a subsidiary system of 'regional protection areas' which makes the detention of migrants a keystone of the filtering mechanisms activated on migratory routes towards Europe (Rodier 2006: 15–16).[13] However, as acknowledged by the Commission itself (European Commission 2005a: 13–15), these waiting areas are far from being safe in terms of the protection they are supposed to afford to detained migrants. In this respect, they seem rather to have a concealed function as buffer zones created to prevent migrants from leaving Africa.

After the conclusion of the AENEAS programme, the Commission continued to support cooperation with Libya in the field of migration and asylum. Projects of the same nature were financed under the Thematic Programme on Migration and Asylum for the period 2007–13. Based on the 2008 selection process for the first call for proposals, Libya benefited from a €2 million project with the UNHCR entitled 'A Comprehensive Approach to the Effective Management of Mixed Migration Flows in Libya'.[14] The specific objective of the project was to strengthen Libya's reception management capacities and its legal and procedural capacities to deal with migration flows, including Libya's capacity to support voluntary repatriations. Furthermore, under the title 'Sahara–MED: Prevention and Management of Irregular Migration Flows from Sahara Desert to Mediterranean Sea', an additional and much more substantial €10 million contract for a project with the Italian Ministry of the Interior had been signed, with the objective to improve border surveillance and fight illegal migration along the Libyan southern borders.

Against this background, concerns have been voiced by the European Parliament over Libya's practice with regard to migrants' fundamental rights, rights of asylum and the principle of *non-refoulement*. In a 2006 study carried out by the European Parliament services, the question has been raised as to the real nature of EU cooperation with Libya on migration matters (Rodier 2006). The study emphasized that, rather than constituting an example of the AFSJ's external dimension fully complying with the approach enshrined in the Hague Programme,[15] the cooperation resembled an attempt at externalizing the EU's asylum and immigration policy, including the management of migration flows, to an unreliable partner. From 2004 a gradual transfer of responsibility took place: on the one hand, through the strengthening of Libyan hosting and protection capacities on the ground and, on the other, through the drawing up, outside any institutional framework, of the abovementioned plans for cooperation in the surveillance of Libya's borders under the AENEAS programme (ibid.: 13, 15). Criticism was raised particularly with regard to the systematic violations of migrants' and refugees' rights as a result of arbitrary arrests, detentions and expulsions operated by the Libyan authorities, as well as – once again – with regard to the deplorable living conditions of people held in camps and the massive repatriations (ibid.: 17–18),[16] thereby concluding that Libya could not be considered as a safe country either for irregular migrants or for refugees.

The study criticized not only the substance of EU–Libya cooperation but also the form of it. In the absence of contractual relations, the European Union had no formal basis upon which to establish a partnership with Libya on migratory issues. The European Parliament underlined that, notwithstanding formal and substantive setbacks, Libya's strategic position on the path of migrants forced the EU to ignore the absence of a legal framework for cooperation and to give priority to geographic and strategic considerations to the detriment of the respect for fundamental rights (Rodier 2006: 17). By putting pressure on third countries to take responsibility for migrants in transit in their territory and by pushing its borders further and further away in order to hold back immigration at its source (ibid.: 20),[17] the EU runs the risk of accepting that migrants be abused or detained in camps such as those existing in Libya. On the ground of both substantial and formal shortcomings of EU–Libya cooperation on migration, the study called for the placing of respect for the fundamental rights of migrants at the heart of the relation between Brussels and Tripoli.

Notwithstanding parliamentary concerns, in October 2010 the EU and the Libyan authorities agreed on yet another informal understanding, this time defined as a migration cooperation agenda, which exemplifies once again the supremacy of strategic objectives over concerns relating to the protection of migrants' rights. Cecilia Malmström, then European Commissioner for Home Affairs, and Štefan Füle, then European Commissioner for Enlargement and ENP, visited Tripoli that year to further define the terms of the increased bilateral dialogue. During their visit an agreement on a migration cooperation agenda was signed which envisaged concrete steps on a border surveillance system, mobility-related issues, smuggling and trafficking in human beings, and a dialogue on refugees and international protection. The proposed initiatives were to be implemented through a variety of means, ranging from the sharing of experience and best practices to the financing of actions, including the acquisition of equipment by the Libyan side (see Carrera *et al.* 2012: 5–6). In order to ensure the effective management of migratory flows, cooperation was foreseen with a view to provide decent treatment, reception and assistance – in line with international standards – to irregular migrants. Also, cooperation was envisaged with regard to offering assisted voluntary return to irregular migrants intercepted or readmitted or to be returned by the Libyan authorities, or stranded in Libya or in the countries of origin, as well as offering support for their social and professional reintegration. With regard to border management, the European Union agreed, on the one hand, to further support the development of Libyan patrolling, search and rescue capacities in its territorial waters and at high sea and the establishment of an integrated surveillance system along the Libyan land borders, with a focus on the areas prone to irregular migration flows. On the other hand, the European Union declared its willingness to explore concrete possibilities of cooperation with the Libyan police, border and migration authorities as regards the return and readmission of irregular migrants (European Commission 2009: 28).

Against this backdrop, the ECtHR condemned in a 2012 ruling the indiscriminate reliance on third countries as a means to manage migration though stricter border controls. In *Hirsi Jamaa and others* v. *Italy* (European Court of Human Rights 2012), the Strasbourg Court construed Italy's bilateral cooperation with Libya as circumscribing its obligations under international human rights law and the principle of *non-refoulement*. Italy's behaviour in this case, which concerned 11 Somali and 13 Eritrean migrants intercepted at sea and returned to Libya without the possibility of requesting asylum, was found to be in breach of, among other things, art. 4 of Protocol 4 ECHR (Council of Europe 1963), which prohibits collective expulsions (European Court of Human Rights 2012: §186). While the case did not directly relate to the EU's cooperation with Libya, it clearly highlights the shortcomings of EBC towards countries whose standard of protection of irregular migrants does not live up to the standards in force within the EU.

Critical aspects of the EU's cooperation with the neighbours of its neighbours in matters of border management

When considering EU cooperation with Libya on migration issues, terms such as externalization, outsourcing, sub-contracting or remote control of migration management appear adequate to describe the transferral of responsibilities from Brussels to Tripoli through supporting Libyan institution- and capacity-building. It is precisely the practice of externalization as exemplified by the cooperation with Libya that poses major problems in terms of the consistency between the internal and the external dimensions of the AFSJ. This should represent an early warning about future developments of EU cooperation with the neighbours of ENP countries in the field of border management.

With regard to cooperation in countering irregular migration, the only legal basis that can be detected in documents concerning EU–Libya cooperation is the one upon which financial measures have been adopted. That is to say, the only legal bases involved are those referring to EU development cooperation policy. Legally, measures foreseeing financial cooperation with Libya are thus the only tools through which the EU's objective of fighting irregular immigration in the context of bilateral relations have been pursued and which are amenable to justice for judicial review.

The European Union's mechanism of externalization as applied to Libya makes EU–Libya cooperation on migration inconsistent with superposed principles of EU law. Indeed, it has so far been at odds with the founding principles of EU legal order and external action, such as the rule of law and respect of fundamental rights, which are unequivocally enshrined in the Treaties. In this respect, EU cooperation with Libya generates contradictions with the internal dimension of AFSJ policies and should therefore be seen as horizontally inconsistent with those. Two different groups of issues, formal and substantive ones, gave rise to inconsistencies in AFSJ-related aspects of the Union's cooperation with Libya.

Formal issues amount to the lack of a formal basis upon which to establish a partnership with Libya on migratory issues. Libya's strategic position on the migratory routes led the EU to overlook the absence of a broader discussion framework with the Libyan authorities and to resort to operational and informal understandings. From a legal point of view, while the prior conclusion of a partnership or association agreement as such cannot be considered as a preliminary requirement to the lawfulness of cooperative arrangements with a third country, this informality nonetheless raises concerns under three different profiles.

First, lacking a legally binding nature as well as a definitive character, informal understandings are not amenable to justice with a view to obtaining judicial review of provisions contained therein in the light of the Treaties. In this sense, the CJEU is deprived not only of its jurisdictional but also of its advisory competence, whereby it assesses the compatibility of a prospective agreement to be concluded by the Union on the ground of the Treaties' provisions. Therefore, the marge of manoeuvre enjoyed by the parties to such understandings appears to be wider than acceptable under the principle of the rule of law by which the conduct of EU institutions must abide.

Second, the lack of judicial control over EU–Libya cooperation adds up to a lack of democratic scrutiny over the content of agreed informal understandings. In this context, the European Parliament, which has acquired a wider treaty-making power under the Lisbon Treaty,[18] is kept out of the loop by the absence of formal arrangements between the Union and the Libyan authorities.

Third, political conditionality is not applied to the kind of informal under-standings that have been analysed here. Even though it is of course no require-ment for the legality of measures establishing cooperation with third countries, conditionality could have helped to safeguard the respect for the EU's founding principles in the cooperation with Libya. This could have been done, for instance, by making EU financial support subject to Libya's abidance by those same principles.

Closely connected with the latter formal considerations, more substantive issues result from the EU choosing to ignore Libyan practices with regard to the treatment of migrants and refugees. The European Union has enhanced Libya's capacities in order to prevent the entry into and the exit from the latter's territory by migrants in general, although only irregular ones were to be the target of cooperation. By externalizing migration control and by moving its southern border further away in an attempt to hold back migration at its sources, the EU has allowed migrants to be denied their fundamental and asylum-related rights.

Concerning asylum rights in particular, the question has been posed as to whether EU cooperation with Libya amounts to an externalization of asylum-related policies as such or to a radical deprivation of related rights. Two con-siderations make the case for the latter thesis. On the one hand, as has already been observed, Libya is not a signatory of the basic international instruments for the protection of asylum-seekers. On the other hand, the practice of haphazard mass expulsions and forced repatriations operated by the Libyan authorities jeopardize the prohibition of *refoulement*, in that not only undocumented migrants get caught but also potential asylum-seekers for whom returning might signify facing persecution and death.

From a strictly legal point of view, two reasons explain the difficulty of estab-lishing that a violation of fundamental and asylum rights has been perpetrated by EU institutions in their informally agreeing to cooperate with a country which does not grant those rights. First, the abovementioned informality of the cooperation grants the Commission and the Council a *de facto* immunity from the CJEU's jurisdiction. Second, even in the presence of formal measures amenable to justice for judicial review, such as an EU–Libya agreement, if one concedes that the measure at stake abides by all the formal and substantial requirements pre-scribed by EU law, it would be difficult for the Court to establish a ground upon which to hold Union institutions responsible for the conduct of the other party, Libya.[19]

Nonetheless, the EU aspiration to set standards on the international scene in matters of protection of fundamental rights is seriously jeopardized by its cooperation with Libya as is the consistency between the internal and external dimension of the AFSJ.

Conclusion

The aim of this chapter was to assess to what extent current forms of EU cooperation with the neighbours of its neighbours in the field of border management qualify as externalization mechanisms and whether this may have an impact on the consistency of the EU's regime of fundamental rights protection. To this end, the concept of externalization as transfer of responsibility, as opposed to externalization as sub-contracting, has been used.

The analysis of both the operational and the development cooperation components of the EU's cooperation with neighbours of its neighbours has allowed the observation that EU priority-setting differs according to the geographical trajectories of cooperation. While cooperation in border management seems to be migration-oriented with countries in the Sahel and the Horn of Africa, a trade facilitation and anti-trafficking approach seems to inspire the EU's cooperation in border control with countries in the Central Asian republics. However, the question to what extent the current forms of cooperation amount to a sufficient critical mass for claiming that border control responsibilities are – even if only partially – externalized towards the neighbours of the EU's neighbours remains open. Future developments of cooperation in this domain will allow a further – and hopefully more conclusive – assessment of the matter.

However, the current state of affairs does not preclude looking at the present forms of cooperation through the lens of horizontal consistency and, by implication, of legitimacy. Particularly when considered in the light of the Libyan precedent, mechanisms like the conclusion of FRONTEX operational arrangements with countries such as Mauritania and EU-financed border-control capacity-building in sub-Saharan Africa seem designed to directly respond to EU concerns over the fight against irregular migration. However, these mechanisms entail the risk of sacrificing migrants' fundamental rights. This jeopardizes in several ways the consistency between the internal and external dimensions of EU fundamental rights protection, particularly in relation to matters of transparency, accountability and access to justice. It remains to be seen how the prospective EU accession to the European Convention on Human Rights and a more flexible interpretation of the admissibility criteria before the Strasbourg Court will make a difference in this respect and whether a change in legal circumstances could let in through the back door those very fundamental guarantees that the EU risks undermining through externalization.

Notes

1 See also Chapter 2 by Sarah Wolff in this volume.
2 These passengers fall within the category of undocumented or irregular migrants, that is, individuals who find themselves in breach of immigration law (Błuś 2013: 413), including those potentially entitled to international protection. The term 'undocumented' or 'irregular' migrant is herein preferred to 'illegal' migrant, whose connotation is problematic to the extent that it contributes to the immediate construction of unauthorized stays or border crossings as criminal offences regardless of the individual's possible entitlement to international protection (ibid.). The chapter will therefore employ the term 'illegal migration' solely when reporting the discourse of EU institutions or other authors.
3 As of April 2013, FRONTEX (2014) had concluded working arrangements with the authorities of 17 countries – the Russian Federation, Ukraine, Moldova, Georgia, the former Yugoslav Republic of Macedonia, Serbia, Albania, Bosnia and Herzegovina, the United States, Montenegro, Belarus, Canada, Cape Verde, Nigeria, Armenia, Turkey and Azerbaijan – and with the CIS Border Troop Commanders Council and the MARRI Regional Centre in the Western Balkans. In addition, following mandates from its Management Board to enter into negotiations, the agency is in various stages of negotiations with the authorities of a further seven countries: Libya, Morocco, Senegal, Mauritania, Egypt, Brazil and Tunisia.
4 According to this geographical definition, 10 countries can be considered neighbours of the EU's neighbours: in the Sahel and the Horn of Africa, Mauritania, Niger, Mali, Chad and Sudan; in the Gulf region, Iran, Iraq and Saudi Arabia; and in Central Asia, Turkmenistan and Kazakhstan. See also the Introduction to this volume.
5 At the Tripoli EU–Africa Ministerial Conference on Migration and Development in November 2006, the EU and its African partner countries adopted for the first time a joint strategy, the Tripoli Declaration, to respond to the challenges and maximize the benefits of international migration. The EU–Africa Action Plan on trafficking in human beings, which was formally endorsed on the same occasion, is part of the comprehensive strategy adopted in Tripoli. See African Union and European Union (2006).
6 For an exhaustive account of all projects financed, see EuropeAid (2006).
7 The DCI Thematic Programme on Migration and Asylum covered the period 2007–13. For an overview of all projects financed, see EuropeAid (2008).
8 This section is largely based on Bonavita (2013), reproduced with permission from Bruylant.
9 The Protocol removed geographical and temporal limitations to the scope of the Convention, thus conferring universal scope to the latter.
10 Art. 33(1) of the UN Convention Relating to the Status of Refugees (United Nations 1966). On the principle of *non-refoulement* as customary international law, see Goodwin-Gill and McAdam (2007: 354).
11 The UNHCR office in Tripoli was eventually closed in 2010 on the grounds that it was carrying out illegal activities. On this point, see the question to the Council by Member of the European Parliament Oreste Rossi (2011).
12 See also Chapter 2 by Sarah Wolff in this volume.
13 This appears to be the case in particular with regard to refugees' resettlement, which involves transferring them from their country of first asylum to a host state with a view to permanent residence. Rodier (2006) expresses concerns in relation to this phenomenon becoming one of the facets of the European asylum system. While resettlement is a demonstration of international solidarity towards the countries of first asylum, it was not conceived to replace the reception of asylum-seekers who arrived by themselves. However, the place given today to resettlement in European programmes suggests that it may eventually be used to justify the adoption of measures

prohibiting the spontaneous arrival of asylum-seekers, therefore resulting in a situation whereby refugees are selected according to the needs of the Member States.

14 As reported in the answer given by Benita Ferrero-Waldner on behalf of the Commission on 5 January 2009 to the written question by Member of the European Parliament Frank Vanhecke (2009).

15 The Hague Programme places partnership with third countries, when pursued in a spirit of shared responsibility, at the heart of its projects. See European Council (2004).

16 Rodier (2006) mentions that more than 20 non-governmental organizations that defend the rights of migrants and asylum-seekers in various European countries and in Morocco have called on the European Union to defer all decisions on cooperation with Libya on matters of immigration, adding that the ratification and the implementation of the international conventions guaranteeing human rights protection on the part of Libya were to be made an essential prerequisite of such cooperation.

17 The study also expresses worries about the possible affirmation of the concept of 'illegal emigration' to describe what possibly arises as a result of illegal immigration or rather the mere fact of taking a route to leave one's country. The study reported a press release from the Conference of the Interior Ministers of the Western Mediterranean, held in Nice on 11 and 12 May 2006, welcoming 'the efforts of the countries of the southern Mediterranean to contain illegal emigration to Europe'. Moreover, the Senegalese authorities announced that they had arrested in their own territory more than 1,500 'potential illegal emigrants' who were preparing to head to the Canaries in pirogues. Such a concept has of course no legitimacy with regard to the Universal Declaration of Human Rights and to art. 13(2) thereof, which stipulates that 'Everyone has the right to leave any country, including his own, and to return to his country'.

18 Art. 218(6)(a) TFEU refers to cases in which the consent of the European Parliament is a mandatory requirement for the conclusion of an agreement by the Council. Since such cases include *inter alia* the conclusion of agreements covering fields to which the ordinary legislative procedure applies, the European Parliament is granted the power to consent to a much wider range of international agreements than in the pre-Lisbon era by virtue of the extension of the ordinary legislative procedure to the vast majority of matters covered by the Union's competence.

19 This remains true, for instance, in relation to the violation of the principle of *non-refoulement*, notwithstanding its extraterritorial application, whereby the principle applies to whatsoever governmental activity, including those carried out outside national borders. In so far as *refoulement* is operated by the Libyan authorities, the prohibition thereof cannot be relied on to support an allegation of *jus cogens* violations by the Union. See United Nations High Commissioner for Refugees (2007: paragraph 24); and Trevisanut (2008).

References

African Union and European Union (2006) 'Joint Africa–EU Declaration on Migration and Development', Tripoli, 22–23 November, http://sa.au.int/en/sites/default/files/Joint%20Africa–EU%20Declaration%20on%20Migration%20and%20Development.pdf (accessed October 2014).

Alegre, S., D. Bigo and J. Jeandesboz (2009) *External Dimension of the Area of Freedom, Security and Justice*, Brussels: European Parliament, PE 410.688.

Błuś, A. (2013) 'Beyond the Walls of Paper: Undocumented Migrants, the Border and Human Rights', *European Journal of Migration and Law* 15(4), 413–446.

Bonavita, V. (2013) 'The FSJ Component of EU–Libya Relations: Building Coherence, Avoiding Contradictions or None of the Above', in C. Flaesch-Mougin and L.S. Rossi (eds) *La dimension extérieure de l'espace de liberté, de sécurité et de justice de l'Union européenne après le Traité de Lisbonne*, Brussels: Bruylant, 575–601.

Carrera, S., L. den Hertog and J. Parkin (2012) *EU Migration Policy in the Wake of the Arab Spring: What prospects for EU–Southern Mediterranean Relations?*, *MEDPRO Technical Report* 15, Brussels: CEPS.

Council of Europe (1963) 'Protocol No. 4 to the European Convention for the Protection of Human Rights and Fundamental Freedoms', Strasbourg, 16 September, amended according to the provisions of Protocol No. 11 (ETS No. 155) as from its entry into force on 1 November 1998.

Council of the European Union (2003) *Mission to Libya Focused on Illegal Immigration – Terms of Reference*, doc. no. 11694/03, Brussels, 22 July.

Council of the European Union (2004) 'Council Regulation (EC) No 377/2004 of 19 February 2004 on the Creation of an Immigration Liaison Officers Network', *Official Journal of the European Union*, L 64, 2 February, 1–4.

Council of the European Union (2005) *Conclusions on Initiating Dialogue and Cooperation with Libya on Migration Issues*, doc. n. 9796/05, Brussels, 6 June.

EuropeAid (2006) *Aeneas Programme: Programme for Financial and Technical Assistance to Third Countries in the Area of Migration and Asylum – Overview of Projects Funded 2004–2006*, Brussels.

EuropeAid (2008) *Migration and Asylum Programme: Thematic Programme on cooperation with Third Countries in the Areas of Migration and Asylum – Overview of projects funded 2007–2008*, Brussels.

European Commission (2005a) *Communication from the Commission to the Council on the Monitoring and Evaluation Mechanism of the Third Countries in the Field of the Fight against Illegal Immigration*, COM(2005) 352 final, Brussels, 28 July.

European Commission (2005b) *Commission Communication: A Strategy on the External Dimension of the Area of Freedom, Security and Justice*, COM(2005) 491 final, Brussels, 12 October.

European Commission (2007) 'Africa–EU Partnership on Migration, Mobility and Employment', http://ec.europa.eu/development/icenter/repository/EAS2007_action_plan_migration_en.pdf (accessed October 2014).

European Commission (2009) 'European Neighbourhood and Partnership Instrument: Libya Strategy Paper and National Indicative Programme 2011–2013', Brussels, 16 April.

European Commission (2010) *Commission Decision on the 2010 Annual Action Programme for the Islamic Republic of Mauritania to be Financed from the 10th European Development Fund*, Brussels, 17 December.

European Commission (2011) *Communication on a Dialogue for Migration, Mobility and Security with the Southern Mediterranean Countries*, COM(2011) 292 final, Brussels, 24 May.

European Council (2004) *The Hague Programme: Strengthening Freedom, Security and Justice in the European Union*, 16054/04, 13 December.

European Court of Human Rights (2012) *Case of Hirsi Jamaa and Others v Italy*, Application no. 27765/09, Strasbourg, Judgment of 23 February.

European External Action Service (2011) 'Strategy for Security and Development in the Sahel', http://www.eeas.europa.eu/africa/docs/sahel_strategy_en.pdf (accessed October 2014).

European Parliament and Council of the European Union (2004) 'Regulation No. 491/2004 of the European Parliament and of the Council of 10 March 2004 Establishing a Programme for Financial and Technical Assistance to Third Countries in the Areas of Migration and Asylum (AENEAS)', *Official Journal of the European Union*, L 80, 18 March, 1–5.

European Parliament and Council of the European Union (2006) 'Regulation No. 1905/2006 of the European Parliament and of the Council of 18 December 2006 Establishing a Financing Instrument for Development Cooperation (DCI)', *Official Journal of the European Union*, L 378, 27 December, 41–71.

European Parliament and Council of the European Union (2010) 'Regulation (EU) No. 439/2010 of the European Parliament and of the Council of 19 May 2010 Establishing a European Asylum Support Office', *Official Journal of the European Union*, L 132, 29 May, 11–28.

European Parliament and Council of the European Union (2011) 'Regulation (EU) No. 1168/2011 of the European Parliament and of the Council of 25 October 2011 Amending Council Regulation (EC) No 2007/2004 Establishing a European Agency for the Management of Operational Cooperation at the External Borders of the Member States of the European Union', *Official Journal of the European Union*, L 304, 22 November, 1–7.

Eurostat (2014) 'Asylum Applicants and First Instance Decisions on Asylum Applications: Second Quarter 2014', *Data in Focus* 11.

Fargues, P. (2013) *EU Neighbourhood Migration Report 2013*, San Domenico di Fiesole: European University Institute.

Fink, M. (2012) 'Frontex Working Arrangements: Legitimacy and Human Rights Concerns Regarding "Technical Relationships"', *Merkourios: Utrecht Journal of International and European Law* 28(75), 20–35.

Frattini, F. (2007) 'Answer Given by Mr Frattini on Behalf of the Commission to Written Question n. E-5006/06 by Robert Kilroy-Silk (NI) to the Commission on Preventing Illegal Immigrants from Mauritania', Brussels, 27 January 2007, *Official Journal of the European Union*, C 293, 5 December, 12.

FRONTEX (2014) 'Third Countries', www.frontex.europa.eu/partners/third-countries (accessed November 2014).

Gammeltoft-Hansen, H. (2010) 'The Externalisation of European Migration Control and the Reach of International Refugee Law', in E. Guild and P. Minderhoud (eds) *The First Decade of EU Migration and Asylum Law*, Leiden: Brill, 1–23.

Gavrilis, G. (2009) 'Beyond the Border Management Programme for Central Asia (BOMCA)', *EU – Central Asia Monitoring* 11, Brussels: CEPS, Madrid: FRIDE.

Goodwin-Gill, G. and J. McAdam (2007) *The Refugee in International Law*, Oxford: Oxford University Press.

McNamara, F. (2013) 'Member State Responsibility for Migration Control within Third States – Externalisation Revisited', *European Journal of Migration and Law* 15(3), 319–335.

Rodier, C. (2006) *Analysis of the External Dimension of the EU's Asylum and Immigration Policies – Summary and Recommendations for the European Parliament*, Brussels: European Parliament, PE 374.366.

Rossi, O. (2011) Parliamentary Question to the Council 'Libya Closes UNHCR Office', E-4582/10 of 18 June 2010, *Official Journal of the European Union*, C 170 E, 10 June, 79.

Slominski, P. (2012) 'The Ambiguities of Legalization of the EU's Strategy of Extraterritorial Border Control', *European Foreign Affairs Review* 17(2/1), 19–34.

Tietje, C. (1997) 'The Concept of Coherence in the Treaty on European Union and the Common Foreign and Security Policy', *European Foreign Affairs Review* 2(2), 211–233.

Trevisanut, S. (2008) 'The Principle of Non-refoulement at Sea and the Effectiveness of Asylum Protection', *Max Planck Yearbook of UN Law* 12, 205–246.

United Nations (1966) *1951 Convention and 1967 Protocol Relating to the Status of Refugee*, attached to United Nations General assembly resolution 2198 (XXI), A/RES/2198 of 16 December.

United Nations High Commissioner for Refugees (2007) 'Advisory Opinion on the Extra-territorial Application of Non-refoulement Obligations under the 1951 Convention Relating to the Status of Refugees and its 1967 Protocol', 27 January.

Vanhecke, F. (2009) Parliamentary Question to the Commission 'Financial assistance for Libya', E-6350/08 of 25 November 2008, *Official Journal of the European Union*, C 316, 23 December, 122.

2 The European Union and the challenges of trans-Saharan migration

Sarah Wolff

Introduction

Since 2011, the 'Arab Spring' and the Syrian crisis have significantly transformed the nature and scope of migratory challenges in the European Union's (EU) broader southern neighbourhood and in particular in the Sahara–Sahel region. This region, which spans from Mauritania, Mali and the Western Sahara to the Horn of Africa, is the new 'arc of instability' for the EU and its Mediterranean neighbours, in particular the Maghreb states.

Historically, the Sahara–Sahel region is a borderless area where nomadic populations such as the Tuaregs have been moving across borders imposed by colonization. Trans-Saharan migration linking the Maghreb to the Sahara and Sahel regions was connected to trans-Saharan trade and has shaped the region. Since the 1970s and 1980s, sub-Saharan migrants have provided labour force to Maghreb countries, for instance to work in the oil industry in Libya (De Haas 2006). Sub-Saharan and African migrants are today settling in Maghreb countries for work and study. In the past, however, the EU has overlooked the impact that its regional or bilateral initiatives such as the 'Barcelona process' and the European Neighbourhood Policy (ENP) towards its Mediterranean neighbours could have on the broader southern neighbourhood and how it could capitalize on cross-regional cooperation. The overemphasis on border control and irregular migration cooperation with the EU's southern neighbours has had a negative impact on the Sahara–Sahel region. Surveillance techniques and joint patrolling at the EU's external borders have disrupted migratory routes, leading migrants to embark on longer and more dangerous journeys. The co-optation of Maghreb law enforcement authorities to stop migrants crossing the Mediterranean has had some negative impacts in the practices of return and readmission to African countries (Wolff 2014).

Today, however, EU policy-makers realize that the borders between Mediterranean countries and their neighbours have become 'disaggregated and partly porous frontiers of [the EU] "empire"' where 'all things destructive, illegal, and potentially dangerous are coalescing' (Del Sarto and Tholens 2013). The intervention of France in Mali in 2013 is a testimony to the weaknesses of nation-states in the region when confronted with borderless criminal and terrorist movements. The rise of the 'Islamic State of Iraq and the Levant' (ISIL) and its activities in Iraq and Syria clearly demonstrate the extension of this 'arc of instability' to the Middle East. According to the Tunisian Ministry of the Interior, 2,400 Tunisians have gone to fight in Syria, and around 80 per cent of them are fighting for ISIL (Jeune Afrique 2014). Moroccan foreign fighters are estimated to number around 1,500 (Masbah 2014). In addition to security threats to states and businesses, the security and safety of migrants is also at stake since they are the first victims of human trafficking and organized crime. The Sahara–Sahel states have been unable to offer 'protection to states and people from the changes that were taking place in the region' in the aftermath of the 'Arab Spring' (Del Sarto and Tholens 2013).

Conceiving the Sahara–Sahel region as a 'new frontier' of the EU, this chapter argues that it is no longer a distant land and ponders the challenges of integrating a cross-regional dimension into the EU's policies towards its broader southern neighbourhood. Paying more attention to the neighbours of the EU's southern neighbours would provide the EU with more leverage in designing and implementing its migration policy instruments such as readmission agreements, Mobility Partnerships, cooperation on border management or visa liberalization and facilitation dialogues.

The first part of this chapter reviews how the Sahara–Sahel region has become a new frontier for EU policy-makers with the conceptualization of a 'Strategy for Security and Development in the Sahel' which on paper comprehensively attempts to bridge the security–development gap (Council of the European Union 2011). So far, though, this strategy has been used more as a crisis management tool than a real development instrument, and it overlooks migratory challenges in the region. The second part of the chapter discusses the policy option of supporting further Maghreb integration and encouraging cross-regional cooperation on migration with sub-Saharan countries. Political challenges in this regard include the Western Sahara conflict and the difference in migration policies between Maghreb and African countries. From a legal point of view, the strengthening of solid legal protection for refugees, asylum policies and migrants' rights in the Maghreb is another key challenge. The third part of the chapter argues that the current EU return and readmission policy presents some political and legal deficiencies that would need to be addressed internally. Engaging the EU's broader southern neighbourhood on migration issues would therefore need to account for those loopholes. This chapter tackles only the issue of refugees, internally displaced people, asylum-seekers and irregular migrants. A comprehensive strategy would necessarily have to include a discussion of the legal migration opportunities for the EU's broader southern neighbourhood.

The Sahara–Sahel region: the 'new frontier' of Europe

The EU's southern neighbours are confronted with immense security and migratory challenges in the Sahara–Sahel region. This new 'arc of instability' is a shared concern in the EU, which has designed an EU Strategy for Security and

Development. This Strategy conceptualizes the region as a 'new frontier' for Europe's security. This securitization of the Sahara–Sahel region without accompanying strong development policies could have some adverse effects on the treatment of migration. Addressing migration as a positive contribution to the resilience of societies in the Sahara–Sahel region and cross-regionally with Maghreb countries would nonetheless be welcomed.

The EU Strategy for Security and Development: still comprehensive?

In the past few years, the international community has been prolific in drafting various strategies for the Sahara–Sahel region. The 'Sahel strategies' designed at EU, regional and international levels mostly address security issues, the lack of governance capacities, the restoration of the nation-state and the provision of humanitarian and development aid. They all display different understandings of the Sahel, 'a way for stakeholders to "map" the Sahel region to fit their own purposes and policies' such as the African Union (AU) Sahel Strategy of 11 August 2014 or the 'Programme de cohérence et d'action régionale de l'Afrique de l'Ouest pour la stabilité et le développement des espaces saharo-sahéliens' of the Economic Community of West African States (ECOWAS) (Barrios and Koepf 2014). The 'Alliance Globale pour l'Initiative Résilience' (AGIR) is an international partnership that was launched in 2012 with support of the European Commission to build resilience in the Sahel region (Council of the European Union 2013). The 2013 Sahel Regional Strategy that brings together UN agencies and non-governmental organizations is the only one to identify early on the problem of refugees and internally displaced people (United Nations 2013).

The EU drafted its own strategy, marking a rupture with prior conceptualizations that had treated sub-Saharan Africa and the Sahel as a 'distant abroad' (Bach 2011). Authoritarian regimes and friendly relations in North Africa acted as a buffer zone. The EU could count on those regimes, with experience in containing radical Islam, to handle security in the Sahel. The proliferation of European hostage-takings, notably by 'Al-Qaeda in the Islamic Maghreb' (AQIM), combined with poverty and a severe food crisis nonetheless compelled Europeans to design a 'Strategy for Security and Development in the Sahel' (Council of the European Union 2011). The hostage-taking in the Algerian gas facility of In Amenas in January 2013 confirmed the spill-over of the security threats from the Sahel to Maghreb countries, and therefore the need for a cross-regional approach to the challenges.

Originally drafted with a strong development component, the strategy was intended to bridge the gap between security and development and provided a comprehensive approach that pooled different resources and expertise in the EU.[1] The comprehensive nature of the strategy was nonetheless undermined by the 2012–13 Malian crisis.

The four axes of the 'Strategy for Security and Development in the Sahel' are: (1) development, good governance and internal conflict resolution; (2) political and diplomatic action; (3) security and the rule of law; and (4) countering violent extremism and radicalization. Migration issues underpin the four axes and yet migration is not a prominent feature of the strategy. Positive aspects of the strategy include the involvement of local civil society and the setting up of a 'Task Force Sahel' within the European External Action Service (EEAS). Directed by the EEAS Department for West and Central Africa, the Task Force Sahel has adopted a horizontal approach and brings together geographic departments and crisis management structures as well as other Directorates General (DGs) of the European Commission such as DG DEVCO (Development and Cooperation), DG ECHO (Humanitarian Aid and Civil Protection) and the EU Counter-terrorism Coordinator (Pirozzi 2013: 12).[2] In March 2013, Michel Reveyrand-de Menthon was appointed EU Special Representative for the Sahel (Council of the European Union 2013). The EU has initially mobilized instruments across the board with €1.5 billion allocated to Mali, Niger and Mauritania for projects in the areas of good governance, rule of law, justice, decentralization, etc. through the Tenth European Development Fund (2007–13) (European External Action Service 2013). The Instrument for Stability was also mobilized to support a project on the fight against money laundering in Ghana, Nigeria, Senegal and Cape Verde (European Commission 2013a).

Inherent weaknesses of the strategy include a lack of indicators to monitor progress, the predominance of an EU internal security focus (including on drug trafficking) and the underestimation of the role of development factors (Wolff 2011). Since the Mali conflict, the strategy has fallen short of initial expectations and has become mostly a tool of crisis management focusing on the Common Security and Defence Policy (CSDP) with the launching of several missions (Pirozzi 2013). The European Union Mission on Regional Maritime Capacity-building in the Horn of Africa, EUCAP Sahel Niger, aims at improving the capacities of the Nigerian security forces (gendarmerie, national police, national guard) to fight terrorism and organized crime. The mandate of the mission specifies that this capacity-building should be undertaken 'in an effective and coordinated manner, with a view to contribute to enhancing of political stability, security, governance and social cohesion in Niger and in the Sahel region' (Council of the European Union 2012). Following the 'Operation Serval' of the French army in Mali, an EU Training Mission was launched to rebuild the Malian armed forces. This has been complemented by an EU capacity-building mission (EUCAP) in Mali that lends support to institutional reforms and the restoration of the authority of the Malian state throughout the country (Council of the European Union 2014a). Security aspects of border management have led to the establishment of 'an inter-service working group to strengthen the implementation of the Sahel Strategy and to develop proposals of greater integration of EU instruments and the EU Member States activities' (Council of the European Union 2014b). The suggestions made by this working group include developing cross-border management cooperation between Maghreb and Sahel–Sahara countries by strengthening inter-agency work. This could be achieved by linking up the work of the EUCAP Sahel Niger and EUCAP Sahel Mali missions to the EUBAM Libya mission. The document calls for coordination with regional initiatives such as the G5 initiated by the leaders of Mauritania, Niger, Mali, Chad and Burkina Faso to anchor security and democracy in the region and create a 'space of solidarity' (Radio France International 2014).

Given the strong French involvement and the appointment of a French defence officer to manage this dossier in the geographical unit of the EEAS, observers have been worried that the strategy's collective European dimension could be weakened. African observers have also voiced a series of concerns which range from the lack of consultation of African countries when drafting the strategy to the overemphasis on security issues by comparison with development issues (Africa Governance Institute 2013). One of the recommendations formulated towards the EU is to redefine the European Neighbourhood Policy, given its inadequacy with regard to the challenges in the Sahara–Sahel region (ibid.: 4). This would also require a clarification of how a renewed EU Sahel–Saharan strategy could be integrated in the post-2020 Cotonou Agreement.

Migration and mobility in the Maghreb–Sahara–Sahel region

The comprehensive nature of the strategy remains therefore mostly at the rhetorical level. While the security situation legitimately required the mobilization of crisis management instruments, the EU also needs to think about the development of the region, including trans-Saharan migration challenges.

The Sahara–Sahel region is undergoing profound changes in migration patterns. If the Tuaregs have always been mobile, today other migratory fluxes go through the desert. While some migrants look for better economic opportunities in the Maghreb or Europe, other populations have been forced to migrate due to a series of security and food crises. In the aftermath of the Libyan conflict, many sub-Saharan families were faced with the disruption of remittances. About 43,000 Chadians returned back home, and money transfers decreased by 57 per cent (Ammour 2012). In combination with the food crisis in the Sahel, future internal displacements and refugee crises are likely to become a common feature in the region.

In 2012, the conflict in Mali led to the displacement of about half a million Malians to neighbouring countries or internally. Internally displaced people are vulnerable when it comes to protection as they do not cross a border but are refugees in their own country, fleeing a war zone or hunger. They remain under the legal responsibility of their governments who are often facing rebellion and lack the capacities to deal with the crisis. 230,000 people chose to return back home between June 2013 and April 2014, while 278,000 remained displaced internally or in neighbouring countries (European Commission 2014). Developing strategies for people who return home is key, especially as the conflict also coincided with a food crisis which has left about 24 per cent of the Malian population in a state of food insecurity (3.7 million people). Around half a million children under five years old were likely to suffer from acute malnutrition in 2014 (European Commission 2014).

The dramatic consequences of the instability in North Africa and in the Sahara–Sahel region make it difficult for the EU external migration policy to ignore its broader southern neighbourhood. In 2011, the UN Refugee Agency declared that the Mediterranean Sea was the most deadly stretch of water in the world, yet the crossing of the Sahara has been as dangerous and the situation could worsen (UNCHR 2012). In 2013, FRONTEX reported the deaths of 92 migrants, mostly women and children, in northern Niger, which has become 'a major corridor for illegal migration and people-trafficking from Sub-Saharan Africa into north Africa and across the Mediterranean into Europe' (FRONTEX 2013: 20). In the last quarter of 2013 detections of irregular West African migrants by FRONTEX decreased, except for Nigerians. However, detections of Eritreans in Italy steeply increased in 2013 and were as high as the numbers of Syrian refugees (FRONTEX 2013: 58). In fact, Eritreans became the second largest group of irregular migrants detected by FRONTEX after the Syrians. The migratory route that they take once again highlights the relevance of the Maghreb–Sahara–Sahel region:

> the vast majority of Eritreans were detected on the Central Mediterranean route (9,926, or nearly 90%), after departing from Libya. Following a similar route, Somalis were also detected in large numbers in 2013 (5,624), which level is comparable to 2012 (5,038). Altogether, [these two groups totalled] 16% of all detections.
>
> (FRONTEX 2014: 30)

Mobilizing cross-regional cooperation on migration in the Maghreb–Sahara–Sahel region seems an obvious recommendation to make. Given the abovementioned challenges, many commentaries put forward the added value of cross-regional cooperation with the Maghreb, an issue which has been absent from the ENP and from the Union for the Mediterranean. Commission President Barroso stressed the importance of cooperation with the Maghreb to face the challenges of instability, and the '5 + 5' group was put forward as one of the best forums to discuss those issues (Agence Europe 2013). A Joint Communication of the European Commission and the High Representative (2012) called for supporting closer cooperation and regional integration in the Maghreb.[3] If such regional cooperation could be reinvigorated, the Maghreb countries could be better anchored in the Joint EU Africa Strategy and on-going initiatives in the field of migration and border management. The Joint Communication also called for a reinvigoration of the Arab Maghreb Union and the possible development of the following initiatives in the field of migration and mobility:

- making further efforts towards the full implementation of existing ministerial declarations and action plans in the area of migration and development between all relevant actors, notably the Euro-African Migration and Development Process (the 'Rabat Process') and the Africa–EU Partnership on Migration, Mobility and Employment;
- supporting legal migration schemes among Maghreb countries as well as between the latter and sub-Saharan states;

- making more systematic use of the opportunities to enhance mobility offered by the EU Visa Code, including for categories such as youth, students or civil society, and increasing understanding via information exchanges on the existing visa regimes;
- promoting regional cooperation in the field of border surveillance and the fight against irregular migration in the Maghreb and the sub-Saharan region including through information-sharing at the regional level, common risk analysis, joint border management and surveillance and police cooperation including on trafficking in human beings and drugs;
- promoting cooperation between the countries of the region in readmission matters, both as regards readmission among Maghreb countries as well as from Maghreb countries to sub-Saharan countries in full respect of migrants' fundamental rights;
- continuing to assist Maghreb countries in the area of asylum and international protection, through capacity-building measures under the Northern African Regional Protection Programme, or by considering possible resettlement options;
- as appropriate, providing information on issues related to EU consular assistance and protection, as well as developing a common understanding in this increasingly important area for EU Member States and Maghreb countries alike (ibid.: 16–17).

Trans-Saharan migration cooperation: the EU's external and internal challenges

Integrating the EU's broader southern neighbourhood requires the consideration of several challenges. First, the Maghreb is a region of closed borders compared to high intra-African mobility, in particular in the case of the ECOWAS countries. Second, the legal challenges in relation to the rights of irregular migrants are multiple.

Maghreb's closed borders vs. ECOWAS intra-regional mobility

In the Maghreb many borders are closed and intra-regional mobility is very low. This is partly explained by the Western Saharan conflict, which has poisoned relations between Algeria and Morocco and affected cooperation with the African Union. The border between the two countries has been closed since their independence, with a few exceptions, and a diplomatic row erupted in summer 2014 with the construction of a fence by Morocco, officially for counterterrorism purposes (France 24 2014). Maghreb countries are indeed wary of the return of nationals fighting with ISIL in Syria. But the border has been closed for many years and as of 2013 Algeria had waived visa requirements for other Maghreb nationals except for Moroccans, Malians and Nigerians (EUI 2013). There is no other regional framework to discuss migration among Maghreb countries besides the '5+5 Dialogue', since Algeria vetoes the membership of

Morocco in the African Union. The Arab Maghreb Union has also not been active for years and Algeria is not a full member of the Rabat Process, a regional consultative process launched in 2006 to discuss migration management and launch concrete initiatives (Collyer *et al.* 2012: 10).

This situation of a 'closed Maghreb' contrasts sharply with the dynamism of intra-African migration. Since the 1980s there has been an acceleration of migratory fluxes from Africa to developed countries (Castles and Miller 2009: 156), but African migration remains mainly intra-regional. Emigrants from Benin, Burkina Faso, Ghana, Guinea, Mali, Mauritania, Niger and Togo go primarily to destinations in West and Central Africa (Awumbila 2009). Like their North African counterparts, some countries such as Ivory Coast, Ghana, Senegal and Nigeria have become the main countries of immigration in Africa (ibid.). The Protocol of Free Movement of ECOWAS allows for 90 days of visa-free stay. Cross-border ethnic groups also explain why mobility is so high in Africa: 'ethnic groups such as the Soninké (of Mauritania, Mali and Senegal), the Mossi (Burkina Faso) and the Dogons (Mali) have traditionally seen short-term migration as a rite of passage or as an important part of personal development' (Westh 2011: 7). Yet although migration is free in West Africa, there is often the problem of a lack of 'comprehensive migration management schemes' (ibid.).

African regional instruments display some best practices in the field of migration. To respond to the African intra-migration flows triggered by internal displacement due to environmental disasters or internal conflicts, the Kampala Convention entered into force in 2012 in the AU countries (African Union 2009). This Convention is a pioneering legally binding instrument which protects internally displaced people on an entire continent. The AU has also engaged in implementing a series of capacity-building and standard-settings initiatives, notably in the field of legal migration and in partnership with the EU. Yet, due to the asymmetry of the AU's relationship with the EU, an evaluation of AU migration initiatives concludes that 'the EU has influenced the development of African frameworks and also influences the type of initiatives the African Union can take, because of the limited amount of funding provided by African member states. This raises questions of ownership and accountability' (Klavaert 2011: 4). The AU has also adopted key texts on migration such as the 'Protocol on the Free Movement of Persons, Right of Residence and Right of Establishment' in parallel to the development of an African Common Market. In 2006 a Common African Position on Migration and Development was adopted (African Union 2006). However, most of those frameworks are not legally binding, apart from the Kampala Convention.

Irregular migrants and refugees: ignored and at risk?

Faced with economic difficulties and democratic transitions, North African governments have tended to focus more on migration issues related to their own nationals than caring for their neighbours' migration problems. In Tunisia, one of the first priorities of the secretary of state for migration and Tunisians abroad after the revolution was to set up a commission to investigate the case of the 'haragas', literally 'those who burn' their lives by crossing the Mediterranean. The EU's discussions on Mobility Partnerships concluded with Morocco in June 2013 and with Tunisia in March 2014 have also mostly concentrated on opportunities and rights for nationals and only a few projects deal with the rights of sub-Saharan migrants. In Morocco, evidence of mistreatment of sub-Saharan migrants has been documented (GADEM 2010; Keygnaert *et al.* 2014) and has led to the departure of 'Médecins sans Frontières' following the publication of a report denouncing violence and abuses against sub-Saharan migrants (Médecins sans Frontières 2010).

Further cross-regional cooperation on migration and any EU policies in this regard need to take into account the rather weak legal framework for migrants, refugees and asylum-seekers in the region. Even though the Maghreb countries are strong advocates for their diasporas abroad and signatories to the Geneva Convention, practices across the region show considerable divergence.

During the 'Arab Spring', 'persons fleeing generalised violence or armed conflict, such as occurred in Libya for example, will frequently fall outside the Convention's definition because of their inability to establish a link between the risk of harm they face and one of the five stated grounds of persecution' (Wood 2012: 8). Other regional instruments have been adopted, such as the 1969 Organization of African Unity Convention Governing the Specific Aspects of Refugee Problems in Africa 'to address aspects of African refugee protection not adequately addressed by the 1951 Convention' (ibid.). Yet the migrants crossing the Mediterranean only fall under the more restrictive 1951 Geneva Convention. According to the United Nations High Commissioner for Refugees (UNHCR 2013a), only Mauritania has a finalized draft national asylum law, which has not yet been adopted; this lack raises serious issues for intra-regional migration. Encouraging these countries to develop migration and asylum legislation should be at the heart of the EU's strategy in supporting democratic transitions.

Following the Libyan conflict, which generated more than 700,000 migrants, around 212,331 returned to their home countries in Burkina Faso, Chad, Ghana, Mali, Niger and Senegal. 'The vast majority of West African returnees were males (98–99%), mostly aged between 20 and 40 years old, of whom a high percentage held low-skilled jobs in Libya, such as labouring, farming and construction' (Naik and Laczko 2012). In Egypt, the numbers of refugees and asylum-seekers coming mostly from Syria, South Sudan, Sudan and Somalia have reached a peak with 267,820 people in January 2015, among whom were 140,000 Syrian refugees (UNHCR 2014). Egypt is also a country of transit towards Israel, which has 'more than 64,000 people of concern to UNHCR, 90 per cent of whom are from Eritrea and Sudan' (UNCHR 2013b). Accordingly, '[t]he number of new arrivals in Israel has declined significantly as a result of deterrence measures which have been put in place, while reports of human rights abuses by smugglers and traffickers in the Sinai desert persist' (ibid.). In Morocco, for instance, not only has irregular migration been criminalized by law, unanimously voted by the Parliament after the 16 May 2003 attacks on

Casablanca (Wolff 2012: 75), but the return of sub-Saharan migrants regularly takes place. Following the 2005 events of Ceuta and Melilla, Morocco recruited 9,000 supplementary agents into the army and adopted a new policy to improve its border control capacities (ibid.; Lahlou 2007: 47). In 2003 Nigerians were returned from the Oudja airport (416 people), Nador (207 people) and Fes-Saïs (480 people), as well as from Tangier and Rabat (Belguendouz 2010). Several other instances have been reported by the 'Groupe Antiraciste d'Accompagnement et de Défense des Etrangers Migrants' (GADEM 2010).

North African countries have had difficulties in shedding their image of 'emigration countries' and are only slowly moving towards the domestic reform of migration. Nonetheless, since 2014 Morocco has embarked upon a reform of its immigration law which should lead to the regularization of sub-Saharan migrants and has led to the processing of refugee applications by the Protection Office for Refugees and Stateless (de Haas 2014). Although this reform has not halted violence against sub-Saharan migrants (Human Rights Watch 2014), it demonstrates that Morocco has acknowledged the importance of integrating them into society and it has responded to international pressure to reform. This also coincides with the geopolitical ambitions of the Kingdom which would like to become a key regional economic player in Africa.

Finally, human being trafficking and environmental migration should also be addressed in the EU's broader southern neighborhood. A European Commission-led task force on the Mediterranean, created in the aftermath of the increase of migrants' influx into Lampedusa in autumn 2013, looked into possibilities of further cooperation between North African countries and their counterparts in the Sahel to combat traffickers' networks:

> In particular, Egyptian authorities should be encouraged to put more attention and to combat more effectively the activities of the traffickers of human beings in the Sinai region; Sudanese authorities should be invited to combat against the criminal organisations operating on their territory and facilitating the smuggling and trafficking of migrants and refugees from the Horn of Africa towards the Mediterranean region; Nigerian authorities should be engaged and assisted to better protecting their most vulnerable nationals from falling victim to the traffickers in human beings.
>
> (European Commission 2013b:6)

The task force also recommends revising Regional Protection Programmes to include Sahel countries (ibid.: 12). Environmental causes of migration have also been underestimated. In the coming years, a country like Mali could lose up to 40 per cent of its agriculture capacity and Sudan up to 50 per cent (Hummel *et al.* 2012: 5). The link between climate change and migration was acknowledged as early as the 1990s and the beginning of the discussions on climate change. Environmental migrations will increase considerably in the near future. Yet there are few projects addressing that.

The challenge of EU return and readmission practices

Migration challenges in the European Union's broader southern neighbourhood cannot be assessed without addressing the EU's inconsistent practices of return and readmission. Return and readmission is governed by the 2008 EU Return Directive, which lays down the minimum conditions for detention and return of irregular migrants (European Union 2008). It constitutes the legal basis for FRONTEX to organize joint return operations. Readmission of irregular migrants is organized through the conclusion of readmission agreements which require a third country to readmit its nationals that have been intercepted in the EU as well as third-country nationals having transited through the third country's territory. Readmission agreements have been since 1999 a Union competence, with several mandates delivered in the 2000s to the European Commission by the Council to open readmission agreements negotiations with third countries. As of 2014, a mandate has been issued for 19 third countries.[5] Yet the main incentives to sign an EU readmission agreement are often of a financial nature and to obtain visa liberalization or facilitation. In the EU's southern neighbourhood this has not yet been the case, except for Turkey. This lack of credible incentives has been a real obstacle to the conclusion of readmission agreements and Mobility Partnerships. The latter are global agreements organizing temporary migration and temporary visa facilitation as well as border management and development aid. Obstacles to the signature of an EU–Morocco readmission agreement were lifted with the signature of a Mobility Partnership in 2013. Visa facilitation for certain categories of travellers such as students and businessmen is part of this political agreement. The conclusion of a readmission agreement is a central element of the agreement on a Mobility Partnership (Wolff 2014).

Given these difficulties, the EU Member States have preferred to rely on informal instruments to return and readmit third-country nationals. Those informal practices compete at times with the negotiation of EU-wide readmission agreements and hamper their negotiations. The myriad of *ad hoc* and informal agreements include police cooperation and law enforcement memorandums of understanding or exchanges of letters with little legal value (Cassarino 2010). Informality and flexibility at the bilateral level imply less parliamentary scrutiny in all countries as well as escaping the 'legal venues' of international and regional conventions. An evaluation of EU readmission agreements highlighted several issues in implementation, among them the fact that Member States do not necessarily resort to this EU instrument and prefer to use older bilateral instruments (European Commission 2011). While the negotiations on the EU–Morocco readmission agreement have not yet led anywhere despite several rounds of negotiations, Morocco has signed several readmission agreements with EU Member States: Germany (1998), Spain (1992, 2003), France (1983, 2001), Italy (1998), Malta (2002) and Portugal (1999).

This internal competition at EU level has had the negative consequence of externalizing such informal practices beyond the EU's southern neighbourhood. Similarly, EU Member States have concluded readmission agreements with

African countries, co-opting them in the control of migration. A Spanish–Malian readmission agreement that entered into force in 2005 helped the Spanish authorities to increase considerably the returns to Mali: before the agreement entered into force (2002–05) a total of five Malian migrants were returned from Spain, while this number increased to 2,567 returnees in 2006–08 (Trauner and Deimel 2013: 25).

This externalization of EU return and readmission practices raises some concerns about fundamental rights. The 2012 case of *Hirsi Jamaa and Others* v. *Italy* condemned Italy for breaching the principle of *non-refoulement*[6] by intercepting in the south of Lampedusa and returning to Libya 11 Somali nationals and 13 Eritrean nationals (European Court of Human Rights 2012). Returning sub-Saharan migrants to a country where their life can be at risk was thus condemned by European judges. However, border management practices sometimes defy legal principles and EU fundamental rights.[7] In February 2014, the Spanish civil guard fired rubber bullets on migrants who were attempting to enter Ceuta and Melilla, two Spanish enclaves on the Moroccan territory. This left 14 migrants dead (Agence Europe 2014).

The EU practice of return and readmission in its southern neighbourhood has therefore had some direct consequences for sub-Saharan migrants. Yet the absence of an efficient 'transregional migration governance' has had a negative impact on the trans-Saharan region (Delcour 2013). Integrating this dimension in the EU's migration policy instruments would certainly help to forge more efficient migration partnerships in the trans-Saharan region.

Conclusion: towards comprehensive cross-regional cooperation

This chapter has reviewed migration challenges in the EU's southern neighbourhood and beyond. The EU has underestimated the need to address these issues comprehensively and cross-regionally. The Sahara–Sahel region has become the 'new frontier' for security issues and controlling the EU's borders and irregular migration.

Migration is nonetheless an issue that should compel the EU to address the topic horizontally across climate change, development, employment, and also its growth strategy. Further work between the EU, the Maghreb and African countries is needed to promote the entrepreneurial role of migrants and diasporas, especially when it comes to development in sending countries. In Africa, remittances have quadrupled between 1990 and 2011, representing around 2.6 per cent of African gross domestic product in 2011 (Ratha *et al.* 2011: 4). Yet remittances are still quite heavily taxed.

Another hurdle for moving migration to the top of the political agenda of the United Nations and linking it to the post-2015 Development Agenda is that the international migration agenda is 'politically unfeasible and too contentious' (Kroll and Klavaert 2012). In spite of the huge impact that a better use of remittances in development aid could have, especially on the eradication of poverty (which is also an EU objective), security-oriented and national approaches to migration remain huge obstacles to a comprehensive global and regional governance of migration. This could be a politically ambitious future agenda addressed by the EU's strategy, together with the ENP countries and the neighbours of the EU's neighbours.

Notes

1 See also Chapter 6 by Tressia Hobeika in this volume.
2 See also Chapter 4 by Gilles de Kerchove and Christiane Höhn in this volume.
3 See also Chapter 9 by Maud Fichet, Enrique Ibáñez and Veronika Orbetsova in this volume.
4 The '5 + 5 Dialogue' is an informal dialogue created in 1990 that gathers Italy, France, Spain, Portugal, Malta, Algeria, Morocco, Tunisia, Libya and Mauritania to discuss political, economic and cultural questions. See http://westmediterraneanforum.org.
5 Hong Kong, Macau, Sri Lanka, Albania, Russia, Ukraine, the Former Republic of Ex-Yugoslavia, Bosnia and Herzegovina, Montenegro, Serbia, Moldova, Pakistan, Georgia, Turkey, Morocco, Algeria, Cape Verde, China and Belarus.
6 Art. 33(1) of the 1951 Geneva Convention specifies that 'no Contracting State shall expel or return ("refouler") a refugee in any manner whatsoever to the frontiers of territories where his life or freedom would be threatened on account of his race, religion, nationality, membership of a particular social group or political opinion'. This principle is reiterated in art. 19(2) of the EU Charter of Fundamental Rights.
7 See also Chapter 1 by Valeria Bonavita in this volume.

References

Africa Governance Institute (2013) 'Note on the European Union Strategy for Security and Development in the Sahel', *Policy Brief* 4, www.westafricagateway.org/files/Policy-Brief-N-4-Sahel-Development-EU-Security.pdf (accessed September 2014).

African Union (2006) 'African Common Position on Migration and Development', Executive Council Ninth Ordinary Session, Banjul, 26 June, EX.CL/Dec.305 (IX).

African Union (2009) *African Union Convention for the Protection and Assistance of Internally Displaced Persons in Africa (Kampala Convention).*

Agence Europe (2013) 'Morocco: Barroso – Significant and Diverse Cooperation Opportunities', *Bulletin Quotidien Europe* 10798, 5 March.

Agence Europe (2014) 'JHA: Spain will Fire No More Rounds of Rubber Bullets Against Migrants', *Bulletin Quotidien Europe* 11027, 26 February.

Ammour, A.L. (2012) 'The Sahara and the Sahel after Gaddhafi', *CIDOB Notes Internationals* 44, Barcelona: Barcelona Centre for International Affairs, January.

Awumbila (2009) 'Intra-Regional Migration in West Africa: Changing Patterns and Dynamics', *DevIssues* 11(2), www.iss.nl/fileadmin/ASSETS/iss/Documents/DevISSues/DevISSues11_2_Nov_09_web.pdf (accessed March 2013).

Bach, D. (2011) 'The European Union and Africa: Trade Liberalisation, Constructive Disengagement, and the Securitisation of Europe's External Frontier', *Africa Review* 3(1), 33–46.

Barrios, C. and T. Koepf (2014) *Re-mapping the Sahel: Transnational Security Challenges and International Responses*, Report 19, Paris: EUISS.

Belguendouz, A. (2010) 'Expansion et sous-traitance des logiques d'enfermement de l'Union européenne: l'Exemple du Maroc', *Cultures and Conflits* 57, 155–129.

Cassarino, J.-P. (2010) 'Unbalanced Reciprocities: Cooperation on Readmission in the Euro-Mediterranean Area', *Viewpoints*, Special Issue, Washington, DC: Middle East Institute.

Castles, S. and M.J. Miller (2009) *The Age of Migration: International Population Movements in the Modern World* (4th edn), Basingstoke: Palgrave Macmillan.

Collyer, M., M. Cherti, E. Galos and M. Grosso (2012) 'Responses to Irregular Migration in Morocco Promising Changes, Persisting Challenges', *Briefing*, London: Institute for Public Policy Research.

Council of the European Union (2011) *Strategy for Security and Development in the Sahel*, Annex to the Council Conclusions on a European Union Strategy for Security and Development in the Sahel, Brussels, 21 March.

Council of the European Union (2012) *CSDP Civil Mission in Sahel*, www.consilium.europa.eu/media/1704249/fact_sheet_sahel_coordinated9_july.pdf (accessed March 2013).

Council of the European Union (2013) *EU Special Representative for the Sahel Appointed*, Brussels, 18 March 2013, Press Release, 6653/13.

Council of the European Union (2014a) *EUCAP Sahel Mali: EU Support Mission for Internal Security in Mali*, Press Release 8773/14, Luxembourg, 15 April.

Council of the European Union (2014b) *Options for CSDP Support to Sahel–Saharan Border Management*, 11601/14, Brussels, 4 July.

De Haas, H. (2006) 'Trans-Saharan Migration to North Africa and the EU: Historical Roots and Current Trends', Migration Policy Institute, www.migrationpolicy.org/article/trans-saharan-migration-north-africa-and-eu-historical-roots-and-current-trends (accessed September 2014).

De Haas, H. (2014) 'Morocco: Setting the Stage for Becoming a Migration Transit Country?', *Migration Information Source*, 19 March.

Delcour, L. (2013) 'The EU: Shaping Migration Patterns in its Neighbourhood and beyond', in D. Kochenov and F. Amtenbrink (eds) *European Union's Shaping of the International Legal Order*, Cambridge: Cambridge University Press, 261–282.

Del Sarto, R. and S. Tholens (2013) 'Conflict at the EU's Southern Borders: The Sahel Crisis', *Open Democracy*, 1 February, www.opendemocracy.net (accessed April 2014).

EUI (2013) *Migration Fact Algeria*, Migration Policy Center, www.migrationpolicycentre.eu/docs/fact_sheets/Factsheet%20Algeria.pdf (accessed September 2014).

European Commission (2011) *Communication from the Commission to the European Parliament and the Council: Evaluation of EU Readmission Agreements*, Brussels, COM(2011) 76 final, 23 March.

European Commission (2013a) *The EU Steps Up its Response to fight Money Laundering and Drug Trafficking in West Africa*, Brussels, IP/13/230, 18 March.

European Commission (2013b) *Communication on the Work of the Task Force Mediterranean*, COM(2013) 869 final, Brussels, 4 December.

European Commission (2014) *Mali Crisis*, ECHO factsheet, June, http://ec.europa.eu/echo/files/aid/countries/factsheets/mali_en.pdf (accessed September 2014).

European Commission and High Representative (2012) *Joint Communication on Supporting Closer Cooperation and Regional Integration in the Maghreb: Algeria, Libya, Mauritania, Morocco and Tunisia*, JOIN(2012) 36 final, Brussels, 17 December.

European Court of Human Rights (2012) Grand Chamber, *Case of Hirsi Jamaa and Others* v. *Italy*, 27765/09, 23 February.

European External Action Service (2013) 'EU Reinforces its Support for the Sahel Region', http://eeas.europa.eu/delegations/un_geneva/press_corner/all_news/news/2013/20131104_sahel_en.htm (accessed September 2014).

European Union (2008) 'Directive 2008/115/EC of the European Parliament and of the Council of 16 December 2008 on Common Standards and Procedures in Member States for Returning Illegally Staying Third-country Nationals', *Official Journal of the European Union*, L 348, 24 December, 98–107.

France 24 (2014) 'La clôture frontalière, nouvelle pomme de discorde entre le Maroc et l'Algérie', www.france24.com/fr/20140730-maroc-algerie-cloture-frontiere-fermeture-diplomatie-mur-barriere-oujda (accessed September 2014).

FRONTEX (2013) *FRAN Quarterly*, Q3, July–September, Warsaw, http://frontex.europa.eu/assets/Publications/Risk_Analysis/FRAN_Q3_2013.pdf (accessed April 2014).

FRONTEX (2014) *Annual Risk Analysis 2014*, Warsaw.

GADEM (2010) *The Human Rights of Sub-Saharan Migrants in Morocco*, Open Society Justice Initiative Report.

Human Rights Watch (2014) 'Abused and Expelled: Ill-Treatment of Sub-Saharan Migrants in Morocco', www.hrw.org/news/2014/02/10/morocco-abuse-sub-saharan-migrants (accessed September 2014).

Hummel, D., M. Doevenspeck and C. Samimi (2012) *Climate Change, Environment and Migration in the Sahel: Selected Issues with a Focus on Senegal and Mali*, MICLE Working Paper 1, Frankfurt: Migration, Climate and Environment.

Jeune Afrique (2014) 'Tunis estime à 2400 le nombre de combatants tunisiens présents en Syrie', www.jeuneafrique.com/Article/ARTJAWEB20140624113446 (accessed September 2014).

Keygnaert, I., A. Dialmy, A. Manço, J. Keygnaert, N. Vettenburg, K. Roelens and M. Temmerman (2014) 'Sexual Violence and Sub-Saharan Migrants in Morocco: A Community-based Participatory Assessment using Respondent Driven Sampling', *Global Health* 10(1), 1–31.

Klavaert, H. (2011) 'African Union Frameworks for Migration: Current Issues and Questions for the Future', *ECDPM Discussion Papers* 108, June, Maastricht: European Centre for Development Policy Management.

Kroll, A. and H. Klavaert (2012) 'Can we Afford to Ignore Migration post-2015?', *ECDPM Talking Points*, 27 July, Maastricht: European Centre for Development Policy Management, www.ecdpm-talkingpoints.org/can-we-afford-to-ignore-migration-post-2015 (accessed March 2013).

Lahlou, M. (2007) 'Migrations transméditerranéeennes et stratégies euro-africaines. Med. 2007. L'année 2006 dans l'espace euroméditerranéen', Barcelona: IEMED, CIDOB.

Masbah, M. (2014) *Moroccan Foreign Fighters*, Carnegie: Sadaa.

Médecins sans Frontières (2013) *Violences, vulnérabilité et migration: Bloqués aux portes de l'Europe*, www2.ohchr.org/english/bodies/cmw/docs/ngos/MSF_Morocco18_fr.pdf (accessed September 2014).

Naik, A. and F. Laczko (2012) 'The Bittersweet Return Home', *Forced Migration Review* 8–9, www.fmreview.org/en/north-africa/wood.pdf (accessed September 2014).

Pirozzi, N. (2013) *The EU's Comprehensive Approach to Crisis Management*, Geneva: DCAF, www.dcaf.ch/Publications/The-EU-s-Comprehensive-Approach-to-Crisis-Management (accessed September 2014).

Radio France International (2014) 'Naissance du "G5 du Sahel" pour le développement et la sécurité', 17 February, www.rfi.fr/afrique/20140217-naissance-g5-sahel-le-developpement-securite-Burkina-Mali-Mauritanie-Niger-Tchad (accessed September 2014).

Ratha, D., S. Mohapatra, Ç. Özden, S. Plaza, W. Shaw and A. Shimeles (2011) *Leveraging Migration for Africa: Remittances, Skills and Investments*, Washington, DC: World Bank.

Trauner, F. and S. Deimel (2013) 'The Impact of EU Migration Policies on African Countries: The Case of Mali', *International Migration* 51(4), 20–32.

UNHCR (2012) 'Mediterranean Takes Record as Most Deadly Stretch of Water for Refugees and Migrants in 2011', *Briefing Notes*, 31 January, www.unhcr.org/4f27e 01f9.html (accessed March 2013).

UNHCR (2013a) *2013 UNHCR Country Operations Profile – Middle East and North Africa (MENA)*, www.unhcr.org/pages/4a02db416.html (accessed March 2013).

UNHCR (2013b) *UNHCR Global Appeal 2013 Update, Middle East and North Africa*, www.unhcr.org/50a9f817b.pdf (accessed September 2013).

UNHCR (2014) *2015 UNHCR Regional Operations Profile – Middle East and North Africa (MENA)*, www.unhcr.org/pages/4a02db416.html (accessed December 2014).

United Nations (2013) *2013 Sahel Regional Strategy*, https://docs.unocha.org/sites/dms/ CAP/2013_Sahel_Regional_Strategy.pdf (accessed September 2014).

Westh, O.A.S. (2011) *Reconsidering West African Migration Changing Focus from European Immigration to Intra-regional Flows*, DIIS Working Paper 21, Copenhagen: Danish Institute for International Studies.

Wolff, S. (2011) 'The Arab Revolts: Reconsidering EU–US Strategies for Freedom, Security and Justice', in P. Pawlack (ed.) *The EU–US Security and Justice Agenda in Action*, EUISS Chaillot Paper 127, Paris: EUISS, 101–113.

Wolff, S. (2012) *The Mediterranean Dimension of the European Union's Internal Security*, London: Palgrave.

Wolff, S. (2014) 'The Politics of Negotiating EU Readmission Agreements: Insights from Morocco and Turkey', *European Journal of Migration and Law* 16(1), 69–95.

Wood, T. (2012) 'Legal Protection Frameworks', *Forced Migration Review* 8–9, www. fmreview.org/en/north-africa/wood.pdf (accessed September 2014).

3 The EU and the neighbours of its neighbours

Security challenges and strategic roles

Alyson J.K. Bailes and Pál Dunay

Introduction

When asked what security role a multilateral organization plays in a given location, it would be normal to begin by stating what security role(s) it plays in general. For the European Union (EU) today, that is precisely one of the hardest questions to answer. Thousands of pages of academic literature have been devoted to such unsolved general riddles as 'Is the EU a power?' and 'Is the EU a force for good?' (Whitman 2013: 171–193).

The way the EU organizes its daily work in Brussels and around the globe hardly helps to clarify matters. The European Union's Common Security and Defence Policy (CSDP) deals almost exclusively with missions of intervention and with the associated needs for military and civilian assets. The longer-standing Common Foreign and Security Policy (CFSP) includes many security-related external activities such as mediation, support for regional cooperation, and the promotion of arms control, disarmament and non-proliferation. Beyond this, however, the EU has many further policies and instruments wielded by the European Commission and specialized agencies, or led by the Council outside the CSDP/CFSP sphere, that not only address its own members' security but also have significant outward-going manifestations. They range from the purely humanitarian – aid in natural disasters and famine, security-related development assistance – through policies on global security challenges such as terrorism, crime or cyber-safety, to the external repercussions of measures taken to defend the EU's own territory against illegal migration and trafficking. These latter, 'softer' (that is, non-military) aspects of EU security policies will be largely covered in other chapters in this book dealing with related social, economic and developmental topics.[1]

When looking at regions two steps away from the EU's territory – the 'neighbours of its neighbours' – we have the luxury of an alternative and simpler approach. Instead of asking what the EU 'is' as a security player, we may examine what it 'does' (what specific strategic role or roles it plays) in given locations, tracking the different security manifestations of EU concern and engagement on the ground. Some of the Union's most powerful security roles and instruments will then be excluded from the start. These are not zones of potential enlargement, where the EU transforms security realities for and within the candidate states as part of the very process of accession. *A fortiori* they are not inside EU territory, where more or less credible guarantees of mutual security aid now apply under the Lisbon Treaty.[2] If we apply the metaphor of the Union as 'empire' (which does have explanatory power, for instance for the dynamics of enlargement; see Zielonka 2005), then the 'neighbours of the EU's neighbours' are beyond even the buffer zone where an empire would normally think it important to manipulate strategic conditions. The potential EU security roles and modes of action that we may look for can thus be reduced to a manageable few: broader (including 'existential' or 'model') strategic roles and influence; conflict-related instruments and actions; armaments-related instruments and actions; and any 'softer' security impacts, including security governance and financial assistance for security-related projects promoting development and stability. The research task for this chapter is to determine how far, in what combination, and with what effects the EU actually plays these roles in the zones in question.

In this chapter we first address the strategic question for all three concerned regions, underlining their differences in the process. The three more specific categories of EU action just enumerated will then be examined for each region in East–West sequence: Central Asia, the Middle East/West Asia, and the relevant African sub-regions. The concluding section touches *inter alia* on the coherence and coordination of the European Union's multifarious policies, instruments and impacts in these zones. It is commonplace to see the lack of such coherence, within and between regions, as one of the EU's chief handicaps as a 'power'. A secondary research question for the present text is to ask whether the cases of the 'neighbours of the EU's neighbours' support this thesis, or whether the importance of coherence – at least in this setting – may be more limited and contingent.

Strategic reality and EU 'strategies'

On the normal definition of strategy, the European Union's strategic position in the three regions considered here is both weak and divergent. It has no direct military or political authority over the states concerned, and only one of them – Djibouti – has a defence agreement with an EU Member State (France). EU strategic influence is further moderated by factors of geography, history, identity, and rivalry or competition with other national and institutional powers. Central Asia is physically the most remote, but the Sahel and the Horn of Africa lie beyond the Mediterranean and a sparsely populated desert. Historically, the Central Asian countries have not been colonies or allies of any European state – barring Russia – since the time of Alexander the Great. The Middle East as far as Iran fell within European (and Turkish) colonial reach, but with results that left as much alienation and division as kinship in their wake. The same is true to a lesser degree for the Horn of Africa and Sahel sub-regions, where decolonization was completed only after the Second World War. In terms of identity and political geography, the intervening EU neighbour countries – the western former Soviet Union, Turkey, the Levant and North Africa – are ones with little or no avocation as eventual EU members; with sub-European political standards; and (Turkey aside) with struggling economies. They are not obvious bridges for diffusing European norms and influences to the next set of neighbours beyond them.

As for rival powers, the prevailing influence in Central Asia is Russia's, followed by Turkey and China, and then by Iran, India and (notably in the Afghanistan connection) Pakistan. All are strong military nations and Russia and China also exert strong economic leverage over their Central Asian partners. In terms of trends, Russia's influence has been somewhat weakening and will not necessarily be enhanced among Central Asians by the recent violence against Ukraine,[3] while Turkey's has not been increasing. China's influence, meanwhile – in concord with global processes – is rapidly growing as a result of fast-rising trade turnover and investments in Central Asian states, three of which border on China. Central Asian states need this kind of economic interaction (Kazakhstan, Turkmenistan and Uzbekistan) and/or support (Kyrgyzstan, Tajikistan) much more than they need Russian help with their external security – though this judgement may be qualified as the significant reduction of foreign military presence in Afghanistan sharpens security concerns, notably for Tajikistan. Finally, the US's bilateral security relations, especially with Kyrgyzstan up to 2014[4] and with Uzbekistan despite often unpredictable oscillations,[5] add a not insignificant twist to the regional power balance.

The Middle East and West Asia have no clear power structure – part of their problem! – but rather a many-sided rivalry between Egypt, Saudi Arabia, Iran and (though temporarily eclipsed) Iraq: a situation further complicated by the contest with Israel and the still-heavy engagement of the United States. Russia's role in settling the Iran nuclear issue and recent behaviour over Syria are a reminder not to leave it out of the picture. Only in the Horn of Africa and Sahel is there no obvious bid for hegemony by competing powers, though inter-state enmities are real and do much to aggravate the transnational security risks.

Model effects and institutional partners

Worldwide, one of the EU's most potent if subtle tools of strategic influence is its model effect for local regional institution-building and its mutually reinforcing cooperation with such groupings when they function well.[6] The resulting Europe–Latin America and Europe–South-east Asia ties, among others, have had real security value. An interesting similarity between the three regions treated here is that their local institutional structures are either (relatively) weak, dysfunctional or hostile to European/Western influence. In Central Asia, inclusive sub-regional fora do exist and some, such as the Kazakhstan-initiated Conference on Interaction and Confidence Building Measures in Asia (CICA) and the Eurasian Economic Community (EurAsEC),[7] extend beyond Central Asia proper. However, their inclusiveness is marred by Turkmenistan's continuing reluctance to engage multilaterally in frameworks of any substance, given its only slowly evolving stance of 'positive neutrality'.[8] Cutting across such local creations and of greater strategic significance are the groups Russia uses to maintain its ties with and protect its interests *vis-à-vis* the former Soviet republics: the Collective Security Treaty Organization (CSTO, including Kazakhstan, Kyrgyzstan and Tajikistan) and the Shanghai Cooperation Organization (SCO, including all these plus China and Uzbekistan) (Bailes *et al.* 2007). Russia has recently put more emphasis on the economic aspect of integration with the former Soviet republics through the Customs Union with Kazakhstan, joined by Kyrgyzstan in 2015, as well as the Eurasian Economic Union taking effect in 2015; but the underlying politico-strategic logic remains clear.

When it comes to Western influence, the EU must contend with the Organization for Security and Cooperation in Europe (OSCE), where all Central Asian states participate and which offers a relatively congenial (consensus-based) forum for their diplomacy, even if their feelings about its intervention in their own affairs – for purposes of democracy-building and attempted crisis resolution – have been mixed.[9] Last but not least, the North Atlantic Treaty Organization (NATO) includes the Central Asians in its Euro-Atlantic Partnership scheme and provides bilateral assistance, covering military reform and governance, terrorism and non-proliferation among other things, through the Partnership for Peace.[10]

In the Middle East it is the absence of any inclusive, efficient collective security provider that stands out. The League of Arab States and the Organization of the Islamic Conference not only exclude Israel but also have political motivations and *modi operandi* rather than those of a cooperative/integrative community. The Arab/Israel split and other local rivalries notoriously complicate initiatives to build cooperation from outside, especially those aiming openly at multilateral security-building such as the EU's 'Barcelona process' (European External Action Service 2014a) with its successor the Union for the Mediterranean (UfM) (European External Action Service 2014b),[11] and NATO's Istanbul Cooperation Initiative of 2004.[12] Progress made in these contexts has been mainly bilateral, while the military interventions leading to Western quasi-takeovers in Iraq and Afghanistan – coupled with the West-versus-Iran nuclear dispute – have had further divisive and polarizing effects.

The one institutional initiative clearly showing some EU inspiration is the Gulf Cooperation Council (GCC) of Bahrain, Kuwait, Oman, Qatar, Saudi Arabia and the United Arab Emirates (UAE), founded in 1981, which has tried (with limited success) to create its own single market and even a common currency.[13] It is, however, strategically divisive to the extent that its members are held together largely by opposition to Iran. In the Horn of Africa and Sahel, the pan-continental African Union (AU)[14] and the sub-regional Intergovernmental Authority on Development (IGAD)[15] have both aspired to serious security roles notably in handling conflict, and they have regular institution-to-institution relationships with the EU (see EU-IGAD 2012). The questions over them are rather about operational capacity and the occasionally fragile political relations between members, which can bring institutional paralysis on the most sensitive issues.

The EU's own 'strategies'

The EU since the 1990s has also used 'strategy' as a term for a class of documents adopted by Member States in the CFSP framework. Art. J 3.2 and 3.3 of the Amsterdam Treaty described 'common strategies to be implemented by the Union in areas where the Member States shall have important interests in common', determining 'objectives, duration and the means to be made available by the Union and the Member States' (European Union 1997).[16] The distinction from the strategic competition discussed above is plain: a strategy for EU external policy starts (or should start) from a recognition of the Union's weak and strong points, possibilities and limitations in the area in focus, and selects targets and tools accordingly.

The overall European Security Strategy adopted in 2003 and updated in 2008 provides general guidelines for EU action, naming 'Building Security in our Neighbourhood' as one of the overarching goals (European Union 2003; 2008). It does not, however, prescribe separately or explicitly for the category of 'neighbours of the EU's neighbours'. Its main relevant remark is that '[i]t is in the European interest that countries on our borders are well-governed' (to avoid 'soft' security risks as well as conflict); and that the EU must 'promote a ring of well governed countries to the East of the European Union and on the borders of the Mediterranean with whom we can enjoy close and cooperative relations' (European Union 2003: 7). Aiming for good government certainly makes sense, in substance and as a realistically limited ambition, both for the ENP countries and the 'neighbours of the EU's neighbours'; but the strategy's mention of specific targets involves only first-tier neighbours and enlargement candidates, countries of special security concern such as Iran and Afghanistan, and larger 'strategic partners' such as Russia. Regional frameworks other than the 'Barcelona process' are not mentioned either.[17]

As to the regions where the 'neighbours of the EU's neighbours' themselves lie, 'The European Union and Central Asia: Strategy for a new Partnership' was adopted by the European Council in June 2007 (European External Action Service 2009: 9–32). Promoted by a German presidency, it reflected the sense of a gap in EU relationships following the latest incarnation of Eastern neighbourhood policy,[18] and the salience of the region during the Afghanistan conflict.[19] The EU's strategic aims were defined as influencing the five states towards improving their governance, human rights, democratization and development performance, while contributing, where possible, to conflict prevention and mitigation and to regional stability. The intrinsic difficulty is that challenges to authoritarian governments in poorly-developed polities are more likely to cause conflict and to destabilize and divide the region than the opposite. Since the end of the Tajik civil war in 1997, in fact, the most serious instability in Central Asia has dogged Kyrgyzstan – arguably the 'stan' most open to democracy. Less controversially, the EU also pursues economic and developmental aims through its individual Partnership and Cooperation Agreements (PCAs), with elements of differentiation based on the Regional Assistance Strategy Paper 2007–13 (European Community 2006) and Indicative

Programmes. Only Turkmenistan's PCA still awaits ratification. All local states except Kazakhstan qualify for EU development assistance, though Turkmenistan's energy income makes it less dependent than the others. Additional dialogues exist on issues such as textiles (linked to cotton exports) for Uzbekistan or energy for Turkmenistan, which relies on gas exports for most of its gross domestic product.

In the Middle East, the EU's strategy-making, like its general involvement, has been led by engagement in the 'classic' (Arab/Israel/Palestinian) Middle East dispute, supplemented by reactions to individual state issues: Iran as a challenge regarding weapons of mass destruction (WMD), Iraq as a conflict, and now Syria as a conflict. Thus we find the papers 'Statebuilding for Peace in the Middle East: An EU Action Strategy' and 'Towards a Comprehensive EU Approach to the Syrian Crisis' presented by the European Commission and the High Representative in 2007 and in 2013 respectively (European Commission and High Representative 2007; 2013). These documents naturally have a strong security focus and do recognize the significance of neighbouring states, but they do not discuss strategic conditions or solutions in the Levant, West Asia or the Gulf region as a whole. They stress partnership with global (United Nations) and other external ('Quartet') groupings, rather than working with or creating regional frameworks. The EU–GCC relationship already mentioned is an exception, but Saudi Arabia is the only major local power covered by it. Western experts have, moreover, criticized the European Union's failure to turn it into something more like a 'strategy' or explicit strategic relationship with the Gulf as such (Brookings 2013).

Following a general 'Joint Africa–EU Strategy' adopted in 2007 (Council of the European Union 2007), a specific EU 'Strategic Framework for the Horn of Africa' was created in November 2011 (Council of the European Union 2011b). Recurring humanitarian crises and Somali piracy appear up-front as special drivers of concern, although conflict, climate change and other 'softer' topics also feature together with the general weaknesses of governance and rule of law. The EU's motivation includes protecting its own citizens from terrorism, piracy, arms proliferation and illegal migration, plus a general recognition of the area's geo-strategic importance. Responding to crisis and conflict is a major EU priority, pursued with CSDP resources and through the financial Instrument for Stability (IfS), but including specialized programmes such as against small arms and terrorist financing. Regional cooperation is to be fostered in pursuance of an EU Horn of Africa initiative from 2007,[20] working especially with the UN, AU and IGAD. The Council Conclusions include approval of a EU Special Representative (EUSR) for the Horn (Council of the European Union 2011b: 3).

An EU 'Strategy for Security and Development in the Sahel' was adopted in March 2011 by the Council in Development Ministers formation, focusing on Mauritania, Mali and Niger and secondarily on Burkina Faso and Chad (Council of the European Union 2011a).[21] As its title suggests, the strategy highlights the interplay between development problems (such as poverty and environmental challenges) and security threats such as terrorism, violent extremism, uncontrolled migration and trafficking – all aggravated by state weakness, poor governance and absent rule of law. A direct interest is identified for the EU in suppressing terrorism and smuggling activity from and through the region. The strategic aims include strengthening security and rule of law and targeting extremism and radicalization, plus strengthening regional cooperation *inter alia* on security. Planned assistance for the three principal states includes increased spending under the 'Security and Rule of Law Line of Action'. Since 2011 the overspill from the Libya conflict, including violence in northern Mali, has sharpened the emphasis on conflict and radicalization within the strategy, as reflected in the Council Conclusions of March 2014 reviewing its implementation (Council of the European Union 2014).

The differences in extent and content between the EU's strategy documents for these three regions are rational enough, given the varied security challenges they present and the amount and nature of EU leverage available. The aims defined in the strategies are also reasonable and in line with broader principles of EU external policy. Where weaknesses can be seen – aside from the underlying limitations of EU influence – they include a failure to distinguish clearly between what is desirable for the regions themselves, and self-regarding EU security interests. The conceptualization of the region as a strategic whole is also weak in the case of the greater Middle East, where EU policy is arguably at its most reactive. The African regions show perhaps the most comprehensive and coherent strategy-building effort, including good handling of the security–development connection; the ex-colonial status of several involved states could be one underlying explanation.

The next three sections will examine and evaluate the EU's three specific security roles, as defined at the outset – conflict intervention, action on weapons-related issues, and 'soft' (non-military) security governance – in turn for each of the regional sets of 'neighbours of the EU's neighbours'.

Specific EU security roles: Central Asia

Conflict intervention

Unlike the neighbouring South Caucasus, Central Asia has been free of lasting, high-intensity inter-state conflicts. Low-intensity conflicts including border skirmishes persist, however, between Uzbekistan on the one hand and Kyrgyzstan and Tajikistan on the other; these often reflecte the arbitrary, illogical frontiers imposed in the Soviet age and are aggravated by massive refugee flows in time of internal conflict (for example in Andijon, Uzbekistan, in 2005) or ethnic violence (between Kyrgyz and Uzbek elements in parts of Kyrgyzstan in 2010).

The EU has no CSDP missions in the region and has generally left the OSCE to take the lead in *ad hoc* conflict mediation or containment efforts. The EU's local programmes are, however, relevant to conflict prevention, notably the Border Management Programme in Central Asia (BOMCA)[22] launched in 2003 and implemented by the United Nations Development Programme (UNDP). Aiming at modernizing border crossing points and creating or modernizing border guard training centres and technical facilities, BOMCA attracts EU funds of over €33 million – out of a total budget of €36 million for 2013–14 (BOMCA 2014). The actual security impact is moot: conditions for *bona fide* travellers may have improved, but border guards and custom services remain corrupt in keeping with local habits,[23] and the Soviet attitude of border guard and customs officers to state authority changes painfully slowly. This especially hampers efforts to fight trans-border criminality and terrorism. As a result, border skirmishes and low intensity hostilities continue along the Uzbek–Tajik and Kyrgyz–Tajik borders (Radio Free Europe/Radio Liberty 2014a; 2014b), and tension is also rising on the Afghan–Turkmen border (Radio Free Europe/Radio Liberty 2014c).

Characteristically, the EU's border-related work is eclipsed by other actors on one of the area's wildest, most porous frontiers – that stretching for over 1,400 km between Tajikistan and Afghanistan, a key focus for concern about spill-over of terrorism, crime and continuing strife from the latter. Aid here comes from Russia (concerned about further spill-over to its own territory) and from the OSCE, which has established a Border Management Staff College in Dushanbe to train Afghan as well as Central Asian officers.

The EU's contribution to conflict mitigation also includes classic diplomatic means such as regular meetings with leaders of the Central Asian states. These address a broad range of issues from human rights to regional cooperation, energy and water management. However, given the pattern of EU interests and lack of an enlargement perspective, it is perhaps unsurprising that forthright talking on human rights and other conflict triggers is the exception more than the rule.[24]

Weapons-related issues

Neither the EU nor other external actors have pursued major weapons-related programmes in Central Asia. The EU has primarily supported local efforts such as the Central Asian Nuclear Weapons Free Zone (NWFZ) created with the Treaty of Semipalatinsk in 2006, and Kazakhstan's particular engagement in clearing up its nuclear legacy and combating proliferation. According to Kazakh assessments, 1.5 million people have suffered health consequences from the four-decades-long existence of the Soviet nuclear (and rocket) test site at Semipalatinsk, damage that persists even after the site's closure in 1991 (Gusev *et al.* 1998; Kassenova 2009). EU funds have contributed to on-going clean-up efforts. Kazakhstan's non-proliferation diplomacy has included offering to establish an international nuclear fuel bank (a CFSP-approved goal), and providing a venue for the EU High Representative to meet Saeed Jalili, the Secretary of Iran's Supreme National Security Council, during nuclear negotiations between Iran and the West in February 2013 (Borger 2013). Kazakhstan's credibility in this field rests not least on having voluntarily returned its stationed nuclear weapons to Russia, and stocks of plutonium to the US, in the 1990s.

As to conventional arms, following the Kyrgyz–Uzbek clashes in southern Kyrgyzstan in 2010 a major weapons collection programme was initiated in order to stabilize the situation. A number of EU Member States helped to finance the project.[25]

'Soft' security and governance

Central Asia is allegedly the transit route for 30 per cent of all Afghan drug exports, which may reach one hundred tonnes (European Commission 2007: 5). The EU's Central Asia Drug Action Programme (CADAP) – also classified as a conflict prevention effort[26] – aims to build local capacities for anti-drug work, including data collection and information strategies, networking and treatment. As with BOMCA, CADAP has a mixed record of achievement: more professionalism in law enforcement agencies, but little impact on governance problems, including endemic corruption, that have left the south–north transit of drugs largely unabated. The success of stopping the spread of drugs at the source remains to be seen.

International efforts for security sector reform in Central Asia have focused less on armed forces and more on actors important for transnational threats – police forces, border guards, customs services – and issues of human security, such as the penitentiary system (Boonstra 2009). On the latter, the EU granted €2.5 million in the period 2009–12 for the reform of Kyrgyzstan's prisons, which a European Commission (2009) report described as facing

> many challenges, among them very poor material conditions, serious difficulties to separate and control the prison population, acute overcrowding, breakdown of prison industries and lack of prison staff training. Cases of tuberculosis among prisoners are 40 times higher than in the general population.

Other Central Asian states doubtless have similar problems but have been shy of advertising them.

More broadly, Brussels seems satisfied to monitor key developments affecting human security in Central Asia, and to maintain a dialogue process, rather than making the effort (or taking the risk) required to transform underlying conditions. It prefers to finance specific projects (for example on human rights, water management or energy), rather than building local capacity in the states most in need, Kyrgyzstan and Tajikistan. The net effect is to leave the region's future in the hands of its current rulers, with little prospect of change unless by the leadership succession process and/or really determined internal contention.

Overall, Central Asia appears as a region of limited EU interests and limited EU influence, a view apparently shared by local residents. An opinion poll of 2012 in Kyrgyzstan showed, for instance, that only 4 per cent of the population ranked the EU among the most influential players in the country, while 87 per cent mentioned Russia, 37 per cent Kazakhstan, 36 per cent the United States and 20 per cent China in that context (International Republican Institute 2012). The EU's practical security actions occur in a set of rather specialized and disparate fields, eschewing both direct physical interventions (CSDP missions) and deeper-reaching political ones. More compelling mutual interests might be hypothesized only in the field of energy security, where – as will be discussed later in this chapter – EU Member States have for long been reluctant to invest in collective approaches. As will also be discussed, a strategic upgrading of the region through the extension of enlargement to the intervening band of states is a low probability, becoming more remote with the latest developments in Ukraine.

Specific EU security roles: Middle East and West Asia

Conflict intervention

As already noted, the conflict of single greatest (and most persistent) concern to the EU in the Middle East is that between Israel and the Palestinians. Aside from the moral and legal issues at stake, this struggle has directly affected European interests through its links with terror, refugeeism, arms trade, strategic overspill (notably to Lebanon) and risks for Mediterranean trade and transport, including oil deliveries. EU responses since 1990 have included political mediation efforts, notably through the 'Quartet' with the UN, US and Russia; humanitarian and reconstruction assistance; efforts for reform and good governance in the Palestinian territories; and two still on-going CSDP missions that were launched in 2005: EU Coordinating Office for Palestinian Police Support (EUPOL COPPS) for the training of Palestinian police[27] and the EU Border Assistance Mission (EUBAM) Rafah to help manage the border crossing at Rafah in Gaza.[28] EU countries also supply over a third of all troops for the United Nations Interim Force in Lebanon (UNIFIL)[29] and have always been represented in the UN's oldest peacekeeping mission, the United Nations Truce Supervision Organization (UNTSO), carrying out observer duties in the Sinai and elsewhere.

The fact that these efforts have not led to peace should not count too heavily against the EU since other actors have succeeded no better, while doing more to make the situation worse. However, this classic 'Middle East problem' has absorbed European diplomatic and material resources to a degree arguably impeding broader European assessments or a wider, more balanced engagement in the Arab world and West Asia. Causation is two-way, as the emblematic importance for Arab states of the Palestinian struggle (not to mention its links with their domestic security) has kept the same issue relentlessly at the top of the agenda in any broader Euro-Arab dialogue. The 'Arab Spring' may have held out some prospect of shifting this focus, but it is early days to gauge the outcome, and the fact that the strongest current concerns are over violence around Israel's own borders – in the Palestinian territories as well as Syria and Iraq – does not particularly help.

Consequently, we do not find the EU as a significant actor in the conflicts before 9/11 – the Iran–Iraq war of 1980–88, the Iraqi invasion of Kuwait and the 'Gulf War' in 1990–91;[30] in tackling actual and potential violence involving Lebanon,[31] Syria and Jordan; or in addressing on-going non-state challenges

Table 3.1 CSDP mission in Iraq

Mission	Duration	Aims	Scale
EUJUST LEX – Iraq	From July 2005, extended to December 2013	Civilian training and support for criminal justice system	66 personnel; €27.15 million common costs, 2012–13

Source: European External Action Service (2014d).

such as the Kurdish question. After 9/11, when Europe rallied to support the US in Afghanistan, NATO became the institutional vehicle. Over Iraq the EU was at first painfully split and paralysed, and when it 'rebounded' to reassert its unity, the fruits were the general progress on the European Security Strategy and CSDP development, and strategies on other regions like the Western Balkans or relations with the UN, rather than the development of a European strategic alternative for Iraq as such (Bailes 2005). EU nations supplying troops there pulled out or stayed to the bitter end as purely national decisions. Only two years after the crisis, in 2005, did the EU agree to launch a still on-going CSDP mission: the EU Integrated Rule of Law Mission EUJUST LEX, a small deployment of civilian trainers to enhance Iraq's criminal justice capabilities (see Table 3.1). For the first six years the training was done in EU countries but since 2011 it has moved mainly to three centres within Iraq, and more than 5,000 individuals have been trained. While admirable and highly relevant to Iraq's challenges after foreign troop withdrawals, this can hardly be considered a decisive strategic input. It may be better seen as a symbol of renewed European unity after the original Iraqi trauma.

Weapons-related issues

In the greater Middle East since the Gulf War of 1990–91, the dominant weapons-related theme has been WMD: efforts to extirpate them in Iraq after that war, the role they played in the Western invasion of 2003, and concerns about possible Iranian acquisition of nuclear weapons capacity. Of these issues the EU has made a strong impact only on the last, where it was arguably driven as much by fears of Washington's and/or Israel's resolving the issue by force as by worries over Iran's own intentions towards Europe or the risks of regional proliferation. Motives aside, however, the European Union has been not only consistent and creative in framing its role, but also ready to learn from Iraq's and Iran's lessons in developing its whole stance on the issue. Telling the full Iran story would demand volumes in itself (see Kile 2005), but we may note three main branches or phases of EU action on the issue:

1   diplomatic negotiations first launched by three European Foreign Ministers with the High Representative in autumn 2003, where the 'carrots' of an EU

cooperative relationship were held out in return for Iranian restraint; these attempts were later joined by the US, Russia and China with UN backing;

2   EU support for UN sanctions when Iran failed to carry out its undertakings and cooperate satisfactorily with the International Atomic Energy Agency (IAEA), plus additional measures taken by the EU itself (last updated in September 2013 but partially suspended up to November 2014 in connection with progress in EU/Iran talks);

3   an EU decision in July 2012 to support efforts for a Middle East Nuclear Weapons Free Zone, notably through meetings where Iranian and Israeli representatives among others could be brought together (Council of the European Union 2012).

In addition, the EU imposed separate sanctions against Iran over its violations of human rights. If all these measures took longer than expected to bear fruit, the EU was – as with the Middle East conflict – hardly the most important party to blame; and its persistence on the diplomatic track undoubtedly helped stave off attempted military actions that could have inflamed the whole region. The EU can also be credited with building broad partnerships and demonstrating the value of institutional approaches, in a field initially overshadowed by US President George W. Bush's 'go-it-alone' mentality.

On the other side, the lessons of 2003 can be given credit not just for the EU's first coherent WMD strategy (Council of the European Union 2003), and the later establishment of an expert European 'non-proliferation consortium',[32] but also for the invention of the 'non-proliferation clause' to be inserted in all 'mixed' EU agreements (agreements covering issues both within and beyond Community competence, such as CFSP matters) with third parties – first seriously tested in the case of Syria – which in turn inspired a similar 'small arms and light weapons' (SALW) clause, regularized in 2008. Finally, general and specific concerns about the impact of Western arms and technology transfers on conflict dangers in the greater Middle East have done much through the years to strengthen motives for tightening the EU's joint strategic export controls, expressed through a regulation for dual-use (WMD-related) items and as a legally binding CFSP Common Position for conventional arms.[33] All these measures have value not only in protecting European security interests, but also in building the Union's credibility and seriousness as an actor – and partner for the US and others – in the 'hardest' spheres of global security governance.

'Soft' security and governance

As the EU's partners in this zone are mainly high-income countries and are also resistant to interference in domestic politics, neither the 'human security' issues of development nor the theme of human rights have lent themselves to much concrete cooperation anywhere outside Iraq. The EU–Iraq Partnership and Cooperation Agreement signed in May 2012 – thus far the only PCA in the region – stresses human rights up-front, provides for a general political–security dialogue, and has detailed provisions on collaboration against terrorism, WMD, small arms trade and war crimes[34] – although its trade clauses were given priority for provisional implementation.

More typically, the EU has used joint fora to put forward its own concerns over state violence and human rights issues, for example in Bahrain during the EU–GCC meeting held there in June 2013 (Gaub and Kistemaker 2013). The place of such normative items in the practical agenda of partnership is taken by topics of energy management, climate, transport, infrastructure and general technology development that could all in some sense be defined as 'security' or security-related ones but that are not articulated as such. The Cooperation Agreement between the European Economic Community and the Gulf Cooperation Council (1988) does express hopes that economic strength will 'reinforce the role of the GCC in contributing to peace and stability in the region', but this may imply nothing more than a view of these states as a relatively benign factor in local balances. In practice, the most lively area of cooperation on a strategic issue currently concerns clean and renewable energy technology, where the EU has used a financial instrument specially designed for cooperation with rich partners – the Instrument for Cooperation with Industrialized and Other High-income Countries and Territories 2007–13 (ICI), now a Partnership Instrument (PI) – to create a Europe–Gulf 'clean energy network'. Further, EU–GCC joint statements routinely contain a blanket condemnation of terrorism and call for peaceful solution of all regional disputes.[35]

The general picture of EU roles in the broader Middle East is one dominated by individual security challenges, often of a single-country or bilateral nature, in which the EU plays a sometimes instrumental role – the Iranian nuclear issue being an example – but is typically side-lined when the time comes for military action or other emphatic applications of power. More subtle weaknesses of the EU approach include the lack of a coherent region-wide perspective and an unwillingness to face the challenge of handling regimes that combine strategic importance for Europe with disregard of European norms. On the other hand, even this partial engagement has been a crucible for the EU's general strategic development, resulting in important strides forward especially in WMD-related policies.

Specific EU security roles: Horn of Africa and Sahel

Conflict intervention

The EU's transition from viewing the African sub-regions of the Sahel and the Horn of Africa as essentially developmental and humanitarian challenges to also stressing their security relevance has clearly been driven first and foremost by the actuality of conflict and especially by violence producing international spill-over, such as Somalia's civil war leading to piracy and the spread of insurrection from Darfur and Libya to Chad and Mali. As a result, the European Union has been drawn in both as a direct actor and in support of AU missions under the

2007 Joint Africa–EU Strategy where 'Peace and Security' is the first area for cooperation (European Commission 2013). Through the Africa Peace Facility Fund created in 2004,[36] the EU has supported not only the former AU intervention in Darfur (African Union Mission in Sudan, AMIS II) – considered as a CSDP operation since European police were directly involved (see Table 3.2) – but also the on-going missions in Somalia and Mali respectively: AMISOM (African Union Mission in Somalia) and AFISMA (African-led International Support Mission to Mali).

As for direct CSDP actions, 2008 was a turning-point both for EU involvement in the Horn and Sahel and in the whole pattern of CSDP activity. It saw not only the short-term European Union Force mission in Chad but also the launch of the EU Naval Force (EUNAVFOR) 'Atalanta', designed to protect commercial shipping and fisheries against piracy from the Somali coast down to the Gulf of Aden. As Table 3.3 shows, reflection on the roots of piracy then drew the EU into a training mission for law and order within Somalia and a multi-nation naval capacity-building programme (EUCAP) for the Horn (European Union Mission on Regional Maritime Capacity building in the Horn of Africa, EUCAP Nestor), followed in 2012–13 by three further training missions in Niger, South Sudan and Mali. As a result, 6 out of 17 on-going CSDP missions in mid-2014 were in the Horn and Sahel, while a seventh in Libya could be considered part of the same nexus.

This rash of new missions and the slanting of the whole CSDP effort towards new African sub-regions is best explained by, first, the higher salience of all conflicts close to or linked with the 'Arab Spring' zone since 2010 and, second, the reinforcement of EU humanitarian motives by others more directly tied to Europe's own interests (Fanta 2012). In the case of Somali piracy, its impact on shipping around the Horn, and the spread of anti-expatriate violence to Kenya, this is obvious, but the mentions of terrorism-related concerns in the EU strategy papers are also not to be taken lightly. As reported by EUROPOL (2013) in the context of an overall rise in European terrorism casualties in 2012, not only have Europeans and their property in the relevant parts of Africa been exposed to new dangers, but EU-based individuals have been traced moving to Somalia, the Sahel countries and Syria to take part in terrorist action and/or training there – raising questions about what happens when they come home. The presence of large numbers of immigrants and recent refugees from these areas on EU soil aggravates concerns about radicalization, as do the Al-Qaeda affiliations of one important transnational group, Al-Qaeda in the Maghreb (AQIM). The sudden break-out into Iraq of the Syria-based Islamic State of Iraq and the Levant (ISIL) group has further raised the profile of the whole 'terrorist tourism' issue and, even if it temporarily distracts notice from other conflict zones, will guarantee continuing Western attention to the problem.[37]

Such self-regarding motives do not *per se* discredit EU activism if its goals are also in the local people's interests; and so far they have been, even if European and African views sometimes diverge on the specific political paths to follow. A more telling criticism would be that the EU's inputs have been limited,

Table 3.2 CSDP missions completed before 2013, Horn of Africa and Sahel

Mission	Duration	Aims	Scale
Support to AMIS II	2005–07 (handed over to African Union–United Nations Mission in Darfur, UNAMID)	Support African Union political, military and police activities in Darfur crisis	Average 30 (military/police)
European Union Force (EUFOR) Chad/Central African Republic	2008–09	Protect civilians, aid flows, UN efforts (plus de-mining and medical aid)	Average 3,700 (military)

Source: European External Action Service (2014d).

Table 3.3 On-going CSDP missions (mid-2013), Horn of Africa and Sahel

Mission	Launch date and mandate length	Aims	Common costs, € millions	Scale
EUNAVFOR Somalia (Atalanta)	2008, renewed 7 December 2010 to December 2014	Protection of shipping, anti-piracy, fisheries	39.65 (2010–14)	6–10 vessels 1,400 personnel
EU Training Mission (EUTM) Somalia	7 April 2010, extended to March 2013	Military training for law and order, anti-crime/terror for forces of the Transitional Federal Government	12.3	126 personnel
EU Aviation Security Mission (EUAVSEC) South Sudan	18 June 2012, 19 months	Training and advice for security of Juba airport	12.5	67 maximum; 49 in September 2013
EUCAP Sahel Niger	16 July 2012, two years	Civilian training and advice for control of territory and development, anti-crime/terror	8.7 (first year)	c.50
EUCAP Nestor	16 July 2012, two years	Civilian training for maritime capacity and law enforcement (including rule-of-law support in Somalia, development of coastguard/maritime capacities in Djibouti, Kenya, Seychelles)	22.8 (first year)	176 maximum; 40 in September 2013
EUTM Mali	18 February 2013, 15 months	Military training to restore order, anti-crime/terror	12.3	500

Source: European External Action Service (2014d).

not just in scale and (so far) duration, but also in their degree of originality, risk and assumption of responsibility. Acting admittedly in a 'heavily crowded field of actors' (van der Zwan 2011: 26) when it comes to conflict prevention and mediation, the EU has tended to choose a secondary and supportive role in political processes such as South Sudan's independence[38] and its coexistence with Sudan, as well as a second-echelon – training and assistance – role in conflict operations and nation-building. The EU also stays one step back from the action when it uses money as its tool, financing peacebuilding activities including reconciliation, refugee aid and reconstruction through the UN, AU and non-governmental organizations – though this could be defended as helping to boost local capacities (for instance in Mali; see Barrios and Koepf 2013). Independent assessors[39] have normally given the local CSDP missions good marks for the coherence of their aims, choice of partners and region-wide vision, and for their practical results. Yet points regularly made on the other side are reactiveness and failure of early warning, lack of local expertise and slow learning curves, inadequate resources, and gratuitous obstacles to efficiency through blockages in Brussels and poor inter-state coordination. Tellingly, problems with local security conditions are cited as an obstacle beyond the EU experts' control (ISIS-Europe 2013): underlining that the EU does not shape strategic realities in these areas today and cannot expect to do so in future, unless with a much larger as well as longer-term investment.

Weapons-related issues

What WMD have been for EU policies in the Middle East, SALW have been for sub-Saharan and also Northern Africa. Both regions were named as high-priority targets in the first full EU SALW strategy of 2006 and continue to attract a sizeable share of related EU funding (Council of the European Union 2006). Their salience seems to owe less to direct EU responsibility – as only 0.8 per cent of EU SALW exports went to the former and 2.7 per cent to the latter in 2005–09 (Poitevin 2011) – and more to concerns about the local impact and inadequate control of such weapons in a region characterized by poor and weak states. Trafficking through and around the region for criminal and terrorist as well as martial purposes is also a concern, as reflected *inter alia* in an EU decision of June 2013 to fund SALW collection and safe-keeping in Libya (Council of the European Union 2013). The EU's relevant action begins outside the region with its support for global and generic measures of SALW restraint, notably the Arms Trade Treaty concluded at the UN in April 2013;[40] continues with efforts to check the illicit movement of such weapons within and from EU territory (export control policy and enforcement); and touches ground with bilateral or regional projects aimed to inculcate international norms and build enforcement capacities among local states. Current examples[41] include cooperation with the Economic Community of West African States (ECOWAS) to get neighbouring states – including Mauritania and Mali – to sign up to a UN convention on illegal manufacturing and trafficking of firearms; funding from the Instrument for

Stability for a Regional Centre on Small Arms and Light Weapons (RECSA) in Nairobi; and grants made through UNDP to strengthen official capacities to control SALW in South Sudan and Niger.

As to the effectiveness of EU policy, coherence in a field once marked by legal challenges over competence between the Commission and Council has much improved, further helped by the implementation of the Lisbon Treaty, and there is no doubt of the seriousness of the Union's intent and willingness to deploy resources. The problem is deeply intractable in itself, however, as arms smuggling has been shown time and again to simply find new paths around obstacles. The fact that the EU's policies are targeted against 'illegal' SALW (Poitevin 2011), also focusing heavily on civilian hand-guns, is arguably ill-suited to weak-state settings where the line between legal or official actors and their opposites, or between 'conflict' and everyday disorder, becomes blurred. Further, as with conflict itself, the EU seems most comfortable in a second-echelon supporting position: no CSDP missions in the region have worked, for instance, at collecting and destroying weapons directly. That said, insofar as gun use is only a symptom of other political and social problems, the EU's emphasis on development as the long-term solution is particularly relevant for these areas.

'Soft' security and governance

Given the developmental perspective and relatively recent influence of 'hard' security concerns, EU policy for these zones places a strong and coherent emphasis on non-conflict-related aspects of security.[42] As an example, a Commission Communication of October 2012 discusses food security for the Horn of Africa and Sahel with a view to improving 'resilience': something the EU aims to do for the former area through a SHARE (Supporting Horn of African Resilience) programme involving cooperation with IGAD, and for the latter through AGIR Sahel (Alliance Globale pour l'Initiative Résilience) with ECOWAS and other regional/functional groupings (European Commission 2012a). The fact that political and physical insecurity and 'geo-political instability' aggravate food security is correctly noted, and a further link is made with environmental security, as addressed by the EU's Global Climate Change Alliance (ibid.). However, the very fact that developmental thinking came first in EU policy evolution means that other prominent issues such as health, infrastructure, education or gender rights are generally not framed in the EU's own discourse (or in its continental and sub-regional partnerships with Africa players) as 'security' ones.[43] They are more likely to be addressed with non-security-related funding instruments and in the framework of general development policies such as the EU's support for the UN Millennium Development Goals. Similarly, support for good governance and human rights is expressed in broad terms and primarily as an obstacle to development in the relevant strategy papers. Further details of EU efforts in such fields are thus best left to other chapters; but it is fair to note that all current CSDP missions except EUNAVFOR have explicit governance-enhancing aims, and that the linkage of conflict management and stabilization with other aspects of human security is fully recognized in EU discourse.

Of the three regions discussed here, that of the Sahel and the Horn of Africa shows the most recent but arguably most coherent build-up of EU security-related activity, spanning the spectrum from CSDP military missions to development programmes with a human security focus. The EU has been reasonably subtle in diagnosing underlying problems, and there is a fair match between its self-regarding concerns (terrorism and migration) and the interests of local development and good governance. The main limitations on EU influence are the limited scale of interventions, their typically reactive nature, and the apparent hesitation over placing EU personnel in really demanding front-line or hands-on roles.

Overarching issues for the three regions

This analysis has brought out the divergent profiles of EU security-related action in the three zones covered, and also the varying relative weight of EU engagement and impact compared with other powers. The European Union clearly occupies a lower, more specialized and circumscribed strategic niche in Central Asia, and among states in the second tier of the Middle East, than it does in the Sahel and arguably (or increasingly) the Horn. This is not just because of a mismatch between its tools and the nature and gravity of the first two regions' security challenges. It also reflects the fact that other powers are relatively less interested and active in the African sub-regions; while those who do act there – the UN, AU and African sub-regional groups – are willing and compatible partners for Europe. The recent colonial history of many local nations helps to enhance both the sense of EU responsibility, thus easing consensus, and the local knowledge and acceptability of EU incomers. Further, the EU's 'money talks louder' in areas where states are smaller, poorer, and facing overwhelmingly developmental problems also in the realm of governance.

It is tempting to suggest, further, that the EU Member States have not recognized a common strategic interest strong enough to force them to overcome these regional variations, or to push them beyond doing 'what comes naturally' in the three different cases of the 'neighbours of the EU's neighbours'. Here, however, we need to recall another point that is basic to EU external policy analysis. There is a world of difference between the EU as such and 'Europe', meaning the aggregation of EU members' national actions and their actions through different international vehicles (UN, NATO, etc.). For 'Europe' in this sense, strategic interest and strategic involvement are as high in the greater Middle East as formal EU involvement is limited. Crude oil imports from Saudi Arabia, Iraq and Iran together made up 14.9 per cent of total EU-27 imports in 2010, making the 'neighbours of the neighbours' the Union's fourth most important suppliers after Russia, Norway and Libya.[44] On the other side, from 2007–12 and despite the export controls mentioned earlier, nine EU Member States supplied Saudi Arabia with a total of US$2,329 million in military equipment, exceeding US sales of US$1,776 million in the same period.[45] Of 30 countries first mentioned by President George W. Bush on 18 March 2003 as a 'coalition of the willing' supporting the invasion of Iraq, 13 were EU members or new members preparing to join in 2004, among whom the UK and Poland participated in the initial military action.

Not only such sharp strategic choices, but other important economic, historical, cultural and human ties, including cross-investments, expatriates, migrants and diasporas, make the EU–West Asia and EU–Gulf relationships intense and sensitive at all times. They have given these regions an extraordinarily powerful influence over the evolution of EU policies and strategies – consider the impact of Iran on EU WMD policy and of the Iraq rift on the Union's whole external stance – even without having formal EU 'strategy documents' allocated to them. But the forces impeding collective EU policy-making and action are the obverse of these realities. Thus far, the interests that the latter create for certain key EU Member States have either not been felt as equally urgent by other (for instance northern and eastern) Member States, or are to some degree in contradiction and competition with each other, or conflict with supposedly agreed EU principles – or all three. Combined with the fateful impact of US policies (the inconstancy of which has lately aggravated the problem), and with the lack of a useful multilateral interlocutor within the region, this is enough to explain the marginal nature of EU institutional action not only today but probably for some time to come.

Central Asia provides a contrasting but equally problematic example. The interests of EU nations largely run parallel there and generate benign policies, but they are slight and essentially contingent compared with Russia's historic engagement and China's encroaching ambitions. In any practical terms the region has secondary importance at best for the EU (or for Europe in general). Little more than 1 per cent of EU trade is conducted with the five Central Asian states (of which 0.9 per cent with Kazakhstan).[46] Reduced European dependence on oil compared with gas and newer energy sources, combined with the collapse of plans for EU-subsidized direct pipelines from Central Asian suppliers (which in itself has affected European credibility), have banished any prospect of this region offering a real chance to diversify EU energy imports.[47] Central Asia meanwhile is looking to faster growing markets: Turkmen gas deliveries to China will rapidly increase in the near future[48] and there are high hopes for a Turkmenistan–Afghanistan–Pakistan–India (TAPI) gas pipeline. Kazakhstan's oil supply infrastructure is to an increasing extent in Chinese hands. Western withdrawal from Afghanistan will further reduce the EU's (and the US's) inclination to make serious investments in or take serious risks for this region.[49] Whether this adds up to a strategic misjudgement by the West, given the possible longer-term implications of Russian/Ukrainian hostilities for energy supplies through the closer neighbourhood zone, will remain to be seen.

If these portrayals of EU strategic limitations have any force, they place the famous issue of 'coherence' in a rather different light. The European Union's own concern for consistency and coordination is shown by both its actions and its pronouncements in the three zones of the 'neighbours of the EU's neighbours'. For example, mandates for CSDP missions given before the entry into force of the Lisbon Treaty contain sections on 'Community Action' designed to ensure synergy notably with developmental inputs, while those adopted after December 2010 speak of 'consistency of the Union's response'. Responsibility for monitoring this is generally given to the Head of a Mission together with the local EU delegation, but is also an important task for any EU Special Representative present. A concern for overall consistency – and its appearance – is further shown by the quick adoption of 'strategies' on emerging challenges such as the spill-over from Libya and the Syrian civil war, while EEAS 'fact-sheets' on regional policies and/or strategy implementation aim to chart all relevant inputs (for example European External Action Service 2014c).

What might be called second-order problems in implementing these good intentions, both in Brussels and on the ground, have been heavily analysed since the Lisbon Treaty came into force. Common criticisms include the continued division of authority and potential competition between the EEAS and European Commission services responsible, for instance, for development, energy, trade and migration; weaknesses of the EEAS itself; inadequate funding and personnel; failure to learn lessons or standardize procedures from one intervention to the next; and more (see, for instance, Bailes *et al.* 2012). The difficulty for local EU delegations of holding things together has also been stressed (Comelli 2011; van Seters and Clavert 2011).

The first-order problem, however, may be better expressed in Michele Comelli's (2011: 10) question 'Real Embassies for a Weak Foreign Policy?'. Where the EU has little strategic influence, few useable tools and partners, and/or internal divisions of (national and institutional) interest, its lack of collective intervention perhaps coupled with non-coherent national involvements will plainly hamper coherence. Where its Member States find little to argue about, limited EU actions with modest goals are easily agreed and coherence as such may be relatively easy to attain. In both cases, however, the EU's engagement and impact may be judged 'weak' in proportion both to the actual needs and to the real or potential impact of other actors. And so long as some fields of operation, whether involving the 'neighbours of the EU's neighbours' or elsewhere, fall into the first of these categories but others into the second, coherence between regions is clearly too much to hope for.

Conclusion

To return to our initial research question, we have seen that in all three regions under study, the EU operates from a relatively weak strategic starting-point shaped by geography, resources, limited historical engagement and the absence of strong institutional partners. The three more specific security roles that it can play in spaces situated at such a remove – CSDP missions, weapons-related measures and efforts for broader security governance – apply differentially across the regions, with CSDP action very limited outside the African zones and with both CSDP and weapons policies largely undeveloped in Central Asia. We have further seen that 'coherence' is a secondary rather than primary factor in the EU's limitations, and that a coherently applied EU strategy can still be a strategically weak and subordinate one. Our dissection of what the EU 'does' in security terms in the three zones studied may illuminate many aspects of EU policy, preferences, strengths and weaknesses in external action.

It would not be safe, however, to extrapolate these findings as a guide to the strength and other key features of EU security action overall. On a geo-strategic view, one would expect the EU to be strongest and most self-aware as a security actor first of all in problem regions that lie on its doorstep and/or are candidates for integration, such as the Western Balkans, and second in its relationships with external powers further afield, such as the US, Russia and China, that affect all Member States' interests (and core EU activities such as trade policy) in comparable ways. Thus it is not surprising if the 'in-between' zones on the European mental map turn out to be ones of relatively limited and heterogeneous EU intervention; where, moreover, the EU's choices seem to be shaped more by local conditions and other actors' agendas than by a single, creative European will.

Could this change? It is hard to make a sensible prognosis for all three cases in question. In West Central Asia and in the second tier of the Middle East, the EU's awareness of its limitations and the dangers of power play are such that an increased EU role may arise, if at all, from 'pulling' rather than 'pushing' – for example from the sudden weakening or de-legitimization of other players' roles, ideally coupled with democratic and sustainable regime change. It is difficult, even so, to imagine a case where some of the power-set Russia, China, India and Iran would not remain doughty rivals in Central Asia, or where all the powers of the greater Middle East would happily choose the EU as arbiter.[50] For both these regions, following the early twenty-first-century age of intervention, a not implausible alternative is that international (including European) attention will simply drift away – leaving local power-play to shape the future.

The only other way the EU's relative strategic role might grow is if its more immediate neighbours participating in the European Neighbourhood Policy became part of a new enlargement zone, a contingency that seems remote in the Eastern Mediterranean and only a little less so in outer Eastern Europe. The wild card is North Africa, where the difficulties are hardly less, but where Western security concerns have lately grown intense and the EU's influence in developmental, general economic, historical and cultural terms is *prima facie* much greater. It might be worth putting a small bet on the possibility that the Sahel and/or Horn of Africa might one day be discussed not as a 'neighbour of the EU's neighbours' but as a direct neighbourhood zone for the EU.

Notes

1 See in particular Chapter 1 by Valeria Bonavita, Chapter 2 by Sarah Wolff, Chapter 4 by Gilles de Kerchove and Christiane Höhn, Chapter 6 by Tressia Hobeika and Chapter 8 by Alexander Warkotsch and Richard Youngs.

2 Namely, art. 42.7 TEU (Treaty on the European Union) on military assistance and art. 222 TFEU on assistance in non-warlike emergencies.

3 Moscow's difficulties in keeping the Central Asian states within its orbit, given their primary concern with economic prosperity and stabilization, help to explain recent Russian 'offers' of a full customs union and of further economic integration through the Eurasian Union. In turn this intensive Russian pressure for economic integration has aroused some partners' suspicions.

4 A US military transit centre at Manas airport in Kyrgyzstan survived several threats to expel it, up to its closure (during the withdrawal process from Afghanistan) in mid-2014.

5 Tashkent has at times used offers of basing facilities *inter alia* to offset criticisms of its human rights record, and would like to receive US equipment left over from Afghanistan.

6 See also Chapter 9 by Maud Fichet, Enrique Ibáñez and Veronika Orbetsova in this volume.

7 For more on CICA and EurAsEc see their respective websites, www.s-cica.org and www.eurasiancommission.org.

8 This declared policy of Turkmenistan naturally rules out membership of a collective defence organization, such as the Collective Security Treaty Organization (CSTO), but should not stop Ashgabat from joining, for instance, the Shanghai Cooperation Organization (SCO).

9 With Kyrgyzstan being a partial exception, the Central Asian countries have received poor marks for election quality and Turkmenistan did not even accept OSCE election observers until December 2013 (see www.osce.org/odihr). Uzbekistan has especially resisted scrutiny and was until recently the only Central Asian state not to have a resident OSCE Centre, but only a 'project coordinator'.

10 Details at www.nato.int/cps/en/natolive/topics_50349.htm (accessed May 2014).

11 Mauritania is included in the UfM.

12 Details at www.nato.int/cps/en/natolive/topics_52956.htm (accessed May 2014).

13 See www.gcc-sg.org/eng.

14 See www.au.int/en.

15 Members: Djibouti, Eritrea, Ethiopia, Somalia, Sudan, South Sudan, Kenya and Uganda (see www.igad.int).

16 Three strategy documents were adopted with direct reference to this provision, on Russia, Ukraine and the Mediterranean respectively. The 'common strategy' as such was, however, found to be an unsatisfactory instrument and was later discontinued.

17 The 2003 text does call for 'A broader engagement with the Arab world' and a closer interest in the 'Southern Caucasus' (European Union 2003: 8). Further, the whole European Security Strategy – without openly discussing Iraq – is 'about' that country insofar as it frames the EU's considered judgement on US actions and doctrines surrounding the March 2003 invasion.

18 As German Foreign Minister Steinmeier told the European Parliament: 'It's a kind of gap in our European consciousness. As far as our common European past is concerned I can't see any stage where people were strongly interested in this region' (cited in Rettman 2007).

19 Interest in Central Asian hydrocarbon resources has also been a factor, becoming more specific as EU energy policy has turned more 'strategic'. In practice, however, only a fraction of European needs are or can be met from these sources – see below and also Chapter 11 by Johannes Theiss in this volume.

20 This initiative aimed to promote regional cooperation on infrastructure and resource management; it was adopted by the European Commission jointly with the IGAD member countries (see www.icafrica.org/topics-programmes/horn-of-africa-initiative, accessed May 2014).

21 The document notes connections with surrounding regions in the broader context of the ENP.

22 See   http://ec.europa.eu/europeaid/where/asia/regional-cooperation-central-asia/border-management-fight-against-drugs/bomca_en.htm (accessed May 2014).

23 The Corruption Perception Index of 2013 (www.transparency.org/cpi2013/results) ranks the five 'stans' (out of 177 states) as follows: Kazakhstan 140, Kyrgyzstan 150, Tajikistan 154, Turkmenistan and Uzbekistan 168.

24 Representatives of civil society in Kazakhstan were disappointed by the lack of attention to human rights violations shown during High Representative Catherine Ashton's 2012 tour of four Central Asian countries, when she met non-governmental figures in only one country. For the EU version see European Commission (2012b).

25 See, for example, Organization for Security and Cooperation in Europe (2013: annex 1). The response of the Kyrgyz head of mission emphasized that the UK has not been the only major contributor to the project (ibid.: annex 2).

26 See http://eeas.europa.eu/delegations/kazakhstan/projects/list_of_projects/projects_en. htm.

27 See www.eeas.europa.eu/csdp/missions-and-operations/eupol-copps-palestinian-territories/ index_en.htm.

28 See www.eeas.europa.eu/csdp/missions-and-operations/eubam-rafah/index_en.htm.

29 UNIFIL webpage at http://unifil.unmissions.org/Default.aspx?tabid=11559&language =en-US (accessed September 2013). France, Italy and Spain are the largest European contributors.

30 However, the independent European defence organization Western European Union – whose competences were subsumed into the CSDP from 1999 – did coordinate Western interventions in 1987–91 for naval de-mining in the Gulf, sanctions enforcement, and aid for Kurdish refugees in Northern Iraq.

31 Revealingly, the current EU-Lebanon Action Plan within the ENP framework (at http://ec.europa.eu/world/enp/pdf/lebanon_enp_ap_final_en.pdf, accessed September 2013) says very little about conflict and then only about the general 'Middle East' problem (foot of p. 7).

32 See www.nonproliferation.eu.

33 See explanations at http://ec.europa.eu/trade/import-and-export-rules/export-from-eu/ dual-use-controls and www.eeas.europa.eu/non-proliferation-and-disarmament/arms-export-control (accessed September 2013).

34 Text at http://trade.ec.europa.eu/doclib/docs/2012/november/tradoc_150084.pdf (accessed September 2013).

35 See, for example, the declaration from the twenty-third joint meeting in Bahrain, June 2013: www.consilium.europa.eu/uedocs/cms_Data/docs/pressdata/EN/foraff/137671. pdf (accessed September 2013).

36 €740 million disbursed since 2004 for capacity-building and early warning as well as mission support: see http://ec.europa.eu/europeaid/where/acp/regional-cooperation/ peace/index_en.htm (accessed September 2013).

37 See also Chapter 4 by Gilles de Kerchove and Christiane Höhn in this volume.

38 In December 2013 High Representative Ashton took a prominent initiative to mediate in South Sudan's outbreak of civil violence. It was the UN peace mission United Nations Mission in South Sudan (UNMISS), however, that was reinforced (to 12,500) to deal with the actual fighting.

39 See, for example, the resources of the International Security Information Service Europe (ISIS Europe) at www.isis-europe.eu/programmes/responding-to-conflict (accessed September 2013).

40 See www.un.org/disarmament/ATT.

41 SALW strategy progress report of May 2013, available with other SALW-related resources at http://eeas.europa.eu/non-proliferation-and-disarmament/documentation/ documents/index_en.htm.

42 See also Chapter 6 by Tressia Hobeika in this volume.

43 See also Chapter 7 by Zuhal Yeşilyurt Güngüz in this volume.

44 Eurostat, 'Main Origin of Primary Energy Imports, EU-27, 2002–2010', http://
epp.eurostat.ec.europa.eu/statistics_explained/index.php?title=File:Main_origin_of_
primary_energy_imports,_EU-27,_2002–2010_%28%25_of_extra_EU-27_imports%
29.png&filetimestamp=20121012131852 (accessed September 2013). The corresponding figure in 2002 was 18 per cent.

45 Figures in 'Trend Indicator Value' (not commercial prices) from the Stockholm International Peace Research Institute (SIPRI) arms transfers database, http://portal.sipri.
org/publications/pages/transfer/splash (accessed September 2013).

46 See http://trade.ec.europa.eu/doclib/docs/2006/september/tradoc_122530.pdf (updated
for end 2012). Kazakhstan's energy exports make it the twenty-seventh largest trading
partner of the EU, but the other 'stans' range between rankings of 85 (Turkmenistan)
and 145 (Tajikistan) place. See also Chapter 5 by Sieglinde Gstöhl in this volume.

47 Experts have concluded that 'The prospect of Central Asian gas reaching Europe in
pipelines that avoid Russia seems as remote as ever' (Melvin and Boonstra 2008: 3),
and 'the dream of Nabucco has all but disappeared as a viable alternative' (Melvin
2012: 2).

48 'CNPC and Turkmengas Ink an Agreement on Boosting Natural Gas Shipments to
China and a Gas Field EPC Contract', www.cnpc.com.cn/News/en/press/newsre-
leases/201309/20130906_C1532.shtml?COLLCC=3672660696& (accessed December 2013).

49 See also Chapter 11 by Johannes Theiss in this volume.

50 This scenario is even harder to imagine without Turkey as an EU Member State.

References

Bailes, A.J.K. (2005) *The European Security Strategy: An Evolutionary History, SIPRI
Policy Paper* 10, Stockholm: Stockholm International Peace Research Institute, http://
books.sipri.org/product_info?c_product_id=190 (accessed May 2014).

Bailes, A.J.K., R. Balfour and M. Kenna (2012) *The European External Action Service at
Work: How to Improve EU Foreign Policy, EPC Issue Paper* 67, 25 January, Brussels:
European Policy Center, www.epc.eu/documents/uploads/pub_1399_the_eeas_at_
work_-_how_to_improve_eu_foreign_policy.pdf (accessed May 2014).

Bailes, A.J.K., V. Baranovsky and P. Dunay (2007) 'Regional Security Cooperation in
the Former Soviet Area', in *SIPRI Yearbook 2007: Armaments, Disarmament and
International Security*, Oxford: Oxford University Press, 165–192.

Barrios, C. and T. Koepf (2013) *Building Peace in Mali: The Elections and Beyond,
EU-ISS Brief* 28, 18 July, www.iss.europa.eu/publications/detail/article/building-peace-
in-mali-the-elections-and-beyond (accessed May 2014).

BOMCA (2014) 'Border Management Programme in Central Asia', www.bomca.eu/en/
about-us.html (accessed May 2014).

Boonstra, J. (2009) *The EU Strategy for Central Asia says 'Security'. Does This Include
Security Sector Reform?, EUCAM Policy Brief* 10, Brussels: EU–Central Asia Monitoring Policy, www.fride.org/descarga/EUCAM_PB10_UE_SRR_ENG_nov09.pdf
(accessed May 2014).

Borger, J. (2013) 'Iran Nuclear Talks in Kazakhstan Go into Second Day', *The Guardian*,
26 February, www.theguardian.com/world/julian-borger-global-security-blog/2013/
feb/26/iran-nuclear-talks-kazakhstan-almaty (accessed May 2014).

Brookings Doha Center (2013) *Towards a Strategic Partnership? The EU and the GCC
in a Revolutionary Middle East*, Event Briefing 21, 24 January, Doha: Brookings Doha
Center, www.brookings.edu/research/papers/2013/01/24-eu-gcc-relations (accessed
May 2014).

Comelli, M. (2011) *Rehashed Commission Delegations or Real Embassies? EU Delega-tions post-Lisbon, IAI Working Paper* 11, July, Rome: Institute of International Affairs, www.iai.it/pdf/DocIAI/iaiwp1123.pdf (accessed May 2014).

Council of the European Union (2003) *EU Strategy Against Proliferation of Weapons of Mass Destruction*, 9 December, http://register.consilium.europa.eu/doc/srv?l=EN& f=ST%2015708%202003%20INIT (accessed May 2014).

Council of the European Union (2006) *EU Strategy to Combat Illicit Accumulation and Trafficking of SALW and their Ammunition*, 13 January, http://register.consilium. europa.eu/doc/srv?l=EN&f=ST%205319%202006%20INIT (accessed May 2014).

Council of the European Union (2007) *The Africa–EU Strategic Partnership, A Joint Africa–EU Strategy*, Lisbon, 9 December, 16344/07 (Presse 291).

Council of the European Union (2011a) *Strategy for Security and Development in the Sahel*, Annex to the Council Conclusions on a European Union Strategy for Security and Development in the Sahel, Brussels, 21 March.

Council of the European Union (2011b) *A Strategic Framework for the Horn of Africa*, Annex to the Council Conclusions on the Horn of Africa, 3124th Foreign Affairs Council meeting, Brussels, 14 November.

Council of the European Union (2012) *Decision in Support of a Process Leading to the Establishment of a Zone Free of Nuclear Weapons and All Other Weapons of Mass Destruction in the Middle East*, 23 July, http://eur-lex.europa.eu/LexUriServ/ LexUriServ.do?uri=OJ:L:2012:196:0067:0073:EN:PDF (accessed July 2014).

Council of the European Union (2013) 'Council Decision 2013/320/CFSP of 24 June 2013 in Support of Physical Security and Stockpile Management Activities to Reduce the Risk of Illicit Trade in Small Arms and Light Weapons (SALW) and their Ammunition in Libya and its Region', *Official Journal of the European Union*, L 173, 26 June, 54–64.

Council of the European Union (2014) *Council Conclusions on Implementation of the EU Strategy for Security and Development in the Sahel*, Foreign Affairs Council meeting, Brussels, 17 March.

EU-IGAD (2012) 'Joint IGAD-EU Communique of 3 April 2012', Fifth Ministerial Meeting, Addis Ababa, http://igad.int/index.php?option=com_content&view=article&i d=421:joint-igad-eu-communique&catid=47:communique&Itemid=149 (accessed May 2014).

European Commission (2007) 'European Community Regional Strategy Paper for Assist-ance to Central Asia for the Period 2007–2013', www.eeas.europa.eu/central_asia/ rsp/07_13_en.pdf (accessed October 2013).

European Commission (2009) 'Governance and Institutional Reform: Supporting Prison Reform in Kyrgyzstan', ec.europa.eu/europeaid/documents/case-studies/kyrgyzstan_ governance_prison_en.pdf (accessed December 2013).

European Commission (2012a) Communication from the Commission to the European Parliament and the Council, *The EU Approach to Resilience: Learning from Food Security Crises*, Brussels, COM(2012) 586 final, 3 October.

European Commission (2012b) 'Catherine Ashton Travels to Central Asia', Press Release, IP/12/1269, Brussels, 26 November, http://europa.eu/rapid/press-release_IP-12-1269_en.htm (accessed May 2014).

European Commission (2013) 'Key Facts on the Joint Africa–EU Strategy', MEMO, 23 April, http://europa.eu/rapid/press-release_MEMO-13-367_en.htm (accessed Septem-ber 2013).

European Commission and High Representative (2007) *Statebuilding for Peace in the Middle East: An EU Action Strategy*, Brussels, 20 November, S378/07, www.

consilium.europa.eu/ueDocs/cms_Data/docs/pressdata/en/reports/97949.pdf (accessed May 2014).

European Commission and High Representative (2013) *Towards a Comprehensive EU Approach to the Syrian Crisis*, JOIN(2013) 22 final, Brussels, 24 June.

European Community (2006) *European Community Regional Strategy Paper for Assistance to Central Asia for the Period 2007–2013*, http://eeas.europa.eu/central_asia/rsp/07_13_en.pdf (accessed May 2014).

European Economic Community and Gulf Cooperation Council (1988) 'Cooperation Agreement between the European Economic Community, of the one part, and the Countries Parties to the Charter of the Cooperation Council for the Arab States of the Gulf (the State of the United Arab Emirates, the State of Bahrain, the Kingdom of Saudi Arabia, the Sultanate of Oman, the State of Qatar and the State of Kuwait) of the other part – Joint Declarations – Declaration by the European Economic Community – Exchange of Letters', *Official Journal of the European Union*, L 054, 25 February 1989, 3–15.

European External Action Service (2009) *EU and Central Asia: The New Partnership in Action*, http://eeas.europa.eu/central_asia/docs/2010_strategy_eu_centralasia_en.pdf, 9–32 (accessed May 2014).

European External Action Service (2014a) 'The Barcelona Process', www.eeas.europa.eu/euromed/barcelona_en.htm (accessed May 2014).

European External Action Service (2014b) 'Union for the Mediterranean', www.eeas.europa.eu/euromed/index_en.htm (accessed May 2014).

European External Action Service (2014c) *The European Union and the Sahel*, Fact Sheet, Brussels, 6 February, 140206/01, http://eeas.europa.eu/statements/docs/2014/140206_01_en.pdf (accessed May 2014).

European External Action Service (2014d) 'Ongoing Missions and Operations', www.eeas.europa.eu/csdp/missions-and-operations/index_en.htm (accessed May 2014).

European Union (1997) 'Treaty of Amsterdam', www.eurotreaties.com/amsterdamtreaty.pdf (accessed May 2014).

European Union (2003) *'A Secure Europe in a Better World'*, European Security Strategy, Brussels, 12 December, www.consilium.europa.eu/uedocs/cmsUpload/78367.pdf (accessed May 2014).

European Union (2008) *Report on the Implementation of the European Security Strategy – Providing Security in a Changing World*, Brussels, 11 December, S407/08, www.consilium.europa.eu/ueDocs/cms_Data/docs/pressdata/EN/reports/104630.pdf (accessed May 2014).

EUROPOL (2013) *EU Terrorist Situation and Trend Report 2013*, www.europol.europa.eu/sites/default/files/publications/europol_te-sat2013_lr_0.pdf (accessed May 2014).

Fanta, E. (2012) *The EU and (Regional?) Insecurity in the Horn of Africa*, EU-GRASP Working Paper 29, January, www.eugrasp.eu/wp-content/uploads/2012/01/EU-GRASPworkingpaper29.pdf (accessed May 2014).

Gaub, F. and B. Kistemaker (2013) *All Quiet on the Bahrain Front?*, EU-ISS Alert, 1 July, www.iss.europa.eu/publications/detail/article/all-quiet-on-the-bahraini-front (accessed May 2014).

Gusev, B.I., R.I. Rosenson and Z.N. Abylkassimova (1998) 'The Semipalatinsk Nuclear Test Site: A First Analysis of Solid Cancer Incidence (Selected Sites) Due to Test-related Radiation', *Radiation and Environmental Biophysics* 37(3), 209–214.

International Republican Institute (Bishkek branch) (2012) 'Kyrgyzstan National Opinion Poll', 4–27 February, www.iri.org/sites/default/files/2012%20April%2011%20Survey%20

of%20Kyrgyzstan%20Public%20Opinion%2C%20February%204-27%2C%202012.pdf (accessed May 2014).

ISIS-Europe (2013) *CSDP-Note: Focus on EUAVSEC South Sudan One Year On*, Brussels: International Security Information Service Europe, www.isis-europe.eu/sites/default/files/publications-downloads/CSDP%20Note%20-EUAVSEC%20-%20LA_0.pdf (accessed May 2014).

Kassenova, T. (2009) 'The Lasting Toll of Semipalatinsks Nuclear Testing', *Bulletin of the Atomic Scientists*, 28 September, www.thebulletin.org/lasting-toll-semipalatinsk-nuclear-testing.pdf (accessed August 2014).

Kile, S.N. (ed.) (2005) *Europe and Iran: Perspectives on Proliferation*, *SIPRI Research Report* 21, Oxford: Oxford University Press.

Melvin, N. (2012) 'The EU Needs a New Values-based Realism for its Central Asia Strategy', *EU – Central Asia Monitoring* 28, October, Brussels: EUCAM.

Melvin, N. and J. Boonstra (2008) 'The EU Strategy for Central Asia@Year One', *EU– Central Asia Monitoring* 1, October, Brussels: EUCAM.

Organization for Security and Cooperation in Europe (2013) 'FSC 718th Meeting 22 May 2013 Statement by the Delegation of the United Kingdom, FSC JOUR/724', www.osce.org/fsc/102024 (accessed December 2013).

Poitevin, C. (2011) Powerpoint on *The European Policy on SALW*, EU Non-proliferation Consortium, 24 May, www.nonproliferation.eu/documents/kickoff/poitevin.pdf (accessed May 2014).

Radio Free Europe/Radio Liberty (2014a) 'Tajik, Kyrgyz Officials Discuss Latest Shooting Incident at Border', 11 August, www.rferl.org/content/tajik-kyrgyz-officials-discuss-latest-shooting-incident.26524669.html (accessed August 2014).

Radio Free Europe/Radio Liberty (2014b) 'Uzbekistan Releases Tajik Shepherds and Livestock', 5 August, www.rferl.org/content/livestock-uzbekistan-tajikistan-border-shepherds-return/26514469.html (accessed August 2014).

Radio Free Europe/Radio Liberty (2014c) 'More Warnings South of the Afghan-Turkmen Border', 14 August, www.rferl.org/content/quishlog-ovozi-afghanistan-turkmen-turmoil/26530471.html (accessed August 2014).

Rettman, A. (2007) 'Steinmeier Sketches New EU policy on Central Asia', *EU Observer*, 23 January, http://euobserver.com/foreign/23329 (accessed May 2014).

van der Zwan, J. (2011) *Evaluating the EU's Role and Challenges in Sudan and South Sudan*, International Alert, September, London: Initiative for Peacebuilding, www.international-alert.org/sites/default/files/publications/092011IfPEWSudan_0.pdf (accessed May 2014).

van Seters, J. and H. Clavert (2011) *EU Development Cooperation After the Lisbon Treaty*, *ECPDM Paper* 123, December, Maastricht: European Centre for Development Policy Management, www.ecdpm.org/Web_ECDPM/Web/Content/Download.nsf/0/49 C7C0C49C73A6AAC125797C002B8A47/$FILE/11-123.pdf (accessed May 2014).

Whitman, R.G. (2013) 'The Neo-normative Turn in Theorising the EU's International Presence', *Cooperation and Conflict* 48(2), 171–193.

Zielonka, J. (2005) *Europe as Empire: The Nature of the Enlarged European Union*, Oxford: Oxford University Press.

4 The fight against terrorism in the EU's broader neighbourhood

Gilles de Kerchove and Christiane Höhn

Introduction[1]

An examination of the terrorist threat in the broader neighbourhood of the European Union (EU) reveals close links and areas of cooperation between terrorist groups in North Africa and sub-Saharan Africa. A successful response has to promote not only capacities at the national level but also a regional dimension with includes both North Africa and the Sahel. Given this interdependence between the direct and the broader neighbourhood,[2] as shown in particular in the aftermath of the conflict in Libya since 2011, the EU is increasingly looking to North and West Africa in a comprehensive regional approach to address the terrorist threat, combining security and development. The EU has developed a separate framework to deal with the Horn of Africa and the terrorist threat there, which is not covered in this chapter (see Barrios and Koepf 2014). This chapter examines how the EU is responding to the terrorist threat in its broader neighbourhood, more specifically in North Africa and the Sahel. Based on a brief analysis of the threat, an inside view of the EU's approach to counter-terrorism in the Sahel and the Maghreb is set out in strategic and practical terms.

The EU's 'Strategy for Security and Development in the Sahel' was the first comprehensive strategy on security and development since the entry into force of the Lisbon Treaty in December 2009 (Council of the European Union 2011a). It has become an example for the EU to follow in other regions, as with the 'Strategic Framework for the Horn of Africa' (Council of the European Union 2011b). It has also set an example for other partners to link security and development in their respective strategies on the Sahel. This approach has been set out more broadly in the Joint Communication by the European External Action Service (EEAS) and the European Commission on the EU's comprehensive approach to external conflict and crises (European Commission and High Representative 2013). In the aftermath of the 'Arab Spring', there is a strong need for the EU to step up its action and start investing heavily in the North African countries. In the Sahel, the EU has increased its response; North and West Africa have become a priority area for EU engagement. The regional dimension is key. Given the lack of regional fora in which all relevant players are involved, a pragmatic approach is needed: using and strengthening different existing fora depending on the issues as well as supporting new and emerging fora, where appropriate.

Among the three regions of the 'neighbours of the EU's neighbours' (North Africa/Sahel, Middle East, and Central Asia), this chapter focuses on North Africa and the Sahel because the EU has developed and implemented an innovative strategic framework over the past years, using the various instruments at the EU's disposal, which has set an example for the EU comprehensive approach since the entry into force of the Lisbon Treaty. Cooperation with both the EU's neighbours and their neighbours is an important part of this strategy.

The 'Islamic State of Iraq and the Levant' (ISIL) has been recognized by the European Council (2014) as a threat to European and regional security. Addressing this threat is a top priority for the EU. Intense work related to foreign fighters has been on-going since the spring of 2013. A comprehensive EU strategic framework to deal with Iraq/Syria/ISIL is being developed at the time of writing in 2014 and events are moving fast, so that any analysis risks being outdated quickly.

After an analysis of the terrorist threat, the chapter will cover various aspects of Security Sector Reform (SSR) in North Africa, including regional cooperation. The EU Strategy for Security and Development in the Sahel will then be discussed, explaining the security and development approach underpinning the strategy and the EU's engagement on security, rule of law and terrorism, and setting out priorities for the EU's future work in the Sahel: further promoting the criminal justice approach in the fight against terrorism, preventing radicalization, and better addressing the terrorism–drugs nexus and the regional dimension.

The terrorist threat in the EU's southern neighbourhood

The terrorism threat in Africa has increased over the past few years. This has also been recognized by the African Union (see, for example, African Union 2014). While the core of Al-Qaeda in Afghanistan and Pakistan has been weakened, regional affiliates of Al-Qaeda or Al-Qaeda-related groups have developed and become stronger and better able to attack. An 'arc of instability' may be developing in Africa. The links between terrorist groups in North, West and East Africa are increasing. North Africa and the Sahel have become a theatre of operations for terrorist groups such as 'Al-Qaeda in the Islamic Maghreb' (AQIM), Al-Mourabitun, Ansar Dine, Ansar al-Sharia groups in North Africa, and Al-Maqtis in the Sinai. Boko Haram and Ansaru in Nigeria have developed links with AQIM and Al-Shabaab and have undertaken kidnappings in neighbouring countries such as Cameroon, which previously had not been affected. In the Horn of Africa, the Shabaab in Somalia have created connections with AQIM and have carried out attacks in Kenya, such as the killings in a shopping mall in Nairobi in September 2013.

Terrorist groups are seeking safe havens in parts of countries where governance is weak. These safe havens are used to train, to regroup, to plan attacks and to acquire and stock equipment such as weapons and vehicles. Such a safe haven existed in northern Mali before the successful French 'Operation Serval' in early 2013.

Today, terrorism is a major obstacle to development in the countries and regions under discussion here. One terrorist attack every six months can be enough to kill tourism, as has happened, for example, in the Sahel countries, which means that a major source of income, in particular for populations living in the Sahara, no longer exists. Development work is hampered when certain areas become off limits for development workers. Investment requires stability and security. Terrorist attacks, which are also directed at critical infrastructures (such as the attack against the Algerian Tigantourine natural gas facility of In Amenas in January 2013 or the kidnappings and attacks against an AREVA uranium mine in Niger as well as against oil tankers in the Suez canal in Egypt and against tourist sites in the Sinai), are obstacles to foreign investment.

Returning fighters and weapons from Libya contributed to the destabilizing of Mali and to the take-over of the north in 2012 first by Tuareg independence-seeking armed groups and then by terrorist groups (AQIM, Mujao at the time, Ansar Dine). A terrorist sanctuary was established and terrorist groups controlled cities, applying the Sharia and destroying Muslim holy sites. France's 'Operation Serval' in early 2013, launched when terrorist groups started moving towards the south in view of conquering the south of Mali, succeeded in considerably weakening the terrorist groups in the north and reestablished control of the cities and territory. However, AQIM and other terrorist groups remain in northern Mali and have spread to other countries in the region, especially to the south of Libya. While this is not a terrorist sanctuary yet, it is a grey zone open to traffickers, not controlled by the state. The south of Libya today is not what the north of Mali was before 'Operation Serval' – the terrorists do not have training camps there (Hofnung 2014), nor the type of quasi-industrial infrastructure they had in the Adrar des Ifoghas. However, terrorist groups are taking root there and the risk exists that Libya could develop into a new centre of gravity for terrorist groups in the region, which are replenishing their arms and vehicle stocks. Financial resources remain strong from ransom payments and direct or indirect links to the drugs trade. Attacks in 2013 in Arlit, Niger, seem to have been planned from Libya. AQIM and Al-Mourabitoun are recruiting from North Africa and the Sahel. The In Amenas attack was planned in Libya and carried out by Belmokhtar's group 'Signed in Blood' (now Al-Mourabitoun), coming from Mali, and the terrorists carrying out the attack represented more than 10 different nationalities.

Niger was less affected by the Libya conflict because the Tuareg went mainly to Mali, as they consider the north of Mali their home. In addition, Niger had put in place an effective strategy, with EU help, to offer disarmament, demobilization and reintegration of fighters and others returning from Libya, especially in the north of the country, and mobilized the military and security forces around its borders. Much of AQIM leadership remains in Algeria. While Algeria is regularly carrying out operations against AQIM, the number of terrorists in the country remains stable. The Sahel region is also a trafficking hub, which further weakens state structures, also in connection with corruption. There are links of convenience, such as the protection of convoys, or more direct links, depending on the terrorist groups.

Due to the dismantling of security services in Libya and Tunisia, Ansar al-Sharia terrorist groups (Salafi jihadist groups subscribing to the Al-Qaeda worldview, engaging both in missionary work – *dawa* – and ultimately in violence) have more room for manoeuvre, especially in Tunisia, where politicians from the opposition have been killed (see, for example, Gall 2013), and Libya, where they have controlled cities and run training camps in East Libya as well as reportedly being involved in the attack on the US Embassy in 2012. The Sinai in Egypt has become a terrorist safe haven as well. The response by the government is overly military (crackdown) and does not narrowly target terrorist groups, but also affects the population. This does not allow an effective fight against terrorism, nor does it win the hearts and minds of the population or prevent radicalization. Sinai-based terrorist groups are now able to strike other parts of Egypt in relatively sophisticated attacks. The labeling of the Muslim Brotherhood as a terrorist group risks being a self-fulfilling prophecy leading to radicalization and recruitment to terrorist violence.

Syria and Iraq have become the most dangerous terrorist hotspot in the wider region. Tens of thousands of so-called 'foreign fighters' have joined in particular the terrorist group 'Islamic State of Iraq and the Levant', which has made major military gains and is now controlling large parts of territory in Syria and Iraq, including oil fields. Some foreign fighters have also joined Jabhat Al-Nusra in Syria. It will be interesting to observe whether and, if so, how the rise of ISIL may cause a realignment of the terrorist landscape, as a number of terrorist groups around the world have now pledged allegiance to ISIL rather than Al-Qaeda. ISIL has unprecedented social media use and revenue mainly due to oil sales and has announced the creation of a so-called caliphate, the 'Islamic State'. ISIL is not an affiliate of Al-Qaeda (on Iraq/Syria/ISIL, see European Council 2014). The foreign fighters include not only Europeans but also thousands of North African origin. The return of foreign fighters to their home countries in the Middle Eastern and North African region may pose the risk of destabilization.

The following trends can be observed: establishment of sanctuaries, recruitment from many nationalities, terrorist groups splintering off and re-grouping, weapons trafficking from Libya playing a major role, and terrorist groups spreading to more countries and establishing links among themselves. A further development is the growth over the last decades of Salafism and Wahhabism, promoted by strong outside financial investment, at the expense of traditional forms of Sufi Islam. Societies in the region are changing, turning their backs on traditional forms of Islam. Many young people who have studied in madrasas and religious universities have not learnt any other skills than the knowledge of the Koran in Arabic and hence cannot find jobs.

Given the terrorist threat, effective counter-terrorism capabilities are important for the countries of the region. Human rights and rule-of-law-compliant counter-terrorism action is most successful in the long term, as it avoids radicalization, disenfranchisement and alienation. Therefore, in North Africa, security sector reform (SSR) is an important part of the transitions since the 'Arab Spring', reforms having been demanded by the citizens.

Security sector reform in North Africa

The EU stands ready to support the transitions in North Africa, including SSR, good governance, institution-building and the promotion of the rule of law and human rights (European Commission and High Representative 2011a; 2011b). Security and counter-terrorism capacity-building and SSR assistance is playing an important role in the Joint Communication on supporting closer cooperation and regional integration in the Maghreb (European Commission and High Representative 2012) and in the related Council Conclusions of 31 January 2013 (Council of the European Union 2013). SSR is crucial for the North African countries to successfully manage the transitions and economic development that the populations have asked for as well as their own security. While initially after the 'Arab Spring' the EU focus was not on security, the EU is starting to engage.

In the remaining part of the chapter, various aspects of SSR will be covered: rule of law and legal frameworks, evidence-based investigation, security expertise, police cooperation and regional cooperation.

Rule of law and legal frameworks

Creating security and justice systems based on human rights and the rule of law, as called for by the citizens in the 'Arab Spring' countries, is not only a political but also a technical challenge. The fight against terrorism was used as a tool for repression by the former regimes, often employing over-broad definitions of the crimes. As a result, after the 'Arab Spring' the repressive terrorism laws were, for example in Tunisia, no longer applied. In addition, the 'political police', the security service, was dismantled. The old systems need to be replaced by new legal, institutional and policy frameworks for counter-terrorism (CT). This is starting in Tunisia, which is in the process of drafting a new CT law.

Security and justice systems that comply with human rights and the rule of law are effective means to fight terrorism, and CT is a crucial part of SSR. A legal framework has to be created which respects the rule of law and human rights, including the definition of terrorist crimes and the procedures that may be used to bring terrorists to justice. Oversight bodies have to be established, including in parliament. SSR starts with the constitution, which is the yardstick against which policies, laws and actions will be measured. A comprehensive security and CT policy needs to be put in place. Training, restructuring and equipment are an important part, and these should feed into legal and policy frameworks.

The Center for the Democratic Control of the Armed Forces (DCAF), which gained considerable experience with the transformations in Central and Eastern Europe after the end of the Cold War, has developed interesting and comprehensive models with regard to SSR, setting out, for example, good practices and require-ments of parliamentary control or intelligence governance.[3]

Civil society plays an important role in SSR as well. A number of local non-governmental organizations have started to engage with SSR-related topics, for example in Tunisia and Morocco. The DCAF is, among others, working with the governments in Tunisia and Morocco and with civil society.[4] Improving the trust of the population in the police, justice and security system, also by increasing transparency, is crucial.

Restructuring the security (intelligence) services of the 'Arab Spring' coun-tries is an important and sensitive challenge. Countries need capable security services, but they may have to learn new ways so that services conform to the rule of law and human rights. Reliable information is key to dismantling terrorist networks. National security remains the sole responsibility of EU Member States according to art. 4(2) of the Treaty on European Union, which means that intelli-gence services remain an exclusive competence of the Member States (within the EEAS, the INTCEN collects strategic intelligence from Member States' ser-vices to produce common strategic assessments for the EU). Therefore, if the EU were asked to support the restructuring of intelligence services in 'Arab Spring' countries, this would have to be done with EU funding and Member States' expertise. In the past, using this model, Common Foreign and Security Policy (CFSP) funding was used to support the restructuring and capacity-building of the Palestine security services (European Union 1997).[5] A number of EU Member States designed and participated in the project. One of the outcomes were lasting relationships between services, which is important in the fight against terrorism.

Evidence-based investigation

In the justice sector, it is crucial to move from confession-based to evidence-based investigations and prosecutions. The EU is promoting a criminal justice approach to terrorism: terrorists are criminals and have to be tried and convicted. This is what happened after the Madrid terrorist attacks in 2004, for example, or with Anders Behring Breivik after his attacks in Oslo in 2012. Treating terrorists as criminals and not as 'warriors' takes the false glamour out of terrorism. A public court hearing provides visible justice to the victims and their families, whose rights are specifically recognized by the Global Counter-terrorism Strategy of the United Nations (United Nations 2006). Indefinite or even secret detention of terrorist suspects without charge or trial not only is against the EU's values and unlawful, but also provides terrorists with distorted arguments (Søvndal et al. 2012).

Relevant international human rights treaties which have to be complied with are the International Covenant for Civil and Political Rights (ICCPR; United Nations 1966) and the Convention against Torture (United Nations 1984). The whole criminal justice chain, from intelligence to police investigations to pro-secutions, trials and prisons, needs to be part of the reforms. An evidence-based approach requires sophisticated tools such as forensics and special investigation techniques. A number of good practices have been set out in the 'Rabat Memorandum on Good Practices for Effective Counter-terrorism Practice in the Criminal Justice Sector' adopted by the Global Counter-terrorism Forum (GCTF) in 2012 (GCTF 2012). Algeria, Morocco and Egypt, for example, participate in the GCTF. The Council of Europe (2005) has made recommendations on special investigation techniques.[6] The case law of the European Court of Human Rights also provices interesting insights into how CT measures are interpreted in respect of human rights, as well as UN soft law such as that of the UN Human Rights Committee. To ensure human rights compliance, it is, for example, important to introduce safeguards to prevent ill-treatment during detention or interrogation and to ensure a sound legal basis and judicial control for detention.

Security expertise

Support for security and justice is different from other development projects. It is a new field for the EU to engage in, and a different type of expertise is necessary. Not all EU delegations have the security experts that are needed to create relationships with their peers in the host countries and to design security and justice projects. The creation of trust and closer relations between security professionals from EU Member States and partner countries is essential for effective cooperation in this area.

Police cooperation

It is also in the EU's interest to involve its agencies EUROPOL,[7] EUROJUST[8] and CEPOL,[9] the European Police College. These have now matured to a point that they can reach out to the EU's neighbourhood. For the partner countries these agencies could become important entry points for operational cooperation on police and justice actions such as investigations, prosecutions and exchange of information. Partner countries could connect to all 28 EU Member States through association with the EU agencies, thereby joining the efforts to fight terrorist groups which operate across borders. This is done first through contact points and then through cooperation agreements. With EUROPOL, partner countries could conclude both strategic and operational agreements. The latter requires a high standard of data protection and allows the sharing of personal data. EUROJUST offers case coordination, for example in the timing of arrests and the exchange of information on cross-border investigations. While countries without cooperation agreements can be associated to such case coordination, they cannot launch them. CEPOL has links to all the police academies of EU Member States and has started to offer training, exchange programmes and study visits to interested countries in the EU's neighbourhood, so far mainly to the eastern partners and the accession countries in the Balkans.

It will be important for the EU to soon offer to the partners in North Africa such opportunities as CEPOL-facilitated study visits, including to EUROPOL

and EUROJUST, exchanges, twinning and joint trainings with EU CT professionals. This would create the necessary networks and trust and would familiarize each side with the other's systems, with the aim of moving on to financially
more intensive and longer-term projects. Cooperation in justice and home affairs
is challenging and sensitive. In the EU, much progress has been made, but more
needs to be done. EUROPOL was created nearly 20 years ago and information
exchange remains a challenge. Therefore, one has to be realistic and must not
expect too much too soon, or disengage because in the security area things take
more time. It is the same in the EU. However, when the EU started to put practitioners together to work on common challenges, progress was made. Therefore,
with the EU's partners in the neighbourhood, it is important to enable practitioners to get together for workshops on topics of common interest, training sessions
and meetings, exchanges and visits.

Other excellent and flexible EU programmes which the countries in the neighbourhood can already apply to with concrete proposals are 'twinnings'[10] (for
example, with a twinning the EU – with Member States' expertise – successfully
assisted Morocco in building its financial intelligence unit) and workshops or
short-term expert visits on topics of particular interest.[11]

With the Euromed Police and Justice projects, the EU brought together security
and justice professionals from around the Mediterranean and EU Member States
over the last few years. These projects were designed before the 'Arab Spring' and
consisted mainly of conferences. They ended in 2014 and are being reviewed. In
the future, a different approach might potentially be considered, which could also
allow the organization of meetings, not conferences, of high-level professionals
around common challenges, followed up on a national basis.

The CT-related topics where fruitful discussions are already taking place are
foreign fighters traveling to and returning from Syria and Iraq, which are a
common challenge to EU Member States and partner countries.

Regional cooperation

In the field of security and justice, it is important to strengthen regional
cooperation, but it is also crucial to improve national capacities and to provide
the possibility for follow-up at national level. The approach needs to be pragmatic: one should start with a few projects that interest both sides and on which
one can build. The EU cannot expect to receive fully fledged SSR reform plans
before the EU starts to engage – this will take time.

In the framework of the joint Communication on the Maghreb (European
Commission and High Representative 2012), the first specific CT project 'Supporting Rule-of-law Compliant Investigations and Prosecutions in the Maghreb
Region' (European Commission 2013b), financed by the European Neighbourhood and Partnership Instrument (ENPI), started in 2014 and is being implemented by the UN Counter-terrorism Executive Directorate (UNCTED) and the
UN Office for Drugs and Crime (UNODC). It provides the opportunity for EU
and Maghreb investigators and prosecutors to get together for workshops on

specific challenges of CT investigations and prosecutions and for national follow-up. It supports evidence-based criminal justice chains, in full compliance with human rights and the rule of law, assisting the on-going reforms in these areas.

Under the rule of law group of the Global Counter-terrorism Forum, the International Institute for Justice and the Rule of Law was established in Malta in 2014.[12] It provides opportunities for the training of justice and other officials in areas related to the evidence-based criminal justice chain and will support in particular countries turning their backs on repression. Initially, beneficiaries are likely to be in particular North, West and East Africa.

The EU has finalized peer reviews of the Ministry of the Interior and of the Ministry of Justice with Tunisia, as well as a borders peer review, which was followed up by the dedication of €25 million to a justice reform support programme.[13] Based on the outcome of the peer reviews, support to reforms will be provided. Now that the constitution is in place it is a good time to engage. Tunisia, with the support of UNODC, is in the process of reforming its CT law, a draft of which has been submitted to the parliament.

The new constitution of Morocco puts emphasis on human rights, security sector and justice reform. A justice reform is on-going, and Morocco has strong CT capabilities. The EU has supported the creation of a financial intelligence unit in Morocco and is ready to provide further support. A counter-terrorism action plan may be developed. The EU participated in both visits by UNCTED to Morocco to ensure support to follow up technical assistance and cooperation. Morocco has a very interesting approach to imam training and supervision as part of a comprehensive approach to the prevention of radicalization. It has also sent 500 imams to Mali. Many justice officials from across the region are being trained in Morocco's judicial school.

In 2005, the EU and Algeria adopted a CT Memorandum of Understanding (MoU) in the context of COTER, the Council Working Party on Terrorism (International Aspects). This MoU will be updated in the future. The EU should explore how it can team up with Morocco and Algeria for joint projects in third countries, for example in the Sahel and the broader Middle East, given the availability of expertise in both countries.

The EU is engaged in Libya on integrated border management through the CSDP operation EUBAM.[14] It has also committed around €10 million to police and justice reform in Libya, and resources have been made available under the Instrument for Stability for strengthening the capacity for criminal investigations. The EU is among the largest partners to fight weapon proliferation and has a number of programmes in the areas of physical stockpile security management, clearance of unexploded ordnances (UXO) and prevention and reduction of armed violence (European Commission 2013a).[15]

The EU strategy for security and development in the Sahel

The Strategy for Security and Development in the Sahel, adopted in 2011, was based on a series of missions by the EU Counter-terrorism Coordinator, the

Director in DG Development at the European Commission at the time[16] and interested Member States, both at political and expert level. The Sahel Strategy is the first comprehensive post-Lisbon EU strategy. It has served as a model for other regions and also as a model for the Joint Communication on the Comprehensive Approach (European Commission and High Representative 2013). It is based on four pillars: political engagement, development, security and the rule of law, and prevention of radicalization. In March 2014, the Council of the European Union (2014b) adopted conclusions on the implementation of the EU Strategy for Security and Development in the Sahel, in which the security and development approach was reaffirmed. In addition to Mali, Mauritania and Niger, Burkina Faso and Chad have been added to the Sahel Strategy. Political dialogue on security issues will also be extended to other relevant countries in West Africa and the Maghreb. The link between the security in the Sahel and Libya has been recognized.

Security and development approach

To sustainably fight terrorism, alternatives have to be offered to young people: economic opportunities (so as not to have to resort to trafficking), education opportunities (to find jobs and to develop critical minds) and social opportunities (leisure, sports facilities). Strengthening the security sector is important, but it is not enough. Development aid is crucial to achieve these aims. It is also crucial to address corruption, which contributes to the weakness of the state, including its security sector. How could this be achieved? Are there possibilities to link further budget support to improvements on the Transparency International list?

In the context of the security and development approach, some funding from the European Development Fund (EDF) has been mobilized to strengthen the security and justice sectors, as well as to provide opportunities for youth. In Mali, before the take-over of the Tuareg and terrorist groups in the north, EU support had been provided to the security and development poles in the north, a promising concept which has not been implemented quickly enough. The idea was that state security forces would redeploy in the north (where they had been largely absent given the 2006 Algiers accords with the Tuareg – which had led to a settlement after earlier conflicts in this region and formed the basis for relations between government institutions and Tuareg in the north since then) and that at the same time, to gain acceptance by the population, social services would be provided and community engagement would be undertaken.

It is important to mobilize development instruments as part of the security and development approach. Much of the assistance the EU is providing in the areas of security, justice and rule of law qualifies as official development assistance (ODA): for example, support to the civilian security and justice systems/SSR and police training, unless the training relates to paramilitary functions such as counter-insurgency work or intelligence gathering on terrorism. Under certain circumstances, the European Development Fund can also finance activities that are not ODA. In the Sahel countries, in addition to support of specific CT capacities, general training, such as evidence collection, is the bulk of what is needed. Some specialized CT training comes on top of this general improvement of capabilities.

According to the OECD-DAC guidelines 'A Development Cooperation Lens on Terrorism Prevention' of 2003, terrorism is a form of violent conflict and conflict prevention is an integral part of the quest to reduce poverty (EU Counter-terrorism Coordinator 2012). The guidelines state that while 'development cooperation cannot and should not target individual terrorists nor combat their networks', it 'does have an important role to play in helping to deprive terrorists of popular support and addressing the conditions that terrorist leaders feed on and exploit' (Organization of Economic Cooperation and Development 2003). A wide variety of measures related to the prevention of radicalization set out in the document qualify as ODA, both general CT-relevant actions and specifically counter-radicalization actions: bolstering accountable security systems and the rule of law; outreach campaigns; and supporting voices such as religious leaders, media and education systems. This includes support to law enforcement and criminal justice which is relevant to CT. Hence, much security support can be carried out under EDF.

The OECD-DAC also assumes that the fight against terrorism is undertaken in the interest of the donor as opposed to the interest of the recipient countries and states: 'Anti-Terrorism – Activities combating terrorism are not reportable as ODA, as they generally target perceived threats to donor, as much as to recipient countries, rather than focusing on the economic and social development of the recipient' (ibid.). Seen in context, this seems to mean that operational CT activities are not considered ODA, while the criminal justice CT response and prevention of radicalization response, most of what EU does, would be possible under ODA. However, this is unclear. Also, the situation has changed, as explained above, and the terrorist threat in African countries today is one of the major obstacles to their own development. Therefore, the EU should have a strong position for the review of ODA criteria at the OECD-DAC in 2014–15 to clarify what capacity-building assistance related to CT can be 'ODA-ble', based on the security threat to the African countries which is hampering their development.

EU engagement in the Sahel on security, rule of law and counter-terrorism

It is crucial to support the civilian approach to the fight against terrorism: terrorist suspects have to be investigated, prosecuted and brought to trial. The criminal justice chain in the Sahel countries tends to be weak: very few terrorists have been convicted in a criminal trial. Basic improvements are needed. For example, as the EU Counter-terrorism Coordinator was informed during visits to Mali, there are very few names in the police database in Mali. In the north of the Sahel countries, in the desert zones, law enforcement authorities are often not present and the military instead carryies out law enforcement functions. It is necessary to support the whole criminal justice chain, from intelligence collection and analysis to investigation, prosecution, trial and imprisonment.

The EU is engaged in a variety of ways to strengthen the law enforcement and criminal justice capacities of the Sahel countries. First, EUCAP Sahel Niger, a civilian mission under the Common Security and Defence Policy (CSDP), was set up in 2012 in order to assist the security forces of Niger to improve their capacities in the fight against terrorism and organized crime. It is the first CSDP operation which includes CT in its mandate. Around 50 EU personnel (advisers, trainers and mission support) are based in Niger and work with the security and defence forces, providing advice and training to the military in some civilian security functions that they perform ('judiciarization').

Second, the EU is training the military in Mali. While this is important in a rule-of-law society, the civilian security forces have to provide security in the country. For the time being, especially in the northern part of the country, this role is fulfilled by the armed forces, given the weakness and the lack of means of the internal security forces. Therefore, the EU is in the process of setting up a civilian CSDP mission, EUCAP Sahel Mali, which will provide training and aim to restructure and regenerate the capacities of the civilian internal security forces in Mali. In support of the Malian government's SSR, the mission will provide basic and more specialized training and strategic advice, including on intelligence functions related to CT, as well as part of the criminal justice chain (collection of evidence, investigations, link to the judiciary).

Third, the EU has provided much-needed capacity assistance to improve integrated border management in Libya (EUBAM Libya). The issue of border management has obvious regional implications, and thus liaison and cooperation with the other CSDP missions in the region was undertaken with the aim of improving mutual awareness in the host countries. Due to the security situation in Libya, activities of EUBAM Libya were suspended in mid-2014.

Addressing border security is a huge challenge and very difficult, and hence a step-by-step approach is necessary. In January 2014, the EU Ministers of the Interior discussed for the first time terrorism and border security (previously, border management issues had been looked at mainly in the context of immigration).[17] Council conclusions on terrorism and border security were adopted under the Greek presidency in 2014 (Council of the European Union 2014a).

It is impossible to fully control the borders in the huge desert zones. Therefore, alternative approaches and compensatory measures have to be explored. The vision needs to include more than just a border control approach: in the EU, there is a lot of experience with the establishment of measures compensating for the lack of controls at the internal borders in the Schengen area. For example, common databases have been developed as well as stronger police and justice cooperation (creation of the EU agencies EUROPOL, EUROJUST and CEPOL), the principle of mutual recognition in the area of judicial cooperation, and the adoption of tools on this basis (such as the European Arrest Warrant, the European Evidence Warrant and the European Investigation Order). The Sahel countries could consider also adopting similar compensatory measures. For example, in the context of the Global Counter-terrorism Forum, best practices on 'hot pursuit' will be developed, and the African Union is working on an African

Arrest Warrant. In addition, strong intelligence is necessary to allow for targeted arrests and border checks. Therefore, support for information gathering, analysis and sharing is fundamental. As with other areas of counter-terrorism, Member State experts would carry out EU-financed projects.

In addition to the four CSDP operations in the region, which show the strong political commitment of the EU, the EU has put other projects in place. The CT Sahel project[18] provides CT assistance to Mali, Mauritania and Niger nationally, including the specialized CT judicial poles where CT cases are prosecuted and adjudicated. In addition, the Sahel Security College is being established as a virtual college, based on the model of CEPOL. With the EU's support, the three Sahel countries have defined the areas in which they want to develop curricula and common training mainly related to the prevention of radicalization. The structures of the college are established by the countries of the region, who have appointed representatives. The EU's WAPIS project carried out by INTERPOL (2012), which created a police network of databases within and among Sahel countries, deserves future support as well. The WAPIS programme is an EU-funded project initiated in 2010 which facilitates the collection, centralization, management, sharing and analysis of police information among countries belonging to the Economic Community of West African States (ECOWAS) and Mauritania.

Through the EDF, the EU also supports security and justice projects in the Sahel countries. A new security project has been launched in Mauritania, which will boost the capacities of the security forces there, including in the area of CT. After 'Operation Serval', the EU provided a €20-million immediate support package through the Instrument for Stability, which included equipment to the security forces as well as support for local radio stations in order to allow the population in the north to hear various narratives and not only the extremist one.

Priorities for the EU's future work in the Sahel

Given the remaining challenges in the Sahel region, in the future the EU needs to focus on areas where more progress is needed. With regard to CT, these are the criminal justice approach to the fight against terrorism; the prevention of radicalization, and the improved addressing of the terrorism–drugs nexus and the regional dimension.

Further promoting the criminal justice approach to the fight against terrorism

While a lot has already been done, considerable weaknesses of the civilian approach to CT remain in Mali, Mauritania and Niger as well as in the neighbouring countries which are now also facing terrorism problems and to which the EU should extend CT capacity-building activities. In particular, the criminal justice chain, including intelligence and prisons, needs further strengthening. In Mali, around 300 detainees have been arrested in the course of the conflict, including terrorist suspects, and they need to be tried. Mali has not yet success-fully prosecuted terrorist suspects in its criminal justice system. It is urgent to assist Mali to investigate and prosecute these terrorist suspects. In addition, work on rehabilitation and reintegration of terrorist detainees would be important.

It is also crucial to support collection of evidence by the military, in particular in Mali, to facilitate prosecutions of terrorist suspects. As it is not realistic that all Sahel countries would establish this capacity nationally, support to a regional for-ensic laboratory which would facilitate terrorist prosecutions could be envisaged.

Dialogue with the private sector should be strengthened, in particular with a view to critical infrastructure protection. Terrorists have attacked energy instal-lations in the Sahel. Given that the installations are run by private companies, increased dialogue with such private operators (for instance through the creation of adequate forums for an exchange of sensitive information) can be helpful both in Europe and in the Maghreb/Sahel region. Such exchanges could contribute to security alertness and could include issues such as updating and verifying security plans and control measures.

As a priority, airport and aviation security in the Sahel should be strength-ened. Aviation and airport security projects need to be set up in the Sahel and Maghreb. This should go beyond core aviation security and include activities to enhance security and response capacities in the broader airport area (MANPAD-threat,[19] protection of public area around airports etc.). Not ensuring aviation security can pose a major risk for economic development.

Prevention of radicalization

The prevention of radicalization is one of the four lines of action of the EU's Sahel Strategy, but the EU is still at the very beginning of providing assistance in the area of 'Prevent'. Current EU programming in the Sahel contains several elements that aim to address radicalization and recruitment but, given that this is a new, sensitive and challenging area, not yet in a comprehensive and structured manner.

Radicalization in West Africa and the Sahel is fuelled by a combination of complex factors and circumstances. It is important to understand that radicaliza-tion is not solely caused by poverty, discrimination, poor economic conditions, and so forth, as it has manifested itself in both impoverished societies and advanced industrialized countries. Hence, the EU's response has to go beyond traditional development work and has to be both 'Prevent'-specific and 'Pre-vent'-relevant.

Prevent-specific activities are aimed at stopping people from turning to ter-rorism. Prevent-relevant activities address the conditions that could be condu-cive to the spread of terrorism and mainly focus on tackling feelings of marginalization, unmet basic needs, unemployment, lack of education, lack of human security, lack of human dignity etc. Tackling these underlying drivers is important as well since they create a sense of grievance – whether such griev-ance is real or perceived. It is exactly that sense of grievance, in combination with the appeal of an inspirational leader or figure that successfully frames these grievances in a particular worldview, that makes people vulnerable and suscepti- ble to exploitation, manipulation and finally radicalization and recruitment. Many of these drivers could be addressed through an appropriate development response – there is no need to label these general development interventions as measures to prevent radicalization. One important area in which the EU should continue to invest is education.

At the same time, it is vital to mainstream 'Prevent' into the EU's develop- ment work and programming in order to focus some of the development pro- grammes on specific geographical areas or communities where radicalization and recruitment are highly concentrated. Hence the EU should consider stepping up existing development programmes in those areas of concern. Strengthening young people's economic prospects and offering alternative educational oppor- tunities may prevent them from being disenfranchised and could make them less vulnerable to extremist narratives. It is known that groups of internally displaced people (IDP) and refugee camps are potential breeding grounds for radicaliza- tion. There are huge numbers of refugees and IDPs in the already poor and under-developed Sahel countries, and there is a risk of growing radicalization and recruitment in these camps (also in neighbouring countries, in particular Senegal, Burkina Faso and Chad).[20]

As mentioned, Prevent-relevant work needs to be complemented with Prevent-specific work because grievances as such may not actually lead to viol- ence in the absence of ideologies and organizations that can frame and channel the relevant grievances in violent directions.

Denmark and Burkina Faso have developed interesting ideas for Prevent- specific work in the Sahel in the context of the GCTF (Center on Global Coun- terterrorism Cooperation 2013). There follow some examples of possible 'Prevent' projects in the Sahel, which are in parts similar to the suggestions in the Danish/Burkino paper.

First, conduct perception studies and assessments of the drivers of radicaliza- tion and violent extremism. Before considering any intervention, it is key to understand the particular context, to assess where and how radicalization is occurring, which groups of people could be most vulnerable and what the main drivers of radicalization are. Such an assessment would – preferably – need to be carried out at the earliest stage of programme development in order for the outcome to be integrated into the assessment of the overall situation in a country and into the programming process.

Second, conduct 'Prevent' training and sensitization for frontline officials and practitioners: The EU could help to develop counter-radicalization awareness trainings for frontline officials and practitioners (law enforcement personnel, prison and probation officers, staff working on areas of development, education, health care etc.). Such training could provide officials working in these different areas with a broad introduction to the challenge of radicalization and how they can contribute to countering it. The Hedayah Centre,[21] set up in Abu Dhabi in the context of the Global Counter-terrorism Forum, could potentially play a leading role in developing such training modules.

Third, conduct awareness-raising and sensitization in the media. It is important to work with civil society organizations to develop training opportunities and materials for media practitioners and to facilitate platforms for the development of voluntary codes of conduct among members of the industry. Such training could focus on investigative methods, training in writing and presenting, developing research and verification skills, and establishing codes of conduct for print and broadcasting.

Fourth, develop rehabilitation and reintegration programmes for former fighters in the Sahel. There is an urgent need to reflect on how to deal with fighters that are willing to lay down their arms and how to reintegrate them into society. Specific programmes could build on good practices developed through other programmes for the demobilization, disarmament, rehabilitation and reintegration of fighters. Such programmes could possibly also include disengagement (de-radicalization) components, but also vocational training, education and aftercare support (for example, counselling, assistance with employment, and support to family members or medical assistance). Such programmes are an integral part of helping to ensure the fighters' re-entry into mainstream society. Closely linked to this is the challenge of dealing with those who have been imprisoned, whether it is for terrorist offences or for petty crime. Prisons are often breeding grounds for radicalization. Good prison standards and a setting where the human rights of prisoners are respected are essential to counter radicalization, as is the professional training of prison staff. For those who are imprisoned for terrorist offences, specific programmes that work with detainees and support their disengagement from violent behaviour or stop them from re-joining terrorist groups upon release could be considered.

Fifth, build the capacity of civil society organizations working with youth. The EU could consider granting scholarships for universities or higher education in European countries, as this could allow students to develop relationships and skills they might not otherwise develop and would bring them into contact with people from different cultures and backgrounds. This experience is likely to be valuable in preparation for future professional activities back in their home countries. The capacity development of youth organizations could also be supported in other ways.

The terrorism–drugs nexus

Already in 2011, drug trafficking in West Africa was considered such a threat to the EU that combating it was made one of the EU's priorities in the fight against organized crime, which is managed through the 2012–13 policy cycle of the Council Standing Committee on Internal Security. With the growing role of criminal networks, West Africa has become in recent years a major hub and transport route for drugs, while local consumption is on the rise. The drug trade has become 'Africanized': locals are now participating and profiting. Income from drug trafficking, which is more profitable than other forms of trafficking, is now considerably higher than the development assistance to the region and provides a regular source of income for terrorists.[22]

Corruption facilitates organized crime in West Africa. Drug trafficking has become a serious problem for security, stability and democratic governance, as well as for human rights, in the countries of the region. The drug problem cannot be addressed with law enforcement and criminal justice assistance alone; it is also a political problem.

As an aggravating factor, terrorism and drug trafficking are more and more interlinked (narco-terrorism): terrorist groups benefit from the drug trade, either through direct involvement, as with Mujao, or indirectly, as with AQIM. Drug trafficking allows terrorist groups to have regular sources of income other than ransoms, for example protection payments for convoys, 'taxes' etc. in the case of indirect involvement of terrorist groups. There may also be links between terrorist and organized crime groups through family ties. This helps terrorist groups to address their rising operational costs (including paying jihadists' salaries).

Therefore, it is important to align the EU's efforts against drug trafficking and terrorism in a truly comprehensive and 'cross-pillar' approach.[23] Many activities could benefit both the fight against crime and the fight against terrorism.

The regional dimension

A regional approach is key to address the security threats. Terrorist groups are moving between the Maghreb and the Sahel and have strong links throughout the region, and hence the threat has to be addressed comprehensively. It is only through a regional dimension including the EU's neighbours and their neighbours that the issues can be fully addressed. No country can solve these problems alone. There is no regional organization today that includes all the players. It is necessary to be pragmatic and develop *ad hoc* fora of 'variable geometry'. As the Maghreb countries are covered by a different financial instrument (European Neighbourhood Instrument) from that covering the Sahel (EDF), it will be crucial to add beneficiaries from both regions to regional projects and find ways to finance them. The EU is currently exploring this. For example, Mauritania is participating in the regional part of the Maghreb prosecutors project (mentioned above) financed by the European Neighbourhood and Partnership Instrument. It is important to recognize the interrelated security challenges in the EU's response.

Countries in the region have taken some interesting initiatives which merit support. First, with regard to intelligence, the African Union's (AU) Nouakchott Process on the Enhancement of Security Cooperation and the Operationalization of the African Peace and Security Architecture in the Sahelo-Saharan Region holds regular meetings at the political level and at the level of heads of intelligence and security services.[24] In this context, the 'Unité de Fusion et de Liaison' (UFL) in Algiers is playing a role and tasks are assigned to it.[25] The UFL serves as model for other sub-regions in Africa, and similar fusion centres have been created in Somalia and in the Great Lakes region. In addition to the seconding of one representative of a security service of each Member State of the UFL, support staff is provided on a voluntary basis (so far mainly by Algeria). The

UFL's mandate includes cooperation among intelligence and security services, such as centralizing and treating intelligence about terrorist and criminal activities, sharing operational intelligence, providing operational intelligence to humanitarian projects, and raising awareness about radicalization of the populations.

Second, for justice, the UN Office for Drugs and Crime set up a Sahel judicial platform, which should be strengthened to improve closer judicial cooperation among the Sahel countries.

Third, with regard to police, the EU-financed Sahel Security College (modeled on the European Police College CEPOL) could provide a regional framework and needs to be beefed up.

Fourth, assistance on border security needs to be stepped up in order to follow up to the meetings in Tripoli,[26] Rabat[27] and Rome (Italian Ministry for Foreign Affairs 2014) on border security over the past years. A conceptual effort is necessary rather than just focusing on border crossings, which cannot be fully controlled given the very long borders in the desert. A more comprehensive vision would need to be developed on borders, where the EU experience could, adapted to the circumstances, play an inspirational role. The EU has a lot of experience to share with regard to measures compensating for lack of border control developed in the Schengen context. In the regional context, more creative approaches should be tried as well, such as regional cross-border economic zones; for example, the economy of northern Mali is more turned towards Algeria than to southern Mali. Processes such as the Tripoli Action Plan with regard to border security in the region, in particular in Libya, merit full support. EUBAM is supporting the Libyan government by setting up a secretariat to oversee the implementation of the Tripoli Action Plan.

Fifth, the UN is convening coordination meetings on security and governance issues in the context of the UN Integrated Strategy for the Sahel. The strategy's second pillar aims at 'strengthening the capacity of national and regional security mechanisms to address cross-border threats' (United Nations 2013). The UN Counter-terrorism Executive Directorate played a role as a convener to bring together high-level security officials of 11 countries in North West Africa (Algeria, Burkina, Chad, Libya, Mali, Mauritania, Morocco, Niger, Nigeria, Senegal, Tunisia) which otherwise have no venue to regularly get together and discuss the threats they face, the responses they have adopted and the next steps.

Sixth, in the context of the Global Counter-terrorism Forum, capacity-building coordination on counter-terrorism is taking place among donors. As the terrorist threat in Africa is growing, a pan-African response, taking into account also the Horn of Africa and the 'arc of instability' across Africa, needs to be added. Hence, it will be important to use the Pan-African Programme to address the increasing security threats in Africa. This allows connection between the EU's neighbours and their neighbours.

Seventh, the presidents of Mauritania, Mali, Niger, Burkina Faso and Chad created the G5 of the Sahel on 16 February 2014 in Nouakchott in order to cooperate and to create an institutional framework to coordinate their policies of development and security.

Conclusion

This chapter has discussed the EU's CT approach to North Africa and the Sahel. A comprehensive development and security approach is needed to address the challenges. Based on the EU's Strategy for Security and Development in the Sahel, which was developed and is being implemented, in partnership with the countries in the region, the EU has devoted considerable resources to the region, ranging from four CSDP operations[28] to development assistance addressing the underlying factors of instability and CT capacity-building.

North-West Africa, the Maghreb and the Sahel are regions where the EU is one of the main and longest-standing partners. It can play an important role, and relations and engagement with the region are priorities for the EU. The security and development of the countries concerned is at stake, as is Europe's own security. Terrorist groups benefit from ungoverned spaces – the creation of new terrorist sanctuaries is a growing threat that needs to be addressed. Given the increased links of the threat between North and West African countries, a response needs to be comprehensive and include both the EU's neighbours and their neighbours, as appropriate. The Maghreb countries have interesting projects of their own in the Sahel, such as the training of justice officials, training on terrorist financing and projects related to prevention of radicalization, so that the EU Member States and the Maghreb countries could cooperate in the Sahel not only politically but also through projects. Strong investment by the EU in security sector reform in the Maghreb is needed. Overall, it is important not to think in silos depending on EU financial or other instruments, but rather to have a vision of what needs to be done and find the means to do it. Security experts in EU delegations can help to create relationships, establish trust and work with the security and justice authorities of the partner countries, as well as helping to design security and justice projects.

The EU is committed to working with its neighbours and their neighbours to assist them in addressing political and development challenges and the terrorist threat in a comprehensive fashion based on the rule of law and human rights. Many Member States are engaged on the ground. It has become a truly European issue which benefits from strong EU coordination and cooperation. The challenge for the EU will now be to learn the development assistance lessons from the past – Mali imploded despite decades of considerable amounts of development assistance – and together with the partners from the region design a security and development approach which will provide viable alternatives to the EU's neighbours and their neighbours, and in particular to their youth populations, who will shape the future of these countries.

Notes

1 Gilles de Kerchove is the EU Counter-terrorism Coordinator, and Christiane Höhn is adviser to the EU Counter-terrorism Coordinator. The views expressed in this chapter are those of the authors alone and do not necessarily reflect the views and positions of the Council of the European Union.

2 See also the Introduction to this volume.
3 See www.dcaf.ch.
4 For DCAF activities in Tunisia, including cooperation with civil society, see www. dcaf-tunisie.org/En/accueil/index/92 (accessed October 2014). For DCAF activities in Morocco, see www.dcaf.ch/Project/Assistance-Programme-Moroccan-Security-Sector-Reform (accessed October 2014).
5 One important focus of COTER was to help the Palestinian intelligence services build an organization with both intelligence-gathering and analytical capabilities.
6 However, since 2005, computer and Internet technology has evolved offering new possibilities to law enforcement.
7 See www.europol.europa.eu.
8 See http://eurojust.europa.eu.
9 See www.cepol.europa.eu.
10 Twinning is an instrument for the cooperation between public administrations of EU Member States and of beneficiary countries. Beneficiaries include (potential) candidate countries as well as countries covered by the European Neighbourhood Policy. See http://ec.europa.eu/enlargement/tenders/twinning (accessed October 2014).
11 TAIEX is the Technical Assistance and Information Exchange instrument managed by the Directorate General of Enlargement of the European Commission. TAIEX supports partner countries with regard to the approximation, application and enforcement of EU legislation. It is largely demand-driven and facilitates the delivery of appropriate tailor-made expertise to address issues at short notice. See http://ec.europa.eu/enlargement/taiex/index_en.htm (accessed October 2014).
12 For more information about the Institute, see www.theiij.org/about-us (accessed October 2014).
13 See http://enpi-info.eu/medportal/opportunities//19478/Tunisia:-Technical-assistance-to-support-the-implementation-of-the-justice-reform-support-programme (accessed October 2014) and www.eeas.europa.eu/delegations/tunisia/eu_tunisia/tech_financial_cooperation/index_fr.htm (accessed October 2014).
14 See http://eeas.europa.eu/csdp/missions-and-operations/eubam-libya/index_fr.htm (accessed October 2014) and Chapter 1 by Valeria Bonavita in this volume.
15 See also Chapter 3 by Alyson J.K. Bailes and Pál Dunay in this volume.
16 Manuel Lopez Blanco, who became the first Sahel Strategy Coordinator in the EEAS.
17 See also Chapter 1 by Valeria Bonavita in this volume.
18 Financed by the Instrument for Stability and carried out by the French agency Civipol linked to the Ministry of the Interior (with experts also from other EU Member States).
19 Man-portable air-defense systems (MANPADS) are shoulder-launched surface-to-air missiles (SAMs). They are typically guided weapons and are a threat to low-flying aircraft, especially helicopters.
20 See also Chapter 2 by Sarah Wolff in this volume.
21 See www.hedayah.ae.
22 See, for example, the studies of the Institute for Security Studies in South Africa, www.issafrica.org.
23 See also Chapter 6 by Tressia Hobeika in this volume.
24 The fourth meeting of the Heads of Intelligence and Security Services of the countries of the Sahelo-Saharan region was held in Niamey, Niger, on 17 February 2014. The following countries participated in the meeting: Algeria, Burkina Faso, Chad, Cote d'Ivoire, Libya, Mali, Mauritania, Niger, Nigeria and Senegal. In addition, the Commission of the African Union, the AU Mission for Mali and the Sahel (MISAHEL), the African Centre for the Study and Research on Terrorism, the Committee of the Intelligence and Security Services of Africa, the Fusion and Liaison Unit (UFL), the Economic Community of West African States (ECOWAS) and the Community of the Sahelo-Saharan States, as well as the United Nations Office for West Africa

(UNOWA) and the UN Multidimensional Integrated Mission for Stabilization in Mali (MINUSMA), attended the meeting.
25 The countries participating in the UFL are Algeria, Burkina Faso, Libya, Mali, Mauritania, Niger, Chad and, given the emerging threat from Boko Haram and the links to AQIM, as of 2011 also Nigeria.
26 Adoption of the Tripoli Action Plan, http://magharebia.com/en_GB/articles/awi/features/2012/03/13/feature-01 (accessed October 2014).
27 Rabat declaration on border security, www.voltairenet.org/article182664.html (accessed October 2014), and www.moroccanembassy.sa/index.php?route=information/news& news_id=83 (accessed October 2014).
28 See also Chapter 3 by Alyson J.K. Bailes and Pál Dunay in this volume.

References

African Union (2014) *Report of the Chairperson of the Commission on Terrorism and Violent Extremism in Africa*, Nairobi, 2 September, http://cpauc.au.int/en/content/report-chairperson-commission-terrorism-and-violent-extremism-africa-peace-and-security-co-0 (accessed October 2014).

Barrios, C. and T. Koepf (eds) (2014) *Re-mapping the Sahel: Transnational Security Challenges and International Responses*, Report 19, June, Paris: European Union Institute for Security Studies, www.iss.europa.eu/uploads/media/Report_19_Sahel.pdf (accessed October 2014).

Center on Global Counterterrorism Cooperation (2013) *Countering Violent Extremism and Promoting Community Engagement in West Africa and the Sahel: An Action Agenda*, July, www.thegctf.org/documents/10299/44331/Action+Agenda+ENG.pdf (accessed October 2014).

Council of Europe (2005) 'Recommendation (2005) 10 of the Committee of Ministers of the Council of Europe to Member States on "Special Investigation Techniques" in Relation to Serious Crimes including Acts of Terrorism', adopted by the Committee of Ministers on 20 April 2005 at the 924th meeting of the Ministers' Deputies, Strasbourg, https://wcd.coe.int/ViewDoc.jsp?id=849269 (accessed May 2014).

Council of the European Union (2011a) *Strategy for Security and Development in the Sahel*, Annex to the Council Conclusions on a European Union Strategy for Security and Development in the Sahel, Brussels, 21 March, http://eeas.europa.eu/africa/docs/sahel_strategy_en.pdf (accessed October 2014).

Council of the European Union (2011b) *A Strategic Framework for the Horn of Africa*, Annex to the Council Conclusions on the Horn of Africa, 3124th Foreign Affairs Council meeting, Brussels, 14 November, www.consilium.europa.eu/uedocs/cms_data/docs/pressdata/en/foraff/126052.pdf (accessed October 2014).

Council of the European Union (2013) 'Conclusions on the Joint Communication "Supporting Closer Cooperation and Regional Integration in the Maghreb: Algeria, Libya, Mauritania, Morocco and Tunisia"', Brussels, 31 January http://register.consilium.europa.eu/doc/srv?l=EN&t=PDF&gc=true&sc=false&f=ST%205896%202013%20INIT (accessed October 2014).

Council of the European Union (2014a) 'Conclusions on Terrorism and Border Security', Luxembourg, 5–6 June, www.consilium.europa.eu/uedocs/cms_data/docs/pressdata/en/jha/143107.pdf (accessed October 2014).

Council of the European Union (2014b) 'Conclusions on the Implementation of the EU Strategy for Security and Development in the Sahel', 17 March, www.consilium.europa.eu/uedocs/cms_data/docs/pressdata/EN/foraff/141577.pdf (accessed October 2014).

EU Counter-terrorism Coordinator (2012) Discussion Paper to the Council of the European Union, June, http://register.consilium.europa.eu/doc/srv?l=EN&t=PDF&gc=true&sc=false&f=ST%209990%202012%20INIT (accessed May 2014).

European Commission (2013a) Staff Working Document Accompanying the Report from the Commission to the European Parliament, the Council, the European Economic and Social Committee and the Committee of the Regions, *2012 Annual Report on the Instrument for Stability*, COM(2013) 563 final, Brussels, 26 July, SWD(2013) 292 final, Volume 2, http://eeas.europa.eu/ifs/docs/comm_staff_work_doc_vol.2_en.pdf (accessed October 2014).

European Commission (2013b) 'Action Fiche for Supporting Rule-of-law-compliant Investigations and Prosecutions in the Maghreb Region', Brussels, http://ec.europa.eu/europeaid/documents/aap/2013/regional_south_part_i_action_fiches_en.pdf (accessed October 2014).

European Commission and High Representative (2011a) Joint Communication to the European Council, the European Parliament, the Council, the European Economic and Social Committee and the Committee of the Regions, *A Partnership for Democracy and Share Prosperity with the Southern Mediterranean*, COM(2011) 200 final, Brussels, 3 March.

European Commission and High Representative (2011b) Joint Communication to the European Parliament, the Council, the European Economic and Social Committee and the Committee of the Regions, *A New Response to a Changing Neighbourhood*, COM(2011) 303 final, Brussels, 25 May.

European Commission and High Representative (2012) Joint Communication to the European Council, the European Parliament, the Council, the European Economic and Social Committee and the Committee of the Regions, *Supporting Closer Cooperation and Regional Integration in the Maghreb: Algeria, Libya, Mauritania, Morocco and Tunisia*, JOIN(2012) 36 final, Brussels, 17 December.

European Commission and High Representative (2013) Joint Communication to the European Parliament and the Council, *The EU's Comprehensive Approach to External Conflicts and Crises*, JOIN(2013) 30 final, Brussels, 11 December.

European Council (2014) 'Conclusions on Iraq/Syria', Brussels, 30 August, www.consilium.europa.eu/uedocs/cms_data/docs/pressdata/en/ec/144538.pdf (accessed October 2014).

European Union (1997) 'Joint Action of 29 April 1997 (97/289/CFSP) Adopted by the Council on the Basis of Article J.3 of the Treaty on European Union on the Establishment of a European Union Assistance Programme to Support the Palestinian Authority in its Efforts to Counter Terrorist Activities Emanating from the Territories under its Control', *Official Journal of the European Union*, L 120, 12 May, 2–3.

Gall, C. (2013) 'Second Opposition Leader Assassinated in Tunisia', *New York Times*, Tunis, 25 July, www.nytimes.com/2013/07/26/world/middleeast/second-opposition-leader-killed-in-tunisia.html?pagewanted=all (accessed October 2014).

GCTF (Global Counter-terrorism Forum) (2012) 'Rabat Memorandum on Good Practices for Effective Counter-terrorism Practice in the Criminal Justice Sector', www.thegctf.org/documents/10162/38299/Rabat+Memorandum-English (accessed October 2014).

Hofnung, T. (2014) 'Le Sud Libyen, nouveau terreau du jihadisme', *Le Monde*, 14 March.

INTERPOL (2012) 'INTERPOL holds Inaugural WAPIS Workshop', 28 November, www.interpol.int/fr/News-and-media/News/2012/N20121128 (accessed October 2014).

Italian Ministry for Foreign Affairs (2014) 'Ministerial Conference on International Support to Libya (Rome, 6 March 2014) – Conclusions', www.esteri.it/MAE/IT/Sala_

Stampa/ArchivioNotizie/Approfondimenti/2014/03/20140306_minconflibconcl.htm (accessed October 2014).

Organization of Economic Cooperation and Development (2003) 'Development Assistance Committee, DAC Guidelines and Reference Series, A Development Cooperation Lens on Terrorism Prevention', Key Entry Points for Action, www.oecd.org/development/incaf/16085708.pdf (accessed October 2014).

Søvndal, V., G. de Kerchove and B. Emmerson (2012) 'Remembering the Victims of Terrorism: A Collective Commitment to Respect for Human Rights', *European Human Rights Law Review* 3, 247–248.

United Nations (1966) International Covenant for Civil and Political Rights, New York, 19 December, www.ohchr.org/Documents/ProfessionalInterest/ccpr.pdf (accessed October 2014).

United Nations (1984) Convention Against Torture, New York, 10 December, www.ohchr.org/EN/ProfessionalInterest/Pages/CAT.aspx (accessed October 2014).

United Nations (2006) 'Global Counter-terrorism Strategy', General Assembly, A/RES/60/288, New York, 8 September, http://daccess-ddsny.un.org/doc/UNDOC/GEN/N05/504/88/PDF/N0550488.pdf?OpenElement (accessed October 2014).

United Nations (2013) 'Report of the Secretary-General on the Situation in the Sahel Region', S/2013/354, 14 June, www.securitycouncilreport.org/atf/cf/%7B65BFCF9B-6D27-4E9C-8CD3-CF6E4FF96FF9%7D/s_2013_354.pdf (accessed October 2014).

Part II

Economic and societal challenges

5 EU trade relations beyond the 'Neighbourhood Economic Community'

Sieglinde Gstöhl

Introduction: trade in the EU's neighbourhood and beyond

With the European Neighbourhood Policy (ENP), the European Union (EU) has for the past decade focused much attention on its post-enlargement neighbours. In light of the EU's 2004 enlargement, the ENP aimed 'to avoid new dividing lines in Europe and to promote stability and prosperity within and beyond the new borders of the Union' (European Council 2002: point 22). Indeed, prosperity can only be achieved and maintained in a stable and secure environment, and in order to become stable, the regions have to become more prosperous as well. 'The European Neighbourhood Policy's vision involves a ring of countries, sharing the EU's fundamental values and objectives, drawn into an increasingly close relationship, going beyond cooperation to involve a significant measure of economic and political integration' (European Commission 2004: 5). Ten years later, it has become clear that the ambitious goal of expanding the 'zone of prosperity, stability and security' beyond the EU's borders is far from being achieved. The EU's neighbourhood has become politically more fragmented and unstable, the pace of economic and democratic transitions has slowed down, and the EU reluctantly finds itself in competition with Russia over the shared eastern neighbourhood, while its engagement in the south has been questioned by the Arab uprisings and their unintended consequences.

Nevertheless, the European Neighbourhood Policy has achieved some progress in the form of domestic reforms, new agreements with the EU (such as trade or visa liberalization), financial support, and various policy dialogues (see European Commission and High Representative 2014). Political conditionality thereby plays an important role:

> The value of the policy does not lie only in the achievements of its individual components (e.g. political reform/democratisation, market integration, better mobility and people-to-people contacts, and sector cooperation). It also anchors countries/societies in transition, and even in crisis situations, to the EU, by proposing a set of values and standards to guide their reform efforts, and generally through the creation of networks linking them to the EU and beyond to other partners.
>
> (Ibid.: 17)

While EU–ENP trade relations have expanded significantly, they tend to reproduce a 'core–periphery' pattern of development in the EU's neighbourhood instead of long-term income convergence as the ENP countries struggle to implement export-led growth strategies which would allow them to compete with the EU in the markets for capital- and knowledge-intensive products (Kallioras 2013). The EU has, in turn, been reluctant to open its markets for agricultural products and labour migration – sectors of major interest for its partners – while showing a propensity to require neighbouring countries to align with the trade-related parts of its *acquis* (Dreyer 2012: 26).

The ENP's long-term goal is 'to move towards an arrangement whereby the Union's relations with the neighbouring countries ultimately resemble the close political and economic links currently enjoyed with the European Economic Area' (EEA) (European Commission 2003: 15). The EEA in 1994 extended the EU's internal market to the countries of the European Free Trade Association (EFTA), covering the free movement of goods, services, capital and persons, competition rules and horizontal and flanking policies. The EEA does not cover the EU's external relations, the common agricultural, fisheries and transport policies, budget contributions and regional policy, taxation or economic and monetary policy. The EEA thus represents less than the internal market but more than a free trade area, and it is not a customs union. It could be considered an economic community, although this notion is not – despite the precedent of the European Economic Community – based on a commonly agreed definition (Gstöhl 2012: 95–97).[1] An economic community constitutes a form of regional integration compatible with the rules of the World Trade Organization (WTO), located somewhere between a free trade area and an internal market, and equipped with a certain degree of collective decision-making capacity (ibid.: 97). An economic community entails 'deep' or 'behind-the-border' integration, in contrast to 'shallow' integration which deals only with the removal of border barriers such as tariffs and quotas. The European Commission (2006: 5) introduced 'a longer-term vision of an economic community emerging between the EU and its ENP partners', which 'would include such points as the application of shared regulatory frameworks and improved market access for goods and services among ENP partners, and some appropriate institutional arrangement such as dispute settlement mechanisms'.[2] Such a Neighbourhood Economic Community (NEC) could be coupled with the concept of a 'security community': 'In a security community members share rational and moral expectations and dispositions of self-restraint, in particular the abstention from the use of force' (Adler 2008: 204). The European Security Strategy, which was drafted at the same time as the ENP, indeed stresses under the heading 'building security in our neighbourhood' the need 'to promote a ring of well governed countries to the East of the European Union and on the borders of the Mediterranean' (European Council 2003: 8).

This chapter aims to compare the EU's trade relations with the ENP countries and those with the neighbours of its neighbours, in order to assess whether in the long run the NEC envisaged for the immediate neighbours could be extended to the broader neighbourhood as well, especially by deepening the linkages between the EU, the ENP countries and their neighbours. In fact, in the same year in which the NEC was first mentioned, the European Commission (2006: 11) had also called for closer cooperation with 'the neighbours of our neighbours'. The ENP is based on geographic proximity to the EU. However, 'a functional approach to neighboring regions based on key EU interests such as trade, energy, migration, and counterterrorism' would require 'a considerably broader concept of neighborhood that includes all of the Middle East, the Horn of Africa, the Sahel, and Central Asia' (Lehne 2014: 6).

As Table 5.1 shows, the African neighbours of the southern ENP countries are, with a gross domestic product (GDP) per capita of not even 3 per cent of the EU's average, clearly the poorest region in the broader neighbourhood. Even if Israel was excluded, the average of the 'ENP south' would still reach around 17 per cent of the EU average in 2012 (and with Israel 25.23 per cent). The eastern ENP countries and the Central Asian republics are on a comparable level, with respectively 13.63 per cent and 13.83 per cent of the EU average. The Middle Eastern region, with 93.78 per cent (105 per cent without Yemen), comes closest to the EU GDP per capita. Even without the small Gulf monarchies – Kuwait, Qatar and the United Arab Emirates (UAE), whose GDP surpasses the EU average – the region would still attain 44.13 per cent.

Unlike in the case of the European Neighbourhood Policy, the EU pursues no overarching policy towards the neighbours of its neighbours as a group. While the 16 ENP partners are already quite a diverse group of countries, the neighbours of the EU's neighbours are even more heterogeneous, ranging from least developed countries (LDCs) to the rich Gulf monarchies. Those better off in the EU's broader neighbourhood primarily owe their wealth to their energy resources. With the neighbours of its neighbours the EU has less far-reaching trade agreements in place with much weaker alignment to EU rules and conditionality. Participation in a future NEC thus seems out of reach for the neighbours of the EU's neighbours, but increased linkages between the European Union, the ENP countries and their neighbours are possible and desirable.

This chapter will first address the emergence of the NEC from a trade perspective. It will then provide an overview of the EU's trade relations with its broader neighbourhood, including a comparison of the EU's trade shares and trade arrangements with the ENP countries and those with its neighbours' neighbours in Saharan Africa, the Middle East and Central Asia. Finally, some conclusions will be drawn with regard to the future of a broader NEC.

The emergence of a 'Neighbourhood Economic Community'

When the ENP was launched, the European Commission (2003: 10) proclaimed that 'all the neighbouring countries should be offered the prospect of a stake in the EU's Internal Market and further integration and liberalisation to promote the free movement of – persons, goods, services and capital (four freedoms)'.[3] The association of the EFTA countries with the EU's internal market – the EEA

Table 5.1 GDP per capita in the ENP countries and their neighbours, 2012

Country	In current US$	% of EU average	Country	In current US$	% of EU average
Armenia	3,354	10.19	Chad	1,035	3.14
Azerbaijan	7,394	22.46	Djibouti	1,575	4.78
Belarus	6,722	20.42	Eritrea	504	1.53
Georgia	3,529	10.72	Ethiopia	467	1.42
Moldova	2,047	6.22	Mali	696	2.11
Ukraine	3,873	11.77	Mauritania	1,043	3.17
ENP East average	**4,486**	**13.63**	Niger	395	1.20
			Somalia		—
Algeria	5,310	16.13	South Sudan	974	2.96
Egypt	3,256	9.89	Sudan	1,695	5.15
Israel	32,567	98.94	**Saharan Africa average**	**932**	**2.83**
Jordan	4,909	14.91			
Lebanon	9,764	29.66	Kazakhstan	12,120	36.82
Libya	13,303	40.41	Kyrgyzstan	1,178	3.58
Morocco	2,902	8.82	Tajikistan	953	2.90
Palestine	2,530	7.69	Turkmenistan	6,798	20.65
Syria (2010)	4,297	13.05	Uzbekistan	1,719	5.22
Tunisia	4,197	12.75	**Central Asia average**	**4,554**	**13.83**
ENP South average	**8,304**	**25.23**			
			Bahrain	23,040	69.99
ENP average	**6,872**	**19.43**	Iran	6,578	19.98
			Iraq	6,625	20.12
			Kuwait	56,367	171.24
			Oman	23,624	71.77
			Qatar	92,633	281.41
			Saudi Arabia	25,946	78.82
			United Arab Emirates	41,692	126.66
			Yemen	1,341	4.07
			Middle East average	**30,872**	**93.78**
European Union average	**32,917**		**ENP neighbours average**	**13,435**	**40.81**

Source: based on World Bank (2014).

– was referred to as a source of inspiration. Moreover, in a non-paper the European Commission (2007b: 4) presented some steps for the development of the long-term vision of a Neighbourhood Economic Community:

- the first phase would focus on the full implementation of the ENP Action Plans;
- in the medium term, the conclusion and implementation of deep and comprehensive free trade agreements would be aimed at;
- in addition, intra-regional integration between the ENP partners themselves should increase;
- and finally, in the long term, the EU member states and the ENP countries would establish the common NEC.

With the exception of Algeria, Belarus, Libya and Syria, all ENP countries have in the past years agreed Action Plans with the EU. Regarding the other proposed steps, trade relations have developed on unilateral, bilateral and regional levels.

Unilateral trade arrangements

The EU's neighbours (except for Israel and the occupied Palestinian territories)[4] benefited from its Generalized System of Preferences (GSP) until the end of 2013. Through the GSP the EU grants developing countries autonomous trade preferences. The 'standard GSP' offers tariff reductions for two-thirds of all EU tariff lines and duty-free access for the rest. The 2014 reform aimed at refocusing the GSP preferences on those countries that needed them most, while also increasing the EU's leverage in trade negotiations (Siles-Brügge 2014). The number of beneficiaries was reduced by half. Algeria, Egypt, Jordan, Lebanon, Morocco and Tunisia are no longer included in the 'standard GSP' because they have market access through bilateral trade agreements with the EU (see below), and Azerbaijan, Belarus and Libya because they have been classified as upper-middle income countries by the World Bank. Hence, in principle only the ENP countries Armenia, Georgia, Moldova, Syria and Ukraine continued to be beneficiaries of the 'standard GSP', as long as no other trade arrangement is in force (European Commission 2014b). Together with Azerbaijan, these countries are also eligible to apply for the second scheme of the GSP, the 'special incentive arrangement for sustainable development and good governance' (GSP+). This offers an additional elimination of tariffs to 'vulnerable' (that is, poorly diversified) economies ready to accept more political conditionality in the form of the effective implementation of 27 international conventions of the United Nations (UN) and of the International Labour Organization, in comparison to 15 core international conventions for the rest of the GSP. In 2014, the GSP+ scheme applied to 13 beneficiaries (out of 34 defined as eligible countries), among which were Armenia and Georgia. Moldova was in 2008 granted special autonomous trade preferences (ATP) as part of the EU–Moldova ENP Action Plan and was thus removed from the GSP list of beneficiaries. These ATP stipulations apply until the end of 2015 and are then to be replaced by the reciprocal preferences of the Deep and Comprehensive Free Trade Area (DCFTA) of 2014 (see below). In a similar way, Ukraine enjoys ATP until the new DCFTA comes into force in 2016.

Bilateral trade agreements

Seven out of the 16 ENP countries were as of 2014 not yet members of the World Trade Organization, but except for Palestine all of them were observer governments and thus in the process of accession to the WTO. The EU considers WTO membership, which guarantees most-favoured-nation treatment, a pre-condition for the conclusion of a free trade agreement (FTA).

With the North African ENP countries (except for Libya and Syria), the EU has since the mid-1990s concluded Euro-Mediterranean Association Agreements (EMAAs) which aim at free trade in industrial goods. The pan-European cumulation system has been extended to the Southern Mediterranean countries, allowing for diagonally cumulative processing in the region in order to obtain preferential treatment.[5] The EU's supplementary bilateral negotiations with these countries have reached different stages with regard to the liberalization of trade in services and the right of establishment, the further liberalization of agricultural, processed agricultural and fisheries products, a more efficient dispute settlement mechanism for the trade provisions of the EMAAs, and Agreements on Conformity Assessment and Acceptance of Industrial Products. Finally, the EU is also embarking upon the negotiation of Deep and Comprehensive Free Trade Areas with Morocco, Tunisia, Egypt and Jordan. The DCFTAs will go beyond the scope of the EMAAs and cover areas such as trade in services, intellectual property rights, public procurement and investment protection, as well as regulatory approximation with the trade-related EU *acquis*.

Even though the eastern ENP countries had in the 1990s only signed Partnership and Cooperation Agreements (PCAs), they have in recent years compared to the southern partners taken the lead in the negotiation of more far-reaching trade agreements. In June 2014 the Association Agreements, including DCFTAs, with Ukraine, Moldova and Georgia were signed, and the DCFTAs with Moldova and Georgia have provisionally been applied since September 2014. In response to the conflict in eastern Ukraine, the provisional application of the Ukrainian DCFTA has, in consultation with Russia, been postponed to January 2016. Azerbaijan is not yet a member of the WTO, and it appears more interested in concluding an enhanced PCA than an Association Agreement with the EU. Finally, not even a PCA is in place with Belarus as due to the domestic political situation the EU had not ratified the agreement concluded in 1995.

The Association Agreements with Ukraine, Moldova and Georgia contain several legislative approximation mechanisms with varying degrees of obligation and different procedures to amend the incorporated rules. In particular, the countries commit to transpose the relevant *acquis* regarding technical barriers to trade and certain services. Also the dispute settlement varies across sectors from consultation, arbitration or mediation to rulings by the Court of Justice of the EU (Van der Loo, Van Elsuwege and Petrov 2014: 14–22). The Association Council monitors the application of the agreement and serves as a forum to discuss new relevant legislation. The DCFTAs are based on far-reaching market access conditionality, which links additional internal market access to the country's progress in implementation. They entail 'a move from the soft law approach based on persuasion and assistance to a comprehensive, binding and detailed legal framework structuring relations between the EU and its Eastern neighbours' (Delcour and Wolczuk 2013: 190).

Regional trade cooperation

The EU promotes intra-regional integration and encourages its neighbouring countries to conclude FTAs among themselves. Some Southern Mediterranean countries are part of intra-regional cooperation schemes such as the Arab Maghreb Union (AMU) created in 1989 (Algeria, Libya, Mauritania, Morocco and Tunisia) or the 1997 Greater Arab Free Trade Area (GAFTA).[6] Moreover, the Agadir Agreement, which entered into force in 2006, has been overseen and financially supported by the EU since its inception.[7] The founding members were Egypt, Jordan, Morocco and Tunisia, but any Arab country that is a member of the Arab League and the GAFTA and linked to the EU through an association agreement can adhere to it. The EU is also seeking closer relations with the AMU. In a Joint Communication the European Commission and High Representative (2012: 3) emphasized the EU's support for sub-regional integration in the Maghreb, 'one of the least integrated regions in the world', and Mauritania's particular 'position at the crossroads between the Arab Maghreb and Sub-Saharan Africa' (see below). A network of DCFTAs between the EU and the Southern Mediterranean countries, 'and also among the Maghreb partners themselves, would contribute to the realisation of the vision of an economic community emerging between the EU and its ENP partners' (ibid.: 10).

In 2000 Russia, Belarus, Kazakhstan, Kyrgyzstan and Tajikistan established the Eurasian Economic Community, while Ukraine and Moldova preferred observer status. Ten years later – *inter alia* in response to the Eastern Partnership initiative that the EU launched in 2009 for the eastern ENP countries – Russia, Belarus and Kazakhstan set up the Eurasian customs union, and the Russian government attempted in particular to attract Ukraine (Delcour and Wolczuk 2013: 191–197). For quite some time Ukraine tried to play the EU and Russia against each other with its 'multivector' foreign policy. In the run-up to the Eastern Partnership Summit in Vilnius in November 2013, the Armenian government announced under Russian pressure its intention of joining the Eurasian customs union instead of signing the Association Agreement and DCFTA that it had negotiated with the EU. The decision of the Ukrainian government to suspend the signature of its agreements with the EU at the Vilnius Summit led to mass protests and a change of government in Kiev. After the Russian Federation had illegally annexed Ukraine's Crimean peninsula in March 2014, the EU and Ukraine signed the political provisions of the Association Agreement and in June 2014 the remaining parts.

Moldova and the Western Balkan states in 2006 formed the Central European Free Trade Agreement (CEFTA) (Dangerfield 2006). The EU has also encouraged trade liberalization in the Black Sea region: its Black Sea Synergy Initiative aims at cooperation with the organization Black Sea Economic Cooperation (BSEC), which comprises Albania, Armenia, Azerbaijan, Bulgaria, Georgia, Greece, Moldova, Romania, Russia, Serbia, Turkey and Ukraine. However, Hajizada and Marciacq (2013) show that cross-regional trade with the EU has become more important than intra-regional trade among BSEC members. Triantaphyllou (2014: 294) argues that

> [t]he tugs of war between Russia and the EU and to a lesser extent between the EU and Turkey are at the core of the challenge of transforming the Black Sea region from being a 'grey zone of instability' to one of peace, freedom, security and prosperity.

As argued by Cottey (2012), the EU's initiatives to promote multilateral regional cooperation in its neighbourhood have for several reasons been rather disappointing: the contested nature of the regions and confusion over the goals of regional cooperation, the gap between the ends sought by the EU and the means available to it, the existence of enduring conflicts in these regions, and, finally, the 'hub-and-spoke' pattern of the relationship between the EU and its partners which militates against regional cooperation.

The following section examines to what extent EU trade with the broader neighbourhood has developed at the unilateral, bilateral and regional levels.

The EU's trade relations with its broader neighbourhood

Taking a geopolitical rather than a strict geographical approach,[8] the 'neighbours of the EU's neighbours' are, on the African continent, the countries of the Sahel strip and the Horn of Africa. Not directly bordering any ENP countries are thereby Djibouti, Eritrea, Ethiopia, Somalia and South Sudan, which gained its independence from Sudan in July 2011. The Horn of Africa is included due to the significant cross-border political and security impact it has on the neighbouring countries in the Southern Mediterranean, the Sahel and the Gulf. In Central Asia, all five republics are taken into account although the Kyrgyz Republic, Tajikistan and Uzbekistan are not direct neighbours of any ENP countries. This approach corresponds to the Central Asia Strategy adopted by the Council of the European Union (2007a) which covers Kazakhstan, Kyrgyz Republic, Tajikistan, Turkmenistan and Uzbekistan. Finally, in the Middle East, the countries of the Arabian Peninsula – the members of the Gulf Cooperation Council (GCC) and Yemen – plus Iraq and Iran are considered, although Bahrain, Kuwait, Oman, Qatar, the UAE and Yemen are not direct neighbours of ENP countries either.

By contrast, excluded from the analysis are Russia and Turkey, which are both immediate neighbours of the European Union and neighbours to ENP countries. Turkey is a candidate country for EU membership, part of the EU customs union, and since 1995 a member of the Euro-Mediterranean Partnership, which has in 2008 evolved into the Union for the Mediterranean (UfM). Russia is a strategic partner of the EU – and with regard to the Eastern Partnership increasingly also a competitor.

For the European Union the share of trade in goods with the ENP countries (Table 5.2) and with their neighbours (Table 5.3) was in 2012 for both regions around 6–8 per cent. Not surprisingly, the Middle East is the EU's biggest trading partner among the neighbours of its neighbours. By contrast, the importance of the EU's internal market for these countries varies considerably. With close to 36 per cent the EU is a very important export market for the ENP countries, both in the east and in the south, whereas the trade shares of the neighbours of the EU's neighbours are considerably lower with an average of only 10 per cent. Quite a number of ENP countries (such as Azerbaijan, Algeria, Libya) and of their neighbours (Saudi Arabia, Kazakhstan, Iran, Iraq and to a lesser extent the other Gulf countries) are important sources of energy for the EU.[9]

Unilateral trade arrangements

The neighbours of the EU's neighbours have in the past benefited from the EU's unilateral Generalized System of Preferences. The 2014 GSP reform has excluded high and upper-middle income countries (Bahrain, Kuwait, Oman, Qatar, Saudi Arabia, the UAE, Iran and Kazakhstan), thus leaving only Iraq, Kyrgyzstan, Tajikistan, Turkmenistan and Uzbekistan in the 'standard GSP'. Together with Iran, these countries would qualify to apply for the 'GSP+' but they have as of 2014 not done so. In addition, 11 least developed countries (LDCs), as defined by the United Nations, benefit from the 'Everything-But-Arms initiative' (EBA), the GSP's third and most far-reaching scheme (European Commission 2014b). It grants duty-free and quota-free market access to the EU's market for all products from LDCs except for arms and ammunition. With the exception of Yemen, the LDCs in the EU's broader neighbourhood are all situated in Saharan Africa (Chad, Djibouti, Eritrea, Ethiopia, Mali, Mauritania, Niger, South Sudan, Sudan and Somalia).

Bilateral trade agreements

All neighbours of the EU's neighbours have in various forms concluded or envisaged trade and cooperation agreements with the EU. Ten out of 24 countries from this group are not yet members of the WTO, but among the non-members only Eritrea, Somalia, Turkmenistan and South Sudan are not yet in the process of accession.

The neighbours of the southern ENP countries belong to the African, Caribbean and Pacific (ACP) group and are contracting parties to the Cotonou

Table 5.2 EU and ENP countries' shares of trade in goods, 2012

	ENP countries' trade with the EU		EU trade with the ENP countries	
	EU share of total exports in %	EU share of total imports in %	Share of total EU exports in %	Share of total EU imports in %
Armenia	39.4	26.5	0.0	0.0
Azerbaijan*	48.3	27.7	0.2	0.8
Belarus*	38.1	20.1	0.5	0.3
Georgia	14.9	31.0	0.1	0.0
Moldova	51.2	43.6	0.1	0.1
Ukraine	24.9	31.0	1.4	0.8
ENP East	**average 36.13**	**average 29.98**	**total sum 2.3**	**total sum 2.0**
Algeria*	55.3	52.4	1.3	1.8
Egypt	26.8	29.8	0.9	0.5
Israel	27.2	34.4	1.0	0.7
Jordan	4.5	17.6	0.2	0.0
Lebanon*	9.9	39.2	0.4	0.0
Libya*	68.3	34.5	0.5	1.8
Morocco	55.7	47.5	1.0	0.5
Palestine*	—	—	0.0	0.0
Syria*	2.9	8.7	0.1	0.0
Tunisia	68.2	59.5	0.6	0.5
ENP South	**average 35.42**	**average 35.96**	**total sum 6.1**	**total sum 5.8**
Total	**average 35.71**	**average 33.57**	**total sum 8.4**	**total sum 7.8**

Sources: based on European Commission (2014c); EUROSTAT (2014).

Note
* Not yet a member of the WTO but observer status as of 2014 (except for Palestine).

Table 5.3 EU and ENP countries' neighbours' shares of trade in goods, 2012

	ENP neighbours' trade with the EU		EU trade with ENP neighbours	
	EU share of total exports in %	*EU share of total imports in %*	*Share of total EU exports in %*	*Share of total EU imports in %*
Chad	0.7	32.9	0.0	0.0
Djibouti	2.6	6.0	0.0	0.0
Eritrea*		—	0.0	0.0
Ethiopia*	32.3	12.1	0.1	0.0
Mali	6.5	25.5	0.0	0.0
Mauritania	26.0	41.6	0.1	0.0
Niger	10.2	26.7	0.0	0.0
Somalia*	0.3	2.1	0.0	0.0
Sudan (including South Sudan)*	2.8	11.9	0.1	0.0
Saharan Africa	**average 10.18**	**average 19.85**	**total sum 0.3**	**total sum 0.0**
Kazakhstan*	54.4	28.0	0.4	1.4
Kyrgyzstan	3.1	5.6	0.0	0.0
Tajikistan	8.3	4.7	0.0	0.0
Turkmenistan*	7.5	18.3	0.1	0.0
Uzbekistan*	3.0	14.1	0.1	0.0
Central Asia	**average 15.26**	**average 14.14**	**total sum 0.6**	**total sum 1.4**
Bahrain	3.7	17.2	0.1	0.1
Iran*	6.5	11.0	0.4	0.3
Iraq*	17.5	13.0	0.3	0.7
Kuwait	5.4	21.1	0.3	0.3
Oman	1.3	14.5	0.2	0.0
Qatar	9.8	26.9	0.4	0.6
Saudi Arabia	10.8	24.3	1.8	1.9
UAE	3.3	20.1	2.2	0.5
Yemen	1.5	9.7	0.1	0.0
Middle East	**average 6.64**	**average 17.53**	**total sum 5.8**	**total sum 4.5**
Total	**average 9.89**	**average 17.60**	**total sum 6.7**	**total sum 5.9**

Sources: based on European Commission (2014c); EUROSTAT (2014).
Note
* Not yet a member of the WTO but observer status as of 2014 (except for Eritrea, Somalia, South Sudan, Turkmenistan).

Agreement. The EU has since 2002 been negotiating Economic Partnership Agreements (EPAs) with them. The EPAs aim at progressively establishing WTO-compatible free trade areas by replacing the non-reciprocal trade preferences of the Cotonou Agreement (Heron 2014; Pape 2013: 733–736). In principle, an EPA covers duty-free and quota-free market access for goods, trade in services, investment and trade-related regulatory issues such as public procurement, competition or intellectual property rights. With the exception of the comprehensive EU-CARIFORUM EPA, all other EPAs so far cover only trade in goods and development cooperation; the remaining issues fall under a 'rendez-vous clause' providing for further negotiations.

Among the neighbours of the EU's neighbours, Djibouti, Ethiopia, Eritrea, Somalia and Sudan are members of the group of Eastern and Southern African states;[10] Mali, Mauritania and Niger are part of the West African group, and Chad participates in the Central African group. Although the EU has reached (interim) EPAs with some African states in these three groups, the neighbours of the ENP countries are not among them, with the exception of the West African countries. One reason certainly is the fact that, as least developed countries, many African ACP countries already benefit from duty-free and quota-free market access under the EBA initiative and have thus weaker incentives to sign up to a reciprocal and more far-reaching EPA. The West African region is the EU's most important ACP trade partner, and the EPA initialled in June 2014 comprises all members of the Economic Community of West African States (ECOWAS) plus Mauritania.

In order to prevent trade disruption when the WTO waiver for the Cotonou Agreement's non-reciprocal preferences expired in January 2008, the EU had adopted a Market Access Regulation to provisionally apply EPA preferences to countries that had concluded a deal by the end of 2007, but were yet to sign, ratify and implement it (Pape 2013: 735). The Market Access Regulation was set to expire on 1 October 2014. As a consequence, any ACP country that had not taken the necessary steps would fall under the less favourable trade regime of the GSP (respectively under the EBA for the LDCs).

The 'east of Jordan' countries – the GCC members, Yemen, Iran and Iraq – maintain more diverse relations with the EU. With the Gulf Cooperation Council and its members Bahrain, Kuwait, Oman, Qatar, Saudi Arabia and the United Arab Emirates, the EU has forged a region-to-region relationship. The 1988 Cooperation Agreement committed them to enter negotiations on a free trade agreement. These negotiations were initiated in 1990, covering, *inter alia*, market access for goods, services, public procurement, intellectual property rights, competition, dispute settlement, human rights, illegal immigration and terrorism. However, they soon reached a standstill over disagreement on liberalizing trade in petrochemicals, services and government procurement as well as human rights and illegal migration clauses (Ayadi and Gadi 2014: 82). Negotiations were resumed in 2002, and one year later the GCC set up a customs union. A few years later the GCC again suspended the negotiations, but informal consultations between the parties continue. The EU–GCC FTA would be the first region-to-region FTA between two customs unions. It remains to be seen whether the exclusion of the GCC countries from the EU's GSP in 2014 provides an incentive for them to advance the negotiations, particularly in view of China's increasing importance as a trade partner for the Gulf.

EU trade with the GCC accounted in 2013 for 3.4 per cent of EU imports and 5.5 per cent of EU exports, while the EU provided 26.1 per cent of GCC imports and absorbed 7.3 per cent of GCC exports, of which three-quarters consisted of – already duty-free – fuels (European Commission 2014a). The GCC is the EU's fifth largest export market, while the EU is the first trading partner for the Gulf. Antkiewicz and Momani (2009) argue that the EU's motives for inter-regional negotiations with the GCC are explained by geopolitical rather than economic interests and by the desire to export its regional model. In comparison to the ENP, neither conditionality policy nor regulatory approximation have played a big role in the Gulf region, which is often seen as impenetrable for 'European' norms and values (Colombo and Committeri 2014: 24).[11] The EU also favours an accession of Yemen to the GCC (ibid.: 229). As a poor and unstable country, Yemen faces many accession difficulties because its political and economic structures are not well prepared and because the GCC members fear massive labour migration and have so far failed to provide clear political guidance (Burke 2012). The EU and Yemen signed a bilateral Cooperation Agreement in 1998, and as an LDC Yemen also benefits from the EBA initiative.

With Iraq the EU signed a Partnership and Cooperation Agreement in May 2012. The PCA is a non-preferential trade agreement that incorporates basic WTO rules, since Iraq is not yet a member of the WTO. The agreement includes trade in goods and services, intellectual property rights, technical barriers to trade, sanitary and phytosanitary issues and a dispute settlement mechanism. By contrast, negotiations for a Trade and Cooperation Agreement between the EU and Iran have been put on hold since 2005, when Iran started to intensify its nuclear activities.

The EU's trade relations with Kazakhstan, Kyrgyzstan, Tajikistan and Uzbekistan are also governed by bilateral Partnership and Cooperation Agreements that were signed in the late 1990s (in 2010 in the case of Tajikistan). The PCA concluded with Turkmenistan in 1998 has for political reasons still not been ratified, but in 2009 the EU adopted an Interim Trade Agreement with the country. Only the Kyrgyz Republic and Tajikistan are currently members of the WTO. In September 2014 the EU concluded negotiations with Kazakhstan on an enhanced PCA which provides for a reinforced political dialogue, trade and investment, cooperation in justice, freedom and security, and cooperation in fields such as foreign and security policy, energy, transport and development.

Central Asia represents a limited market for the EU, and the bilateral relationship remains dominated by the hydrocarbon sector. Central Asian energy resources, also coveted by China and India, offer the EU the opportunity to diversify its energy providers and thus circumvent Russia. Besides the lure of oil and gas resources, post-9/11 security concerns reaching across Central Asia into

Afghanistan and a certain path dependency (all former Soviet Union states were offered PCAs) may help explain the EU's Central Asia Strategy. As in the case of the Gulf, the EU's human rights and democracy policy in Central Asia has largely been dominated by the *realpolitik* of security, political stability and energy security (Crawford 2008). Anceschi (2014: 2) argues that 'the tension between values and interests translated into EU reluctance to attach conditionality to the offers of cooperation made to the Central Asian political elites'.[12]

Regional trade cooperation

The negotiation of tailor-made Economic Partnership Agreements with regional ACP groupings was intended to support regional integration in order to facilitate integration into the world economy, boost regional trade and attract foreign investments. In Africa, the EU's attempt at concluding region-to-region EPAs risks to some extent undermining sub-regional integration due to differences in memberships. The way in which African countries have organized themselves for the negotiations is inconsistent with some integration schemes, and even within the EPA groups states have chosen different trade schemes. Theoretically at least, if all North and Saharan African countries concluded DCFTAs or EPAs with the EU, this could in long run lead to free trade with all of them.

It is also worth mentioning that with the Abuja Treaty (1991: art. 6(5)), the African Union aims at creating an African Economic Community by 2034. The various regional blocs in Africa, also known as Regional Economic Communities, should form the 'pillars' of the African Economic Community. As part of the Joint Africa–EU Strategy of 2007, the EU supports this pan-African integration process with the Africa–EU Partnership on Trade, Regional Integration and Infrastructure (Council of the European Union 2007b: 10–12). The cooperation *inter alia* includes private sector development, improvement of infrastructure, regulatory convergence, and aid for trade.

The EU Strategic Partnership with the Mediterranean and the Middle East (SPMME) launched in 2004 embraces the countries of North Africa, the GCC, Yemen, Iraq and Iran (European Council 2004). This was a first step in the direction of greater coherence for the EU's policy towards the region of the Middle East and North Africa (MENA). Although the Strategic Partnership still distinguishes between the countries of the Euro-Mediterranean Partnership and those 'east of Jordan', it considered the progressive future establishment of regional free trade agreements, such as the linking of the (future) Euro-Mediterranean and EU–GCC FTAs. However, the EU's intention to develop a policy towards the 'east of Jordan', coherent with its Mediterranean policy, has not prospered, and the SPMME was soon forgotten. In a similar vein, the expectations of the European Commission (2007a: 3) to create a close link between the Black Sea approach and the EU Strategy for Central Asia, including 'substantial inter-regional elements', have not been fulfilled (Duhot 2012).

In 2011, Russia proposed to develop its customs union with Belarus and Kazakhstan into a Eurasian (Economic) Union that could extend to the post-Soviet space. Hence, Russia is *de facto* compelling countries in the common neighbourhood to choose between this project and a DCFTA with the EU, unless the EU were instead to conclude an FTA with the entire Eurasian customs union (Delcour and Kostanyan 2014: 5). Russia's annexation of Crimea and its role in the conflict in eastern Ukraine in 2014 have prompted the EU to halt many joint activities with this strategic partner, including the negotiations on a new agreement replacing the PCA, launched in 2008, and to adopt sanctions. As a result of Russia's policy, 'in some cases dividing lines pass through partner countries such as Georgia (with South Ossetia and Abkhazia), Moldova (with Transnistria) and Ukraine (with Crimea)', and in the future 'new lines may appear, such as through Gagauzia and eastern/southern Ukraine' (ibid.: 10). However, the economic benefits of the Eurasian Economic Union launched in 2015 are questionable given the high tariff levels that will make imports from the EU and China more expensive and will call into question the commitments of the WTO members Armenia and Kyrgyzstan, while complicating Kazakhstan's negotiations on WTO accession. Russia therefore offers a range of subsidies to its (potential) partners in the form of cheaper gas or loans and access to its labour market (Popescu 2014: 11–14).

On the whole, on all levels – unilateral, bilateral and regional – the EU's trade relations with the neighbours of its neighbours provide a very mixed and fragmented picture.

Conclusion: a broader 'Neighbourhood Economic Community'?

This chapter has compared the European Union's trade relations with its immediate and broader neighbourhood to the east and south. Whereas the EU has over the past decade developed the European Neighbourhood Policy, no comparable 'umbrella approach' or strategy is available beyond the ENP countries. While in Africa an EU approach of multilateralism (Cotonou Agreement) and (emerging) inter-regionalism (EPAs) prevails, cooperation in the Middle East is characterized by inter-regionalism and bilateralism and in Central Asia solely by bilateralism (Gstöhl 2014). Hence the relationships between the EU and the neighbours of its neighbours appear to be looser from west to east.

Table 5.4 summarizes the current trade relations, which range from unilateral trade preferences to bilateral and inter-regional trade and cooperation agreements. Generally they tend, over time, to shift from PCAs to FTAs (in case of WTO membership), except for LDCs which may prefer continue relying on the EBA initiative. DCFTAs may be embedded in bi- or multilateral association agreements (EMAAs, Cotonou Agreement). In addition, the EU supports subregional integration, which may also link ENP countries and their neighbours.

With the European Neighbourhood Policy the EU has primarily created a 'hub-and-spoke bilateralism' in trade with its immediate neighbours (Gstöhl 2012: 100). While the connections 'between the spokes' still need to be reinforced, the EU's

Table 5.4 EU trade relations with the ENP countries and their neighbours, 2014

Country	EU trade relations with immediate neighbourhood	Country	EU trade relations with broader neighbourhood
ENP East		**Saharan Africa**	
Armenia	GSP+; PCA (Association Agreement with DCFTA not signed)	Chad	EBA
		Djibouti	EBA
Azerbaijan*	GSP (eligible for GSP+); PCA to be replaced by enhanced PCA (Association Agreement with DCFTA)	Eritrea*	EBA
		Ethiopia*	EBA
		Mali	EBA (EPA West Africa)
Belarus*	No trade agreement (conditionality); suspended from GSP (conditionality) and excluded as of 2014	Mauritania	EBA (EPA West Africa)
		Somalia*	EBA
Georgia	GSP+; PCA to be replaced by Association Agreement with DCFTA	Sudan	EBA
		South Sudan*	Not yet in EBA nor in Cotonou Agreement
Moldova	ATP; PCA to be replaced by Association Agreement with DCFTA	**Central Asia**	
Ukraine	ATP; PCA to be replaced by Association Agreement with DCFTA	Kazakhstan*	PCA, to be replaced by an enhanced PCA; GSP until 2014
ENP South		Kyrgyzstan	GSP (eligible for GSP+); PCA
Algeria*	EMAA; GSP until 2014	Tajikistan	GSP (eligible for GSP+); PCA
Egypt	EMAA to be complemented by DCFTA; GSP until 2014	Turkmenistan*	GSP until 2016 (eligible for GSP+); PCA pending (conditionality); interim trade agreement
Jordan	EMAA to be complemented by DCFTA; GSP until 2014	Uzbekistan*	GSP (eligible for GSP+); PCA
Israel	EMAA	**Middle East**	
Lebanon*	EMAA; GSP until 2014	Bahrain	EU–GCC Cooperation Agreement (FTA pending); GSP until 2014
Libya*	No trade agreement (conditionality, negotiations pending); GSP until 2014	Iran*	GSP until 2014 (eligible for GSP+); Cooperation Agreement pending (conditionality)
Morocco	EMAA to be complemented by DCFTA; GSP until 2014	Iraq*	GSP (eligible for GSP+); PCA
		Kuwait	EU–GCC Cooperation Agreement (FTA pending); GSP until 2014
Palestine*	Not in GSP; interim trade agreement (to be complemented by Association Agreement)	Oman	EU–GCC Cooperation Agreement (FTA pending); GSP until 2014

Syria*	GSP (eligible for GSP+); signature of 2008 Association Agreement suspended (conditionality); 1977 Cooperation Agreement
Tunisia	EMAA to be complemented by DCFTA; GSP until 2014
Qatar	EU–GCC Cooperation Agreement (FTA pending); GSP until 2014
Saudi Arabia	EU–GCC Cooperation Agreement (FTA pending); GSP until 2014
United Arab Emirates	EU–GCC Cooperation Agreement (FTA pending); GSP until 2014
Yemen	EBA; Cooperation Agreement

Source: author's compilation.

Note

* Not yet a member of the WTO (as of 2014).

trade pattern with the neighbours of its neighbours is more diverse. The latter's trade volumes are, except for energy imports, not very significant. These relationships are, however, often at the intersection of other important policy areas and EU interests such as the trade–development or trade–security nexus. The economic heterogeneity among the neighbours of the EU's neighbours, ranging from many extremely poor to a few extremely rich countries, is bigger than among the already diverse ENP countries. This is reflected not only in the lack of an overarching policy towards the neighbours of its neighbours but also in less far-reaching trade arrangements with the EU and much weaker alignment to EU rules and conditionality policy.

Since the end of the Cold War the European Union has introduced, and strengthened step by step, political conditionality in its trade policy (Gstöhl 2010). This policy is – despite all its weaknesses in practice – much more systematic and stronger in the ENP than with regard to the neighbours of the EU's neighbours. The ENP typically combines positive political conditionality (promising rewards for future desired action) with negative conditionality (withholding benefits in case of non-compliance) in a 'carrot and stick' policy. The revised ENP of 2011 was to reinforce the 'more for more' approach although in practice the EU's preference for positive over negative measures still persists. *Ex ante* conditionality has in the past been applied to the countries which had for political reasons no new bilateral agreements in force yet, such as Belarus (democratic reforms), Libya (lifting of UN and EU sanctions), Syria (cooperation with regard to regional stability), Iran (nuclear issue) and Turkmenistan (human rights). A typical case of *ex post* conditionality is the application of a human rights clause. The EU has more or less consistently introduced such clauses in trade agreements, in the GSP and in financial instruments. Yet so far, the EU has – based on human rights clauses in agreements suspended only financial aid, especially with regard to ACP countries in response to military *coups* or other violations of democratic processes, but not trade benefits. In 2007 Belarus had its unilateral GSP trade preferences withdrawn due to non-compliance with its International Labour Organization obligations relating to the freedom of association for workers. However, this sanction has now lost relevance as Belarus – classified as an upper middle-income country – would in 2014 anyway have been excluded from the standard GSP. There have been calls for an investigation into a temporary withdrawal of GSP preferences from Uzbekistan due to forced child labour in the cotton production, and the European Parliament (2011) for this reason withheld its consent to extending the PCA with Uzbekistan to cover bilateral trade in textiles.

An inclusion of the neighbours of the EU's neighbours in the ENP does not appear to be a realistic future option.[13] Could the Neighbourhood Economic Community in the long run be widened to the EU's broader neighbourhood? The concept of economic community has been used for various regions and purposes: from the European Economic Community, the African Economic Community and the Eurasian Economic Community to the Neighbourhood Economic Community. If an economic community is understood as a WTO-compatible form of regional integration somewhere between a free trade area and an internal market, and equipped with a certain degree of collective decision-making capacity, developing an NEC already constitutes a big challenge for the ENP countries, let alone for the neighbours of the EU's neighbours. Nevertheless, the systematic development of linkages between the European Union, the ENP countries and the neighbours of the EU's neighbours is feasible and desirable.

The different EU initiatives should generally reinforce pan-regional dynamics instead of cross-cutting them and should open the possibility to build bridges across policy frameworks. When the European Council of March 2009 (annex 2) adopted the Eastern Partnership, for instance, it underlined the 'effective complementarity between the Eastern Partnership and existing regional initiatives in the EU's neighbourhood, in particular the Black Sea Synergy' and the fact that third countries would be eligible for participation on a case-by-case basis in concrete activities. The SPMME of 2004, which included the countries of North Africa, the GCC, Yemen, Iraq and Iran, had envisaged the possibility to couple the future Euro-Mediterranean and EU–GCC FTAs. The Cooperation Agreement with Yemen explicitly foresees that economic and other cooperation may extend to activities under EU agreements with other countries of the same region. Some cross-regional programmes and networks already permit the connecting of the EU with its immediate and more distant neighbours and are funded by more than one EU financial instrument.[14] INOGATE (Interstate Oil and Gas Transport to Europe), for instance, supports the development of energy cooperation between the European Union, the littoral states of the Black and Caspian Seas and their neighbouring countries,[15] while the TRACECA programme (Transport Corridor Europe–Caucasus–Asia) develops international transport between Europe and Asia across the Black Sea, the South Caucasus, the Caspian Sea and Central Asia.[16] Hence, with a functional approach to the extended neighbourhood which allows for 'variable geometry', the EU could engage subsets of its partners in function of both sides' interests. This approach could be embedded in an overarching strategy for the neighbours of the EU's neighbours that draws as well on the already existing regional strategies for parts of the broader neighbourhood (Gstöhl 2014).

Notes

1 Economics and international economic law distinguish a free trade area abolishing tariffs and quotas; a customs union involving, in addition, common external tariffs *vis-à-vis* non-members; and a common market which also removes restrictions on factor movements (Balassa 1961: 2).
2 Smith and Weber (2007: 12) argue that an economic community 'entails a deliberate banding together of actors to create a centralised political structure with genuine decision-making power'.
3 Art. 26:2 TFEU defines the internal market as 'an area without internal frontiers in which the free movement of goods, persons, services and capital is ensured'.
4 As a result of the 1994 Oslo Accords, Israel and the Palestinian Authority act under a customs union managed by Israel, which – as a high-income country – is not eligible for the GSP. Palestinian exports have basically duty-free access to the EU market based on the Interim Association Agreement on Trade and Cooperation of 1997 and

the additional agreement of 2011 for the liberalization of agricultural and fishery products. Palestinian products might also be exported into the EU under Israeli certificates of origin.

5 Diagonal cumulation means that materials from anywhere in the region that qualify as originating can be used to manufacture a product without losing duty-free access. The pan-Euro-Mediterranean system of cumulation of origin also includes Turkey, the Western Balkans and the EFTA countries.

6 GAFTA members include Algeria, Bahrain, Egypt, Iraq, Jordan, Kuwait, Lebanon, Libya, Morocco, Oman, Qatar, Palestine, Saudi Arabia, Sudan, Syria, Tunisia, the UAE and Yemen. See Romagnoli and Mengoni (2009).

7 See Chapter 9 by Maud Fichet, Enrique Ibáñez and Veronika Orbetsova in this volume.

8 See the Introduction to this volume.

9 See also Chapter 11 by Johannes Theiss in this volume.

10 South Sudan is in the process of joining first the ACP group and then the Cotonou Agreement.

11 See Chapter 8 by Alexander Warkotsch and Richard Youngs in this volume.

12 See also Chapter 8 by Warkotsch and Youngs in this volume.

13 At least for Kazakhstan, the ENP had at some point been considered (Anceschi 2014: 8).

14 See Chapter 10 by Alessandro Carano in this volume.

15 INOGATE covers the European Union, Armenia, Azerbaijan, Belarus, Georgia, Kazakhstan, Kyrgyzstan, Moldova, Tajikistan, Turkmenistan, Ukraine and Uzbekistan. See www.inogate.org.

16 Full parties of TRACECA are Armenia, Azerbaijan, Bulgaria, Georgia, Iran, Kazakhstan, Kyrgyzstan, Moldova, Romania, Tajikistan, Turkey, Ukraine and Uzbekistan. See www.traceca-org.org.

References

Abuja Treaty (1991) Treaty Establishing the African Economic Community, Abuja, 3 June, www.africa-union.org/root/au/Documents/Treaties/Text/AEC_Treaty_1991.pdf (accessed October 2014).

Adler, E. (2008) 'The Spread of Security Communities: Communities of Practice, Self-restraint, and NATO's Post-Cold War Transformation', *European Journal of International Relations* 14(2), 195–230.

Anceschi, L. (2014) 'The Tyranny of Pragmatism: EU–Kazakhstani Relations', *Europe–Asia Studies* 66(1), 1–24.

Antkiewicz, A. and B. Momani (2009) 'Pursuing Geopolitical Stability through Inter-regional Trade: The EU's Motives for Negotiating with the Gulf Cooperation Council', *Journal of European Integration* 31(2), 217–235.

Ayadi, R. and S. Gadi (2014) 'EU–GCC Trade and Investment Relations: What Prospect of an FTA between the Two Regions?', in S. Colombo (ed.) *Bridging the Gulf: EU–GCC Relations at a Crossroads*, Rome: Istituto Affari Internazionali, 47–88.

Balassa, Bela (1961) *The Theory of Economic Integration*, Homewood, IL: Richard D. Irwin.

Burke, E. (2012) ' "One Blood and One Destiny"? Yemen's Relations with the Gulf Cooperation Council', *Research Paper, Kuwait Programme on Development, Governance and Globalisation in the Gulf States* 23, London: LSE.

Colombo, S. and C. Committeri (2014) 'Need to Rethink the EU–GCC Strategic Relation', in S. Colombo (ed.) *Bridging the Gulf: EU–GCC Relations at a Crossroads*, Rome: Istituto Affari Internazionali, 19–45.

Cottey, A. (2012) 'Regionalism and the EU's Neighbourhood Policy: The Limits of the Possible', *Journal of Southeast European and Black Sea Studies* 12(3), 375–391.

Council of the European Union (2007a) *The European Union and Central Asia: Strategy for a New Partnership*, Brussels, 21–22 June.

Council of the European Union (2007b) 'The Africa–EU Strategic Partnership, A Joint Africa–EU Strategy', Lisbon, 9 December, 16344/07 (Presse 291), www.consilium.europa.eu/uedocs/cms_data/docs/pressdata/en/er/97496.pdf (accessed October 2014).

Crawford, G. (2008) 'EU Human Rights and Democracy Promotion in Central Asia: From Lofty Principles to Lowly Self-interests', *Perspectives on European Politics and Society* 9(2), 172–191.

Dangerfield, M. (2006) 'Subregional Integration and EU Enlargement: Where Next for CEFTA?', *Journal of Common Market Studies* 44 (2), 305–324.

Delcour, L. and H. Kostanyan (2014) 'Towards a Fragmented Neighbourhood: Policies of the EU and Russia and their Consequences for the Area that Lies in Between', *CEPS Essay*, 17, Brussels: Centre for European Policy Studies, 17 October.

Delcour, L. and K. Wolczuk (2013) 'Eurasian Economic Integration and Implications for the EU's Policy in the Eastern Neigbhourhood', in R. Dragneva and K. Wolczuk (eds) *Eurasian Economic Integration: Law, Policy, and Politics*, Cheltenham: Edward Elgar, 179–203.

Dreyer, I. (2012) 'Trade Policy in the EU's Neighbourhood: Ways Forward for the Deep and Comprehensive Free Trade Agreements', *Studies and Research* 90, Paris: Notre Europe, May.

Duhot, H. (2012) 'The Black Sea Synergy Initiative: The Reflection of EU's Ambitions and Limitations in the Region', in E. Lannon (ed.) *The European Neighbourhood Policy's Challenges/Les défis de la politique européenne de voisinage*, Brussels: P.I.E. Peter Lang, 323–344.

European Commission (2003) Communication from the Commission to the Council and the European Parliament, *Wider Europe – Neighbourhood: A New Framework for Relations with Our Eastern and Southern Neighbours*, COM(2003) 104, Brussels, 11 March.

European Commission (2004) Communication from the Commission, *European Neighbourhood Policy – Strategy Paper*, COM(2004) 373, 12 May.

European Commission (2006) *Communication from the Commission to the Council and the European Parliament on Strengthening the European Neighbourhood Policy*, COM(2006) 726 final, Brussels, 4 December.

European Commission (2007a) Communication from the Commission to the Council and the European Parliament, *Black Sea Synergy – A New Regional Cooperation Initiative*, COM(2007) 160 final, Brussels, 11 April.

European Commission (2007b) *ENP – A Path towards Further Economic Integration, Non-paper Expanding on the Proposals Contained in the Communication to the European Parliament and the Council on 'Strengthening the ENP*, COM(2006) 726 final, 4 December 2006, Brussels, June.

European Commission (2014a) DG Trade, 'European Union, Trade in Goods with GCC (6)', 28 August, http://trade.ec.europa.eu/doclib/docs/2006/september/tradoc_113482.pdf (accessed October 2014).

European Commission (2014b) 'The EU's Generalised System of Preferences (GSP)', October, http://trade.ec.europa.eu/doclib/docs/2014/november/tradoc_152865.pdf (accessed November 2014).

European Commission (2014c) DG Trade statistics, http://ec.europa.eu/trade/statistics (accessed October 2014).

European Commission and High Representative (2012) Joint Communication to the European Parliament, the Council, the European Economic and Social Committee and the Committee of the Regions, *Supporting Closer Cooperation and Regional Integration in the Maghreb: Algeria, Libya, Mauritania, Morocco and Tunisia*, JOIN(2012) 36 final, Brussels, 17 December.

European Commission and High Representative (2014) Joint Communication to the European Parliament, the Council, the European Economic and Social Committee and the Committee of the Regions, *Neighbourhood at the Crossroads: Implementation of the European Neighbourhood Policy in 2013*, JOIN(2014) 12 final, Brussels, 27 March.

European Council (2002) *Presidency Conclusions*, Copenhagen, 12–13 December.

European Council (2003) *European Security Strategy: A Secure Europe in a Better World*, Brussels, 12 December.

European Council (2004) 'Final Report on an EU Strategic Partnership with the Mediterranean and the Middle East', June, http://consilium.europa.eu/uedocs/cmsUpload/Partnership%20Mediterranean%20and%20Middle%20East.pdf (accessed October 2014).

European Council (2009) *Declaration by the European Council on the Eastern Partnership, Presidency Conclusions of the Brussels European Council*, 19–20 March.

European Parliament (2011) 'EC-Uzbekistan Partnership and Cooperation Agreement and Bilateral Trade in Textiles', European Parliament Resolution of 15 December 2011 on the Draft Council Decision on the Conclusion of a Protocol to the Partnership and Cooperation Agreement Establishing a Partnership between the European Communities and their Member States, of the one part, and the Republic of Uzbekistan, of the other part, Amending the Agreement in order to Extend the Provisions of the Agreement to Bilateral Trade in Textiles, Taking Account of the Expiry of the Bilateral Textiles Agreement (16384/2010 – C7–0097/2011–2010/0323(NLE)), P7_TA(2011)0586, Strasbourg, 15 December.

EUROSTAT (2014) database, http://epp.eurostat.ec.europa.eu (accessed October 2014).

Gstöhl, S. (2010) 'The Common Commercial Policy and Political Conditionality: "Normative Power Europe" through Trade?', *Studia Diplomatica* 63(3–4), 23–41.

Gstöhl, S. (2012) 'What is at Stake in the Internal Market? Towards a Neighbourhood Economic Community', in E. Lannon (ed.) *The European Neighbourhood Policy's Challenges/Les défis de la politique européenne de voisinage*, Brussels: P.I.E. Peter Lang, 85–108.

Gstöhl, S. (2014) 'Conclusion: Models of Cooperation with the Neighbours of the EU's Neighbours', in S. Gstöhl and E. Lannon (eds) *The Neighbours of the European Union's Neighbours: Diplomatic and Geopolitical Dimensions Beyond the European Neighbourhood Policy*, Farnham: Ashgate, 269–289.

Hajizada, M. and F. Marciacq (2013) 'New Regionalism in Europe's Black Sea Region: The EU, BSEC and Changing Practices of Regionalism', *East European Politics* 29(3), 305–327.

Heron, T. (2014) 'Trading in Development: Norms and Institutions in the Making/Unmaking of European Union–African, Caribbean and Pacific Trade and Development Cooperation', *Contemporary Politics* 20(1), 10–22.

Kallioras, D. (2013) 'Trade Activity Between the EU and the ENP Countries: A "Reproduction" of the "Core-periphery" Pattern?', *SEARCH Working Paper* 2/06, September, www.ub.edu/searchproject/wp-content/uploads/2013/09/SEARCH_Working-Paper_2.06.pdf (accessed October 2014).

Lehne, S. (2014) *Time to Reset the European Neighbourhood Policy*, Brussels: Carnegie Europe, February.

Pape, E. (2013) 'An Old Partnership in a New Setting: ACP–EU Relations from a European Perspective', *Journal of International Development* 25(5), 727–741.

Popescu, N. (2014) *Eurasian Union: The Real, the Imaginary and the Likely*, Chaillot Paper 132, Paris: EUISS, September.

Romagnoli, A. and L. Mengoni (2009) 'The Challenge of Economic Integration in the MENA Region: From GAFTA and EU-MFTA to Small Scale Arab Unions', *Economic Change and Restructuring* 42(1–2), 69–83.

Siles-Brügge, G. (2014) 'EU Trade and Development Policy beyond the ACP: Subordinating Developmental to Commercial Imperatives in the Reform of GSP', *Contemporary Politics* 20(1), 49–62.

Smith, M.E. and K. Weber (2007) 'Governance Theories, Regional Integration and EU Foreign Policy', in K. Weber, M.E. Smith and M. Baun (eds) *Governing Europe's Neighbourhood: Partners or Periphery?*, Manchester: Manchester University Press, 1–20.

Triantaphyllou, D. (2014) 'The European Union and the Black Sea Region in Search of a Narrative or a New Paradigm', *Journal of Balkan and Near Eastern Studies* 16(3), 286–299.

Van der Loo, G., P. Van Elsuwege and R. Petrov (2014) 'The EU–Ukraine Association Agreement: Assessment of an Innovative Legal Instrument', *EUI Working Papers*, LAW 2014/09, Florence: European University Institute.

World Bank (2014) *World Development Indicators* database, http://databank.worldbank.org (accessed October 2014).

6 The EU and state fragility in its broader neighbourhood

Development cooperation in the name of the 'security–politics–development nexus'

Tressia Hobeika

Introduction: the 'security–politics–development nexus' in the EU's fragile neighbourhood

On the outskirts of the European Union's (EU) neighbourhood lie the most fragile hotspots in today's world. Long-ignored swathes of the Sahel–Sahara region burst into flames in 2012 after Mali's *coup d'état* and Libya's slip into anarchy. Droughts and famines, coupled with enduring insurgencies in newly independent South Sudan, Sudan, Ethiopia and Somalia, continue to be the order of the day in the Horn of Africa. As Yemen faces secessionist and rebel movements, the 2011 Syrian unrest has stoked the creation and expansion of extremist groups in Iraq and Syria, overriding the century-long lines drawn by the Sykes-Picot Agreement. That is the so-called 'arc of instability' writ large. Once defined as stretching from Afghanistan through Pakistan to the Middle East via Iraq and Yemen (Turse 2011), it is now rapidly expanding to encompass the Sahelian belt running from the Atlantic Ocean to the Red Sea basin along the southern reaches of the Saharan desert.

However diverse these contexts are, belonging to the 'arc' entails common symptoms of a 'fragility syndrome' – weak governance, endemic corruption, mounting factionalism, low human development, poor economic performance, extensive interference by external actors, and in most cases the breakout of armed insurgencies (Menkhaus 2010a: 175). Even more, 'waves' of fragility in the form of 'refugees, warring groups, contagious diseases and transnational criminal networks that traffic in drugs, arms, and people' turn these countries into 'bad neighbours' or make them easy prey to bad neighbourhood effects (Zoellick 2008: 68). A prime illustration is the fallout of the Libyan crisis in the Sahel or the spillover from the Syrian civil war into Iraqi soil.[1]

'Bottom billion countries' are also no easy terrain (Collier 2008) – not only for their citizens but also for international actors seeking to sow the seeds of stability and welfare in these arid fields. Traditional development cooperation strategies have simply not delivered. 'Fixing failed states' (Ghani and Lockhart 2008) henceforth requires a major shift from 'development as usual' to development reaching 'beyond aid' (Manning and Trzeciak-Duval 2010), that is, a secured and political development. In other words, a development that is sensitive to its security outcome, a development that is guided by 'politically smart methods' (Carothers and De Gramont 2013).

Heretofore a mere afterthought in policy circles, linking security and development has become the foreign policy issue *du jour* in Western capitals in the last decade. The so-dubbed 'security–development nexus' is increasingly guiding engagement in fragile settings. What remains more of an uphill struggle in the international aid community, however, is the recent addition of 'politics' to the 'nexus'. The 'security–politics–development nexus', although one of the 10 'Principles for Good International Engagement in Fragile States' introduced by the Development Assistance Committee (DAC) of the Organization for Economic Cooperation and Development (OECD), is being received with less enthusiasm in aid bureaucracies (OECD-DAC 2007). 'Thinking and acting politically' does in fact require them to go beyond the 'temptation of the technical' to a more uncertain and less straightforward path to development (Carothers and De Gramont 2013).

In recognition of the aid effectiveness agenda, reflections on past shortcomings in the delivery and impact of aid in faltering countries have prompted international actors to change the way they responded to the plight of these countries. The European Union, for example, has recently made concrete efforts to adapt its wide array of policies, instruments and *modi operandi* to the myriad of development challenges assailing fragile states, with a particular focus on the countries lying on the fringes of its immediate neighbourhood. The 'nexus' has therefore gained steam through, for instance, the EU's 'Strategy for Security and Development in the Sahel' (Council of the European Union 2011a) and 'Strategic Framework for the Horn of Africa' (Council of the European Union 2011b).

It is against this background that this chapter probes the EU's efforts to integrate security and politics in its development cooperation with the fragile states of its broader neighbourhood. It specifically seeks to comprehend how and to what extent the EU deals with the 'security–politics–development nexus' in the Sahel, the Horn of Africa and the Arabian Peninsula, namely through its policies, *modi operandi*, foreign aid instruments and integration of politics in its development assistance. It argues that the EU, albeit well equipped to deal with the nexus in the broader neighbourhood, has not gone overboard in strategically capitalizing on its toolbox.

It is worth noting that this chapter's basic premise is that, while fragility remains a conundrum and fragile states face real and daunting challenges, these are not insuperable. First, engagement in such settings is not a fool's errand and the EU has the potential to succeed in its endeavour to help these states get on their feet – 'as it is, and in spite of what it is' (Vennesson and Büger 2009: 4). Second, engagement is most effective when the fragile state is relevant to the EU's (and its Member States') values and interests and when the intervention is likely to have an impact (Carment, Prest and Samy 2010).

The chapter proceeds by sketching the debate around fragility and the nexus between politics, security and development. It then provides a broad-brush overview of the symptoms of state fragility in the EU's broader neighbourhood, namely in the Sahel, the Horn of Africa and the Arabian Peninsula. While a thorough analysis of all countries and regions lies beyond the scope of this chapter, reference to some examples of 'insecurity–politics–underdevelopment' challenges reveal their historical roots and their regional implications in the broader neighbourhood and, beyond, in the EU's immediate neighbourhood. The chapter thus sifts the evidence from the above dynamics in order to delve into the EU's toolbox attending to the 'security–politics–development nexus' in the fragile countries of its broader neighbourhood, including its development-related policies, institutional setup and instruments as well as its political mainstreaming work and engagement in its development assistance.

Disentangling the nexus

This section introduces fragility as the chapter's analytical vehicle, by conceptually placing it at the heart of the nexus. It then unpacks the relations between security, politics and development.

Fragility at the heart of the nexus

Albeit a self-evident syndrome, fragility is politically and conceptually contested. Stigmatizing fragile countries tends to be politically contentious, particularly by creating 'a self-fulfilling prophecy' (Collier 2008: 3–16) or causing 'detrimental effects' on a country's status on the international scene (Barakat and Larson 2014: 22). However, the recent 'g7+' grouping of self-declared fragile states came to epitomize the effort to go beyond the labelling taboo to a 'nothing-about-us-without-us' attitude (Nussbaum, Zorbas and Koros 2012).[2] On the other hand, while the definitional and conceptual contours of state fragility are difficult to pin down, there is little disagreement over the main dimensions of fragility.[3]

As a conceptual framework, fragility offers an adequate analytical vehicle that unpacks the relations between security, politics and development, thereby ensuring more coherent words and deeds in fragile settings. Nonetheless, caveats remain. As it remains amorphous and ill-defined, the fragile state concept can be easily used to oversimplify the portrayal of complex dynamics of fragile environments (Barakat and Larson 2014). The same framework is also widely used to justify the stabilization agenda of international donors under the sky of a 'Global War on Terror' (Muggah 2010). According to this post-9/11 doctrine, fragile states pose security threats to the international system, hence the urgent need for an external intervention. Yet the causal relationship between state fragility and transnational threats remains 'an exaggerated one' (Chandler 2006) with relatively little empirical analysis behind it (Patrick 2007).

The use of 'fragility' classifications is also riddled with controversies.[4] Not only does the calculation of differential capacity render the phenomenon of failure ahistorical and Eurocentric, but it also leaves behind the reporting of present external interventions, thereby perpetuating the phenomenon of remotely designed technical policies and programmes (Jones 2013; Tschirgi 2009).

After all, fragile countries tend to figure at the bottom of every ranking, irrespective of the indicators and the methodologies. There is also little dispute over the complex brew of costs and effects of fragility that tend to be 'substantial, widespread and persistent in different settings', with little purchase for Westphalian notions of the colonial modern-day borders (European Report on Development 2009: 18). While sparse literature documents the regional impact of fragile states, the 'bad neighbourhood' phenomenon has been widely acknowledged in policy and academic circles.[5]

The fragility syndrome not only exacts its toll on its carriers and neighbours, but also has proved to be particularly impervious to donor interventions. In their search for remedies for the ills of fragile states, donors have generated a growing corpus of rules and recommendations to guide their engagement in fragile settings. OECD-DAC considerations place fragility at the heart of the 'security–politics–development nexus' debate, by dedicating one of the 10 'Principles for Good International Engagement in Fragile States' to the nexus.[6]

While recognizing the need to juxtapose fragility with its historical origins in each context, this chapter regards state fragility as a challenge not only to the country itself but also to development actors or neighbours vying for influence in their backyard. That being said, the challenge is not only of a socio-economic nature but also of a security and political one.

Development, security and the nexus

Stern and Öjendal (2010: 6) confirm it: the security–development nexus 'matters'. However, if security and development are nowadays 'inextricably linked' (United Nations 2004: viii) – in the words of Kofi Annan – their confluence remains a 'conceptual jungle' in its own right (Büger and Vennesson 2009: 6–9). Uncertainties remain over what it should look like, how the concept can be used, what can be attained, by whom and for whom. The lines between development and security are more than ever blurred.

Still, the idea of the nexus has increasingly provided academic scholars, think tanks and policy-makers alike with a more cogent framework to describe, analyse and prescribe processes or even determine outcomes in fragile settings, and in most cases a 'taken-for-granted point of departure' for intervention (Stern and Öjendal 2010: 6). In their view, there exists a certain correlation between underdevelopment and insecurity, whereby insecurity is 'development in reverse' and fragile countries are caught in a mesh of 'vicious circles' (World Bank 2003).

While this chapter does not challenge the correlation between insecurity and underdevelopment, it focuses on how a foreign donor uses the nexus in fragile settings. In that sense, doing development in the name of the nexus entails more than merely grasping the nexus, rhetorically committing oneself to the nexus and tweaking policy-making mechanisms in accordance with the nexus.

It most importantly requires being backed by strategic policy-making and agility in fragile settings. Otherwise, the foreign donor would run the risk of subscribing to what Chandler (2007) rightly called an 'anti-foreign policy'. Accordingly, if we think of development as one of the many foreign policy tools at hand, any international actor in its development clothes – any development actor – would be 'retreat[ing] from *strategic policy-making* towards a more inward-looking approach to foreign policy, more concerned with self-image than the policy consequences in the areas concerned' [emphasis added] (ibid.).

Development, politics and the nexus

Adding 'politics' to the nexus – albeit less popular in policy circles – generates a different kind of debate. It compels the development actor to be 'politically smart' when operating in fragile and insecure settings. In that sense, 'just' being security-sensitive is not enough. As Carothers and De Gramont (2013) point out, a politically smart development actor is bound to grapple with the political complexities on the ground as well as the essentially political nature of developmental change, particularly in insecure arenas.

Taking local politics into account requires exploring and adopting 'politically smart methods', which go beyond mere technocratic approaches to designing and implementing aid (Carothers and De Gramont 2013). This includes, among other things, recognizing that the problem of state fragility is not a 'matter of low capacity', which often leads to the assumption that an 'off-the-shelf' patchwork of technical projects and programmes would change the local rules of the game (Menkhaus 2010a: 176). While alleviating some of the symptoms of fragility, the development actor runs the risk of unwittingly contributing to the perpetuation of underdevelopment and insecurity, by assuming 'the position of bystander, colluder, fashion setter, provider of substitute services, or dictator of policies' (Ghani and Lockhart 2008: 66).

Comprehending the local or regional dynamics of fragile contexts, including the political economy of state failure, therefore entails a systematic use of analytical tools in the programming and implementation of development assistance, whereby the involvement of relevant stakeholders is key to identifying change agents and reaching the expected development outcomes.

The EU's broader neighbourhood: an 'arc of fragility'

Whether self-declared or not, state fragility is a challenge: to the country itself, to its neighbours and to any development actor seeking to intervene in the name of the 'security–politics–development nexus'. State fragility can also be nurtured by pivotal neighbouring states vying for influence in their region. In such precarious contexts, socio-economic challenges are only a part of the story. They are 'inextricably linked' to local and regional security and political (sometimes personal) concerns.

This section does not seek to give a detailed analysis of the 'insecurity–politics–underdevelopment' challenges besetting the countries and regions of the 'arc of fragility'. The variety and complexities of these challenges in such intricate configurations make a concise overview a somewhat challenging endeavour. Rather, the intention is to give a broad-brush account of the abovementioned dynamics through some examples from the three regions at hand – the Sahel, the Horn of Africa and the Arabian Peninsula.

Setting the stage: the fragile countries of the 'arc'

Regardless of the definition, classification, indicators or methodologies, 11 countries of the 'arc' hit the bottom of most rankings (Tables 6.1 and 6.2).[7] These countries, although diverse in nature and size, share many characteristics with other fragile countries in the world in terms of authority, service and legitimacy failures. They differ, however, in terms of their growth, life expectancy and foreign debt, among other factors (European Report on Development 2009; Stewart and Brown 2009). Their geographical ubiquity also varies from one region to another. In the Sahel, for instance, all countries are in fragile situations.[8]

Sahelistan: 'le couloir de tous les dangers'[9]

The tag 'Sahelistan' would not raise eyebrows in the wake of the recent events in the Sahel: fragility has proven to be ubiquitous in the southern fringes of the European Union's neighbourhood.[10] A no-man's-land today, an inhospitable stretch separating North Africa from the rest of the continent, the Sahara was long 'an inland sea' for the populations of the Maghreb 'crossed by camel caravans bringing gold, salt, ostrich feathers, and slaves northwards' (Joffé 2012: 137–138). In many ways, and with just a 'stroke of an international pen', the scramble for Africa and the colonial experience were to deeply alter the fate of the region – of both Sahelian states and societies (Collier 2009). Not only were the eyes of North African states diverted from the Sahara northwards but, more importantly, bifurcated and extractive colonial state structures were carved up in such a way as to transfer resources to the colonial powers rather than foster local development (European Report on Development 2009: 49–56). 'Born dirt poor

Table 6.1 Fragile states of the EU's broader neighbourhood

	Sahel	*Horn of Africa*	*Arabian Peninsula*
'g7+'	Chad	Somalia South Sudan	—
'non-g7+'	Mali Mauritania Niger	Ethiopia Eritrea Sudan	Iraq Yemen

Table 6.2 Key development indicators in the 'arc of fragility'

	Average annual population growth (%, 2010–2015)	Gross national income per capita (US$ purchasing power parity, 2011)	Population below poverty line (% purchasing power parity, 2000–2012)	UNDP Human Development Index (rank out of 187, 2013)	Education Development Index* (rank out of 120, 2010)	Failed States Index (rank out of 178, 2013)
Chad	2.6	1,622	62	184	—	6
Eritrea	2.9	1,147	—	182	115	23
Ethiopia	2.1	1,303	30.6	173	116	19
Iraq	3.1	14,007	2.8	120	—	13
Mali	3.0	1,499	50.4	176	118	36
Mauritania	2.2	2,988	23.4	161	107	28
Niger	3.5	873	43.6	187	120	19
Somalia	2.6	—	—	—	—	2
South Sudan	—	—	—	—	—	1
Sudan	2.4	3,428	—	166	—	5
Yemen	3.0	3,945	17.5	154	—	8

Sources: author's own compilation based on United Nations (2014; 2012); and Fund for Peace (2014). Based on a poverty line of US$1.25 per day.

Note

* The Education Development Index (EDI) value for a given country is the arithmetic mean of four indicators: primary adjusted net enrolment ratio, adult literacy rate, quality of education (survival rate to Grade 5) and gender (gender parity indexes for primary education, secondary education and adult literacy). The higher the EDI value, the closer the country is to achieving 'education for all' as a whole.

and with a weak sense of common identity' (Boukhars 2013: 120), the limited development orientation of today's Sahelian fragile states, a lingering colonial legacy, surfaces for example in the divide between northern Mali and the southern 'Mali utile' – a French colonial idea that would survive decolonization and usurp subsequent Malian decision-making in the years to come (Marty 2013).

Today's developmental landscape is daunting. All the Sahelian states figure in the bottom 30 of the United Nations Development Programme's (UNDP) Human Development Index (HDI), with Niger faring worst (rank: 187) in the world. All these countries' populations are trapped in a quagmire of poverty, with more than 62 per cent of Chadians living below the income poverty line, on the fringes of society. Gender inequalities are also a source of poverty in Mauritania, where women enjoy fewer rights than men in terms of education, health-care and access to the labour market (Simon *et al.* 2012: 20), as epitomized by an HDI rank of 161 (Table 6.2).[11]

Such entrenched socio-economic challenges are further worsened by frail state institutions unable – or unwilling – to penetrate their societies or to stretch their presence to their border- and hinterlands: basic public services are lacking, the informal economy is rife, and corruption is rampant. Mauritania is the example *par excellence*, where pervasive corruption and weak governance exacerbate long-standing ethnic and social grievances of the Haratins – the so-called black Moors – whose basic rights have long been denied and who still face severe socio-economic conditions (Boukhars 2013).

Moreover, 'closely knit ethnic communities stretch along state borders and allegiance to kinsmen is often stronger than allegiance to the state' (Wehrey 2013: 3). Porous borders in vast tracts of hostile terrain, along with the dysfunctional capacities of the states in the region, facilitate the proliferation of illicit networks, transnational criminality and the implantation of radical Islamism in the form of Salafism in Mauritania or 'Al-Qaeda in the Islamic Maghreb' (AQIM). Compounding these regional illicit dynamics is state connivance in organized crime and trafficking markets in practically all Sahelian countries (Lacher 2013). AQIM not only roams freely in the vast swathes of the Sahel but also taps into societal fabrics splintered by grievances and poor socio-economic conditions in places such as northern Mali, Chad and Mauritania. AQIM also looks 'north'.

It was not until the uprisings roiled the Arab world as of 2010 that the deep links of the Sahel with its neighbouring region to the north were brought to the fore. The fault-lines of Saharan state fragility had nonetheless long run deep north through, *inter alia*, perpetual waves of Chadian refugees or African migrants to Libya.[12] Northern pivotal states had long set the rules of the game in the region, thereby cultivating fragility in their backyard. The meddling of Libya's president Gaddafi in Chad's affairs and the support of Tabu Chadian insurgents against the government in Ndjamena in the 1970s is a case in point. While Gaddafi's original plan to unify the Sahel had a deep impact on his southern neighbours, it was his orientation toward Africa in the 1990s – while under Western sanctions – that was to engrain his legacy to the present day. The

Tuaregs of Malian and Nigerian origins, for example, were to be increasingly recruited into the Libyan army.[13] And it was these same Tuaregs that were to fuel the rebellion of 2012 in Mali upon their return, in the wake of the Libyan crisis (Cole 2013).

The Horn of Africa: crisis as usual

The story of a fragile Horn is no different from those of its neighbours to the west, although the crises in the Horn are far from being new, perhaps except for piracy. Famine, radical Islamism and state failure have all had particular resonance for the region since the early 1970s. For all, history matters: some crises find their roots in the historic Horn centred on Abyssinia (modern-day Ethiopia) and predate the colonial era, while others are an imprint of European colonization, which left contested – and porous – borders behind (Woodward 2013).

The prospects for meeting the Millennium Development Goals are as dim as ever. The 'wickedness' of state and environmental fragility is particularly apparent in the countries of the Horn, beset by acute poverty, hunger and recurrent droughts and floods resulting in waves of displaced populations (Menkhaus 2010b). The countries at the tip of East Africa also fare worst in terms of human development: they all figure at the bottom of the UN's HDI, with Eritrea securing the rank of 182 and 31 per cent of Ethiopia's population blighted by extreme poverty (Table 6.2). Food security challenges are also daunting. In 2011, the Food and Agriculture Organization declared a state of famine in southern Somalia, affecting 3.5 million people around the country, following the worst drought in more than half a century in East Africa (Maxwell and Fitzpatrick 2012).

Severe and recurring droughts have aggravated the already feeble political institutions, marred by a poor record of governance and a high frequency of *coups d'état* and violent regime change. Current regimes in Eritrea, Ethiopia, Somaliland, Sudan and South Sudan were all induced by *coups* or civil wars (Soliman *et al.* 2012). As for Somalia, Siad Barre's legacy still weighs on the clash of 'clannish identities', mired by piracy in the Gulf of Aden and an Islamist insurgency – Al-Shabaab – in its rural areas (Woodward 2013).

These states differ in their capabilities to face the sources of their 'wicked' fragility, but none has managed to overcome 'clannish' and ethnic resistance to their territorial and authority control. They also have a rich history of nurturing fragility and domestic instability in each other's territories, thereby exacerbating their interlocking vulnerabilities. Ethiopia's support to Barre's enemies, especially in northern Somaliland, was to increasingly weaken his regime – with his downfall in 1991 engendering the worst crisis in the history of the Horn of Africa, bringing with it massive and recurrent waves of refugees, at times exacerbated by droughts and food crises.

At the crossroads between Africa and the Arabian Peninsula, the Horn of Africa is bound to the Gulf states, and particularly Yemen, not only by the thin waters of the Red Sea but also by social, cultural, trade and even piracy connections. However, the Arab country with the longest-standing link to the Horn of

Africa has been Egypt, perhaps because of its historical and colonial connections. In that sense, Egypt's interests in the Horn have always been guided by its water concerns, particularly with Sudan and Ethiopia with regard to the management of Nile waters.

Yemen and Iraq: fragility in a sea of prosperity

Although geographically situated in the Arabian Peninsula, Yemen's challenges are often seen through the Horn's lenses, particularly in connection with Somalia. After all, both countries have proven to be no stranger to intermittent crises. After years of Ottoman and British rule, the creation of the Republic of Yemen in 1991 did not herald a new era of prosperity (Phillips 2011). Instead, Yemen has been plagued by a myriad of development and security problems, compounded by a weak central government in Sana'a and a contestation of its territorial control outside the capital. The Shiite Houthis's rebel movement in the north and a rising Al-Qaeda in the Arabian Peninsula insurgency seek to embolden themselves in the midst of foreign interference in Yemeni domestic affairs, notably by Saudi Arabia and Iran. Yemen's fragility is also compounded by its destabilizing links with the Horn of Africa, such as arms smuggling, piracy off its coast and a constant inflow of refugees from Somalia and other African countries seeking a better life in oil-rich Gulf countries (Atarodi 2010).

While sectarian strife is one of the numerous challenges in Yemen, these are increasingly shaping post-2003 Iraq – the last bit of the 'arc of fragility'. Iraq is somehow the exception in the 'arc', where the 2003 war had a major impact on its socio-economic conditions and societal fabric. With the highest gross national income per capita (US$14,007) and HDI (rank 120) in the 'arc', yet one of the most fragile states, Iraqi society remains splintered by simmering sectarian-based grievances, paving the way for Sunni militant campaigns such as Al-Qaeda and the 'Islamic State of Iraq and the Levant' (ISIL) to assert themselves in confrontation with a Shiite-dominated, increasingly authoritarian government (Table 6.2; International Crisis Group 2013). Here, the Syrian uprising followed by a war with sectarian undertones similar to the ones in Iraq has spilled across the porous border, with the creation in 2014 of ISIL's self-proclaimed caliphate over Iraq and Syria.[14]

This brief tour of the EU's broader neighbourhood uncovers a looming 'arc of fragility'. Its fragility lies at the intersection of underdevelopment and insecurity, themselves prime ingredients for an emergency state of permanent crises. Both drivers and consequences of the 'wicked' problem of state fragility in the 'arc' reveal their historical roots, their regional implications and their close connections with the EU's immediate neighbourhood. In that sense, fragility as such – a challenge to development and security policies alike – is unlikely to respect the EU's nexus policy, let alone its institutionalization with regards to the 'arc of fragility'.

The nexus at work in the 'arc': the EU way

This section unpacks the EU's toolbox dedicated to the 'security–politics–development nexus' in the fragile states of its broader neighbourhood.

When development meets security in the nexus: signs of anti-foreign policy

With the passing of a few decades of international debate on the fragility concept, security has gradually seeped into the development equation of donors' engagement, leading to a gradual recognition of a 'security–development nexus' in their work in fragile settings. The EU has followed suit, not only in its rhetorical or financial commitment to fragile states but also in its *modi operandi* and a wide range of development-related instruments. The 'arc of fragility' is particularly salient in this regard.

A commitment in progress

The EU's fragility lexicon has clearly evolved in the last decade in order to address the linkages between its development and security policies. While development policy is clearly present in the EU's own jargon since the Treaty of Rome and a shared parallel competence between the European Union and the Member States, the EU's security policy has ever since remained in the Member States' own hands (Overhaus 2013). The Treaty of Lisbon did not eliminate the clash between the Union's delimitation of competences and the converging rationale between security and development but gave the EU a strong legal basis for its work in fragile states (art. 21 TEU).

In the meantime, however, not only had the EU clarified its understanding of fragility through a number of policy documents, but it had also enriched its nexus development policies along three lines: international references and commitments, EU policy frameworks, and geographical or regional strategies.

The EU's international commitment was given a firm standing through its endorsement of the 2007 OECD-DAC 'Principles for Good International Engagement in Fragile States' and its backing of the 2011 Busan New Deal for Engagement in Fragile States, along with its Peacebuilding and Statebuilding Goals (PSGs) and the voluntary association of the 'g7+' countries.[15] In its broader neighbourhood, for example, the EU was the 'co-leader' of the Somali 'New Deal Compact' and an 'active partner' in the 'South Sudan Compact' (Interview VII).[16]

These international references were also reflected in the EU's own extensive policy framework, including its 'security and development bibles' such as the 2003 'European Security Strategy', the 2005 'European Consensus on Development' or the 2009 'Agenda for Change' (Gänzle 2012: 118–120).[17] Statements such as '[t]he security development nexus has been firmly established in the EU's political priorities' (European Commission, 2009: 78) are also echoed in the two sets of Council Conclusions on the 'EU Response to Situations of

Fragility' (Council of the European Union 2007a) and 'Security and Development' (Council of the European Union 2007b).

The nexus is also put forward in a number of geographical or regional policies in relation to the EU's broader neighbourhood, such as the Cotonou Agreement of 2000 and its successive revisions in 2005 and 2010 or the two regional strategies: the 'Strategy for Security and Development in the Sahel' (Council of the European Union 2011a) and the 'Strategic Framework for the Horn of Africa' (Council of the European Union 2011b).

It is worth noting that the abovementioned policy documents, among others, not only stress the importance of the nexus but also emphasize the need for a 'more strategic' approach to aid in fragile contexts – mantra-like words recurrently stressed by European Commission officials (Cornaro 2012). For others, however, 'there is [simply] no strategic culture in Brussels yet' (Interview II). The regional strategies in the broader neighbourhood are a case in point.

In the Sahel, for example, the strategy clearly identifies four 'strategic' lines of action, all directly or indirectly linked to the EU's development policies.[18] However, the very region for which the EU had a reasonably good strategy collapsed because of unforeseen destabilizing shockwaves and a lack of policy agility. The regional fallout of the Libyan conflict had been 'severely underestimated' and the 'preventive' objective of the strategy had not prevented the EU from being a 'slow' actor, leading to a deteriorating situation on the ground, 'beyond the point of prevention' (Simon, Mattelaer and Hadfield 2012: 28). Other weaknesses were identified in the strategy's poorly defined regional geographical framing, which failed to reflect the interlinked nature of the underdevelopment and insecurity issues in the Sahel (Bello 2012). In that sense, the EU's focus on the three 'core states' (Mauritania, Mali and Niger) within a broader framework encompassing the Maghreb (and West Africa) rendered uncertain the way to bring the 'pivotal' states of the neighbourhood (Algeria and Libya) on board and failed to suggest concrete operational linkages between these core and pivotal states.

The 2013 Joint Communication on the 'EU's comprehensive approach to external conflict and crises' adds up to the abovementioned list of nexus-related policy documents designed to guide the EU's work in fragile contexts 'in a strategic manner' (European Commission and High Representative 2013). The release of this much-awaited document was depicted as an attempt to institutionalize the nexus (Zwolski 2013). While the comprehensive approach holds the promise to systematically place the EU's development policy within a broader nexus-sensitive foreign policy toolbox, it is also seen as an 'updated wording ... [which could] mask ... incoherencies in supposedly development friendly European policies' (Helly and Rocca 2013: 6). Are we witnessing, in the words of Chandler (2007: 368), a set of policy statements covered by the nexus that 'read more like rhetorical wish lists than seriously considered policy options'? Is 'fusing security and development just another euro-platitude' (Youngs 2007)?

Rhetorical commitments to the nexus may display signs of 'anti-foreign policy' in the fragile broader neighbourhood, but the financial commitment does tell a different story. The EU and its Member States remain one of the largest donors to most of the 'arc' countries, with a share of official development assistance (ODA) of 48.7 per cent to Niger in the Sahel, 47.2 per cent to Somalia in the Horn of Africa and 36.2 per cent to Yemen in the Arabian Peninsula (Table 6.3).

While the financial commitment in the region is far from being window-dressing, the 'broad agreement on the principles underpinning [the] nexus contrasts with the difficulties encountered in their implementation' (European Commission 2009: 62). Here, the abovementioned treaty-based divide between development cooperation and security and defence policy makes it difficult to draw the line between security and development, a difficulty that then trickles down to the institutional operationalization of the nexus (Merket 2012).[19] Making sense of the nexus in practical terms remains a struggle to most EU officials despite the willingness to converge both areas in their work (Keukeleire and Raube 2013). Some officials claim that there is an internal recognition of the nexus 'while challenges remain' (Interview V), whereas others perceive the nexus-related regional strategies as a 're-labelling' of previous and on-going development action in the Sahel: 'building a road was relabelled as contributing to security' (Interview VI) or 'education was relabelled [in accordance with the Sahel Strategy] when most education-related projects were on-going' (Interview V). In other words, 'the thinking [on the nexus] in fragile contexts was already there' (Interviews V and VII). For others, while 'development' is more appropriate for the development world and 'security' for the military world, 'fragility' could be the middle ground for both communities (Interview VIII).

With Commission officials calling for the 'need to achieve a common understanding on key policies ... [related to] the development side of the comprehensive approach' (Cornaro 2012), the nature of the EU as a 'multi-cephalous actor' means that the institutional reality of the nexus remains that of a fragmented responsibility over the EU's diverse financial and non-financial instruments (Banim 2009).

A fragmented institutional setup

When engaging with the fragile states of the 'arc', there are at least three institutional focal points of EU foreign aid at the intersection of security and development (Table 6.4). Here, the Lisbon Treaty equipped the EU to better deal with the development side of the nexus, by disabling the pillar structure and enabling, in theory, a cross-pillar and cross-policy foreign policy formulation, including security and development (Keukeleire and Raube 2013). The Treaty also adapted the EU's aid decision-making mechanisms in the 'grey area' of the nexus, in such a way as to bring development closer to security in the nexus's institutional hierarchy.

The first and foremost institutional innovation in that domain is the new function of the High Representative of the Union for Foreign Affairs and Security

Table 6.3 Bilateral ODA to the fragile countries, 2012 (share in million US$ at current prices and in % of gross national income)

	EU institutions' share	DAC EU members' share	All donors	EU and EU Member States' share (%)
Chad	121.3 (1.24%)	72.9 (0.75%)	478.6 (4.91%)	40.6
Eritrea	8.7 (0.29%)	7.5 (0.24%)	133.8 (4.37%)	12.1
Ethiopia	226.4 (0.53%)	775.8 (1.8%)	3,261.3 (7.58%)	30.7
Iraq	91.6 (0.04%)	113.1 (0.05%)	1,300.8 (0.61%)	15.7
Mali	85.7 (0.87%)	239.8 (2.44%)	1,001.3 (10.21%)	32.5
Mauritania	61.7 (1.52%)	125.4 (3.08%)	408.3 (10.04%)	45.8
Niger	223.8 (3.47%)	215.5 (3.34%)	901.9 (13.985%)	48.7
Somalia	170.9 (—)	300.1 (—)	998.7 (—)	47.2
South Sudan	46.9 (0.58%)	402.6 (5.01%)	1,578 (9.65%)	28.5
Sudan	192 (0.35%)	217.7 (0.4%)	983.2 (1.81%)	41.7
Yemen	64.2 (0.19%)	192.6 (0.57%)	709.4 (2.11%)	36.2

Source: author's own compilation based on OECD (2012).

Table 6.4 EU staff dealing with foreign aid in the fragile countries, 2014

Unit/Division	Geographical/regional	Thematic	Horizontal	Other
EEAS	Sahel and Horn of Africa [MD II] Africa	Conflict prevention, peace building and mediation instruments	[VI.B.2] Development cooperation coordination	Commission Foreign Policy Instruments service
	Yemen and Iraq [MD IV] North Africa, Middle East, Arabian Peninsula, Iran and Iraq			
DG DEVCO	Horn of Africa [D] East and Southern Africa and ACP Coordination Sahel [E] West and Central Africa Yemen and Iraq [H] Asia, Central Asia, Middle East/Gulf and Pacific	[B5] Instrument for Stability, nuclear safety	[07] Fragility and crisis management	
EU delegations	• Sahel: Mauritania, Mali, Niger and Chad • Horn of Africa: Sudan, South Sudan, Ethiopia, Eritrea and Djibouti • Middle East: Yemen and Iraq			

Sources: author's own compilation based on Tannous (2013); Soliman *et al.* (2012); EEAS organization chart (September 2014); DG DEVCO organization chart (July 2014); and Interviews III, IV, VII, VIII (2013).

Note
Indications in square brackets are taken from the source charts and are used there to identify the units or divisions of the organization.

Policy and Vice-President of the European Commission (HR/VP) and the establishment of the European External Action Service (EEAS). The HR/VP accordingly serves as 'a formal institutional linkage' for foreign policy matters between the Council and the European Commission (Smith 2013: 1302), thereby placing development at the 'heart of the EU's external action', closer to security and defence policy (Tannous 2013: 334). The convergence between development and security was further echoed in the EEAS Council Decision, which conferred on the EEAS competences both in development and in Common Foreign and Security Policy (CFSP) and brought together staff from the European Commission, the General Secretariat of the EU Council and the Member States with security- and development-oriented portfolios (Council of the European Union 2010; Merket 2012). The EEAS became – on paper – the institution *par excellence* for strategy formulation and the coordination of EU foreign aid at the interface of development and security objectives.

The centrality of development within the EEAS is also stressed through the work of a small horizontal unit responsible for development cooperation coordination, whereas a Fragility and Crisis Management unit places the nexus at the heart of the development policy of the Directorate General for Development and Cooperation – EuropeAid (DG DEVCO) (see Table 6.4). In other words, 'development and security policy overlap in the new system' (Furness and Gänzle 2012: 12). By the same token, the DG DEVCO fragility unit is itself endowed with the mission to 'address the security–development nexus' in its formulation of policy orientations for cooperation with countries in fragile or crisis situations, in coordination with other services, particularly the EEAS Conflict Prevention, Peace-Building and Mediation Instruments Division (Interview VIII). It was also an 'added value' regarding the conflict in Mali, as it convened and chaired weekly meetings with all relevant stakeholders from the corresponding institutions (Interview V).

Second, with the transfer of the country desks of the pre-Lisbon Commission DG for Development to the EEAS, post-Lisbon DG DEVCO was left with the remaining Commission policy units, which were merged with the former EuropeAid Cooperation Office (Tannous 2013). Beyond DG DEVCO and the EEAS, another important institutional player in relation to the nexus is the Foreign Policy Instruments (FPI) service, a Commission service directly reporting to the HR/VP.

In an attempt to further reconcile development and security objectives, interorganizational structures were established, such as the 'Conflict Prevention Group' chaired by the EEAS Conflict Prevention division and composed of representatives from the EEAS, the FPI service, DG DEVCO and the Directorate General for Humanitarian Aid and Civil Protection (DG ECHO) (Gavas *et al.* 2013). In the same line, an EEAS 'Sahel Task Force' was set up to gather staff from relevant institutions, who meet informally two or three times per month under the leadership of the Managing Director for West and Central Africa. The task force was initially charged with the preparation of the EU Sahel Strategy and recently with the evaluation of the Strategy's performance (Simon, Mattelaer and Hadfield 2012; Bello 2012).

The third institutional focal point feeding into the nexus is the network of EU delegations, the EU's 'eyes and ears' on the ground, providing the countries they operate in with a 'point of contact and conduit to Brussels' (Furness 2012: 84). The EU external diplomatic corps is well represented in the broader 'arc', with the exception of Somalia, as the delegation operates from Kenya. There was, however, a clear sign of the EU's willingness to 'fly the flag in Somalia' with the approval of a budget for a representative office in Mogadishu (Soliman *et al.* 2012: 30). 'Why don't they come to Mogadishu?' was also a question raised by Somali stakeholders (Interview I). As for South Sudan, the EU is set to open a delegation in Juba as soon as 'the necessary conditions are fulfilled' (Interview VII). EU delegations in the Horn of Africa are comprised of both EEAS and DG DEVCO staff, with a much larger ratio of development officials to political officials. It is telling to note that there is only one political officer, which means that in certain instances, DG DEVCO staff takes on the supposedly political responsibilities of EEAS staff.[20] Does this mean a greater willingness on the part of the European Commission to cope with security-related aspects of development cooperation or just a lack of resources? For a DG DEVCO official, it is a mere 'strategic choice' (Interview VII; Soliman *et al.* 2012). The same ratio applies for EU delegations in the Sahel, as illustrated by the delegation in Niger. According to a European Parliament official, the walls between development and security actors in Niger are quite high, where personnel of the civilian mission under the Common Security and Defence Policy (CSDP) were found to be isolated from the delegation (Interview II). The political section in the delegation in Chad is also small (OECD-DAC 2012: 130). Even more, there is only one officer for West Africa looking at security issues (Barrios 2013: 15). In the fragile countries of the Arabian Peninsula, the recent establishment a full-fledged delegation in Sana'a with beefed-up human resources on the ground is a paramount indication that the EU is indeed 'getting its hands dirty' while coping with the nexus on the ground.

The above-described institutional restructuring has engendered a complex programming process with regard to the EU's foreign aid instruments (Van Seter and Klavert 2011). While art. 9 of the EEAS Council Decision left some room for interpretation about the 'joint' EEAS – European Commission preparation of proposals for external instruments 'under the responsibility of the Commissioner for Development', the working arrangements of January 2012 set out the modalities for cooperation between the two institutions (Council of the European Union 2010; European Commission and European External Action Service 2012; Görtz and Keijzer 2012).[21] This holds true for the European Development Fund (EDF) (Sahel and Horn of Africa) and the Development Cooperation Instrument (DCI) (Yemen and Iraq) but not for the Instrument for Stability (IfS) (long-term measures), as the responsibility of its strategic programming lies within the EEAS in consultation with the Commission (Table 6.5).[22] What this programming process between the EEAS and DG DEVCO entails for the balancing of development and security in the 2014–20 Multiannual Financial Framework (MFF) is telling. Even though, in theory, the EEAS is in charge of strategic

Table 6.5 EU financial instruments for funding the 'nexus' in the broader neighbourhood

Instrument	Scope	Focus	Responsibility for strategic programming	Budget 2014–2020
Instrument for Stability and Peace (IfSP)	Thematic	Conflict prevention, crisis response, global and trans-regional threats	*Short-term*: non-programmable, managed by FPI service *Long-term*: EEAS in consultation with the European Commission	€2,339 million
EDF African Peace Facility	Geographical/thematic	Capacity-building (African Peace and Security Architecture); AU-led peace support operations	Joint preparation EEAS and European Commission (outside EU budget)	€26,980 million (eleventh EDF)
EDF B-Envelope	Geographical (Sahel and Horn of Africa)	Exogenous shocks with a cross-country dimension		
Development Cooperation Instrument (DCI)	Geographical (Gulf region)	Poverty eradication with priority to 'countries most in need', including countries in crisis, post-crisis, fragile and vulnerable situations	Joint preparation EEAS and European Commission	€19,662 million

Source: author's own compilation based on EU public documents.

Note
Budget 2014–2020 refers to commitments in million € at current prices.

planning, DG DEVCO's officials interviewed were clear about the fact that the line is not really drawn but cooperation is rather left to personal contacts between the EEAS and DG DEVCO desks. After all, 'the EEAS is responsible for the programming, but between brackets; they do not have the money' (Interview VII). Collaboration between Horn of Africa desks proved to be more tightly knit because of the balance between development and security (ibid.).

While the nexus seems to draw both institutions closer in the case of some fragile states of the 'arc', the complex nature of the EU's bureaucracy cannot but generate inter-institutional tensions, and policies towards the 'arc' of the broader neighbourhood are no exception. Although regional strategies were expected to ease up the work in the current programming cycle, it seems that the pre-Lisbon coordination problems were not solved, but 'merely repackaged ... into a new bureaucracy' (Smith 2013: 1309). The statement 'we do the same thing, but slightly differently' when referring to the role of the EEAS and DG DEVCO in the programming of EU financial instruments is a compelling example of the above (Interview III and IV). After all, the confluence between development and security is largely contingent upon institutional dynamics; a 'diffused institutional responsibility' over a wide gamut of external relations instruments remains the backcloth against which the EU does development in the name of the nexus (Merket 2012: 630).

Instruments at the service of the nexus

In order to provide assistance to the fragile states of the 'arc' in a timely and strategic way, specific arrangements include two 'nexus-related' financial instruments – the Instrument for Stability and the African Peace Facility (APF) – and the use of more flexible procedures in crisis situations.[23] The new MFF regulations introduce a greater flexibility into the standard instruments and the nexus-relevant instruments alike.[24] Non-financial 'beyond-aid' instruments are equally vital vehicles for nexus-related assistance in fragile settings, including development-friendly political/policy dialogue and EU Special Representative (EUSR) interventions.

While standard instruments can indirectly address the nexus through the EDF's B-envelope or the DCI's referral to 'situations in crisis, post-crisis and fragile states', it is the IfS and APF that explicitly fund activities at the intersection of security and development in the fragile countries of the 'arc' (Table 6.5).

The IfS, re-named the Instrument for Stability and Peace (IfSP) for the period 2014–20, is the EU's main financial instrument addressing conflict prevention as part of the security–development nexus (European Parliament and Council of the European Union 2014b; European Commission 2014). It replaced the Rapid Reaction Mechanism in 2007 and vowed to equip the EU with a 'strategic tool to address a number of global security and development challenges' as its main horizontal tool in countries affected by crises and conflict (European Commission 2007; 2012). The IfS has become the only instrument addressing needs that cannot be otherwise tackled under any other instrument, whether because of the global or transnational nature of the problem, its ineligibility for ODA or the urgency of the response (European Commission 2011a: 6).[25] As such, the IfS reduces the EU's 'reaction time' in its response to crisis situations with a link to long-term development, thanks to its short-term and long-term components. In other words, it 'speaks to the time dimension of the security–development nexus' (Gänzle 2012: 133).

With its global coverage, the IfS has funded nexus-related activities in all the regions of the 'arc'. In line with the Sahel Strategy, the IfS provided, in 2012, support to the northern regions of Niger and Mali in order to mitigate the impact of the Libyan fallout (European Commission 2013a). Under its long-term component, the IfS also continued funding, in 2012, the implementation of the project 'Contre Terrorism Sahel' along with a host of capacity-building interventions in Niger and Mauritania (ibid.). In the Horn of Africa, stabilization and early recovery projects were funded in Somalia in addition to long-term recovery projects in the framework of the 'Critical Maritime Routes' programme, which seeks to enhance information-sharing capacities and maritime law enforcement in coastal states such as Djibouti, Yemen and Somalia (ibid.). As for the Arabian Peninsula, the IfS funded the design of Yemen's reform plans (ibid.).

In contrast with the IfS, the APF is – as its name suggests – geographically limited to Africa, including the Sahel and the Horn of Africa in the 'arc'. It is specifically designed to finance security-related activities in the framework of the European Development Fund. As such, the 'APF is an exceptional policy framework in the context of the development policy of the EU' since development euros are spent on 'non-DAC-able' military means (Keukeleire and Raube 2013: 560). The APF provides support to the African Union's (AU) 'African Peace and Security Agenda/Architecture', specifically dealing with conflict prevention and resolution in Africa. However, the bulk of APF funding has since 2004 supported peace operations, mostly in the Horn of Africa, including the AU Mission in Somalia (AMISOM) and the AU Mission in Sudan (AMIS) in 2006–07. In this light, financial support to AMISOM, under the guidance of the 'Strategic Framework for the Horn of Africa', was seen as an integral part of the EU's comprehensive approach to supporting the AU's security and development efforts or, in other words, the nexus (Soliman *et al.* 2012). In the Sahel, the APF is set to contribute around €50 million to Malian troops (Helly and Rocca 2013: 9).

Standard financial instruments indirectly funding the nexus in the 'arc' have also seen their provisions gradually evolve toward more flexibility and agility in fragile situations. For instance, unallocated funds foreseen in the EDF's 'B-Envelope' were transferred to DG ECHO for humanitarian use during the recent famine in the Horn of Africa or have supplemented EDF local development (OECD-DAC 2012: 91). On top of the simplification of rules and procedures of external action instruments, the MFF foresees unallocated funds for the DCI, which means more flexibility in the Arabian Peninsula (European Parliament and Council of the European Union 2014a; 2014c). Flexible procedures should also apply to all crisis and emergency countries of the European Commission's confidential 'crisis declaration list' (Interview VIII). These include the application of a number of exceptions to some basic rules for grants, such as the non-obligation of annual programming or the awarding of grants without a call for proposals (ADE 2011; European Commission 2013b).

With the above enhanced flexibility measures, the EU's development assistance is better equipped to speak to the time dimension of the nexus. Its 'spatial dimension' remains, however, less developed. While the nexus-sensitive development programmes set out above take into account the cross-border or regional nature of fragility, these remain confined to the geographical contours of the 'arc'. In other words, programmes and projects such as the 'Critical Maritime Routes' in the Horn of Africa, the assistance to Nigerian authorities in their coping with the fallout of the Libyan crisis in the Sahel or even APF-funded peace operations – albeit conceptually connected to the EU's immediate neighbourhood – remain operationally restricted to the EU's broader neighbourhood's confines, whether on a country or regional level. After all, the EU's neighbours and their neighbours are governed by 'totally different' policies, let alone funding mechanisms, as confirmed by a DG DEVCO official: 'Our instruments prevent us from looking North in the Sahel', although the fallout of the Libyan crisis in Mali did trigger discussions in DG DEVCO and the Council's Political and Security Committee (PSC) on how to build bridges between the EU's immediate and broader neighbourhoods in terms of its development policy (Interview V).

The remaining instruments coping with the nexus in the 'arc' are of a non-financial nature. These are particularly important in the 'arc's' context of fragility, as they allow the EU to promote development that moves beyond classical or technical aid to a truly security-sensitive development. They most importantly allow the EU to be a real 'player' – and not just a 'payer' – in crisis prevention and management, a player that builds on the potential political leverage of its financial support.

Pro-development political dialogue, for instance, was recognized in the 2005 'European Consensus on Development' as 'an important way in which to further development objectives' thanks to its 'preventive dimension' (European Parliament, Council of the European Union and European Commission 2006: 4). In the Sahel and the Horn of Africa, political dialogue is an essential component of the Cotonou Agreement, based on 'policies to promote peace and to prevent, manage and resolve violent conflicts' (European Commission 2010: art. 8). Moreover, political dialogue became systematic under the 2005 revised agreement, to be held before the consultation procedure with each recipient country (ibid.: art. 96). On the ground, however, even though the European Commission was found to have increasingly used preventive political dialogue, the absence of political sections in the delegations constrained the use of such instruments (ADE 2011). As already noted, political sections, not to mention political officers, are not widely available in the delegations of the 'arc'. Nonetheless, EU ambassadors are more boldly and increasingly using development aid leverage in political dialogue and *vice versa*, as in the case of the ambassador in Chad who had come from a development-related Commission post (OECD-DAC

2012: 130). Development-friendly political dialogue should also aim to involve regional pivotal actors if it is to account for the 'bad neighbourhood' effects of fragile states. In the Sahel, bilateral relations with Algeria, 'often tainted by ambiguous post-colonial ties', prevent a genuine political dialogue on the fragile countries in its backyard (Helly and Rocca 2013: 11). That being said, the EU was not keen to conduct genuine dialogues with pivotal states in the Sahel, including Algeria, and instead dispatched fact-finding missions to the region in 2009–10 in preparation for the Sahel Strategy (Bello 2012).

Borrowing from the CFSP toolbox for nexus-related development could also be of strategic added value for the EU, as for example in the appointment of EUSRs in the regions of the 'arc'. The EUSR's function is in fact perceived by EU officials as to 'bring together the more security policy oriented aspects with the more political work of the [EEAS] desks and then ... connect it to DG DEVCO', thereby enhancing the link between development and security in fragile settings (Henökl and Webersik 2013: 9). The EUSR for the Horn of Africa is expected to develop and implement an EU approach to piracy, 'encompassing all strands of EU action', including development policy (Council of the European Union 2011b).

While the 2013 Communication on the Comprehensive Approach holds promise for coordinating financial with non-financial foreign policy and aid instruments at the EU's disposal in fragile situations, it also vows to render EU development policy more political and more strategic (European Commission and High Representative 2013).

When development meets politics in the nexus: more thinking, less acting

Beyond the EU's will and capacity to put the nexus at work, the real spoilers or drivers of change are above all local. The EU – like any other international donor – can unwittingly be a real facilitator, a mere bystander or even a colluder when it comes to processes of change in any fragile country, including in the neighbouring 'arc' (Ghani and Lockhart 2008). After all, 'state-building is an indigenous political process; [the EU] cannot and should not change it according to [its] own viewpoint', reminds a DG DEVCO official (Ionete 2013). However, by being 'politically smart', a development actor is better able to navigate the local rules of the game. This entails thinking and acting politically: in other words, adding 'politics' to the nexus.

Thinking politically means above all thinking outside the technical 'box' of development aid. It requires 'mainstreaming political understanding' to all sectors of development assistance, or what Carothers and De Gramont (2013: 225–251) call the 'integration' of politics. In this context, the post-Lisbon institutional reshuffle has created a 'window of opportunity' for the EU to inject politics into its development assistance, particularly through the creation of DG DEVCO's Fragility unit, the EEAS Conflict Prevention division or the European Commission's FPI service (Table 6.4). These 'focal points' on fragility and conflict have taken numerous steps to 'integrate' politics into the

EU's development work, mainly through analysis and experience sharing (Carothers and De Gramont 2013: 233). Guidance notes, for instance, have been developed on the 'use of conflict analysis in support of EU external action' as well as on 'addressing conflict prevention, peace building and security issues' in the strategic programming of external cooperation instruments (European External Action Service and European Commission 2013a; 2013b).[26] In their 'integration' efforts, these units have also assisted development staff in taking up politics in their work through capacity-building and training (European Commission 2011b).[27]

Although these mainstreaming efforts have increased attention to politics, some officials across EU institutions continue to see such activities as specific to governance-related projects and not applicable to projects focusing on economic development (Interview VII). Opinions are split on whether there is enough 'in-house' local political knowledge and on the benefits of more in-depth local insights (Hauck, Galeazzi and Vanheukelom 2013: 11).

Acting politically, on the other hand, means acting upon one's political understanding by shifting to political engagement in development assistance. This entails employing politically savvy methods, such as *inter alia* the systematic and structured use of analytical tools, which should put political complexities of local contexts at the heart of development programming and implementation (Carothers and De Gramont 2013: 125–154). Whereas the EU's development assistance was found to be insufficiently conflict-sensitive in the past 10 years, the aforementioned 'focal points' worked on developing two analytical tools, namely the EEAS's 'light touch conflict analysis' and DG DEVCO's 'Political Economy Analysis' (ADE 2011; European External Action Service and European Commission 2013a; 2013b).[28] The use of the latter was, however, recently discontinued, after its testing in six pilot countries, thereby bringing to the fore the EU's struggle to move beyond 'the temptation of the technical' and turn its rhetorical political understanding into practical political engagement. In fact, such analysis is not only sensitive to donor–beneficiary relations. It also 'confronts donor agencies with their own political economy analysis' by explicitly unravelling what the EU prefers 'not to put too formally on the table', such as the interests of its Member States or the unintended consequences of its assistance (Bossuyt 2013).

The evidence generated by the use of politically smart analytical tools is above all to be systematically fed into the programming and implementation of development work. After all, the 'Political Economy Analysis' exercise was discontinued because it was found very difficult to turn the evidence into useful recommendations (Interview V). In that sense, the EU itself recognizes that 'planning and programming documents have often contained elements of formal conflict analysis, but not always in a systematic and structured manner' (European External Action Service and European Commission 2013a: 2). The Sahel Strategy, for instance, acknowledges that 'a coherent and systematic action linking political, security and development aspects … [remains] insufficient' (Council of the European Union 2011a: 3). In this regard, a Country Evaluation in Chad concluded that the European Commission's approach was not specifically tailored to the context of fragility (ECO Consult 2007). In the Horn of Africa, the EU was found to reduce Somalia's complex gamut of stakeholders to 'plain black-and-white images' (Henökl and Webersik 2013: 14) in its 'Strategic Framework for the Horn of Africa', through its policy of distinguishing between terrorist groups, pirates and the new Somali government, itself made up of former warlords and supported by businessmen maintaining their private militias. In Yemen, Hout (2010: 154) argues that 'the Commission did not dig deep enough' to understand the root causes of fragility.

It follows that, while political thinking is more and more present, acting politically remains contingent upon a better linking up of analyses with programming. And evidence generated by smart tools often requires 'unpalatable political choices' (Faria and Sheriff 2009: 11) that neither the EU nor its partners are willing or able to make (Bossuyt 2013).

Conclusion: a toolbox without a strategy

Far from being a mere outlying stretch flanking the EU's immediate neighbourhood, an 'arc of fragility' is now the order of the day in the broader neighbourhood. Countries in the 'arc' not only display the 'wicked problems' of state fragility but also are more than ever entwined with their littoral Mediterranean neighbours, in an ever-deeper negative feedback loop of underdevelopment and insecurity.

Dealing with 'wicked' symptoms at the intersection of development and security is anything but straightforward; and development cooperation is no exception. It requires strategic policy-making, agility and political thinking and acting. Most of all, it entails more than just development as usual, but rather a certain kind of development beyond aid. Otherwise, the development actor runs the risk of descending into what Chandler (2007) termed 'anti-foreign policy'.

In this light, this chapter has probed the EU's efforts to integrate security and politics in its development cooperation with the fragile states of its broader neighbourhood. It has specifically sought to comprehend how and the extent to which the EU uses its toolbox to cope with the 'security–politics–development nexus' in the Sahel, the Horn of Africa and the Arabian Peninsula.

The European Union, albeit well equipped to deal with the nexus in the broader neighbourhood, has not gone overboard in strategically capitalizing on its toolbox. In recognition of the nexus, the EU has upped its financial commitment, fine-tuned its *modi operandi* and adapted its foreign aid instruments to the fluid nature of fragile settings. While these institutional fixes have proved to be seminal steps for a better engagement, strategic considerations have not yet found their way into the EU's development assistance in the fragile states of the 'arc'.

In that sense, its foreign aid speaks more to the time dimension of the nexus and less to its spatial dimension, although the case of the 'arc' reveals an ever more intertwined neighbourhood stretching from the Mediterranean to the southern reaches of the Sahara desert. Beyond aid, non-financial development instruments are not widely used and, where they are used, not strategically. Pro-development political dialogue, although increasing, leaves regional pivotal states aside. The CFSP toolbox, such as the appointment of EUSRs, is not particularly employed to promote pro-development policies in the 'arc'.

Conversely, the integration of politics remains a challenging endeavour for the EU. Political thinking in connection with fragility in the 'arc' is progressively finding fertile ground in EU institutions. Acting politically, however, which entails using smart tools and producing evidence, has not found particular resonance in Brussels yet. And while the long-awaited set of principles on the comprehensive approach holds promise for better engagement in fragile settings, the EU remains bereft of a consistent strategic vision for the 'arc'. Regional comprehensive approaches pile up on its officials' desks, but the EU's development assistance still displays signs of 'anti-foreign policy'.

Notes

1 The concepts of 'fragile', 'failed' or 'precarious' states are not consensual among donors. The terms 'state failure' and 'fragile states' are used interchangeably in this chapter, in concordance with the EU's fragility lexicon or jargon. For a more comprehensive analysis, see Banim (2009).

2 The 'g7+' group, inaugurated in Dili (Timor-Leste) in 2010, is an association of 18 fragile and conflict-affected countries. The group called for a New Deal for engagement in fragile states based on five peace-building and state-building goals at the 2011 Fourth High Level Forum on Aid Effectiveness in Busan. 'Nothing about us without us' was an expression used by a 'g7+' representative in Busan (Nussbaum *et al.*: 583).

3 Stewart and Brown (2009) argue that most definitions in the existing literature rally around authority, service and legitimacy failures as the main facets of state fragility.

4 The Fund for Peace 'Failed State Index' (2014) is one example of a 'fragility' classification. See http://ffp.statesindex.org.

5 Lambach (2007), for example, distinguishes between structural and dynamic cross-border linkages in order to grasp the interaction between in-house failure and its consolidation in neighbouring states.

6 Principle 5 calls for recognition of 'the links between political, security and development objectives', or the so-called 'politics–security–development nexus' (OECD DAC 2007).

7 The compilation in Table 6.1 is based on a harmonized list of fragile and conflict-affected countries drawn from the World Bank's Country Policy and Institutional Assessment for 2014, the African Development Bank's list, the UNDP Human Development Index, the Ibrahim Governance Index, the Country Indicators for Foreign Policy by Carlton University, the Fund for Peace Failed State Index and the Centre for Systemic Peace. For more information, see Cilliers and Sisk (2013).

8 Fragile states are located in only three out of the four regions of the EU's broader neighbourhood. Central Asia is therefore excluded from the analysis.

9 Or 'the strip of all threats', as described by a senior Algerian security officer. See Zoubir (2012: 452).

10 The term 'Sahelistan' has been used in the media in the wake of the French 'Operation Serval' in Mali in 2013.

11 See also Chapter 7 by Zuhal Yeşilyurt Gündüz in this volume.

12 See also Chapter 1 by Valeria Bonavita and Chapter 2 by Sarah Wolff in this volume.
13 The Tabus (like the Tuaregs) are Libya's Sahelian non-Arab minorities spreading across southern Libya and northern Chad and Niger, while the Tuaregs spread across Mali, Niger, Algeria, Libya and Burkina Faso. Culturally and ethnically different from their Libyan Arab compatriots, both Tabus and Tuaregs have faced intermittent political, economic and social exclusion from the modern government. See Cole (2013).
14 See also Chapter 4 by Gilles de Kerchove and Christiane Höhn in this volume.
15 The New Deal's five PSGs in fragile countries are: legitimate and inclusive politics, security, justice, economic foundations, and revenues and services.
16 The 'Somali Compact', launched in Brussels in September 2013, is a 'political, security and development architecture framing the future relations between Somalia, its people, and the international community' backed by pledges of €1.8 billion (Federal Republic of Somalia 2013: 3). South Sudan was expected to sign its New Deal Compact in late 2013 but hiccups in the consultations, such as the non-application of conditions imposed by the International Monetary Fund (Interview VII), delayed the process.
17 European Consensus on Development: 'Without peace and security development and poverty eradication are not possible, and without development and poverty eradication no sustainable peace will occur' (European Parliament, Council of the European Union and European Commission 2006: 7).
18 (1) Development, good governance and internal conflict resolution; (2) political and diplomatic; (3) security and the rule of law; and (4) fight against and prevention of violent extremism and radicalization.
19 The difficulties related to the institutional operationalization of the nexus are clearly illustrated by a famous dispute between the European Commission and the Council of the European Union on the legality of Council Decision 2004/833/CFSP, which was meant to provide support to the Economic Community of West African States (ECOWAS) (Merket 2012). The European Commission found that such assistance should be adopted in accordance with art. 11(3) of the Cotonou Agreement in the framework of the EU's development policy. The ruling of the European Court of Justice consequently annulled the above Decision (Council of the European Union 2004).
20 The head of the political section is the only political officer in the EU delegations of the Horn (Interview VII).
21 The inter-service agreement is confidential but main aspects on the modalities in relation to development cooperation were outlined by a DG DEVCO representative to the European Parliament's Development Committee on 25 January 2012. See www.europarl.europa.eu/ep-live/en/committees/search?legislature=7&start-date=25–01–2012&end date=25–01–2012&committee=DEVE (accessed November 2013).
22 Note that Somalia, Sudan and South Sudan are not signatories to the revised Cotonou Agreement and are therefore not eligible for development assistance under the EDF.
23 Other nexus-relevant instruments are the CFSP and the Athena instruments, but are not considered foreign aid as they are used to finance operational and military costs of CFSP/CSDP missions, therefore explicitly defending EU interests abroad (Furness and Gänzle 2012). Note that the fragile countries of the Arabian Peninsula (Yemen and Iraq) are not entitled to funds under the African Peace Facility.
24 A Common Implementing Regulation for the Union's six external instruments replaces the previous scattered rules and procedures and provides clear provisions on their complementarity, flexibility and coherence, among other things (European Parliament and Council of the European Union 2014c).
25 ODA reporting excludes, for example, peacekeeping and military aid.
26 The guidance notes were jointly developed by the EEAS Conflict Prevention division and the European Commission's Fragility unit.

27 For example, DG DEVCO 07 organizes training courses on 'Fragility, Security and Development'. Six sessions for about 360 EU security and development staff have been delivered since 2012.
28 Political economy analysis is employed where in-depth analysis of the political and economic processes, relationships and dynamics at work is required; it combines extensive desk and field research. Light-touch conflict analysis is a rather quick response to a conflict-affected setting, informing critical decision-making.

References

ADE (Aide à la Décision Economique) (2011) *Thematic Evaluation of European Commission Support to Conflict Prevention and Peace-building*, Brussels: EuropeAid/1228888/C/SER/Multi, October.

Atarodi, A. (2010) *Yemen in Crisis – Consequences for the Horn of Africa*, Stockholm: Swedish Defence Research Agency.

Banim, G. (2009) 'EU Responses to Fragile States', in S. Weiss, H.-J. Spanger and W. van Meurs (eds) *Diplomacy, Development and Defense: A Paradigm for Policy Coherence*, Gütersloh: Verlag Bertelsmann Stiftung, 303–351.

Barakat, S. and A. Larson (2014) 'Fragile States: A Donor-serving Concept? Issues with Interpretations of Fragile Statehood in Afghanistan', *Journal of Intervention and Statebuilding* 8(1) 21–41.

Barrios, C. (2013) *The Future of Security – development Cooperation between the EU and the African, Caribbean and Pacific States*, London: Conference 'Navigating the Nexus: The Interplay of EU Security and Development Policies in Africa', London: Chatham House.

Bello, O. (2012) *Quick Fix or Quicksand? Implementing the EU Sahel Strategy, Working Paper* 114, Madrid: FRIDE.

Bossuyt, J. (2013) *Is There a Future for Political Economy Analysis in the European Commission?* Maastricht: ECDPM Talking Points, www.ecdpm-talkingpoints.org/is-there-a-future-for-political-economy-analysis-in-the-european-commission (audio, accessed December 2013).

Boukhars, A. (2013) 'The Drivers of Insecurity in Mauritania', in F. Wehrey and A. Boukhars (eds) *Perilous Desert: Insecurity in the Sahara*, Washington, DC: Carnegie Endowment for International Peace, 119–143.

Büger, C. and P. Vennesson (2009) *Security, Development and the EU's Development Policy*, Florence: European University Institute.

Carment, D., S. Prest and Y. Samy (2010) *Security, Development and the Fragile State: Bridging the Gap between Theory and Policy*, London: Routledge.

Carothers, T. and D. de Gramont (2013) *Development Aid Confronts Politics: The Almost Revolution*, Washington, DC: Carnegie Endowment for International Peace.

Chandler, D. (2006) *Empire in Denial: The Politics of Statebuilding*, London: Pluto Press.

Chandler, D. (2007) 'The Security–Development Nexus and the Rise of "Anti-Foreign Policy"', *Journal of International Relations and Development* 10(4), 362–386.

Cilliers, J. and T.D. Sisk (2013) *Prospects for Africa's 26 Fragile Countries*, African Futures Paper 8, Denver: Institute for Security Studies and Freferic S. Pardee Center for International Futures.

Cole, P. (2013) 'Borderline Chaos? Stabilizing Libya's Periphery', in F. Wehrey and A. Boukhars (eds) *Perilous Desert: Insecurity in the Sahara*, Washington, DC: Carnegie Endowment for International Peace, 35–59.

Collier, P. (2008) *The Bottom Billion*, Oxford: Oxford University Press.

Collier, P. (2009) *Wars, Guns, and Votes – Democracy in Dangerous Places*, New York: Harper Collins Publishers.

Cornaro, M. (2012) Speech, Brussels, Orientation Course on Security, Fragility and Development in the Context of EU External Action, http://capacity4dev.ec.europa.eu/public-fragility/event/orientation-course-security-fragility-and-development-context-eu-external-action#sthash.m1aTiHTn.dpuf (accessed November 2013).

Council of the European Union (2004) 'Council Decision 2004/833/CFSP of 2 December 2004 Implementing Joint Action 2002/589/CFSP with a View to a European Union Contribution to ECOWAS in the Framework of the Moratorium on Small Arms and Light Weapons', *Official Journal of the European Union*, L 359, 2 December, 65–67.

Council of the European Union (2007a) *Council Conclusions on a EU response to situations of fragility*, 2831st External Relations Council meeting, Brussels, 19–20 November.

Council of the European Union (2007b) *Council Conclusions on Security and Development*, 15097/07, Brussels, 20 November.

Council of the European Union (2010) 'Council Decision of 26 July 2010 Establishing the Organisation and Functioning of the European External Action Service (2010/427/EU)', *Official Journal of the European Union*, L 201, 3 August, 30–40.

Council of the European Union (2011a) *Strategy for Security and Development in the Sahel*, Annex to the Council Conclusions on a European Union Strategy for Security and Development in the Sahel, Brussels, 21 March.

Council of the European Union (2011b) *A Strategic Framework for the Horn of Africa*, Annex to the Council Conclusions on the Horn of Africa, 3124th Foreign Affairs Council meeting, Brussels, 14 November.

DG DEVCO organisation chart (2014) https://ec.europa.eu/europeaid/organisational-structure-dg-devco_en (accessed October 2014).

ECO Consult (2007) *Evaluation de la coopération de la Commission européenne avec la République du Tchad*, EVA 2007/geo-acp, Brussels, 12 September.

EEAS organisation chart (2014) http://eeas.europa.eu/background/docs/organisation_en.pdf (accessed October 2014).

European Commission (2007) *The Instrument for Stability: Strategy Paper 2007–2011*, Brussels.

European Commission (2009) *Commission Staff Working Document Accompanying the Report from the Commission to the Council EU 2009 Report on Policy Coherence for Development*, SEC(2009) 1137 final, Brussels, 17 September.

European Commission (2010) 'Agreement Amending for the Second Time the Partnership Agreement Between the Members of the African, Caribbean and Pacific Group of States, of the one part, and the European Community and its Member States, of the other part, Signed in Cotonou on 23 June 2000, as First Amended in Luxembourg on 25 June 2005', *Official Journal of the European Union*, L 287, 4 November, 3–46.

European Commission (2011a) 'Proposal for a Regulation of the European Parliament and the Council Establishing an Instrument for Stability, COM (2011) 845 final, 2011/0413 (COD)', Brussels, 7 December.

European Commission (2011b) *Fiche Contradictoire: Evaluation of European Commission Support to Conflict Prevention and Peace-building*, Brussels.

European Commission (2012) *Instrument for Stability: Thematic Strategy Paper 2012–2013; Assistance in the Context of Stable Conditions for Cooperation*, Brussels.

European Commission (2013a) *2012 Annual Report on the Instrument for Stability*, COM (2013) 563 final {SWD (2013) 292 final}, Brussels, 26 July.

European Commission (2013b) *Annex A11a: Guidelines on Contractual Procedures to be Used in Cases of Crisis Situations under the General Budget and EDF. Practical Guide to Contract Procedures for EU External Actions (PRAG)*, Brussels.

European Commission (2014) *Commission Implementing Decision on the Annual Action Programme 2014 for the Instrument Contributing to Stability and Peace – Conflict Prevention, Peace-building and Crisis Preparedness Component (Article 4) to be Financed from the General Budget of the European Union*, C(2014) 5706 final, Brussels, 12 August.

European Commission and European External Action Service (2012) *Working Arrangements between Commission Services and the European External Action Service in Relation to External Issues*, SEC (2012) 48, Brussels, 13 January [unpublished].

European Commission and High Representative (2013) *Joint Communication to the European Parliament and the Council: The EU's Comprehensive Approach to External Conflict and Crises*, JOIN (2013) 30 final, Brussels, 11 December.

European External Action Service and European Commission (2013a) *Guidance Note on the Use of Conflict Analysis in Support of EU External Action*, Brussels.

European External Action Service and European Commission (2013b) *Addressing Conflict Prevention, Peace-building and Security Issues under External Cooperation Instruments*, Brussels.

European Parliament and Council of the European Union (2014a) 'Regulation (EU) No 233/2014 of the European Parliament and of the Council Establishing a Financing Instrument for Development Cooperation for the Period 2014–2020', *Official Journal of the European Union*, L77, 15 March, 44–76.

European Parliament and Council of the European Union (2014b) 'Regulation (EU) No 230/2014 of the European Parliament and of the Council Establishing an Instrument Contributing to Stability and Peace', *Official Journal of the European Union*, L77, 15 March, 1–10.

European Parliament and Council of the European Union (2014c) 'Regulation (EU) No 236/2014 of the European Parliament and of the Council Laying Down Common Rules and Procedures for the Implementation of the Union's Instruments for Financing External Action', *Official Journal of the European Union*, L77, 15 March, 95–108.

European Parliament, Council of the European Union and European Commission (2006) 'The European Consensus on Development', *Official Journal of the European Union*, C46, 24 February, 1–19.

European Report on Development (2009) *Overcoming Fragility in Africa*, Florence: European University Institute.

Faria, F. and A. Sheriff (2009) 'EU Policies to Address Fragility in Sub-Saharan Africa', paper prepared for the conference 'Moving Towards the European Report on Development 2009', Florence, 21–23 June.

Federal Republic of Somalia (2013) *The Somali Compact*, www.pbsbdialogue.org/The%20Somali%20Compact.pdf (accessed July 2014).

Fund for Peace (2014) *Failed States Index*, http://ffp.statesindex.org.

Furness, M. (2012) 'The Lisbon Treaty, the European External Action Service and the Reshaping of EU Development Policy', in S. Gänzle, S. Grimm and D. Makham (eds) *The European Union and Global Development: An Enlightened 'Superpower' in the Making?*, Basingstoke: Palgrave Macmillan, 74–93.

Furness, M. and S. Gänzle (2012) *The European Union's Development Policy: A Balancing Act Between a 'More Comprehensive Approach' and Creeping Securitisation*, ISL working paper 11, Agder: University of Agder.

Gänzle, S. (2012) 'Coping with the "Security–Development Nexus": The European

Union and the Instrument for Stability', in S. Gänzle, S. Grimm and D. Makham (eds) *The European Union and Global Development: An Enlightened 'Superpower' in the Making?*, Basingstoke: Palgrave Macmillan, 116–135.

Gavas, M., F. Davies, A. Mckechnie, O. Brown and E. Hefer (2013) *EU Development Cooperation in Fragile States: Challenges and Opportunities*, Brussels: European Parliament, 26 April.

Ghani, A. and C. Lockhart (2008) *Fixing Failed States*, Oxford: Oxford University Press.

Görtz, S. and N. Keijzer (2012) *Reprogramming EU Development Cooperation for 2014–2020*, Discussion Paper 129, Maastricht: European Centre for Development Policy Management.

Hauck, V., G. Galeazzi and J. Vanheukelom (2013) *The EU's State Building Contracts: Courageous Assistance to Fragile States, but How Effective in the End?*, Briefing Note 60, Maastricht: European Centre for Development Policy Management.

Helly, D. and C. Rocca (2013) *The Mali Crisis and Africa-Europe Relations*, Briefing Note 52, Maastricht: European Centre for Development Policy Management.

Henökl, T. and C. Webersik (2013) *The EU Strategic Framework for the Horn of Africa: Approaches to a Joint Humanitarian-Development Framework in the EU's Post-Lisbon Institutional Setting*, Working Paper, Kristiansand: University of Agder, www.sgir.eu/warsaw/uploads/JHDF%20paper_Hen%C3%B6kl_Webersik%20%2028%2008%20 2013.pdf (accessed November 2013).

Hout, W. (2010) 'Between Development and Security: The European Union, Governance and Fragile States', *Third World Quarterly* 31(1), 141–157.

International Crisis Group (2013) *Make or Break: Iraq's Sunnis and the State*, Middle East Report 144, Brussels/Baghdad.

Interview I, Member of the Federal Parliament of Somalia, Brussels, 8 November 2013.

Interview II, European Parliament Official, Brussels, 25 November 2013.

Interview III, EEAS Official, Brussels, 3 December 2013.

Interview IV, EEAS Official, Brussels, 3 December 2013.

Interview V, DG DEVCO Official, Brussels, 4 December 2013.

Interview VI, DG DEVCO Official, Brussels, 4 December 2013.

Interview VII, DG DEVCO Official, Brussels, 13 December 2013.

Interview VIII, DG DEVCO Official, Brussels, 13 December 2013.

Ionete, D. (2013) *Speech: EU Development Cooperation in Fragile States*, Brussels, European Parliament Development Committee, 18 December.

Joffé, G. (2012) 'The EU, the Maghreb and the Mediterranean', in A. Abedajo and K. Whiteman (eds) *The EU and Africa: From Eurafrique to Afro-Europa*, London: Hurst and Co., 137–152.

Jones, B.G. (2013) '"Good Governance" and "State Failure": Genealogies of Imperial Discourse?', *Cambridge Review of International Affairs* 26(1), 49–70.

Keukeleire, S. and K. Raube (2013) 'The Security–Development Nexus and Securitization in the EU's Policies towards Developing Countries', *Cambridge Review of International Affairs* 26(3), 556–572.

Lacher, W. (2013) 'Organized Crime and Conflict in the Sahel–Sahara Region', in F. Wehrey and A. Boukhars (eds) *Perilous Desert: Insecurity in the Sahara*, Washington, DC: Carnegie Endowment for International Peace, 61–85.

Lambach, D. (2007) 'Close Encounters in the Third Dimension: The Regional Effects of State Failure', in D. Lambach and T. Debiel (eds) *State Failure Revisited I: Globalization of Security and Neighbourhood Effects*, INEF Report 87, Duisburg: Institute for Development and Peace, 32–52.

Manning, R. and A. Trzeciak-Duval (2010) 'Situations of Fragility and Conflict: Aid Policies and Beyond', *Conflict, Security and Development* 10(1), 103–131.

Marty, A. (2013) 'Aux fondements de la crise malienne: la formation inachevée de la nation', symposium 'Quelle nouvelle gouvernance au Mali?', Paris: Assemblée Nationale.

Maxwell, D. and M. Fitzpatrick (2012) 'The 2011 Somalia Famine: Context, Causes, and Complications', *Global Food Security* 1, 5–12.

Menkhaus, K. (2010a) 'State Failure and Ungoverned Space', in M. Berdal and A. Wennmann (eds) *Ending Wars, Consolidating Peace: Economic Perspectives*, London: International Institute for Strategic Studies, 171–188.

Menkhaus, K. (2010b) 'State Fragility as a Wicked Problem', *PRISM* 1(2), 85–100.

Merket, H. (2012) 'The European External Action Service and the Nexus between CFSP/CSDP and Development Cooperation', *European Foreign Affairs Review* 17(4), 625–652.

Muggah, R. (2010) 'Stabilising Fragile States and the Humanitarian Space', in M. Berdal and A. Wennmann (eds) *Ending Wars, Consolidating Peace: Economic Perspectives*, London: International Institute for Strategic Studies, 33–52.

Nussbaum, T., E. Zorbas and M. Koros (2012) 'A New Deal for Engagement in Fragile States', *Conflict, Security and Development* 12(5), 559–587.

OECD (2012) *Stat Extracts*, stats.oecd.org.

OECD-DAC (OECD Development Assistance Committee) (2007) *Principles for Good International Engagement in Fragile States and Situations*, Paris: OECD, 4 April.

OECD-DAC (2012) *Peer Review 2012: European Union*, Paris: OECD, 28 March.

Overhaus, M. (2013) 'Security–Development Nexus: Perspectives for the EU's Next Financial Framework', *European Foreign Affairs Review* 18(4), 511–528.

Patrick, S. (2007) 'Failed States and Global Security: Empirical Questions and Policy Dilemmas', *International Studies Review* 9(4), 644–662.

Phillips, S. (2011) 'Introduction: How did it Come to This?', *Adelphi Series* 51(420), 11–24.

Simon, L., A. Mattelaer and A. Hadfield (2012) *A Coherent EU Strategy for the Sahel*, Brussels: European Parliament, DG External Policies PE 433.778, 11 May.

Smith, M. (2013) 'The European External Action Service and the Security–Development Nexus: Organizing for Effectiveness or Incoherence?', *Journal of European Public Policy* 20(9), 1299–1315.

Soliman, A., A. Vines and J. Mosley (2012) *The EU Strategic Framework for the Horn of Africa: A Critical Assessment of Impact and Opportunities*, Brussels: European Parliament, DG External Policies PE 433.799.

Stern, M. and J. Öjendal (2010) 'Mapping the Security Development Nexus: Conflict, Complexity, Cacophony, Convergence?', *Security Dialogue* 41(1), 5–30.

Stewart, F. and G. Brown (2009) *Fragile States*, Working Paper 51, Oxford: Centre for Research on Inequality, Human Security and Ethnicity.

Tannous, I. (2013) 'The Programming of EU's External Assistance and Development Aid and the Fragile Balance of Power between EEAS and DG DEVCO', *European Foreign Affairs Review* 18(3), 329–354.

Tschirgi, N. (2009) 'The Security–Politics–Development Nexus: The Lesson of Statebuilding in Sub-Saharan Africa', paper prepared for the conference 'Moving Towards the European Report on Development 2009', Florence, 21–23 June.

Turse, N. (2011) 'Obama's Global Arc of Instability', *The Nation*, 19 September.

United Nations (2004) *A More Secured World: Our Shared Responsibility*, Report of the Secretary-General's High-level Panel on Threats, Challenges and Change, New York: UNDP.

United Nations (2012) *Youth and Skills: Putting Education to Work*, EFA Global Monitoring Report 2012, Paris: UNESCO.

United Nations (2014) *Sustaining Human Progress: Reducing Vulnerabilities and Building Resilience*, Human Development Report 2014, New York: UNDP.

Van Seter, J. and H. Klavert (2011) *EU Development Cooperation after the Lisbon Treaty: People, Institutions and Global Trends*, Discussion Paper 123, Maastricht: European Centre for Development Policy Management.

Vennesson, P. and C. Büger (2009) 'Coping with Insecurity in Fragile Situations', Paper prepared for the conference 'Moving Towards the European Report on Development 2009', Florence, 21–23 June.

Wehrey, F. (2013) 'Introduction', in F. Wehrey and A. Boukhars (eds) *Perilous Desert: Insecurity in the Sahara*, Washington, DC: Carnegie Endowment for International Peace, 1–5.

Woodward, P. (2013) *Crisis in the Horn of Africa: Politics, Piracy and the Threat of Terror*, London: I.B. Tauris.

World Bank (2003) *Breaking the Conflict Trap: Civil War and Development Policy*, Washington, DC: World Bank.

Youngs, R. (2007) *Fusing Security and Development: Just Another Euro-Platitude?* Working Document 277, Brussels: Centre for European Policy Studies.

Zoellick, R.B. (2008) 'Fragile States: Securing Development', *Survival: Global Politics and Strategy* 50(6), 67–84.

Zoubir, Y. (2012) 'The Sahara–Sahel Quagmire: Regional and International Ramifications', *Mediterranean Politics* 17(3), 452–458.

Zwolski, K. (2013) *Defining the Relationship between Security and Development*, London: Chatham House, Conference 'Navigating the Nexus: The Interplay of EU Security and Development Policies in Africa'.

7 'Gendering the neighbours'

The European Union's policies on gender and equality in Saharan Africa and Central Asia

Zuhal Yeşilyurt Gündüz

Introduction

This chapter draws on a conceptual framework from gender studies and critical security studies, especially the meaning of security and the concept of human security, in order to examine the situation of women in two very different regions of the broader neighbourhood of the European Union (EU): Saharan Africa and Central Asia. It deals with three interrelated issues that are vital for both regions: colonialism and neo-colonialism; patriarchy and body politics; and women in politics. The chapter then turns to EU policies on 'gendering the neighbours' and asks how the EU constructs gender within and outside its own borders. It briefly looks at gender during the enlargement processes and within the European Neighbourhood Policy (ENP) before critically evaluating how important gender is for the EU's policies regarding 'the neighbours of its neighbours'. The chapter argues that although gender equality is a core value for the EU, it is not a 'norm' followed during the enlargement processes or neighbourhood policies. As policy-making and its processes are gendered, gender inequality is thus being reproduced again and again. The last part aims at providing well-intentioned recommendations for a more gender-inclusive, human-centred and just approach on the part of the EU towards its neighbours near and far.

Conceptual background

This section aims to present important concepts such as gender, security and human security and to introduce a gender perspective.

Gender

It was only after the 1970s that in international relations feminists began to ask the question 'where are the women?'. Women had been silenced for so long that this was difficult to answer, as in fields of power such as politics and economics, women were virtually absent. Feminists demanded the inclusion of gender in *all* spheres and the recognition that daily life and the private sphere are political.

Still, women are often ignored; if they are referred to, they are mostly considered as a homogeneous group or as passive bystanders and victims (Waylen 2006: 148). Most studies reveal a 'gender blindness, with little acknowledgement ... that gender is a constitutive force' (ibid.: 150–151).

For Judith Butler (1990: 140), 'doing' gender stands above 'being' gender, as gender is not biological but 'performative'. Gender 'is something that one does, and does recurrently in interaction with others' (West and Zimmerman 1987: 125). Thus people are 'doing gender' and society expects the constant realization of gender. As gender is constructed and performed within social, cultural and historical restrictions, it becomes an ideology that justifies social organization forms (Steans 2010: 75). By doing gender, men also 'do dominance' and women 'do deference'. This leads to a social order that legitimizes and strengthens hierarchy, as gender 'is a powerful ideological device, which produces, reproduces, and legitimates the choices and limits that are predicated on sex category' (West and Zimmerman 1987: 147).

Going beyond biological distinctions of being male or female in the term 'sex', 'gender' deals with its socio-political meanings (Shepherd 2010: 8) and includes 'the social constructions of maleness and femaleness which often translate into power relations between men and women' (Kameri-Mbote 2004: 84). Gender as an analytical concept exposes culturally shaped and learned definitions about femininity and masculinity. In most cultures gender differences signify relations of inequality, the power and dominance of men and the oppression of women (Cockburn 2010: 108). Gender is 'also a logic, which is produced by and productive of the ways in which we understand and perform global politics' (Shepherd 2010: 5).

Gender leans on patriarchy, going beyond the 'rule of the father' to a more general 'rule by men' in the private and the public area. Patriarchy 'uses law, tradition, force, ritual, customs, education, language, labour (etc.) to keep women governed by men in both public and private life' (Salami 2012b). Femininity has to be formed so as to ensure women's conformity and alliance in this 'patriarchal project'. It is clear that the hierarchical patriarchal social orders, where 'men and masculinity are authoritative, combative and prone to coercion, while women and femininity are submissive, supportive and nurturing, are particularly fitted to the needs of militarist and nationalist societies and cultures' (Cockburn 2010: 108).

Security

Until the 1990s, the notion of security in international relations has been state-centric, with 'security' meaning the security, protection and territorial integrity of the state. Security was thought to be the absence of violent conflict, no more and no less. With the end of the Cold War, hopes for a more peaceful world did not come true as territorial, ethnic and religious conflicts arose. Moving beyond the limitations of national security, new ideas about 'common security' emerged (King and Murray 2002: 588), which include political, economic and ecological factors and entail the 'elimination of physical, structural, and ecological violence' (Tickner 1992: 22). This consideration goes beyond the dichotomy between war and peace and the simplistic definition of peace as absence of war. Indeed, 'from the masculine perspective, peace for the most part has meant the absence of war' (Reardon 1990: 137). But this is a minimalistic version of peace – 'negative peace' – that cannot be sustained, let alone developed.

In violent conflicts and wars, women and children suffer most. Leading to refugee crises, systematic war rape and prostitution, wars have detrimental effects on women (Tickner 2001: 47–61). Whereas at the beginning of the twentieth century around 10 per cent of war casualties were women and children, the percentage rose to 80 to 90 per cent by the end of the century (Tickner and Sjoberg 2007: 193). Even when a war ends, nothing is over – poverty, starvation, diseases follow wars, and women suffer the most.

For peace scholar Johan Galtung (1969: 167–191), systematic exclusion, marginalization and exploitation lead to structural violence, which is a situation where marginalized people are destined to have shorter, less wealthy and less healthy lives because of the unequal and unjust distribution of resources. Structural violence refers to people's economic insecurity resulting from internal and international structures of political and economic oppression. Consequently, peace researchers doubt that states' territorial and economic security is identical with people's physical and economic security (Tickner 1992: 69).

For women, security means absence of all kinds of violence, 'whether it be military, economic or sexual' (ibid.: 66), and security from sexism, discrimination, poverty, domestic and state violence. It entails the realization of positive peace, internalizing 'conditions of social justice, economic equity and ecological balance' (Reardon 1990: 138), where all violence, conflict and war-related factors are abolished and then a real, lasting peace can emerge. Security thus incorporates the elimination of poverty, environmental degradation, and economic and social concerns (Mwagiru 2004: xv). Consequently, real security can only be realized when gender relationships of dominance and subordination are eradicated (Tickner 1992: 22–23) and a multilevel security is constructed that eliminates violence at all levels – physical, structural and ecological (Tickner and Sjoberg 2007: 193).

The contemplation of multi-layered violence enables a critical review of conventional definitions of the state and the connection of domestic violence to regional, state and global violence. For women, security can be defined as 'freedom from danger, fear or anxiety' (Kameri-Mbote 2004: 84). Considering security from this perspective reveals that insecurity is built upon unjust economic development and access to resources. With disregard for their contributions to production, women mostly are set apart from decision-making, resulting in a worsening of their insecurities and the perception of women as victims of insecurity instead of active agents who are able to enhance security and peace (ibid.: 86).

Considering the ties between social, military, economic and environmental security, it becomes clear how gender hierarchies and their connection with race, ethnicity and culture intensify women's insecurities (Tickner and Sjoberg 2007: 192). Gender as an analytical and political device reveals that accounts about femininity are also accounts about masculinity. Consequently, changing conceptions about women's security alter insights into men's security, too. A feminist definition/re-definition of security, where the existence of one rests on the safety of another, would boost both women's and men's security and well-being (Hudson 2005: 156).

Feminists try to challenge and overcome disparities (Waylen 2006: 147) as to realize social justice, including women's equal participation in economic and political power (Duncan *et al.* 2002: 453). Economic, social, military and ecological insecurities can only be terminated when hierarchical social and gender relations are overcome. Consequently, achieving 'peace, economic justice, and ecological sustainability is inseparable from overcoming social relations of domination and subordination; genuine security requires not only the absence of war but also the elimination of unjust social relations, including unequal gender relations' (Tickner 1992: 128). There is no separation between gender insecurities and other insecurities. By defeating women's oppression, these insecurities will also be ended, as 'social justice, including gender justice, is necessary for an enduring peace' (ibid.: 129).

Human security

2014 marked the twentieth anniversary of a concept that still waits to be implemented globally – the vision of 'human security'. In 1990, the United Nations Development Programme (UNDP) initiated its Human Development Reports (HDRs).[1] Since then, UNDP has been publishing the annual HDRs with a Human Development Index (HDI) based on available data on longevity, education and standards of living.

The 1994 HDR introduced and defined human security as 'safety from such chronic threats as hunger, disease and repression' and 'protection from sudden and hurtful disruptions in the patterns of daily life – whether in homes, in jobs or in communities' (UNDP 1994: 23). It underlined that '[f]or most people today, a feeling of insecurity arises more from worries about daily life.... Job security, income security, health security, environmental security, security from crime, these are the emerging concerns of human security' (ibid.: 3). This notion is very close to feminist ideas of the personal being political.

For supporters of human security, the realist state-centric definition of security has become outdated, as it disregards how much states themselves are sources of insecurity for people and conceals the many non-military threats people face in their daily lives (Thomas 2001: 161). Therefore, human security alters the focus of security from state-centric to people-centric and highlights the state's responsibility to care for the lives, rights and well-being of its citizens. The two main goals of human security – 'freedom from fear' (protection) and 'freedom from want' (empowerment) (UNDP 1994: 24) – symbolize the principles of guaranteeing survival and basic human needs as well as human dignity.

Human security also means liberation from repressive power structures at the social, local, national or global levels (Thomas 2001: 161–162). A gender-sensitive vision of human security connects women's daily practices with regional, national and global political structures and processes and reveals the responsibility of states/global governance structures for humans'/women's insecurities (Hudson 2005: 164).

A gender perspective

The United Nations has adopted some important international instruments, such as the Universal Declaration of Human Rights (1948), the International Covenant on Civil and Political Rights (1966) and the International Covenant on Social, Economic, and Cultural Rights (1966). All these instruments entail a broad range of rights, such as the right to life and access to health care, education and water. Women achieved the acceptance of the indivisibility of human rights and the significance of all categories of rights, as 'there is no respect for human rights if people can vote but not eat, or if people have access to health care but cannot say what they think' (Kaiser 2006: 475–476). Women's activism made possible attainments such as the Convention on the Elimination of all forms of Discrimination Against Women (CEDAW, 1979) and the Vienna Declaration (1973), stating that women's rights are human rights.

In 1997 the UN's Economic and Social Council defined the concept of gender mainstreaming as the 'process of assessing the implications for women and men of any planned action, including legislation, policies or programmes' and highlighted the importance of 'making women's as well as men's concerns and experiences an integral dimension of the design, implementation, monitoring and evaluation of policies and programmes in all political, economic and societal spheres' (UN ECOSOC 1997) with the final goal of reaching full gender equality.

Women have rights as humans as well as rights as women. Women's rights are 'two sides of the same coin: they are an integral part of the fundamental human rights of all human beings, and they are about safeguarding the specific needs of women' (EuroMeSCo 2006: 13). As gender discrimination is entangled in political, social, cultural and economic structures, it goes deeper than legal restrictions. Offering formal equality by legal amendments and reforms cannot therefore be enough, as it does not consider women's special needs and problems. By applying special treatment, distributive justice could be advanced to reach real gender equality (Kameri-Mbote 2004: 88). Consequently, art. 4 CEDAW states these 'temporary special measures aimed at accelerating de facto equality between men and women shall not be considered discrimination' (quoted in ibid.: 88–89). What is necessary is a true gender approach that bears in mind the gendered varieties of roles, responsibilities and access to resources. Gender mainstreaming requires evaluation of the differing implications of policies and the planning and implementing of policies that promote and enhance gender equality.

Ethnocentricism vs. cultural relativism

A study of gender issues in different regions has to be aware of two connected dangers. First, the study should not be ethnocentric. Ethnocentrism is the tendency of societies to put their own cultures at the centre and to consider these to be superior to other cultural practices.[2] Postcolonial feminists warn 'white' Western feminists of repeating what men have so often done: namely to write (his)story/ies from their perspective. Postcolonial feminism is a critique of Western depictions of 'Third World' women as pitiable, un- or undereducated, victimized and passive bystanders (Tickner and Sjoberg 2007: 192). Hence, accounts on gender in differing regions should be aware of evaluation from an ethnocentric, standardized perspective.

Second, the study should also avoid cultural relativism, which is a method by which diverse cultures or societies are evaluated without applying the values and norms of one's own culture to judge and evaluate, on the principle that cultures can only be appreciated when they are studied in terms of their own values and norms. Cultural relativism refers to the idea that purpose and significance of any social characteristic is relative to its own cultural background.[3] However, cultural relativism could include other dangers, such as accepting a lower, subordinated position by claiming that this is the 'maximum' to be reached for women in this or that region. Here the danger of discrimination and belittling become clear.

To avoid ethnocentrism some go as far as to doubt whether the attempt to improve gender equality on a global basis is an 'unnecessary interference from Western do-gooders, and is tantamount to cultural imperialism' (Constanza 2011). Relativist arguments, such as those that women appear to be oppressed according to Western values, but not by 'their own' values, can then be put forward. However, this view disregards that gender roles constantly assign women oppressed positions and men dominating powers and thus restrain women's choices. Cultural relativism and its consequences can even imply that varying ideals ought to be applied to varying groups, depending on their regions. This then would mean that the rights that women in the West enjoy need not be spread to women elsewhere, due to their specific cultures. Consequently, this would mean that women in some places are being denied the rights that women in other places take for granted (ibid.).

Feminism appreciates differing ways of viewing the world and sees multiple layers of identities. As gender is entangled with other identities such as ethnicity, class and nationality, feminists triumph over the dichotomy between cultural relativism and universalism and unite individuals' experiences with broader regional and global structures or processes (Hudson 2005: 158). Feminism is thus the way to overcome ethnocentrism and cultural relativism.

Gender issues in the EU's neighbours' neighbours

This section deals with three interconnected topics that have so far mostly been neglected in the EU's neighbourhood policies but that have affected Saharan

Africa and Central Asia deeply from the past to today, namely colonialism and neo-colonialism, patriarchy and body politics, and women in politics.

Gender issues in Saharan Africa

Saharan Africa, extending from the Atlantic Ocean to the Horn of Africa on the Red Sea, experiences drought, poverty, human rights problems and low human development.[4] Women face a 'power gap' (Okome 2013). At the same time, Saharan Africa has women state leaders and high female representation in parliaments. Hence, there is a wide diversity that needs to be understood. Studies have to avoid simplification as 'generalisation inevitably leads to inaccuracies. The perception of African cultures as necessarily similar, and inherently beset by misogyny, is misguided and damaging' (Constanza 2011).

Colonialism/neo-colonialism

Western constructions of Africa are often those of backwardness and

> indigenously-generated poverty.... But from the perspective of many Africans, the starting point ... originates from the fact that Europeans landed with a loud crash in the middle of their neighbourhoods and required the local population to start doing things differently.
>
> (Flynn 2013)

Colonization is destructive. 'Foreigners overrun a territory with force and take it over. They install their own government, staffed by their own nationals. The inhabitants are forced ... to adopt the colonizers' cultural practices' (Goldstein 2005: 472). The end of colonization brings formal independence, but it is not a real end; rather it is the beginning of neo-colonialism – 'the continuation of colonial exploitation without formal political control' (ibid.: 475).

African leaders opted for Western types of patriarchy instead of their own traditional cultural forms that allocated women larger partaking in decision-making, which worsened women's positions (Mikell 1997). The idea of 'male head of household' and the conservative Western division of labour along gender lines was introduced by development aid programmes. Esther Boserup's research on the consequences of modernization policies on women reveals the disastrous effects of those policies and reviews critically the notion of development as *the* big remedy to poverty and key to growth (Tickner 1992: 76). She highlights that rural women's position deteriorated the further this process went and the more Western capitalism and culture were forced upon them, as women's traditional ways of cultivating crops were belittled by colonizers.

However, more than half of the world's food – in sub-Saharan Africa even up to 80 per cent – is produced by women (Food and Agriculture Organization n.d.). Women plant subsistence crops, the basis for their survival, whereas men (are forced to) prefer cash crops for generating limited income. Considered to be 'unscientific', rural women's traditional agricultural knowledge is ignored by development experts. Western development policies concentrated on industrialization for economic growth. Here, however, gender hierarchies became even more pronounced as many women found themselves in unskilled, badly paid and insecure factory jobs (Tickner 1992: 77).

The neoliberal development model, focusing on the market, free trade and export-led growth strategies, that was forced upon many less developed countries, entails continued high growth rates in order for poverty to decline. Disregarding the difficulties of sustaining growth, it is not evident how high growth rates can directly reduce poverty, how benefits and costs will be distributed or whether this model can really improve the lives and human security of people (Thomas 2001: 160–161). Besides, this model resulted in unemployment increases, the shutting down of many small firms in traditional sectors, the movement from subsistence crops and food production for local markets to export-oriented cash crops (with which a state cannot feed its population) and increasingly heavy burdens of government debt (Sassen 2001: 101–102).

Eliminations of state subsidies, cuts in life-sustaining areas (nutrition and housing) and cuts in essential investments for a better future (health and education) had detrimental effects on women. The unequal distribution of resources and power hindered their development and put them under pressure to find ways to ensure their families' survival. Among the alternatives were subsistence crops and food production, informal work, migration and prostitution (ibid.: 102–103).

Patriarchy and body politics

Africa has been facing high and fast population growth for a long time, which makes it difficult to provide public goods for more and more people. The prime reason behind this rise is patriarchy – here in the form of body politics, with the state, government, society, institutions, families, husbands all cooperating to control women's bodies. The perseverance of sexism and social and institutional gender inequality can be blamed on resistance to change. As gender is a vital component of culture, changing visions about it for many are identical to deserting their cultures and identities, which is the greatest impediment to equality and clarifies 'why women are often as culpable as men in perpetuating gender inequality' (Constanza 2011).

Gender norms forced upon women demand early marriages and large families. Women mostly are not in a position to decide about childbearing as social pressures require big families to boost one's social standing. The 'unmet need for contraception' (Zlatunich 2011) due to poor health systems, lack of information and social norms leads to high fertility and high maternal mortality rates. Moreover, lacking access to contraceptives causes unintended pregnancies. The earlier a girl gets married, the more pregnancies and the higher health risks she is likely to have. Most probably this will halt her education process, which will make it difficult for her to find better job opportunities. In this way the poverty cycle will be perpetuated.

Another predicament and human rights violation is the widespread tradition of female genital mutilation, performed on young girls before puberty. Estimates state globally 140 million girls and women undergo this torture (Salami 2013a). One hundred million were Africans, with the highest rates in Sudan and Somalia, which are among the nine countries (alongside Cameroon, the Democratic Republic of the Congo, Gambia, Liberia, Mali, Nigeria and Sierra Leone) that have not outlawed it so far. Hereby the whole or a part of the clitoris is removed surgically to limit or end women's sexual drives (ibid.). This sexist practice is continued because 'total control of a woman's life must be achieved, even at the expense of her mental and physical health' (Henry 2010).

Rape is another predicament women face. Moreover, HIV/AIDS affects women in the region immensely. Patriarchal structures lead to male dominance, which puts women under higher risk of contracting HIV as their subordinated position hinders them from refusing sexual relations with an infected partner or insisting on the use of condoms (Steinitz and Ashton 2007: 217).

Women in politics

Whereas gender mainstreaming was debated globally in the 1980s, it had been raised by Jacqueline Ki-Zerbo from Burkina Faso as early as 1960 at a UN meeting (Tripp 2013). African women's organizations have carried out unique campaign methods and battles for quotas and constitutional reforms. By doing so, they have influenced and inspired international feminism. 'Far from following a trajectory that seeks to "catch up" with Western feminism, several African countries and social groups have forged their own conceptions of equality and provided models for the rest of the world to follow' (ibid.).

The African Union (AU) has named this decade (2010–20) the 'Decade of African Women' (Frostrup 2011). And indeed, women have already achieved a lot in this decade. With Ellen Johnson-Sirleaf, Africa saw its first woman president in Liberia in 2006. In 2012, Joyce Banda became president of Malawi; in September 2013, Senegal elected its first woman prime minister, Aminata Touré. 2013 marked the fiftieth Anniversary of the AU. This was also the year when the AU Commission elected a woman as its head, Nkosazana Dlamini-Zuma, who highlights that '[t]he African continent is increasingly seen as the continent of the future and we need to applaud the prominent role that women are playing in running the affairs and shaping the destiny of the continent' (quoted in Lythgoe 2013). It is interesting to note that in 1999 *The Economist* had defined Africa as the 'hopeless continent', whereas in 2011 its headline proclaimed: 'Africa Rising: The Hopeful Continent' (ibid.).

Women's representation in legislatures in many African countries is very high – higher than in many 'developed' countries. In the 2008 national elections, Rwanda had achieved 56 per cent female representation; in the 2013 elections this rose to a global record of 64 per cent (Salami 2013b). In Senegal, Seychelles and South Africa women's representation is over 40 per cent, in Angola, Mozambique, Tanzania and Uganda over 35 per cent (Tripp 2013). 'Unlike many other rights, which are dictated from a top-down international (and often Western) level, Africa has actively enhanced global understandings of feminism' (ibid.).

Feminism is as much a component of Africa as the fight against imperialism and injustice (Salami 2012a). Women participated in liberation struggles against colonialism and patriarchy. However, after independence was won, women's organizations were bound to patronage politics of the single-political party state and concentrated on issues such as welfare and development, mostly shunning political engagement. Grassroots activism focused on increasing literacy, farming, income-generating projects and cultural activities (Tripp 2013).

The UN Decade for Women 1975–85 strengthened women through feminist activism and scholarship (Salami 2013c). The 1985 UN Conference on Women in Nairobi and the 1995 UN Conference on Women in Beijing provided new impetus for women's movements and activists. In addition, international donors, aware of state corruption and misuse, transferred their resources to non-governmental organizations, especially women's organizations. After the 1990s feminists broadened their agendas towards political involvement and legislative changes and were active in the democratization processes. The road towards multiparty systems and the general diminishing of violent conflict after 2000 facilitated women's rights (Tripp 2013) and led to feminism spreading into policy, legislation and culture via grassroots and intellectual activism (Salami 2013c).

Women's mounting presence in African parliaments and governments led to global debates about novel methods to increase women's political representations. In Senegal, as an example, the percentage of women parliamentarians climbed from 23 per cent to 43 per cent in the elections of 2012 as a result of the new parity law, which guaranteed that candidate lists would rotate female and male candidates. The 'Conseil Sénégalais des Femmes' had campaigned for this law for over a decade. Following this line, instead of the incremental model of rising women's representation which brought many women into Nordic parliaments after the 1970s, the innovative 'fast track' African model with electoral quotas was adopted by many countries. Another successful method, followed by other states, was the implementation of 'gender budgets' in many African countries to turn gender connotations into a main concern of national spending (Tripp 2013).

2014 marked also the twentieth year of democracy in South Africa. Whereas during the apartheid regime women suffered triple oppression on the basis of colour, gender and class, 'gender equality is now a constitutional imperative' (Williams 2013). Progressive legislation such as the Promotion of Equality and Prevention of Unfair Discrimination Act, the Domestic Violence Act and the Sexual Offences Act all aimed at improving women' position. Before the first democratic elections in 1994 women had a representation of 2.7 per cent; in 1994 the number rose to 27.7 per cent; in 1999, 30 per cent; in 2004, 32.7 per cent; in 2009 it reached 42 per cent (Williams 2013); and in the 2014 elections it climbed up to nearly 50 per cent (Johnston 2014).

Gender issues in Central Asia

Kazakhstan, Kyrgyzstan, Tajikistan, Turkmenistan and Uzbekistan are the five former Soviet republics commonly referred to as Central Asia. In December 1991 they gained their independence, but they remained connected by social infrastructure. They have in common countless impacts from their Soviet past despite varying social, political and economic conditions (Swan 2009). Deeply attached by shared aims and common hopes, they have their own distinctive characteristics and challenges on gender. As elsewhere, times of transition affect women more than men (Bassiuoni 2011: 32–33).

In Kazakhstan minor steps towards democratization have been made, but the road remains long. This is even truer for the other four republics (Shakirova 2007: 1). Rather than seeing the region as a similar 'bloc', divergences between Tajikistan, Uzbekistan and Turkmenistan on the one hand and Kazakhstan and Kyrgyzstan on the other should be noticed, as the first three reveal increasing conservatism, which leads to 'reconsolidation of traditional gender roles [that] became a part of the new national identity' (Güneş-Ayata and Ergun 2009: 215).

In the early excitement about the end of the Cold War, scholars neither in the East nor in the West expected gender issues to be among the most challenging issues of transition. Yet this has indeed been the case. Women outnumber men in unemployment and are at the margins of governmental, political and public spheres. Still, thanks to women's universal literacy, their participation in the labour force and politics and their involvement in global women's movements, they have tried to respond to these developments and are not only victims in this process but also agents of change and transformation (Ishkanian 2003: 474–475).

Colonialism and neo-colonialism

Colonialism and its legacy have left their mark in all parts of Central Asia. The Soviet intrusion into Central Asian societies, including social institutions and conceptions, had both its advantages and disadvantages. The Soviet goal of gender equality led to the building of egalitarian institutions and resulted in unique chances for women in education and work. Conversely, Soviet efforts of equality and emancipation led to an increase in conservative roles for women as signs of cultural and national identity (Ishkanian 2003: 477–478).

Communist Party leaders did not much consider feminism or gender issues. What they contemplated was the anticipated economic and political alteration of the society following the transformation of women (ibid.: 477–478). With this aim, the regime in the 1920s abolished restrictions on women's rights and freedoms and adopted legislation on civil marriage, divorce, maternity payments, childcare services etc. By doing so, it offered women social and economic gains such as education, employment and political representation via a quota system. Formally, women received equal rights. However, this did not bring real gender equality, as they had to carry the double burden of domestic work and care work along with paid employment. The leaders' aim was not their liberation, but to turn them into workers within the Communist system (ibid.: 478–479) and to construct an economically dynamic, well-educated and Russified/Sovietized population (Swan 2009).

By 1926, the Soviet regime considered legislative reforms to be inadequate and decided to run the brutal, interventionist Hujum campaign (Ishkanian 2003: 480). On International Women's Day of 8 March 1927 women were forced to publicly drop their head-to-toe veils and burn them. This campaign went furthest in Uzbekistan and Tajikistan. 'Given the varied meanings applied to the veil, the tenacity with which it was both attacked and defended becomes more understandable' (Northrop n.d.). With Hujum, the Soviet elite tried to restrict traditional culture to the private sphere, while in public the new secularized Soviet identities were presented (Akiner 1997: 261) as part of the transformation of society. No other Soviet policy in Central Asia had resulted in such vehement opposition (ibid.: 271). While unveilings strengthened Muslim resentment towards the Soviet regime, they made cultural change harder as antagonism against women's liberation became more visible (Northrop n.d.).

By the 1930s, indoctrination and violence had stopped public resistance against Soviet reforms; in private, however, traditional behaviour, including gendered roles, were kept. Women began tertiary education and joined professional employees. Pro-women employment preferences initiated promotions in business and politics. Maybe the transformations were perceived as being too quick, which made women persevere more firmly with customs and traditions at home. Thus, gender roles could not be completely redefined and Central Asia was, and still is, a mixture of tradition and Western(ized) modernity (Swan 2009).

The end of Communism and Soviet rule in 1991 brought new opportunities but also tough impediments. Although the transformation towards free market economies and parliamentary democracies affected all, women were more deeply distressed, for instance by cuts in social services benefits in education and health. The revitalization of traditional conservative ideals made women's lives harder. Many suffered violence, oppression and discrimination. Besides, Central Asia endures human rights problems that affect women indirectly, such as corruption, nepotism, economic insecurities, pervasive poverty, insufficient infrastructure in education, health services and transportation, and media censorship (Bassiuoni 2011: 32–33).

Patriarchy and body politics

Universal literacy was a goal that was largely reached during Soviet times, with women being even better and more highly educated than men. By the 1980s they made up 54 per cent of students in higher education and over 61 per cent of professional experts with higher or specialized education (Ishkanian 2003: 482). Still, however, as in other regions, women had to carry the double burden of employment and homework. Since independence women face predicaments in trying to achieve all – jobs plus care for families and homes (Akiner 1997: 281).

The impact of free market reforms on women was tougher since conventional gender concepts about women's and men's roles and responsibilities outline the types of employment that these can take, which is true even in the former Soviet states. Due to their governments' economic maladministration, women suffered a deterioration of living standards and faced sexism, discrimination and violence. According to a report by the World Bank (2014), '[w]omen's low participation in politics, gender inequality under the law, and gender-based violence remain the top areas of concern, and where more work is needed'.

What had been promised and what had come true were two differing stories. Absolute poverty and social polarization increased. Although women's economic activity remains quite high with around 80 women per 100 men, they often receive only 60 to 80 per cent of men's average salaries and are limited by the 'glass-ceiling effect' that keeps them away from decision-making positions and politics (International Labour Organization 2008).

Women suffered most from the economic transition towards a free market economy, facing high unemployment, increases in poverty and loss of socio-economic safety provisions, including maternal and childcare aid and worsening gender inequalities. Even a decade after their independence, the former Soviet republics in Central Asia were still among the 'Medium Human Development' grouping in the UNDP Human Development Index and thus among 'developing' countries. This process, known as de-development or de-modernization, led to concerns and worries among people (Ishkanian 2003: 483).

Besides, the capitalist reforms and neoliberal economic principles themselves are in no way gender-neutral. As they aim at a free market economy, untouched by state intervention, and the growth of profit as opposed to the well-being of humans, they do not lead to collective economic programmes aiming at equality and solidarity – ideals that would make women's lives easier. For international financial institutions, which insist on those neoliberal reforms, the distresses are unavoidable and just temporary. However, in Central Asia, a long time has passed, but people still suffer and try to survive poverty, with women suffering more as adjustment policies hit them harder (Moghadam 2000: 31–32). Thus the transition towards capitalist economies has disadvantaged women and worsened gender inequality. The decline in employment possibilities and the deterioration of working conditions made finding employment so difficult for women that they are more inclined to work in less prestigious jobs such as small-size shuttle trade or as merchants in markets and bazaars (Ishkanian 2003: 485).

Religion is being ever more politicized. In Tajikistan, increased Islamization led to demands on women and girls 'to abandon their European clothes in favour of native costumes, or in other words to "desovietize" themselves' (Ishkanian 2003: 486). This was considered as a move towards a return and restoration of women's pre-Soviet identities. Women in Central Asia therefore face two opposing legacies – that of the former Soviet Union and that of the emancipation process, including the politicization of Islam. In these circumstances, some want to keep their personal freedom while others wish to return to religious roots (Akiner 1997: 263).

Women in politics

Central Asian countries are characterized by strong presidential rule, propped up by family and clan ties and patronage relations. The leaders have a strong say and control over public life, which generated some stability over the transition period. Remembering the past, people are suspicious of politicians and politics, which limits political participation (Akiner 2002: 21).

All five countries have signed international treaties for gender equality and women's rights, such as the CEDAW. The signing was necessary for their integration with the West, 'thereby becoming a yardstick for a country's prestige in the international community' (Güneş-Ayata and Ergun 2009: 220) and thus aimed at showing that they were on their road towards 'Westernization' and globalization. However, quite often the requirements of international agreements are not implemented and 'many believe it's little more than a cosmetic attempt to enhance the countries' images abroad' (Altymysheva and Krastev 2014).

Even though women were decisive in the independence movements in Central Asia, since independence they have lost their former high representation in local and national governments. In particular the double burden of job plus household, gendered roles and responsibilities and the thought that politics is 'men's work' and 'dirty' all lead to low female participation. Although this problem is not restricted to the region, considering the Soviet legacy on women's rights and participation, a greater political representation of women at local and national levels could at least be expected. Instead, women mostly prefer non-governmental organizations, where they can work toward personal and social goals while simultaneously reiterating gender roles and gendered divisions of labour (Ishkanian 2003: 487).

Although Central Asian states are criticized for their poor human rights records[5] and high corruption, one thing applauded by many is the gender balance in politics. As an example, Uzbekistan, usually at the lowest levels in human rights and transparency indexes, set up a 30 per cent quota for female parliamentarians. In Tajikistan, government agencies have to take on at least one woman to a high-ranking position. Kazakhstan and Turkmenistan do not have quota systems, but try to achieve gender balance and posit women in many high-ranking posts (Altymysheva and Krastev 2014). Women are considered to be less corrupt and more responsible, 'cleaner' indeed, which leads to more encouragement of women. In white-collar professions and among university students, gender balance has been kept successfully, too. But the growing impact of Islam also changes ideas about women's responsibilities with an increase in conservative notions (ibid.). Most women in high positions still come from the generation that received education during Soviet times. Quotas facilitate the upholding of women's rights. Nevertheless, women may be present within the government, but they are nearly absent from 'powerful' ministries and mostly to be found in 'softer' – more feminine? – fields such as health, education or culture. Sometimes gender quotas are misused by government officials to install their female family members in posts for which they may or may not be qualified (ibid.).

The media, by constantly presenting women's predicaments, such as poverty, unemployment, discrimination and violence, constructs women as a 'negative problem'. Feminists demand change in order to reach social policies and social justice (Shakirova 2007: 2). Problematic are also statements about democratic change that do not acknowledge that 'development does not change the essence of political and public patriarchy. We lived and still live in a political environment that is unfriendly to the idea of gender equality and democratic parity' (ibid.: 3).

Anara Moldosheva, a Kyrgyz gender expert, names gendered prejudices and the prevalent power system as main targets of the women's movement. She compares mainstream organizations' tactics with the fairy tale figure Dyuimovochka Thumbelina, the tiny little girl, who is 'a weak victim of circumstances who waits for her prince (i.e. social protection, state paternalism, men's patronage)' (quoted in Shakirova 2007: 3). Yet there are many women's movements that cooperate actively with global networks and can quickly mobilize women for actions (ibid.: 3–4). So far, however, laws on gender equality and domestic violence were adopted quite slowly. There is also a discrepancy between political rhetoric on gender and its practical implementations. Alexandra Sorokopud highlights that gender equality

> should not be artificially imposed from outside. It should be exercised in line with the needs of every cultural group, its realities and a situation as related to gender, class, ethnos and culture with a preservation of local philosophy, background and identities.
>
> (quoted in ibid.: 5)

The influence of Western women's movements in the region has been limited as many women consider them as 'yet another colonial ideology' (ibid.: 5). Over time, however, with sustainable development being ensured, women's positions can advance and they can find their own balance between family-orientated custom and personal freedom and development (Swan 2009).

The EU and 'gendering' the neighbourhood (policy)

Gender on the EU level

As 'a young normative power, which is slowly transforming itself from an economic community into a post-national political actor' (Peto and Manners 2006: 98), the EU constructs its identity on universal human values. On the EU level, equality between men and women is a fundamental right in the Charter of Fundamental Rights and a core value of the EU's founding Treaties.

Formal equality is among the most advanced areas within EU policy action. Especially in social and employment policy, the EU is a leader in promoting formal equality. This goes back to the Rome Treaty art. 119, which stated that '[e]ach Member State shall ... ensure and subsequently maintain the application of the principle that men and women should receive equal pay for equal work'. This was the starting point for further gender equality legislation, including social security measures, child-care facilities etc. However, it brought a predicament with it: 'because equality of sexes was defined in an employment context, this pre-determined the site and the means through which gender equality might be achieved' (Peto and Manners 2006: 98).

The UN Decade for Women 1975–85 led the European Commission to launch its rather conservative 'Women in Development' approach. During the UN's Fourth World Conference on Women in Beijing in 1995, the EU's emphasis shifted towards 'Gender and Development' and gender mainstreaming aimed at involving women's voices and integrating gender issues in development cooperation (Peto and Manners 2006: 108). The EU put forward an advanced commitment to gender equality in the Amsterdam Treaty, art. 3(2), which made gender equality no longer only a recommendation but a principle that required mainstreaming into all Community policies (ibid.: 100). Aiming at gender equality, the Council of Europe defined gender mainstreaming as the

> (re)organisation, improvement, development and evaluation of policy processes, so that a gender equality perspective is incorporated in all policies at all levels and at all stages.... In concrete terms, this implies that the needs, interests, competence and skills of both women and men are taken into account.
>
> (Council of Europe 1998: Appendix 2)

This principle incorporated the vision that women would not be asked to adjust to institutions that advantage men, but that 'gendered structures shall be changed in order to become more women friendly' (Roth 2004: 120). Bretherton (2002: 6) highlights that gender mainstreaming measures do not 'merely seek to add women to a particular context ... [but] seek to change the context itself' and to alter 'the systems and structures of discrimination' (Peto and Manners 2006: 99).

Gender in enlargement policies

The EU approaches norms about gender on a multi-layered basis – from 'very committed' at the EU level to 'less and less interested' in the relations with its neighbours. As gender equality is such a well-recognized and well-promoted legal norm within the EU, the EU could be expected to be 'a powerful values actor and indeed a norm entrepreneur' (David and Guerrina 2013: 56) and to encourage the principle outside its borders among its neighbours.

During each enlargement process, expectations of the new EU members have changed according to their own achievements in the area of gender equality. Whereas Scandinavian women were troubled that membership would water down gender equality laws, applicants with less developed women's rights anticipated an improvement in gender equality and women's representation (Roth

2004: 119). However, the top priority of EU accession negotiations was not gender, but 'social and economic reforms based on neo-liberal principles that were lacking a gender perspective' (ibid.: 121). The fact that negotiations were continued and finalized even in cases where accession states did not accomplish the gender *acquis* reveals that the EU was not able to promote its own gender norms and 'failed either to extend or consolidate these norms' (David and Guerrina 2013: 53).

Gender in the European Neighbourhood Policy

The ENP's main aims were laid down in the Commission Communication on 'Wider Europe': '1. to enhance relations … on the basis of shared values; 2. to develop a zone of prosperity and friendly neighbourhood – a ring of friends; and 3. to promote reform, sustainable development and trade' (European Commission 2003). Thus the EU aimed at defining its borders and finalizing future enlargement in addition to answering challenges and concerns regarding security. Further, through the ENP, the EU attempted to respond to critique about the EU as a hegemonic and imperialistic power (David and Guerrina 2013: 57–58). One unintended consequence of these three objectives, however, was 'releasing the EU from the need to press further in respect of adhering to its own norms' (ibid.: 57).

Whereas the accession process necessitates a 'conditionality' to adhere to, in its relations with its neighbours the EU has altered its policies towards 'joint ownership', which highlights 'co-existence of differences' and 'otherness' (ibid.: 58). Thus, the EU did not ask those states to adhere to EU principles. This can be seen in the 2004 Communication, which highlights that 'joint ownership of the process, based on the awareness of shared values and common interests, is essential. The EU does not seek to impose priorities or conditions on its partners' (quoted in ibid.: 58).

By taking this position, however, the EU practices cultural relativism and legitimizes inequality on the ground of 'cultural difference'. Yet whereas initially cultural relativism was considered to be an alternative to ethnocentricism and a way to fight Western cultural dominance, it became a means to defend laws that violate human rights and women's rights and perpetuate discrimination. In fact, there are values such as those of the CEDAW that are widespread, universal and common values, fought for by women's groups all over the globe (EuroMeSCo 2006: 9–10).

Instead of pushing for those universal values, the EU, by paying lip-service to gender mainstreaming, acts inconsistently and may even be indicted as trying to 'deceive' others (David and Guerrina 2013: 60). On this line, the Euro-Mediterranean Human Rights Network (EMHRN 2012) asked the EU to follow up on its commitments stemming from the 2011 ENP and 2012 EU human rights package by focusing on democratization and human rights, together with gender equality, in its relations with partners. The EMHRN also demanded the EU to insist on its Mediterranean partners to include women's rights and gender inequality in legislation and to implement the CEDAW without reservation. It also asked the EU to assist democratic forces 'if it wants to regain lost credibility with the citizens of the region, who aspire to democracy, respect of human rights and a life in dignity' (ibid.). Thus the EU has no less than its credibility in the region at stake.

When it comes to solid policies towards its neighbours, the main focus of gender policies is on women's employment. This reveals that the EU's main reason for 'extending equal rights to women is an economic one', which suggests, with regard to gender equality at least, that 'the EU is not the normative actor it purports to be' (David and Guerrina 2013: 60). 'Thus, equality is construed in narrow and limited terms and gives something of a lie to the EU's expressed commitment to mainstreaming' (ibid.: 61).

Action Plan on Gender Equality

In EU documents there is a double construction and dual justification when it comes to gender – gender equality as a fundamental human right and as a prerequisite for economic development. In its 2007 Communication on gender equality and women's empowerment, the EU stated that '[l]egislation ensuring equal rights for all women and men is critical … in order to protect the fundamental human rights of women and also to enhance the reduction of poverty and economic growth' (European Commission 2007). 'It has to be clearly seen that measures to increase Gender Equality, in addition to increasing social cohesion and enhancing the protection of women's human rights, have a strong impact on economic growth, employment and poverty reduction' (ibid.).

In its Action Plan on Gender Equality and Women's Empowerment in Development for the period 2010–15, the EU

> reiterates its strong commitment to gender equality as a human right, a question of social justice and a core value of the EU development policy.… Gender equality, women's political and economic empowerment and women's enjoyment of human rights are essential for poverty reduction and sustainable development.
>
> (Council of the European Union 2010)

The Strategy for Equality between Women and Men (2010–15) states that '[e]quality is one of five values on which the Union is founded. The Union is bound to strive for equality between women and men in all its activities' (ibid.: 8). 'The EU will continue to use its development policies to promote gender equality and women's empowerment' (ibid.: 28).

In all EU documents we find evidence of the dual justification, leading to the question why the goal of gender equality cannot be a discrete goal for the EU. Why does the EU add poverty reduction and development policies?

Gender in the EU's mind-set

Allwood (2013: 50) highlights that in many of the EU documents gender is only considered within 'a very narrow range of issues, such as employment and sex trafficking. Women are constructed as needing special consideration in certain circumstances, often because they are "vulnerable" or "victims", and they are often listed along with other groups'. Another problem is that the question of gender competes with many more topics, 'raising the possibility of mainstreaming overload, or the dilution of gender into a long list' (ibid.). As an example, in the 2010 Review of the Cotonou Agreement, the list of thematic or crosscutting themes to mainstream was in art. 20 expanded from 'gender issues and institutional development and capacity building' to 'human rights, gender issues, democracy, good governance, environmental sustainability, climate change, communicable and non-communicable diseases and institutional development and capacity building' (ibid.).

Gender mainstreaming and accompanying hopes for gender equality are complicated by 'structural inequality and the constructed nature of gender' (Peto and Manners 2006: 109). As gender is deeply embedded in cultural meanings and social structures, power and hegemony are reproduced in gender relations. This, however, reduces policy-makers and others' capability to question hegemonic discourses and act differently so as to reach (real) gender equality (Allwood 2013: 45). As gender is constructed and (re-)produced, ideas about gender are deeply entrenched so that various inclinations 'reflect the institutionalization of masculine principles. In consequence, attempts to "mainstream" gender equality are confronted by pervasive understandings and practices supportive of male dominance' (Bretherton 2001: 62).

The EU may declare its commitment to values such as gender equality. However, there is a 'lack of coherence between policy declarations and practice with regard to achieving gender equality and women's empowerment' (Karadenizli 2007: 58). Applied in a fruitful manner, gender mainstreaming necessitates the constant implementation of its principles in all EU policies, so that these principles become institutionalized over time. Unfortunately, 'the processes of institutionalization are selective, and receptiveness to new ideas and principles is to a large degree a reflection of interests' (Bretherton 2001: 72). Gender equality initiatives are kept at the margins and fight against 'the "tide" of neo-liberal market principles' (ibid.: 73).

Gender mainstreaming is also complicated by 'inadequate allocation of human and financial resources, evaporation of policy commitments at the level of programme implementation, limited gender competence among staff members, absence of political leadership and political will' (Karadenizli 2007: 7). Even worse, the aims of gender equality, women's empowerment and women's rights are often openly incompatible with the EU's trade liberalization policies (ibid.). With the Lisbon Treaty and the modification of development policy in the Agenda for Change in 2012, aid efficiency and the focus on economic growth for developing was given even more prominence (Allwood 2013: 48). However, the restrictive focus on economic growth misses seeing the gendered nature of economic lives and the impact of liberalization policies on women, such as driving them into insecure, exploitative and temporary forms of work. As long as women are not included in decisions about donor support in various sectors, they will be held back economically, socially and politically. A 'one-size-fits-all' strategy will result in serious negative implications for the development of these countries. The simplistic view that trade liberalization leads to poverty eradication and social development needs to be challenged (Karadenizli 2007: 37). The effects on men and women may differ fundamentally, as women mostly engage in small crop farming and men mostly in the production of agricultural products for international markets (Allwood 2013: 48).

Conclusion: commonalities and well-intentioned recommendations

This chapter has tried to provide a conceptual understanding of gender, security and human security and to examine vital gender issues among the neighbours of the EU's neighbours, specifically Saharan Africa and Central Asia. It has aimed at revealing how the EU 'genders' its neighbourhood policy and how gender is dealt with within various processes such as enlargement, the ENP and beyond so as to disclose the very concept of gender in the EU's mind-set.

Gender is performative, constructed, internalized and reproduced. The notion of security should go far beyond state security, as for women security incorporates the lack of *all* types of violence and security from discrimination, oppression, poverty and domestic as well as state violence. Incorporating the ground-breaking idea of 'freedom from fear' and 'freedom from want', the concept of human security includes all these and more, namely the responsibility of the state to care for the lives, safety and well-being of its citizens.

The chapter has shown that women in Saharan Africa and in Central Asia, as elsewhere, face patriarchy, discrimination, inequality, subordination and domination. Some commonalities of these regions can be summarized as follows. To begin with, both regions face colonial legacies that still affect and influence them. Colonial influence brought in changes in women's positions. In the case of Saharan Africa women's status deteriorated, whereas in the Central Asian case it improved. After the end of colonialism, women's positions altered again. In both cases it was women who suffered most from transition periods, environmental degradation and economic predicaments. Another similarity is the fact that whereas women were active during the independence movements of their countries, after independence nationalism trumped feminism and provided little reward for women. More conservative interpretations of tradition, customs or religion contribute to and increase men's domination of women. This growing conservatism leads to the subordination of women and traditional constructions of gender roles. Women's representation is more limited now than in the past in Central Asia, whereas in Saharan Africa their political representation is on the rise. A central predicament is body politics: the politics and practices through which those in power, such as the state, government, society, fathers and husbands, regulate and control women's bodies. They are the ones to decide upon marriages, pregnancies, bodies, clothes, employment, education and all other issues, too. This is, however, degrading for women, and it is far away from the vision of human security, which entails human dignity.

The last part of the chapter dealt with gender in the EU's policies towards its neighbours' neighbours. It revealed that although gender equality is a core value for the EU itself, it has not become a 'norm' to adhere to either during enlargement processes or within the EU's neighbourhood policies. A look at EU pronouncements regarding gender equality in various official documents or action plans reveals a dual justification – gender equality as fundamental human right *and* as a prerequisite for economic development.

There is also a huge gap between the many policy declarations and high rhetoric regarding gender equality and women's empowerment and the practice in reality. Also important is the fact that policy-making and its processes are gendered and lean on gendered ideas, which then leads to the reproduction of gender inequality.

What the EU needs to do is to concentrate on the realization of human security, with which survival, basic human needs and human dignity can be achieved and oppressive structures at local, national and global levels can be eliminated. Real security incorporates security from domestic, physical, military, economic, sexual, ecological and structural violence. It can only be achieved when gender relations of dominance and oppression as well as poverty are eradicated.

The EU's neoliberal development and trade policies, however, marginalize people's needs and endanger their human security. Instead, what is needed is a 'people-centred notion of policy coherence which implies that EU trade policy must be transformed into a development framework of social justice, guaranteeing the enforcement of human and women's rights and eradication of all forms of inequalities, discrimination and poverty' (Karadenizli 2007: 58).

A development that is just has to concentrate on projects that promote women and the subsistence food sector. Therefore, a basic needs approach is essential, one that ensures an inclusive definition of basic needs, so that material needs for survival and the political contribution and involvement of women are promoted. This can empower women to improve their lives and increase their securities by strengthening their positions as active agents providing for their own physical and economic security. For this, it is essential that women partake at all levels of economic planning and that their knowledge is recognized (Tickner 1992: 94–96).

What is desperately needed are 'more resources, better training, greater awareness' and 'the struggle is to retain or re-insert a feminist theoretical understanding of gender and gender equality' (Allwood 2013: 50). Therefore, feminism itself provides the key to the solution as '[f]eminism is the voice of half the members of humankind, dominant groups acted to silence for thousands of years. ... It is a call for inclusion, respect for diversity and human dignity' (Staik 2005: 205–206).

Notes

1 See http://hdr.undp.org/aboutus.
2 See www.sociologyguide.com/basic-concepts/Ethnocentrism.php.
3 See www.sociologyguide.com/basic-concepts/Cultural-Relativism.php.

4 See also Chapter 6 by Tressia Hobeika in this volume.
5 See also Chapter 8 by Alexander Warkotsch and Richard Youngs in this volume.

References

Akiner, S. (1997) 'Between Tradition and Modernity: The Dilemma Facing Contemporary Central Asian Women', in M. Buckley (ed.) *Post-Soviet Women: From the Baltic to Central Asia*, New York: Cambridge University Press, 261–304.

Akiner, S. (2002) 'History and Politics in Central Asia: Change and Continuity', in M. McKee, J. Healy and J. Falkingham (eds) *Health Care in Central Asia*, Buckingham: Open University Press, 12–30.

Allwood, G. (2013) 'Gender Mainstreaming and Policy Coherence for Development: Unintended Gender Consequences and EU Policy', *Women Studies International Forum* 39, 42–52.

Altymysheva, Z. and N. Krastev (2014) 'Do Central Asia's Gender Quotas Help Or Hurt Women?', 13 January, *Radio Free Europe. Radio Liberty*, www.rferl.org/content/Do_Central_Asias_Gender_Quotas_Help_Or_Hurt_Women/1977535.html (accessed July 2014).

Bassiuoni, S. (2011) *Briefing Note on the Situation of Women in Central Asia*, Working Paper, Paris: UNESCO, www.unesco.org/new/fileadmin/MULTIMEDIA/HQ/BSP/GENDER/Working%20Paper_BriefingWorking%20Paper_S%20Bassiuoni_Situation%20of%20Women%20in%20Central%20Asia.pdf (accessed July 2014).

Bretherton, C. (2001) 'Gender Mainstreaming and EU Enlargement: Swimming Against the Tide?', *Journal of European Public Policy* 8(1), 60–81.

Bretherton, C. (2002) 'Gender Mainstreaming and Enlargement: The EU as Negligent Actor?', National Europe Centre Paper 23, https://digitalcollections.anu.edu.au/bitstream/1885/41760/3/bretherton.pdf (accessed August 2014).

Butler, J. (1990) *Gender Trouble: Feminism and the Subversion of Identity*, Abingdon: Routledge.

Cockburn, C. (2010) 'Militarism and War', in L.J. Shepherd (ed.) *Gender Matters in Global Politics: A Feminist Introduction to International Relations*, Abingdon: Routledge, 105–115.

Constanza, G. (2011) 'The State of Gender Relations in Africa: An Assessment of the Multi-faceted Issue of Gender in Africa', *Think Africa Press*, 1 April, http://thinkafricapress.com/article/state-gender-relations-africa (accessed March 2014).

Council of Europe (1998) *Message of the Committee of Ministers to Steering Committees of the Council of Europe on Gender Mainstreaming*, 628th meeting, 15–16 April, Strasbourg, www.coe.int/t/dghl/standardsetting/equality/03themes/gender-mainstreaming/CM-Message-Appendix2-1998_en.pdf (accessed July 2014).

Council of the European Union (2010) *Strategy for Equality between Women and Men 2010–2015*, September, http://ec.europa.eu/justice/gender-equality/files/strategy_equality_women_men_en.pdf (accessed August 2014).

David, M. and R. Guerrina (2013) 'Gender and European External Relations: Dominant Discourses and Unintended Consequences of Gender Mainstreaming', *Women's Studies International Forum* 39, 53–62.

Duncan, W., B. Jancar-Webster and B. Switzky (2002) *World Politics in the 21st Century*, Rochester: Pearson.

Euro-Mediterranean Human Rights Network (2012) 'EU Policies towards Southern Mediterranean Countries: Implementation of the "New ENP Approach" should Match

Commitments', 10 December, www.euromedrights.org/eng/2012/12/10/eu-policies-towards-southern-mediterranean-countries-implementation-of-the-new-enp-approach-should-match-commitments (accessed August 2014).

EuroMeSCo (2006) *Women as Full Participants in the Euro-Mediterranean Community Democratic States*, EuroMeSCo Annual Report 2006.

European Commission (2003) Communication from the Commission to the Council and the European Parliament, *Wider Europe – Neighbourhood: A New Framework for Relations with Our Eastern and Southern Neighbours*, COM(2003) 104, Brussels, 11 March.

European Commission (2007) Communication from the Commission to the European Parliament and the Council, *Gender Equality and Women Empowerment in Development Cooperation [SEC(2007) 332]*, COM(2007) 0100 final, Brussels, 8 March.

Flynn, D. (2013) 'African Migrants Aren't Just Fleeing to Europe, They're Fleeing from Europe's Legacy in Africa', *Think Africa Press*, 11 November, http://thinkafricapress.com/senegal/blog/what-la-pirogue-tells-us-about-tragic-stories-african-migration-europe (accessed July 2014).

Food and Agriculture Organization (n.d.) 'Women Feed the World', www.fao.org/docrep/x0262e/x0262e16.htm (accessed July 2014).

Frostrup, M. (2011) 'Feminism's Global Challenge: With One Voice', *Observer*, 6 March, www.theguardian.com/society/2011/mar/06/feminism-global-challenge-one-voice (accessed July 2014).

Galtung, J. (1969) 'Violence, Peace, and Peace Research', *Journal of Peace Research* 6(3), 167–191.

Goldstein, J. (2005) *International Relations*, Rochester: Pearson Education.

Güneş-Ayata, A. and A. Ergun (2009) 'Gender Politics in Transitional Societies: A Comparative Perspective on Azerbaijan, Kazakhstan, Kyrgyzstan, and Uzbekistan', in L. Racioppi and K. O'Sullivan (eds) *Gender Politics in Post-Communist Eurasia*, Michigan State: East Lansing, 209–236.

Henry, K. (2010) 'Gender Issues in Sub-Saharan Africa', *Open Salon*, 6 July, http://open.salon.com/blog/spywoman70/2010/07/06/gender_issues_in_sub-saharan_africa (accessed September 2014).

Hudson, H. (2005) ' "Doing" Security as Though Humans Matter: A Feminist Perspective on Gender and the Politics of Human Security', *Security Dialogue* 36(2), 155–174.

International Labour Organization (2008) 'Gender', Decent Work Technical Support Team and Country Office for Eastern Europe and Central Asia, www.ilo.org/public/english/region/eurpro/moscow/areas/gender.htm (accessed July 2014).

Ishkanian, A. (2003) 'Gendered Transitions: The Impact of the Post-Soviet Transition on Women in Central Asia and the Caucasus', *Perspectives on Global Development and Technology* 2 (3–4), 475–496.

Johnston, H. (2014) 'Voting for Change? Women and Gender Equality in the 2014 South African Elections', 5 May, http://za.boell.org/2014/05/05/voting-change-women-and-gender-equality-2014-south-african-elections (accessed July 2014).

Kaiser, S. (2006) 'Why Women's Day?', *Peace Review: A Journal of Social Justice* 18(4), 475–477.

Kameri-Mbote, P. (2004) 'Gender, Conflict and Regional Security: African Regional Security in the Age of Globalisation', in M. Mwagiru (ed.) *Gender, Conflict and Regional Security*, Nairobi: Heinrich Böll Foundation, 1–9.

Karadenizli, M. (2007) *Who Decides? Gender Mapping the European Union's Policy and Decision-making in the Areas of Development, External Relations and Trade*, WIDE,

Globalising Gender Equality and Social Justice, Brussels, http://wideplusnetwork.files. wordpress.com/2012/10/who-decides-def20073.pdf (accessed August 2014).

King, G. and C.J.L. Murray (2002) 'Rethinking Human Security', *Political Science Quarterly* 116, 585–610.

Lythgoe, L. (2013) 'Experts Weekly: Africa's Leading Women', *Think Africa Press*, 18 February, http://thinkafricapress.com/gender/experts-weekly-africas-leading-women (accessed July 2014).

Mikell, G. (ed.) (1997) *African Feminism: The Politics of Survival in Sub-Saharan Africa*, Philadelphia: University of Pennsylvania Press.

Moghadam (2000) 'Gender and Economic Reforms: A Framework for Analysis and Evidence from Central Asia, the Caucasus, and Turkey', in F. Acar and A. Ayata (eds) *Gender and Identity Construction*, Leiden: Brill Publishers, 23–43.

Mwagiru, M. (ed.) (2004) *African Regional Security in the Age of Globalisation*, Heinrich Böll Foundation.

Northrop, D. (n.d.) 'Down With The Veil! The Limits Of Liberation In The Soviet Union, 1919–1935', http://ultimatehistoryproject.com/down-with-the-veil.html (accessed July 2014).

Okome, M.O. (2013) 'Experts Weekly: Africa's Leading Women', *Think Africa Press*, 18 February, http://thinkafricapress.com/gender/experts-weekly-africas-leading-women (accessed July 2014).

Peto, A. and I. Manners (2006) 'The European Union and the Value of Gender Equality', in S. Lucarelli and I. Manners (eds) *Values and Principles in European Union Foreign Policy*, Routledge: London, 97–113.

Reardon, B. (1990) 'Feminist Concepts of Peace and Security', in P. Smoker, R. Davies and B. Munske (eds) *A Reader in Peace Studies*, Oxford: Pergamon Press, 136–157.

Roth, S. (2004) 'Opportunities and Obstacles – Screening the EU Enlargement Process from a Gender Perspective', *International Law Review* 2(1), 117–127.

Salami, M. (2012a) 'Feminism has Always Existed in Africa', 1 June, *MsAfropolitan*, blog, www.msafropolitan.com/2012/06/feminism-has-always-existed-in-africa.html (accessed June 2014).

Salami, M. (2012b) '7 Key Issues in African Feminist Thought', 6 August, *MsAfropolitan*, blog, www.msafropolitan.com/2012/08/7-key-issues-in-african-feminist-thought. html (accessed January 2014).

Salami, M. (2013a) 'What Makes a Clitoris Dangerous?', *MsAfropolitan*, blog, 17 August, www.msafropolitan.com/2013/08/fgm.html (accessed January 2014).

Salami, M. (2013b) 'African Women are Blazing a Feminist Trail – Why Don't we Hear their Voices?', *The Guardian*, 23 September, www.theguardian.com/commentis-free/2013/sep/23/african-women-rwanda-feminism (accessed January 2014).

Salami, M. (2013c) 'A Brief History of African Feminism', *MsAfropolitan*, blog, 2 July, www.msafropolitan.com/2013/07/a-brief-history-of-african-feminism.html (accessed July 2014).

Sassen, S. (2001) 'The Excesses of Globalisation and the Feminisation of Survival', *parallax* 7(1), 100–110.

Shakirova, S. (2007) 'Women's Movement and Feminism in Central Asia: From a Not Comforting Forecast to Efficient Strategies', http://globalstudies.trinity.duke.edu/wp-content/themes/cgsh/materials/WKO/v2d2_Svetlana.pdf (accessed January 2014).

Shepherd, L.J. (2010) 'Sex or Gender? Bodies in World Politics and Why Gender Maters', in L.J. Shepherd (ed.) *Gender Matters in Global Politics: A Feminist Introduction to International Relations*, Abingdon: Routledge, 3–16.

Staik, A. (2005) 'Gender Theories, Partnership, Global Transformation', *Peace Review: A Journal of Social Justice* 17, 197–206.

Steans, J. (2010) 'Body Politics: Women's Human Rights in International Relations', in L.J. Shepherd (ed.) *Gender Matters in Global Politics: A Feminist Introduction to International Relations*, Abingdon: Routledge, 74–88.

Steinitz, L. and D. Ashton (2007) 'The Face of AIDS is a Woman', in S. LaFont and D. Hubbard (ed.) *Recommendations for Action Unravelling Taboos: Gender and Sexuality in Namibia*, Legal Assistance Center, 216–233.

Swan, A. (2009) 'Educating Women in Post-Soviet Central Asia', *On Campus With Women* 37(3), www.aacu.org/ocww/volume37_3/global.cfm (accessed January 2014).

Thomas, C. (2001) 'Global Governance, Development and Human Security: Exploring the Links', *Third World Quarterly* 22(2), April, 159–175.

Tickner, J.A. (1992) *Gender in International Relations*, New York: Columbia University Press.

Tickner, J.A. (2001) *Gendered World Politics: Issues and Approaches in the Post-Cold War Era*, New York: Columbia University Press.

Tickner, J.A. and L. Sjoberg (2007) 'Feminism', in T. Dunne, M. Kurki and S. Smith (eds) *International Relations Theories*, Oxford: Oxford University Press, 185–202.

Tripp, A.M. (2013) 'How African Feminism Changed the World', *Think Africa Press*, 8 March, http://thinkafricapress.com/gender/how-african-feminism-changed-world (accessed September 2014).

UNDP (1994) *Human Development Report1994 – New Dimensions of Human Security*, New York: United Nations Development Programme.

UN ECOSOC (United Nations Economic and Social Council) (1997) *Gender Mainstreaming*, OSAGI: Office of the Special Advisor on Gender Issues and Women's Advancement: *Gender Mainstreaming Competence Development Framework: Summary*, www.un.org/womenwatch/osagi/gmgenericsummframe.htm (accessed March 2014).

Waylen, G. (2006) 'You Still Don't Understand: Why Troubled Engagements Continue between Feminists and (Critical) IPE', *Review of International Studies* 32(1), 145–164.

West, C. and D.H. Zimmerman (1987) 'Doing Gender', *Gender and Society* 1(2), 125–151.

Williams, P. (2013) *Celebrating Our Women's Liberation*, blog by South African Government, 30 July, www.info.gov.za/blogs/2013/women_130731.html (accessed September 2014).

World Bank (2014) *Empowering Women – Where Does Europe and Central Asia Stand?*, 20 May, www.worldbank.org/en/news/feature/2014/05/20/empowering-women--where-does-europe-and-central-asia-stand (accessed September 2014).

Zlatunich, N. (2011) 'Healthy Numbers: The Gender Dimension', *Think Africa Press*, 14 September, http://thinkafricapress.com/population-matters/demographic-growth-health-and-gender-africa (accessed February 2014).

8 The limits of EU democracy support

Central Asia and the Gulf Cooperation Council

Alexander Warkotsch and Richard Youngs

Introduction

The European Union (EU) faces especially difficult challenges in extending its democracy and human rights policy instruments from its immediate periphery into the 'neighbours of its neighbours'. This chapter examines the nature of the EU's democracy and human rights policies in Central Asia and the Arab states of the Gulf Cooperation Council (GCC). We compare these two regions because they present similar kinds of challenges, related to strategic priorities, energy politics and regimes demonstrating firm authoritarian resilience. Our core research aim is to explore how far geopolitical and geo-economic interests prevail over political reform considerations in these two regions. The chapter finds that EU policy has evolved in both Central Asia and the Gulf, but that no more than a very circumspect commitment to democracy and human rights is detectable. The EU's tepidness is indeed explained by well-known security and energy calculations. In the context of this volume, the chapter's significance is to demonstrate how far policy dynamics beyond the immediate neighbourhood retain a notable geopolitical ethos. The nature of politics, economics and society in Central Asia and the Arabian Gulf militate against any smooth expansion of European Neighbourhood Policy (ENP) initiatives.

The chapter first considers Central Asia, looking in turn at: the state of democracy in the region; the evolution of EU policy; and the explanation for the nature of EU policy. The same three part structure is then applied to the Gulf.

EU democracy support in Central Asia

The state of democracy

Central Asia provides a tough test and ample reason for the EU's commitment to democracy and human rights promotion. In most states, presidents rule by decree. Parliaments and courts are weak and routinely ignored. Opposition has been circumscribed, co-opted and/or repressed. Almost all elections have had dubious legitimacy and the emergence of independent mass media has been hindered; in short, substantive democracy is either absent or falls short of the mark. Uzbekistan, which is still governed by a former first secretary of the Soviet Communist Party, shows a well-documented atrocious human rights record. Like its neighbour Turkmenistan, Uzbekistan ranks among the world's most repressive societies (Freedom House 2012: 6). Semi-authoritarian Kazakhstan has never held an election that was considered free or fair by the Organization for Security and Cooperation in Europe (OSCE). In 2010 – ahead of its OSCE chairmanship – Kazakhstan adopted a 'Path to Europe' programme and its first National Human Rights Action Plan but little progress has been recorded. Human rights watchdogs report a downward trend in basic freedoms and rights, in particular due to the banning of several media outlets following a harsh crackdown on labour disputes in late 2011 (Boonstra and Tsertsvadze 2013). In Tajikistan President Emomali Rahmon – also a former senior Communist Party member – has established a degree of authoritarianism that ranks between the outright dictatorships in Uzbekistan and Turkmenistan and semi-authoritarian Kazakhstan. As a prelude to presidential elections in November 2013, Tajik authorities have widened their crackdown on members of the political opposition and democracy activists, imprisoning or intimidating opposition party leaders and stepping up efforts to extradite political opponents from abroad. The government has also restricted media freedom, with state media relentlessly providing a positive view of President Rahmon and virtually no coverage of opposition candidates or critical views on Tajik government policy (Human Rights Watch 2013a). The region's poorhouse Kyrgyzstan is a fragile counterpoint to the rest of Central Asia. It is the only Central Asian country where the idea of popular sovereignty has been taking a limited hold. In the early 1990s it was dubbed the 'Switzerland of Central Asia' due to comparatively favourable democracy and human rights rankings. In summer 2010 Kyrgyzstan became the first country in Central Asia to adopt parliamentary democracy.

Notwithstanding most Central Asian republics' obvious non-conformance with liberal principles, the EU's attempts at the promotion of human rights and democracy in the region give the impression of tameness, little exertion of pressure on the incumbent elites and generally a policy approach that is high on rhetoric but low on delivery. This analysis will start with a short overview of democracy and human rights promotion in the official EU Central Asia Strategy (Council of the European Union 2007: 1). It will then describe the policy instruments that the European Union has at hand to further that goal. Finally, the analysis offers explanations for the EU's cautious approach and limited democratization impact by referring to Member State interests, particularities of Central Asian society, and cost–benefit calculations on the part of Central Asian regimes.

The framework of EU democracy promotion in Central Asia

The promotion of human rights and democracy has been incorporated into the network of the EU's bilateral and regional agreements with the Central Asian republics, purportedly as a shared value and objective. For example, the bilateral Partnership and Cooperation Agreements (PCAs) between the EU and the Central Asian countries, concluded in the 1990s, start with a declaration on 'general principles'. They declare that 'respect for democracy, principles of international law and human rights ... as well as the principles of a market economy, underpin the internal and external policies of the Parties and constitute an essential element of partnership of this Agreement'. Moreover, art. 1 of all PCAs explicitly refers to the 'consolidation of democracy' as a main objective of cooperation. The EU's Regional Strategy Paper for Central Asia includes similar passages (European Community 2006). For example, it states with regard to its overall objectives that the 'EU strives in particular to promote prosperity, solidarity, human rights and democracy' (ibid.: 4). At the level of technical assistance, the Development Cooperation Instrument (DCI) 'serves to promote democracy, good governance and respect for human rights and the rule of law' (European Commission 2014). Finally, the EU's Central Asia Strategy, which was adopted in 2007 and serves as the centre-piece document and overall guidance for EU policy in Central Asia, highlights 'good governance, the rule of law, human rights, and democratisation' as 'key areas' for EU support (Council of the European Union 2007: 1). EU policy to foster human rights, democracy and good governance in Central Asia centres on two main instruments: political and human rights dialogue and technical and financial assistance.

Political and human rights dialogue

The EU's political and human rights dialogue rests on assumptions of Habermasian social theory as well as on insights from social psychology. It claims that the targets of political dialogue – the socializees – do not so much calculate cost and benefits but rather that they engage in argument about their respective interests and preferences as 'correct' interpretations of the world. The mechanism postulates that community norms are normatively valid claims argumentatively justified by the socialization party towards the target states. Thanks to the 'power of the better argument', the target actors are persuaded by the legitimacy of the validity claims and change their identity and interests accordingly (Risse and Sikkink 1999: 1–6).

Obviously, an important condition for successful socialization is constant interaction. However, before the adoption of the EU's Central Asia Strategy in 2007 dialogue was hardly a prominent instrument for the EU's democracy promotion. The frequency of meetings has been very low. PCA dialogue is mainly conducted through the Cooperation Council, which functions as a steering committee for EU–Central Asian cooperation. It consists of members of the Council of the European Union, since the Lisbon Treaty the European External Action Service (EEAS), the European Commission and high-ranking officials from Central Asia. With only one meeting per year, the Cooperation Council dialogue is not intense – at least compared to, for example, the dialogue conducted through the Euro-Mediterranean Partnership. Interesting to note is that only the

Uzbek PCA directly links political dialogue to issues of democracy by stating that

> [t]he political dialogue ... shall foresee that the Parties endeavour to cooperate on matters pertaining to the observance of the principles of democracy, and the respect, protection and promotion of human rights, particularly those of persons belonging to minorities and shall hold consultations, if necessary, on relevant matters.
>
> (European Communities 1999: 24)

EU Council talks are conducted in a reserved manner, and it has always been a struggle to find high-level EU officials to attend the Cooperation Council meetings, while many Central Asia delegations would typically be composed of the Prime Minister or the Foreign Minister (International Crisis Group 2006: 18). On the ground, representation which is necessary to continue dialogue outside Cooperation Council meetings is limited. For example, in Turkmenistan, the region's worst human rights offender, the EU has no EU delegation in place. It only runs a so-called 'Europa House' which functions as an implementation and management support office for EU relations with Turkmenistan. However, in Uzbekistan – the region's other major human rights offender – the EU opened a delegation in 2011.[1]

A first important step towards increasing the dialogue capacity has been the appointment of an EU Special Representative for Central Asia in 2005 who was tasked not only with coordinating the efforts of various EU actors in the region but also with furthering the development of political dialogue.[2] This was followed by the 'Strategy for a New Partnership' and its new focus on dialogue commitments, including a high-ranking and regular regional political dialogue and a bilateral 'result-oriented' human rights dialogue. However, as Melvin and Boonstra (2008: 3) point out, the strategy for this dialogue is top-down: the European Union confined its dialogue with Central Asia to discussions between EU officials and representatives of the incumbent elite. The European Union does not seek in a significant way to engage civil society organizations and their representatives in Central Asia. Nonetheless, it is certainly laudable that with the new dialogue structure in place the intensity of high-level contacts has reached an unprecedented level in Central Asia. For example, in 2012, the EU held three ministerial conferences with Central Asia and also conducted one human rights dialogue with each of the five Central Asian states. In 2013, however, the intensity of high-level talks decreased again to one ministerial conference held in Brussels.

Technical and financial aid

As regards technical and financial assistance, democracy in Central Asia in its narrower sense is promoted through the European Initiative for Democracy and Human Rights (EIDHR). Funding is made available for three tracks with a clear focus on supporting civil society actors: (1) combating torture, xenophobia and minority and ethnic discrimination; (2) fostering human rights; and (3) supporting the democratic process. Funding is equally spread across the three tracks with a slight focus on fostering human rights (Warkotsch 2011: 107). In addition, assistance for non-state actors/local authorities (NSA/LA) as part of the EU's Development Cooperation Instrument and the Institution Building Partnership Programme (IBPP) targets the non-governmental sector and local governing authorities with a focus on strengthening capacity in the fields of poverty reduction and basic services provision. The focus of the NSA/LA and IBPP on dealing with the consequences of political, social and economic transition allows for the integration of projects with democracy-building activities but the emphasis is on socially oriented projects and not on democracy and human rights (Axyonova 2012: 2–3). EIDHR and NSA/LA operate primarily in Kazakhstan, Kyrgyzstan and Tajikistan. As a result, democracy and human rights funding in its narrower sense concentrates on regimes where reforms are already underway and where aid is less needed than in dictatorial Uzbekistan and Turkmenistan. Uzbekistan continues to benefit from the IBPP, a funding mechanism that was phased out for other countries with the introduction of the DCI. Between 2008 and 2011 the EU allocated a total of €15.2 million in democracy and human rights assistance to Central Asia (see Table 8.1).

No EU democracy and human rights instruments are targeted at Turkmenistan, as government policies there make it impossible for the EU to reach adequate partner organizations. Interesting to note is a distinct feature of IBPP support to Uzbekistan where the EU and the recipient country have to sign annual financial agreements before project implementation can begin. This is an effective tool for Uzbekistan to co-decide about the allocation of funds to certain programme themes. But also in Kazakhstan, Kyrgyzstan and Tajikistan human rights and democracy project implementation is anything but a smooth process. This is not so much due to government intervention but a result of complex conditions for grant application and project implementation. For example, EIDHR and NSA/LA projects demand that local non-governmental organizations (NGOs) face a mandatory cost-share of 10 per cent of project costs. Even for EU small grant projects (varying between €10,000 and €300,000) this equals a minimum of €1,000 from an NGO's own resources. For many Central Asian

Table 8.1 EIDHR, NSA/LA and IBPP assistance to Central Asia 2008–11 (in million €)

	EIDHR	*NSA/LA*	*IBPP*
Kazakhstan	2.4	2.3	not active
Kyrgyzstan	2.7	1.95	not active
Tajikistan	1.8	1.85	not active
Turkmenistan	not active	not active	not active
Uzbekistan	not active	not active	2.2

Source: based on Axyonova (2012: 2).

NGOs this is a prohibitively high amount. Furthermore, grant application often requires, for example, English language knowledge which is an additional barrier for many local organizations. Therefore, it is often only the well-established NGOs that are in a position to apply for external funding, which thus unnecessarily inhibits EU assistance from reach a wider target audience (ibid.: 3).

An important tool of external democratization policy is political conditionality. The EU generally prefers a positive approach and considers the release and amount of funds conditional upon the extent to which reform targets are met. Though such a positive conditionality approach is enshrined in many of the EU's strategy documents, commitment to it seems half-hearted at best. According to the EU's Central Asia DCI indicative budget for 2011–13, average annual country allocations were as follows: Tajikistan €20.7 million, Kyrgyzstan €17 million, Uzbekistan €14 million, Turkmenistan €10 million, and Kazakhstan €10 million (European Commission 2010a: 13). At first sight, this reflects the region's pattern of economic development and social well-being with the poorhouses Tajikistan and Kyrgyzstan well ahead at the top of recipients and Kazakhstan, the region's most developed country, at the end. On a per capita basis, however, the picture changes. Turkmenistan, the region's worst democracy and human rights performer, received per capita DCI aid of €2.01, which is much closer to the amount Tajikistan (€2.58) and Kyrgyzstan (€3.06) obtained (European Commission 2010a: 13).[3] With the exception of Uzbekistan, harsh measures such as sanctions have never been applied. And even in a rare case of the EU taking a tough stand on human rights, after the Andijon uprising, the EU lifted sanctions in October 2009 without getting a long-demanded independent investigation of the massacre.[4]

Finally, although EU assistance has been significantly increased since the implementation of the EU's Central Asia Strategy, overall technical and financial assistance is still relatively low compared to other regions. For example, the national indicative envelope for technical and financial assistance to the Ukraine for the period 2011–13 was €470 million (European Union 2010: 8). This contrasts with an amount of €321 million in DCI assistance for all of the five Central Asian republics for the same time frame. It can easily be imagined that this low level of overall assistance impairs the EU's position at the bargaining table when advocating progress in human rights and democracy in exchange for technical and financial assistance.

Explaining EU policy

The brief examination above has shown that EU democracy promotion in Central Asia is high on rhetoric but relatively low on delivery. First, although EU policy documents and agreements with the Central Asian republics make aid conditional on the respect for human rights and democratic principles, in practice, disbursement is rather unconditional. Second, high-level EU–Central Asian dialogue is both rare and relatively tame. Third, the general level of democratization aid to Central Asia is low compared to other recipient countries. This section outlines three features in EU–Central Asian relations which offer explanations for the EU's 'rhetoric–reality gap' in democracy promotion by examining EU Member State interests, particularities of Central Asian society, and cost–benefit calculations by Central Asia regimes.

First, the EU's democracy promotion policy often conflicts with Member States' national interests, in particular a 'Russia-first' policy as well as security interests related to military engagement of the North Atlantic Treaty Organization (NATO) in Afghanistan. Russian-led initiatives such as the Eurasian Customs Union or the Eurasian Economic Union are recent examples of Russia being an increasingly assertive actor throughout the Commonwealth of Independent States (CIS).[5] The aim is to rebuild a 'Greater Russia' by establishing an extensive web of economic, cultural and military dependencies in Russia's 'near abroad' (Nygren 2007) and possibly to reintegrate these near abroad regions into Russia, as manifested by the annexation of Crimea in 2014 and the subsequent conflict in eastern Ukraine. Russia is well aware that a very important factor in helping to consolidate its influence in the region is the extent to which the political trajectories in the CIS follow a pattern similar to Putin's concept of a 'guided democracy'. Hence it came as little surprise that in 2005 former Russian Defence Minister Sergei Ivanov, during a speech at the Foreign Relations Council in New York, stated that Russia 'would react very sharply to the export of [democratic] revolutions to the CIS countries' (Eder and Halbach 2005: 7). Within the EU the bigger Member States, Germany, France, and Italy, have shown great leniency in dealing with such Russian ambitions.

Germany is also taking the centre stage when it comes to trading human rights and democracy interests in Central Asia for security interests related to the war against terror in Afghanistan. Germany is dependent on using the Uzbek airbase in Termez as a logistical hub for transporting troops and material to and from Afghanistan. Fears of having to close that airbase have resulted in a very doveish attitude towards the Karimov regime, manifesting itself, for example, in Germany lobbying for lifting EU sanctions that were put in place after the Andijon massacre in 2005 (*The Guardian* 2007). The continued cooperation between Berlin and Tashkent amid Uzbekistan's blunt ignoring of basic human rights and democracy standards once prompted the German news magazine *Der Spiegel* (2006) to call Uzbek president Karimov 'Germany's favourite despot'. Though NATO's International Security Assistance Force (ISAF) mission came to an end in 2014, German policy is unlikely to change: it has signalled its willingness to continue a military presence in Afghanistan as part of NATO's follow-up mission 'Resolute Support'.

Second, as regards the particularities of Central Asian societies, their social fabric is made up of an intermixture of traditional institutions such as family, kinship and clan affiliations and loyalties. The underlying culture of these networks is barely democratic, but authoritarian, patrimonial and personal; all of them hardly compatible with democratic norms.[6] Furthermore, the absence of recognition in Islamic thought of the legitimacy of an independent political and public sphere, separate from the sacred realm of God, is not particularly conducive to individualism and makes Central Asian societies rather inhospitable places for the emergence of democracy. According to a Council Common Position, increased democracy support is to be considered where positive changes have taken place, that is, where democratization aid falls on fertile ground (Council of the European Union 1998). Given the rather bleak picture of democracy in most of the Central Asian states as well as bleak prospects for future democratization due to an unfavourable social fabric, the fertile ground condition may be another impediment for more significant EU democratization support.

Third, the EU's choice of instruments tends to be influenced by the resource relations between the EU and the target country (Jünemann and Knodt 2007): generally speaking, we can observe that with an economically potent partner, there are no strong instruments applied and only a very weak political dialogue is set up. In such cases the EU tries to push through its values via alternative arenas, such as the World Trade Organization, the United Nations and the OSCE. At first sight, EU Central Asian economic relations are hardly overwhelming; trade is lopsided, with 20 per cent of Central Asian exports (including energy) going to the EU, making the Union the second largest Central Asian export destination after Russia (Eurostat 2012: 154). On the other hand, only about 0.7 per cent of EU exports are shipped to the region. However, the EU's stakes appear significantly increased when energy issues are included in the calculation as part of a larger trade dimension.[7] Though Central Asia's energy potential has occasionally been overestimated, the region is nonetheless part of a 'strategic energy ellipse' (Kemp and Harkavy 1997) reaching from the Persian Gulf to the Caspian Sea and Russia.[8] Three of the five Central Asian states have significant energy reserves. Kazakhstan has by far the largest share with oil reserves in the global top ten and gas in the top fifteen (British Petrol 2014). Turkmenistan has huge unexplored gas reserves that rank in the global top five (ibid.: 20). Uzbekistan is also a significant gas producer but uses most of its resources for domestic demand. In the late 1990s Europe started to think of Caspian resources as a potential 'additional filling station'. Since EU gas demand is likely to increase more sharply than oil demand, Turkmenistan is of particular interest to Europe. Turkmenistan produces roughly 62 billion cubic metres of natural gas every year (ibid.: 22). This equals about 20–25 per cent of total EU gas imports (European Commission 2010b: 31).

Furthermore, Central Asia, in particular Kazakhstan, holds vast untapped reserves of rare earths. In February 2012, German Chancellor Merkel and Kazakhstan President Nazarbaev signed a strategic partnership that guarantees Germany the right to search for and mine rare earths and other raw materials in Kazakhstan in exchange for technological and other investments (*New York Times* 2012). The agreement involves about 50 separate accords worth a total of €3 billion (ibid.). The signing of the agreement came only several months after violent clashes between security forces and demonstrators in Zhanaozen. The confrontation between striking oil workers and police resulted in the deaths of at least 16 unarmed protesters and, according to Human Rights Watch, detainees made credible and serious allegations of torture (International Crisis

Group 2013: 13; Human Rights Watch 2013b). But Germany is not the only country that is cosying up to Kazakhstan. On 1 July 2013 British Prime Minister David Cameron visited Astana to sign a package of business deals totalling up to £700 million in the fields of energy, infrastructure and transport. Like Chancellor Merkel, Cameron 'pre-emptively' stressed that during the visit human rights concerns and the need to adhere to democratic principles had been discussed (Nichol 2013: 11; *New York Times* 2012). In response to British criticism, Nazarbaev stated that democracy in Kazakhstan was in fine shape and that building democracy and human rights was in any case a long-term process that had also taken hundreds of years in the United Kingdom (quoted in Nichol 2013: 11). Adding to Kazakh self-confidence in dealing with normative demands from Britain is probably also the fact that Kazakhstan is part of a transportation route that is vital for Britain to ship military equipment home from Afghanistan.[9]

It is hard to rule out the conclusion that the choice of democratization instruments is influenced by interests in resources and security on the part of Member States or of the EU as a whole, tempting the Union to refrain from the employment of negative conditionality or even sanctions. This is most certainly true for Kazakhstan, where human rights and democracy standards have significantly deteriorated over the last couple of years. The EU nevertheless has since 2011 been trying to forge closer bilateral relations with Kazakhstan by negotiating an enhanced Partnership and Cooperation Agreement, with only the European Parliament (2012) advocating for an improved human rights record before signing such an agreement.

EU democracy support to the Gulf Cooperation Council

Many of the same patterns evident in Central Asia can be seen in the Gulf. The hope raised by the 'Arab Spring' has not extended into the Gulf states of Saudi Arabia, Kuwait, Bahrain, Qatar, the United Arab Emirates (UAE) or Oman. While the EU has been keen to prise open any modest possibilities for reform, the region's strategic importance has gradually pulled policy back toward familiar *realpolitik* thinking. The larger EU Member States remain more prominent players than the EU as such, and their concerns have tilted back towards security issues as post-2011 changes have bred a more unstable region. Recent events related to the 'Islamic State of Iraq and the Levant' (ISIL) have militated even further against the prioritization of democracy support.[10]

The state of democracy

Notwithstanding the 'Arab Spring', authoritarianism in the Gulf region remains largely undimmed (Gause 2011). Saudi Arabia has led the counter-revolution, reforms here impeded by the long-standing trinity of oil rents, loyal security forces and an Islamist establishment aligned with and not against the regime. Increased regime subsidies have failed entirely to quell discontent across the

Gulf. As a result, regimes have gradually switched to more draconian repression. Gulf leaders talk enthusiastically about North Africa's 'Arab Spring' in part to keep revolts away from the Gulf. Sectarianism has weakened the preconditions for reform in the Gulf. Nervous Gulf regimes have clamped down hard on Muslim Brotherhood affiliates. Some GCC states have removed citizenship rights from opposition members.

In Qatar the Emir committed to a partially elected Shura Council. A 60 per cent pay rise was given to public sector workers in Qatar to pre-empt any unrest. The Emir's decision to step down in 2013 and hand power to his son did nothing in itself to increase democratic freedom, although the symbolism of a healthy and popular ruler relinquishing power was significant. Political space has contracted particularly in the UAE, where hardline leaders in Abu Dhabi have gained ascendency over relatively more open tendencies in Dubai. The UAE has stamped down hard on small-scale protests and civil society has not been strong or organized enough to retain any momentum.

Human rights advocacy has increased in Saudi Arabia. One group of activists announced the creation of the kingdom's first political party; the regime has gradually arrested prominent activists and the founders of the party. Protests have fizzled out, obstructed by the security services. A clampdown on Saudi Shias was justified as a reaction to the revolts in Bahrain. Shia communities have become far more actively organized in protest against the regime, although Sunni groups have recoiled from allying with them in a common pro-democracy front (Mathiesen 2012). A US$97 billion package has aimed subsidies and benefits at the sectors engaged in protest, while also creating 60,000 new security posts; 2012 saw a record budget surplus thanks to rising oil prices. Delayed municipal elections took place with no advances in free political competition and with women still excluded. Crucially, the most powerful sectors of the clerical establishment have decided not to break ranks with the regime (Lacroix 2011).

Bahrain was the one Gulf state where mass protests broke out in 2011 and posed a serious challenge to the regime. Protests initially involved both Sunni and Shia. They then assumed a sectarian character, the majority Shia calling for the minority Sunni autocracy to be overthrown. Activists insist the problem was not minority rule but the Al-Khalifa monopoly; Sunnis also signed reform petitions. Shia leaders accepted the need for constitutional guarantees for the Sunni minority. Saudi and UAE tanks rolled in to help quash the protests. Many of those arrested were tortured. The government successfully mobilized the Sunni community. Thousands of protestors were subsequently dismissed from their jobs in government and government-owned companies. The regime convened a National Dialogue. The Shia Al-Wefaq soon pulled out, leaving the process bereft of any genuine reform potential. The National Dialogue still struggles to move beyond basic points of procedure.

Kuwait has a lively parliament that often challenges the government. In March 2011 demonstrations called for the Prime Minister to step aside because of incompetence; remarkably, the regime bowed to this pressure. The new Parliament was even more critical of the government. The Emir suspended the

Parliament, but the Court overturned his decision and required new elections to be held. The government has moved on corruption issues, but still refuses to open up key ministerial posts to candidates from outside the ruling family. Criticism of the Emir remains a red line; opposition parties are not mass movements; and restrictions on the media have tightened.

EU policy evolution

In the wake of the 'Arab Spring', the EU did to some extent show a greater willingness to criticize human rights abuses in the Gulf. The EEAS and the European Parliament issued strongly worded statements on abuses in both Bahrain and the UAE in 2013. The UK created a Gulf Initiative in the summer of 2010; at the end of 2011 it promised to 'adjust' this initiative to put more pressure 'on supporting long-term political and economic reform across Gulf states' (House of Commons 2011: 46, 61). The UK has launched projects in Kuwait on political corruption, effective opposition and state administrative reform. It temporarily tightened export controls on arms sales to Bahrain and Yemen. Sweden's Defence Minister was forced to resign in March 2011 over leaked plans to fund an arms facility in Saudi Arabia. EU Member States pushed the regime in Bahrain to launch the National Dialogue. The UK insisted that in Bahrain it linked a continuation of cooperation to the opposition's inclusion in the National Dialogue on reform.

In general, however, policies have followed the same broad contours as existed prior to the 'Arab Spring'. The UK in particular still doubts the value of supplanting national with EU policy frameworks, including the 'neighbours of the neighbours' concept. The UK insisted on excluding the Gulf from the remit of the new EU Special Representative for the 'Arab Spring' on the grounds that the factors at play there are fundamentally different from those in the Maghreb and Mashreq.[11] Other Member States read this as implying that the UK was not keen on seeing unpredictable change in its Gulf allies. The British role in Oman is perceived by Omanis to be entirely based on supporting the person of the Sultan, a post the UK effectively invented. Power is highly concentrated, with the Sultan himself occupying all major ministerial portfolios and refusing to contemplate succession plans; yet the UK has not pressed even for a limited dispersal of some powers. A UK ministerial visit to Oman in February 2013 brought gushing praise for the Sultan and new strategic cooperation.

The EU has pushed the GCC to engage in more meaningful human rights dialogue but has done little to counter Gulf resistance to this idea or push any specific reforms – with the exception of women's voting in municipal elections in Saudi Arabia. The approach in the Gulf is that these countries' political systems are highly distinctive and that the EU can and should do no more than gently cajole reform from within. Experts suggest that continuing Western patronage is a more potent explanation of the paucity of reform in Arab monarchies than any cultural or institutional differences with reforming republics (Gause and Yom 2012).

Much new local-level mobilization has taken shape in the Gulf, but it is based on a bottom-up, leaderless youth and volunteer activism that the main European aid donors (such as the UK, Germany, France and the Netherlands) have not targeted for support or systematic engagement. Protests erupted again in the summer of 2013 in Saudi Arabia, leading to further arrests. The EU response was muted. In general, US diplomats tend to meet with activists more than do European member state governments. EU governments did not exert critical pressure on Saudi Arabia for its active support of the Egyptian army's *coup d'état* in June 2013, even though Saudi money did much to undercut Western efforts to get the Egyptian transition back on track.

Although raising concerns, Member States continued security and commercial cooperation with Bahrain in the aftermath of the democracy uprising. The British ambassador who met with opposition leaders early in the protests in Bahrain was moved to Oman to smooth waters. Bahraini officials noted that the UK then played a cautious mediating role between the regime and opposition, and was far less confrontational than the US. The UK voted against a proposed UN resolution criticizing the Bahraini government. Some embassies wound down cooperation with the Bahraini opposition, reflecting a fear that the legacy of the 'Arab Spring' might be to unleash a wave of Shia hostility across the region (Brookings Doha Centre and FRIDE 2013).

UK diplomats based in Kuwait admit that their policies did not change significantly after the beginning of the 'Arab Spring'.[12] Kuwait is regarded as a model for democratization in the region, with a powerful elected parliament. Locals comment that much of the UK's welcome pro-reform work sat uneasily with a new 2013 contract for British companies to sell internet surveillance technology to the Kuwaiti regime. Nordic states retain a focus on human rights but representatives of countries such as Spain acknowledge that their concerns are commercial. Members of the Kuwait Society for Human Rights complain strongly at the insipidity of EU and US pressure for reform.

Aid funding for human rights and democracy has little place in EU policies in the Gulf, due to both the region's wealth and the obstacles placed in the way of democracy assistance by regimes. Across the Gulf, EU Member States offer low-key human rights funding only, while channelling resources towards infrastructure and development projects. No new EU political reform projects have commenced in the Gulf since 2011. The UK supported little more than a small pilot project on judicial reform in Bahrain and Oman. EIDHR projects are not funded in the Gulf. No new funding has supported the Bahraini opposition.

Explaining EU policy

In the Gulf, the EU priority lies in maintaining defence deals and military cooperation. The absence of pressure on Gulf states reflects a stability-oriented strategic perspective. In the words of one EU diplomat: 'the equation of values and interests coinciding is still different in the Gulf'.[13] EU–GCC security cooperation has deepened in response to the civil conflict in Yemen, piracy, arms control and the scheduled talks on a Middle East nuclear free zone. In 2012, the EU further deepened strategic dialogue with the GCC on Iran, Palestine and Syria – even if it did not follow through on the European Parliament's call for a formal Strategic Partnership. High Representative Catherine Ashton and her team have made a significant effort to boost diplomatic engagement with GCC states on regional challenges, in what they insisted amounted to a more preferential strategic relationship; this apparently bought into Gulf regimes' discourse of the 'Arab Spring' being a highly positive event taking place outside the GCC and having little pertinence to domestic politics in the Arabian Peninsula.

The UK has upgraded its 'Two Kingdoms Dialogue' with Saudi Arabia to the status of a formal bilateral strategic partnership. The House of Commons Committee on Arms Exports Controls criticized the UK government for issuing an increased total of 288 licenses for arms sales to Saudi Arabia in 2011, along with 97 licenses to Bahrain. Evidence collected at a parliamentary hearing showed that the Prime Minister's visit to Kuwait was seen in the region as symbolic of a continuity in the 'bad old ways' as he lectured on the importance of human rights trailed by a delegation of arms companies (even if the government pointed out that it revoked a record 158 licences in 2011) (House of Commons 2012: chapter 4, para. 6). The UK signed a new security pact with Bahrain in October 2012 and beefed up its support for the Kuwaiti Military Staff College.

The UK remains ambivalent about an enhanced EU role. Some observers suggest that the extent of the UK's increased military presence in the region almost takes it back to an 'east of Suez' doctrine: an upgraded airbase in the UAE; enhanced cooperation with the Emirates; the Royal Navy's increased use of facilities in Bahrain; and a beefed-up presence in Jordan. This is driven in part by a desire to assist the US's pivot to Asia by demonstrating UK utility to Washington – albeit perhaps raising expectations beyond what Britain can actually deliver in terms of security protection for the region (Stansfield and Kelly 2013).

EU governments relied on the UAE and Qatar for help in Libya. Spanish diplomats insist that geo-strategy prevents the EU from applying a reform logic to the Gulf (Youngs 2014). The inter-linkage of Gulf and Spanish royal families weighs heavily, together with a defence cooperation deal between Spain and the UAE and Saudi Arabia. The French government has signed several defence accords with Gulf regimes. Qatar buys four-fifths of its defence equipment from France. In July 2011 Germany agreed to sell 200 tanks to Saudi Arabia – despite the echo of Saudi tanks having just gone into Bahrain to quell pro-democracy protests. Germany used increased arms exports as a strategic tool, to enable allies in a context where it remained unwilling to become a stronger security actor itself (ibid.).

At the time of writing, the focus is on the new threat posed by the jihadist group of the 'Islamic State in Iraq and the Levant', which has taken control of large swathes of territory in Iraq and Syria. With Western governments cooperating with Saudi Arabia and the UAE in pushing back against ISIL, there is clearly even less appetite for pushing these states on their own democratic shortcomings. Indeed, the challenge of dealing with ISIL appears to have brought European policies right back to their pre-'Arab Spring' focus on counter-terrorist containment.

Coordinated action against ISIL is in its early stages and it is not clear how it will unfold; evidently, however, the role of Saudi Arabia, the UAE and other Gulf states as 'allies' in the turbulent reshaping of Middle East politics has put the onus back on traditional security and alliance-building.[14]

Gulf investment has, of course, become important to crisis-stricken EU economies. The GCC's exports now prioritize Asia but its imports still come overwhelmingly from Europe and its foreign direct investment is oriented even more heavily towards Europe in the aftermath of the Eurozone crisis. The UK's stated aim is to be 'the Gulf's commercial partner of choice' (Youngs 2014). It has put in place a network of bilateral accords across the region to help British businesses win more contracts. The UK's ambitious target is to increase trade to the Gulf by two-thirds by 2015; the UK already exports more to the Gulf than to China (Howell 2012). Far from reacting critically to the Saudi protest-quashing incursion into Bahrain, in early March 2011 the UK sent a trade mission to Saudi Arabia. In November 2012, David Cameron made a second extensive trip around the Gulf to build on the 20 per cent increase in exports to the region registered in 2011. He backed a British Aerospace bid for a new five-year aircraft supply deal with Saudi Arabia. In the UAE he lobbied (unsuccessfully) in favour of a possible US$10 billion contract for Typhoon fighters against French and US competition. British Aerospace is now more dependent on Gulf and Saudi contacts in particular, as new procurement contracts within Britain itself have dried up. Spain won a high-speed train contract for the Mecca–Medina line only after personal lobbying from King Juan Carlos; this deal was termed locally 'the contract of the century'. The king also visited Kuwait once a year from 2008 to push infrastructure projects on the behalf of big Spanish companies.

Compounding the effect of security links, EU governments judge Gulf regimes to have remained cooperative players within global energy markets – important at a time of tensions in relations with Russia. The Gulf is set to be increasingly important as an energy provider to European markets. Qatar's share of gas trade expanded dramatically, from a 1 to a nearly 10 per cent share of EU imports between 2001 and 2011, taking market share from Russia (British Petrol 2012: 14). For all the changes to international energy markets and non-conventional sources, Saudi Arabia remains the world's swing producer, the only state with sufficient capacity significantly to temper fluctuations in world oil prices.

The EU has proposed extending the Energy Community Treaty and raised the prospect of a memorandum of understanding for the Gulf, of the type signed with Egypt, Algeria, Ukraine, Azerbaijan and Kazakhstan. The European Commission has also advocated support for building pipelines across the Arabian Peninsula to reduce the amount of oil that had to pass through the vulnerable Straits of Hormuz (Luciani 2007: 15). In practice, as Europe's financial crisis coincided with a period of renewed oil price hikes, EU Member States have recently been in greater need of liquidity from cash-rich Gulf states than the latter have required European investment in energy infrastructure. Gulf states are increasingly interested in partnership with Asian markets. By 2011, China and Japan were the two largest markets for Gulf oil exports; 80 per cent of Asia's oil imports now come from the Middle East, compared to only 25 per cent of the EU's imports; and 65 per cent of Gulf oil is exported eastwards (Youngs 2014). The EU's hand has palpably weakened.

Conclusions

This chapter has explored the relationship between democracy and geopolitics in EU policies towards Central Asia and the Gulf. It has found that in both regions geopolitical interests continue to militate against more ambitious democracy support policies. The kind of policy instruments that the EU has developed in the ENP have not been easily extended into these two crucial 'neighbours of the EU's neighbours' regions. This may be a relatively unsurprising conclusion; but it does caution against any easy optimism that the ENP can simply be extended outward without taking into account the set of very different strategic and political factors encountered in more distant regions.

Notwithstanding their obvious differences, Central Asia and the Gulf both demonstrate the limits of EU commitments to democracy and human rights. Three observations can be drawn from this analysis. First, Central Asia and the Gulf are both regions where geopolitical and geo-economic calculations still compromise the EU's focus on democracy promotion. This is perhaps not a novel observation, but in the context of this volume it is significant to point out that political trends in ENP countries have not necessarily spread outwards to the broader 'neighbours of the EU's neighbours' band of states. This not to say that such geopolitics are not prominent within the ENP or Saharan Africa; but the challenges of standard EU democracy instruments gaining space in Central Asia or the Gulf appear to be especially daunting. Second, even if the EU's commitment was stronger, the two regions house states whose domestic political regimes do not seem propitious to pro-reform influences. Third, leading on from this, some of the basic principles of the European Neighbourhood Policy have little traction in these two regions; this is the case in particular with the uploading of EU rules and proposed integrative initiatives. These three conclusions constitute a sober assessment for the prospects of an effective and coherent 'neighbours of the neighbours' policy – that is, for implementing the broadening of the ENP's scope.

Notes

1 See Delegation of the European Union to Uzbekistan, http://eeas.europa.eu/delegations/uzbekistan/eu_uzbekistan/political_relations/index_en.htm (accessed March 2013).
2 In April 2014, High Representative Catherine Ashton appointed Janos Herman as EU Special Envoy to Central Asia. The appointment followed the resignation of Patricia Flor, former EU Special Representative for Central Asia from 2012 to 2014 (European External Action Service 2014).

3 Per capita calculation builds on population figures taken from World Bank (2012).
4 During the Andijon uprising some 1,500 protesters are believed to have been killed by Uzbek security forces.
5 See also Chapter 5 by Sieglinde Gstöhl and Chapter 9 by Maud Fichet, Enrique Ibáñez and Veronika Orbetsova in this volume.
6 See also Chapter 7 by Zuhal Yeşilyurt Gündüz in this volume.
7 See also Chapter 11 by Johannes Theiss in this volume.
8 See also Chapter 3 by Alyson J.K. Bailes and Pál Dunay in this volume.
9 According to the *Guardian* (2013), 'Kazakhstan's human rights record may look woeful, but Nazarbayev has good spin doctors. Chief among them is Tony Blair, who has a multimillion-pound contract with Astana to advise on governance'.
10 See also Chapter 4 by Gilles de Kerchove and Christiane Höhn in this volume.
11 Based on interviews by Richard Youngs in Brussels 2014.
12 Based on interviews by Richard Youngs in Kuwait 2014.
13 Based on interviews by Richard Youngs in Brussels 2014.
14 See also Chapter 3 by Alyson J.K. Bailes and Pál Dunay and Chapter 4 by Gilles de Kerchove and Christiane Höhn in this volume.

References

Axyonova, V. (2012) 'EU Human Rights and Democratisation Assistance to Central Asia: In Need of Further Reform', *EUCAM Policy Brief* 12, Brussels: EUCAM.

Boonstra, J. and T. Tsertsvadze (2013) 'Kazakhstan: rising star or falling short of results', *EurActiv*, 31 May, www.euractiv.com/global-europe/kazakhstan-rising-star-falling-s-analysis-528175 (accessed May 2014).

British Petrol (2012) *BP Statistical Review of World Energy June 2012*, London, www.bp.com/content/dam/bp/pdf/Statistical-Review-2012/statistical_review_of_world_energy_2012.pdf (accessed September 2014).

British Petrol (2014) *BP Statistical Review of World Energy June 2014*, London, www.bp.com/content/dam/bp/pdf/Energy-economics/statistical-review-2014/BP-statistical-review-of-world-energy-2014-full-report.pdf (accessed September 2014).

Brookings Doha Centre and FRIDE (2013) *Toward a Strategic Partnership? The EU and the GCC in a Revolutionary Middle East*, Event Briefing, January.

Council of the European Union (1998) 'Common Position of 25 May 1998 concerning Human Rights, Democratic Principles, the Rule of Law and Good Governance in Africa (98/350/CFSP)', *Official Journal of the European Communities*, L 158, 2 June, 1–2.

Council of the European Union (2007) *The EU and Central Asia: Strategy for a New Partnership*, 10113/07, Brussels, 31 May.

Der Spiegel (2006) 'Germany's Favourite Despot', 2 August.

Eder, F. and U. Halbach (2005) *Regime Change in Kyrgyzstan and the Specter of Coups in the CIS*, Policy Brief (C16), Berlin: German Institute for International and Security Affairs.

European Commission (2010a) *Central Asia DCI Indicative Programme 2011–2013*, www.eeas.europa.eu/central_asia/docs/2010_ca_mtr_en.pdf (accessed June 2013).

European Commission (2010b) *EU Energy and Transport in Figures*, Statistical Pocketbook, Brussels.

European Commission (2014) 'EuropeAid – Development and Cooperation' website, http://ec.europa.eu/europeaid/where/asia/overview/index_en.htm (accessed May 2014).

European Communities (1999) 'EC, ECSC, Euratom: Council and Commission Decision of 31 May 1999 on the Conclusion of the Partnership and Cooperation Agreement

Establishing a Partnership between the European Communities and their Member States, of the one part, and the Republic of Uzbekistan, of the other part', *Official Journal of the European Union*, L 229, 31 August, 1–2.

European Community (2006) 'European Community Regional Strategy Paper for Assistance to Central Asia for the period 2007–2013', http://eeas.europa.eu/central_asia/rsp/07_13_en.pdf (accessed May 2014).

European External Action Service (2014) 'Catherine Ashton appoints Special Envoy to Central Asia', Press Release, 140409/01, Brussels, 9 April, http://eeas.europa.eu/statements/docs/2014/140409_01_en.pdf (accessed July 2014).

European Parliament (2012) 'Kazakhstan must Improve Human Rights Record to get Closer Ties with the EU', Press Release, 22 November, www.europarl.europa.eu/pdfs/news/expert/infopress/20121116IPR55719/20121116IPR55719_en.pdf (accessed June 2013).

European Union (2010) 'European Neighbourhood and Partnership Instrument: Ukraine: National Indicative Programme 2011–2013', http://ec.europa.eu/world/enp/pdf/country/2011_enpi_nip_ukraine_en.pdf (accessed June 2013).

Eurostat (2012) *Yearbook 2012: The Statistical Guide to Europe*, Luxembourg: Office for Official Publications of the European Communities.

Freedom House (2012) 'Worst of the Worst: The World's Most Repressive Societies', Washington, DC, www.freedomhouse.org/sites/default/files/Worst%20of%20the%20Worst%202012%20final%20report.pdf (accessed May 2014).

Gause, F.G. (2011) 'Why Middle East Studies Missed the Arab Spring: The Myth of Authoritarian Stability', *Foreign Affairs* 90/4, 81–90.

Gause, F.G. and S.L. Yom (2012) 'Resilient Royals: How Arab Monarchies Hang On', *Journal of Democracy* 23(4), 74–88.

Guardian (2007) 'Germany Pushes for Lifting of EU Sanctions on Uzbekistan', 14 May.

Guardian (2013) 'Kazakhstan: Strategically Valuable but Democracy is "Work in Progress" ', 30 June.

House of Commons (2011) *British Foreign Policy and the 'Arab Spring': The Transition to Democracy*, London: Foreign Affairs Committee, October.

House of Commons (2012) *British Foreign Policy And the Arab Spring*, London: Foreign Affairs Committee, July.

Howell, D. (2012) 'UK Relations with the GCC Region: A Broadening Partnership', speech, Foreign Office Minister, GCC and the City conference, 20 June.

Human Rights Watch (2013a) 'Tajikistan: End Crackdown Ahead of Election', 22 October, www.hrw.org/news/2013/10/21/tajikistan-end-crackdown-ahead-election (accessed May 2014).

Human Rights Watch (2013b) 'World Report 2013, Country Chapter on Kazakhstan', www.hrw.org/world-report/2013/country-chapters/kazakhstan (accessed March 2013).

International Crisis Group (2006) *Central Asia: What Role for the European Union?*, *Asia Report* 113, Osh and Brussels.

International Crisis Group (2013) *Kazakhstan: Waiting for Change*, Asia Report 250, Osh and Brussels.

Jünemann, A and M. Knodt (2007) *Externe Demokratieförderung durch die Europäische Union European External Democracy Promotion*, Baden-Baden: Nomos.

Kemp, G. and R. Harkavy (1997) *Strategic Geography and the Changing Middle East*, Washington, DC: Brookings Institution Press.

Lacroix, S. (2011) 'Is Saudi Arabia Immune?', *Journal of Democracy* 22(4), 48–59.

Luciani, G. (2007) 'The Economics and Politics of the "Dire Straits" ', *GRC Security and Terrorism Research Bulletin* 6, Dubai: Gulf Research Centre, August.

Mathiesen, T. (2012) 'A Saudi Spring? The Shi's Protest Movement in the Eastern Province 2011–2012', *Middle East Journal* 66(4), 628–659.

Melvin, N. and J. Boonstra (2008) 'The EU Strategy for Central Asia at Year One', *EUCAM Policy Brief* 1, Brussels: EUCAM, www.fride.org/download/OP_The_EU_Strategy_ENG_oct08.pdf (accessed May 2014).

New York Times (2012) 'Germany and Kazakhstan Sign Rare Earths Agreement', 8 February.

Nichol, J. (2013) 'Kazakhstan: Recent Developments and U.S. Interests', Congressional Research Service, Washington, DC, 22 July.

Nygren, B. (2007) *The Rebuilding of Greater Russia: Putin's Foreign Policy Towards the CIS Countries*, Milton Park: Routledge.

Risse, T. and K. Sikkink (1999) 'The Socialization of International Human Rights Norms into Domestic Practices', in T. Risse, S.C. Ropp and K. Sikkink (eds) *The Power of Human Rights: International Norms and Domestic Change*, Cambridge: Cambridge University Press, 1–39.

Stansfield G. and S. Kelly (2013) *A Return to East of Suez? UK Military Deployment to the Gulf*, RUSI Working Paper, London, April.

Warkotsch, A. (2011) 'Human Rights, Democratization and Good Governance', in A. Warkotsch (ed.) *The European Union and Central Asia*, London: Routledge, 102–114.

World Bank (2012) *World Development Report 2012*, Washington, DC.

Youngs, R. (2014) *Europe in the New Middle East: Opportunity or Exclusion?* Oxford: Oxford University Press.

Part III

Opportunities for connecting the neighbours' neighbours

9 Building, bridging, blocking

The EU's approach towards sub-regional integration in its broader neighbourhood

Maud Fichet, Enrique Ibáñez and Veronika Orbetsova

Introduction: building, bridging and blocking sub-regional integration

The number of regional integration processes has exponentially increased since the second half of the twentieth century. Although the scope, objectives and level of integration of these processes vary greatly, this wave of 'regionalism' has resulted in a plethora of (sub-)regional organizations, some of which have turned out to be significant international actors like the European Union (EU). This is in line with the evolution from 'old regionalism' to 'new regionalism' identified by Söderbaum and Sbragia (2010: 571): whereas the former was structured around the Cold War equilibrium and dominated by nation-states, the latter has flourished in the wake of the collapse of the 'Iron Curtain', accentuating the economic nature of regionalism and allowing non-state actors to become relevant players as well. Regionalism can be defined as the 'elaboration of agreed rules and collective institutions by the governments of a region; generally these are formal trade and economic integration agreements but could extend to other areas' (Holden 2011: 160). Recent literature on the topic has also developed the concept of 'open regionalism', which seeks to make the development of regional integration and an active participation in the international markets compatible (Shui and Walkenhorst 2010: 269).

As Holden (2011) notes, (sub-)regional integration can take many forms ranging from a pure economic rationale to including political and security issues. Table 9.1 at the end of this chapter provides an overview of the regional integration schemes in the EU's broader neighbourhood stretching from sub-Saharan Africa to the Middle East and Central Asia. In line with the reasoning by Söderbaum and Sbragia (2010), which attributes more importance to the economic nature of (sub-)regional integration, and taking into account the EU's own nature as first and foremost a huge single market, this chapter will primarily focus on economic integration processes. As an economic power, the EU has indeed stronger incentives to interact with predominantly economic regionalization. Following Mattli (1999: 41), regional economic integration is understood as the process of 'voluntary linking in the economic domain of two or more formerly independent states to the extent that authority over key areas of domestic regulation and policy is shifted to the supranational level'. This definition can also be applied to the phenomenon of sub-regional integration, with sub-regions being the 'geographical-political spaces which are subsets of a larger regional space' (Cottey 2009: 5). In this chapter, the notions of sub-regional and regional integration will be used interchangeably, as there is a difference only in the geographical scope.

The process of (sub-)regional economic integration can be divided into several stages, each of which is an enhanced version of the previous one. Following Balassa's (1961: 2) categorization, a free trade area or agreement (FTA) encompasses the abolition of tariffs and quotas between its members; a customs union adds the harmonization of tariffs *vis-à-vis* non-members; a common market removes restrictions on the movement of production factors, notably labour and capital; and ultimately an economic union (with a common currency) adds harmonized economic policies and possibly a unified monetary policy as a result of the single currency. The regional integration processes will be examined in light of this progression.

This chapter thus examines why and how the EU is engaging with subregional economic integration processes in its broader neighbourhood. To answer this question, a comparative approach will be used in which three different sub-regions of the EU's broader neighbourhood will be analysed, namely the Southern Mediterranean region, the Gulf and the post-Soviet space.[1] Although the Southern Mediterranean is covered by the European Neighbourhood Policy (ENP), and therefore does not belong to the broader neighbourhood *per se*, we will focus on this region rather than on sub-Saharan Africa because membership in the current sub-regional integration schemes in the Southern Mediterranean is open to the neighbouring African countries, whereas no other real sub-regional integration scheme has developed in the Sahel or the Horn of Africa.

We argue that, contrary to the assumption commonly found in the literature whereby the EU is generally expected to 'reproduce itself ... advocating its own form of regional integration' (Bretherton and Vogler 2006: 95), because it is the 'best way of managing social and political conflict, fostering the economic wealth of a society and ensuring peace and stability' (Börzel and Risse 2009: 22), the EU has taken a different stance towards sub-regional integration depending on the region at hand. More precisely, as will be set out below, the EU has adopted a 'three-B' approach: a 'building' strategy in the Southern Mediterranean, a 'bridging' strategy in the Gulf and a 'blocking' strategy in the post-Soviet space.

An analysis of this 'three-B' approach towards sub-regional integration that can be observed in the EU's broader neighbourhood requires an investigation of the EU's dominant interests in each case. The 'building' approach in the Southern Mediterranean region may be understood as a firm support of integration initiatives not only as declared support but also at financial and technical levels. It is based on the EU's own integration experience and mainly determined by the regions' geographical proximity to the EU. This policy is based on the assumption that a greater degree of integration among the countries would boost economic growth and therefore reduce potential problems (immigration, terrorism, political instability, etc.). On the other hand, the 'bridging' approach adopted towards the Gulf results in a support of sub-regional integration processes as well, as long as these would serve the EU's primary foreign policy objectives in the region, namely the securitization of energy resources. Finally, the 'blocking' approach used by the EU *vis-à-vis* the post-Soviet space, and other sub-regional integration schemes which include Russia for that matter, derives from the incompatibility of the EU's model with the integration model promoted by Russia, the other great governance exporter of the region (Dragneva and Wolczuk 2012: 9). The EU, then, tries to block any sub-regional integration scheme in the post-Soviet space that is not based on its own model or rules, as it is seen as a potential threat for its economic and political objectives. This attitude is to a large extent linked to the mutual distrust and the talking at cross-purposes that increasingly characterize the EU–Russia relationship (Bachkatov 2012: 324).

This chapter first introduces an analytical framework to study the motivations that lead the EU to engage with sub-regional economic integration schemes. Then the framework is applied to one case of economic integration in each of the three regions. The case studies have been selected after an extensive mapping exercise, which is reflected in Table 9.1. This will allow for a comparative analysis between both the evolution of the three processes and the EU's approaches toward each of them. Finally, conclusions will be drawn concerning the effectiveness of the strategies adopted by the EU in accordance with its interests.

Why does the EU normally promote sub-regional integration?

As a primary example of regional market integration, the EU sets among its top priorities the fostering of (sub-)regional integration in other areas of the world (Börzel and Risse: 21) as 'preconditions for political stability, economic development and the reduction of poverty and social divisions' (European Commission 2003: 3). The EU has repeatedly stressed its desire to actively contribute to the stability, security and prosperity of its neighbourhood (European Commission 2006: 8). The 'export' of these three values constitutes, indeed, the ENP's main objective. This stated positive approach toward (sub-)regional integration is increasingly seen 'as the "normal way" … to address issues of common interests' (Bicchi 2006: 287).[2]

The question that arises is why the EU is interested in pursuing interregionalism. Although the motivations of the EU to foster (sub-)regional integration are interlinked and to some extent overlapping, for heuristic reasons, this study divides them into two broad categories: (1) economic motivations and (2) political and security motivations. Both categories of motivations are related to the perceptions of power which the EU, as an international actor, seeks to project.

Within the economic motivations, four main drivers can be identified: (a) convergence of policies and regulatory approximation to the EU; (b) market opening, trade defence and commercial diplomacy; (c) competition with other norm exporters; and (d) prosperity in the EU's neighbourhood.

The first economic driver is linked to Chad Damro's concept of 'Market Power Europe', according to which the EU 'exercises its power through the externalisation of economic and social market-related policies and regulatory measures' (Damro 2012: 682). Indeed, as Momani (2007: 5) points out, the EU prefers to foster 'intraregional agreements to facilitate policy harmonization, easing the way for EU investment in other regions'.

This relates directly to the second driver which can be referred to as market access and which re-groups motivations related to market opening, trade defence and commercial diplomacy. By establishing convergent rules and standards, EU firms can gain easier access to diversified markets, especially in a context of economic downturn.

Gaining access to foreign markets is also essential for the third economic motivation – competition with other norm exporters. In today's world, where a high degree of economic liberalization has already been attained, states concentrate their efforts on establishing their own rules and standards. This is what Strange (1988: 24–25) defines as 'structural power', or 'the power to shape and determine the structures of the global political economy, within which other states (and regions) ... operate'. Although being a huge market is a clear advantage for the EU, it has to counter the offers of other standard-setting international actors, both at a global level (mainly the US) and at a more regional level (Russia and increasingly other emerging economies such as China or Brazil).

The fourth economic motivation consists in ensuring the prosperity of the regions in proximity to the European Union by promoting cooperation between developing countries, or 'south–south cooperation', in addition to the EU's own development cooperation. This motivation is based on the assumption that increased intra-regional trade helps the achievement of economic growth and development. It should be noted, though, that some of the schemes that the EU has already put in place follow a 'north–south' or 'hub-and-spoke' pattern instead, which, according to Wippel (2005: 6),

> [c]an be extremely detrimental as they impede horizontal exchange by vertically binding individual countries in a region to an already integrated core with a series of bilateral FTAs instead of creating a multilateral FTA network with all the countries concerned.

As far as the political and security motivations are concerned, three main driving forces may be identified: (a) stability in the EU's neighbourhood; (b) security in the EU's neighbourhood (in relation to both traditional and non-traditional threats); and

(c) exporting the belief system and principles of the EU as well as its model of integration.

The first variable is self-explanatory and was stated for the first time in the European Security Strategy (ESS) of 2003: 'It is in the European interest that countries on our borders are well-governed' (European Council 2003: 7). This was complemented by a Communication of the European Commission (2006: 11) in which it aspired to 'look beyond the Union's immediate neighbourhood, to work with "the neighbours of our neighbours"' in order to foster regional cooperation and avoid negative spill-over effects from the 'second ring' of neighbours to the EU's immediate neighbourhood.

Narrowly linked to the concept of stability, security is a second essential political driver that explains the EU's interest in other (sub-)regional integration mechanisms. Indeed, while underlining the crucial role of regional organizations in combating global threats to peace and security, the ESS stresses the importance of ensuring 'security and stability in [the EU's] neighbourhood and beyond' (European Council 2003: 10). Ensuring energy security is of vital importance for the EU since it is relatively poor in natural resources and thus heavily dependent on imports from its neighbouring regions to sustain its economy and competitiveness.[3] This is why the Council of the European Union (2013: 3, 8), in its review of developments on the external dimension of the EU energy policy, urges the development of 'cooperation with neighbouring countries' in general and with 'countries in the Western Balkans, Eastern Europe and other neighbouring countries willing and able to implement the relevant EU *acquis*' in particular. Moreover, the newly adopted European Energy Security Strategy states that 'fundamental political decisions should be discussed with neighbouring countries' (European Commission 2014a: 17).

Finally, exporting the EU's guiding principles and belief system based on its own model of integration and thus exercising what Ian Manners (2002: 235–258) named 'normative power' constitutes a third main political motivation for promoting sub-regional integration. This tendency to 'reproduce itself' (Bretherton and Vogler 2006: 49) rests on the assumption that the EU projects externally its internal solutions (Lavenex 2004: 695), resulting in what Bicchi (2006: 287) defines as an 'our size fits all' approach. By doing so, the EU exports its (moderate) neo-liberal model – free market with some degree of state intervention – and its belief system, *inter alia* enshrined in art. 21 TEU: democracy, rule of law, human rights and fundamental freedoms, respect for human dignity, equality and solidarity, and respect for the principles of the UN Charter and international law.

In sum, whether the motivations are economic or rather political and security-related, it could be argued that the EU promotes (sub-)regional integration to achieve 'gains [that it] has been unable to reap through more traditional multilateral and bilateral channels' (Aggarwal and Fogarty 2005: 342).

Mapping sub-regional economic integration in the EU's broader neighbourhood

The choice to focus on three sub-regional integration schemes, one in North Africa, one in the Gulf and one in the post-Soviet space among the schemes listed in Table 9.1, lies in the motivations of the EU. Taking into consideration the abovementioned motivations, one would expect that the EU would have a similar supportive approach towards all sub-regional integration efforts in its immediate or broader neighbourhood. However, we argue that different motivations prevail.

First of all, it is important to acknowledge that the sub-regional distinction presented here is somewhat artificial and mainly serves an analytical purpose. It is based on the geopolitical division that informs the EU's own understanding of its neighbourhood. Nevertheless, it must be noted that some countries participate in several sub-regional integration schemes, which are not always classified as belonging to the same region (see Table 9.1).

Sub-regional integration in the Mediterranean and in the Gulf region is not a new phenomenon but dates back to the processes of decolonization. Common economic, linguistic and cultural features among countries in the region have facilitated sub-regional integration initiatives, ranging from simple bilateral agreements to more sophisticated schemes (Shui and Walkenhorst 2010: 269–70). The case study selected for the Mediterranean region is the Agadir Agreement, a process undertaken by the ENP countries Morocco, Tunisia, Egypt and Jordan (see Table 9.1), with membership open to their sub-Saharan neighbours. Several reasons inform this choice. First, the Agadir Process is composed of those Mediterranean countries whose commercial relationship with the EU is the most integrated (Ayadi and Gadi 2013: 8): all of them have concluded Association Agreements (AA) and ENP Action Plans, and they are also members of the World Trade Organization (WTO) (Boussetta 2005: 174). Second, it groups countries with no common border among themselves and belonging to different sub-regions: Morocco and Tunisia to the Maghreb; Egypt and Jordan to the Mashreq. And third, it has garnered the support of the EU not only at a declaratory level, but also in terms of financing and technical expertise.

In the Gulf region, the focus will be put on the Cooperation Council of the Arab States of the Gulf (GCC) as the most prominent sub-regional organization. It centralizes decisions to initiate or repel economic, political and security integration processes. The GCC is also at the heart of the EU's strategy for the region, and the EU is, indeed, focusing on the GCC so as to consolidate regionalism. Consequently, and even in the face of current difficulties, it remains the most relevant organization to study in this region (Antkiewicz and Momani 2009: 217–235).

When it comes to the post-Soviet space, three preliminary observations are in order. First, the notion of 'post-Soviet space' seems more appropriate than that of 'Eurasia', not only because it allows to define the region in geographical, socio-economic and political terms, but also because it introduces a historically embedded perspective, indispensable for the understanding of the processes in the region. Second, it is important to note the dominant role of Russia, as all sub-regional integration involving this country is bound to be asymmetric due to its sheer size and economic characteristics (Cooper 2013: 15–34). Third, since sub-regional integration was quite advanced during the Soviet period (Warsaw Pact, COMECON), it seems more appropriate to talk about 're-integration'. This would imply that sub-regional integration should be easier and speedier than in other regions. However, since all of the states in the post-Soviet space are 'newly independent' states, they share concerns about safeguarding their sovereignty which is why they are dubious about both the ambitions of Russia and its hege-monic position. In this region, the focus has been on the formation of a Eurasian Economic Union (EEU) as of 2015. This process has strongly accelerated in the past decade, making it the most dynamic integration process in the region. More-over, the geopolitical changes and the conflict in eastern Ukraine in 2014 have brought this process to the attention not only of the EU, but also of the rest of the world.

Building regional integration: the Agadir Process

This section applies the analytical framework presented above to study the main motivations that have led the EU to promote sub-regional integration in the Southern Mediterranean region, using the Agadir Agreement as a case study.

Origins

At the fourth Euro-Mediterranean conference – the periodic meeting of foreign affairs ministers of the members of the Euro-Mediterranean Partnership (EMP) – held in Marseilles in November 2000, the final conclusions welcomed the desire expressed by Morocco, Tunisia, Egypt and Jordan to conclude an FTA among themselves and underlined the back-up role the EU should play (Fourth Euro-Mediterranean Conference 2000). Following the Marseilles conference, the 'Agadir Declaration' of May 2001 paved the way towards the establishment of an FTA between these countries. The membership to this FTA, though, was not exclusive; it was left open to '[a]ny Arab state member of the Arab League and the … [GAFTA], linked to the EU through an Association Agreement or a free trade agreement' (Agadir Agreement 2004).[4]

Initialled in Amman in 2003, where the secretariat, known as the Agadir Technical Unit (ATU), was established, the agreement was signed in Rabat on 25 February 2004 and entered into force in July 2006. The agreement is based on two premises: (1) deeper economic integration, including trade in goods and services, as well as enhancing investment opportunities, and (2) wider integra-tion with the EU (Casero and Seshan 2010: 299). The deepening and widening of integration with the EU is best exemplified by the adoption of the EU rules of origin by the contracting parties of the Agadir Agreement. For some authors this constitutes a real added value as it could help to maximize the benefits of the

AAs that these countries have concluded with the EU by facilitating their access to the EU's market (Ghoneim 2013: 3).

The creation of an FTA among these four countries served several purposes. First, the Agadir Agreement was supposed to help attain the objective set in the 'Barcelona Declaration' of establishing a Euro-Mediterranean FTA (EMFTA) by 2010 (Euro-Mediterranean Conference 1995; European Commission 2010: 199). This EMFTA was to be gradually established by concluding FTAs between the EU and the Mediterranean Partner Countries (MPCs) and then among the MPCs themselves, and finally by regionalizing those into a greater FTA (De Ville and Reynaert 2010: 195).

Second, the Agadir Agreement was also supposed to boost intra-regional trade among the MPCs, which to the date had 'remained limited and well below potential' (Bayar 2006: 4). In the late 2000s, the level of intra-Maghreb trade barely reached 2 per cent of the sub-region's combined gross domestic product (GDP) and accounted for only about 3 per cent of the region's total trade, representing one of the lowest intra-regional trade exchanges in the world (Akhtar and Rouis 2010). Several economic reasons have been put forward to explain these underperforming intra-regional trade flows (Shui and Walkenhorst 2010: 273). However, there seems to be a consensus that rather than economic impediments, the main hampering factor was (and still is) the lack of real political will (Boussetta 2005: 176). The Agadir Agreement was also conceived as a way to circumvent the Arab Maghreb Union (AMU), which had been paralysed mainly due to the opposition of Algeria to go further in the integration process. The Agadir Process emerged, thus, as a political message to the rest of the MPCs that only those willing to move towards more sub-regional integration would earn the support of the EU.

The EU's role

The approach that the EU has taken towards the Agadir Process can best be described as a 'building' approach, in that the EU has supported this integration scheme from the beginning. At a declaratory level, the main EU institutions, namely the European Parliament, the European Commission and the Council of the EU, expressed their firm support for the Agadir Process which galvanized along two lines: the first one led EU officials to acknowledge that its creation would help the establishment of the EMFTA by 2010, as the then Commissioner for External Relations, Chris Patten (2001), stated: '[t]his sort of sub-regional integration … is the best practical method to move ahead in our partnership towards the overall objective of a Euro-Med free trade area by 2010'. The second line of support stressed the readiness of the European Commission (2004) to support the establishment of the Agadir Process by both financial and technical means. Again, Commissioner Patten (2001: 4) stated that the EU was willing to help the participating countries 'in any way we [the EU] can, political, technical and financial'. Along the same lines, Trade Commissioner Peter Mandelson (2008) reiterated this position by offering 'help and experience' to the participating countries.

Until 2012, the EU disbursed a total amount of €8 million in support of the Agadir Process. This was done first within the framework of the MEDA programme, the main financial instrument covering the EMP established in 1996, and then through the European Neighbourhood and Partnership Instrument (ENPI, 2007–13; as of 2014 the European Neighbourhood Instrument, ENI, 2014–20), the main financial instrument of the ENP.[5] For the first phase (2004–08) of the 'Support Project to the Agadir Agreement' an amount of €4 million was allocated to help setting up the ATU and to finance other activities outlined in this document. The second phase (2008–12), equally funded with €4 million, sought to consolidate the ATU. The third phase of the project, 'Support to trade development in the Southern Mediterranean programme', approved by the Commission in July 2013, also foresees €4 million to secure progress in various fields such as 'nontariff barriers …, rules of origin, services and investment, competition, intellectual property rights, dispute settlement, anti-dumping and regional trade facilitation' (European Commission 2013: 1). Moreover, over the period 1995–2009, the four countries received around 60 per cent of the EU's total Official Development Assistance (ODA) to the region (Ayadi and Gadi 2013: 8).

EU motivations

Drawing on the analytical framework presented in the introduction to this chapter, four main motivations can be identified for the EU to act as a regional integration builder in the case of the Agadir Process. Two of them fall under the economic motivations of our analytical framework and two under the political and security dimension. Some limitations and shortcomings of the Agadir Agreement are also pointed out at the end of this section.

Among economic motivations, working towards obtaining regulatory and legislative approximation to the EU is arguably the strongest. Empirically, this is supported by the fact that the Agadir countries adopted the pan-Euro-Mediterranean protocol on cumulation of origin, which was approved by the Council of the EU in October 2005 (Lannon and Martín 2009: 32), instead of implementing the pan-Arab cumulation system applied within GAFTA. Harmonization of rules of origin in the Mediterranean basin is crucial for the establishment and functionality of the EMFTA. It is precisely the lack of harmonization in rules of origin – and not the level of protection of customs duties which has been decreasing gradually – that hinders further integration in the region (Galal and Reiffers 2012: 56–57).

The second motivation within the economic dimension is linked to the EU's interests in promoting sub-regional integration as a way to counter the models of integration of other norm exporters. Although it is the most important trading partner, the EU is not the only actor that has concluded FTAs in the region: the US has signed FTAs with Jordan and Morocco; Turkey with all Agadir participants except for Jordan; and of particular importance is the increasing presence of China in the region as a main exporter since the 2000s (Ghoneim 2013: 2). In addition, the influence of the Gulf countries in the Southern Mediterranean has been enhanced since the 'Arab Spring' as they have offered significant amounts of financial and material help to the countries in the region (Al-Sayed 2013).

Turning to the political and security side of our framework, an important driver for the EU's support of sub-regional integration was the attainment of stability in the region, clearly related to the previous motivation, that is, competing to become the norm setter in the regions covered by the ENP. In this sense, geographical proximity is a decisive element, as the EU fears turmoil in its main backyard. Illegal immigration, terrorism networks or organized crime are just a few examples of transnational threats that the Union wants to reduce at its borders.[6] Fostering sub-regional integration is a way to link these countries' economies and make them cooperate (Bayar 2006: 8).

The second political motivation for the EU was to promote its own belief system, that is, the establishment of a free-market economy with a certain degree of state intervention. As Commissioner Mandelson (2008) stated, the aim with the Agadir Process was to create a 'regional market place along the southern shore of the Mediterranean, to echo the single market we have on the northern side'. It should be noted that the EU supported this process also as a way to bypass the AMU, which was not delivering any positive results, mainly due to the blocking position of Algeria. Therefore, the support to the Agadir Process needs to be understood also as a political message sent to Algeria and other countries in the region conveying the idea that isolation and non-engagement would not be rewarded.

Considering how the process was conceived, the active involvement that the EU showed and the high stakes the EU had in the region led many authors to rightly point out the enormous potential of the Agadir Process (Bayar 2006; Boussetta 2005; Handoussa and Reiffers 2002). First of all, it was an agreement linking two sub-regions, the Maghreb and the Mashreq, which could serve as a stepping stone to GAFTA, and it also had the advantage to reinforce South–South cooperation. Second, it was backed by full political, financial and technical support from the EU. Third, it was seen as 'an avant-garde initiative' that brought together those Arab countries most interested in economic reforms (Wippel 2005: 16). And finally, it was an ambitious agreement that went beyond trade in goods, extending its scope to trade in services and dealing as well with regulatory and legislative approximation.

In spite of these promising features, the assessment of the Agadir Process today is quite nuanced mainly because many sub-regional agreements in the Middle Eastern and North African (MENA) region 'look stronger on paper than in practice' (Shui and Walkenhorst 2010: 295). First of all, the Agadir Process has enhanced closer integration with the EU, but it has failed to deliver on the objective of boosting intra-regional trade. For Liargovas (2013: 18), this is due to the 'absence of "one single" regionalism in the North Africa/Middle East area', which leads him to conclude that the Agadir Process, in spite of being the most important commercial initiative in the region, 'has not contributed to the creation of a deep and comprehensive free trade area with its current members'.

A second obstacle is the slow pace of liberalization in agricultural products and services. Paradoxically, the MPCs have been more receptive to open up their markets in services to the EU than to grant the same access to their Mediterranean neighbours in the Maghreb (Brunel and Hufbauer 2008: 69). A similar situation arises regarding agricultural products. Although the MPCs have notably reduced their tariffs to a regional average of 22.3 per cent for agricultural products, some countries still apply disproportionately high tariffs. The prime examples are three of the four contracting parties of the Agadir Agreement: Morocco (42.1 per cent), Tunisia (40.9 per cent) and Egypt (70.7 per cent) (Kadhim 2013: 71–73).

A third reason is to be found in the regulatory area. Although the adoption of the pan-Euro-Mediterranean protocol was a step in the right direction, Lannon and Martín (2009: 32) consider that the system 'has foundered due to the existence of non-tariff barriers'. In addition, the system is blocked as a result of the proliferation of agreements and the differences in their regulatory systems, which are at the origin of the erosion of preferential treatment (Brunel and Hufbauer 2008: 75).

Conclusions on the Agadir Process

In the light of what has been presented above, it is safe to argue that the EU's motivations for promoting sub-regional integration in the Southern Mediterranean constitute a balanced mix of economic motivations on the one side and political and security motivations on the other. The economic motivations, especially regulatory approximation, derive from the stated objective of establishing the EMFTA in the region, whereas the political and security ones are clearly shaped by the geographical proximity of the region to the EU. It is in the 'first ring' of neighbours where the EU had to learn that the attainment of economic integration cannot be delinked from the political stability and the security of the region. The high stakes the EU has in both dimensions (economic and political/ security) of our framework help explain the 'building' approach to sub-regional integration. It can be concluded that the EU has engaged in promoting sub-regional integration in the Southern Mediterranean because it was in both its economic and political best interests. It has done so by adopting a proactive approach, defined here as a 'building' approach, supporting the initiative from the beginning at both a declaratory and a financial level.

Bridging regional integration: the Gulf Cooperation Council

This section looks at how the EU engaged with a region neighbouring its own neighbours, namely the Arab Peninsula, with the Gulf Cooperation Council as a case study.

Origins

The GCC is comprised of six oil-producing monarchies of the Arabic Peninsula: Saudi Arabia, Bahrain, Qatar, the United Arab Emirates (UAE), Kuwait and Oman. Soon after the GCC was established in Riyadh in 1981, the founding members signed a Unified Economic Agreement (UEA). Ambitious objectives were put forward, aimed at increasing the economic interdependence of the members by establishing an intra-Gulf FTA, enforcing a customs union, ensuring non-discrimination between members on labour issues and capital flows, and achieving a common investment policy (Lawson 2012: 20). According to Partrick (2011: 5), however, internal and regional security fears also drove the integration process. Notwithstanding considerable delays and difficulties, the GCC inaugurated its customs union in 2007. In 2008, the GCC members formally launched the common market and allowed free movement of goods, capital and labour. Complete realization of this free movement still has to be achieved.

The EU–GCC Cooperation Agreement signed in 1988, which entered into force in 1990, aimed at broadening and consolidating 'economic and technical cooperation relations' and encouraging economic diversification between the EU and the GCC (European Community 1989: 4). The ultimate objective was the establishment of an FTA between the two blocs. The Cooperation Agreement also established annual inter-ministerial meetings (Joint Council), as well as regular exchanges at the level of officials (Joint Cooperation Committee). Thematic working groups cover energy, economic issues and air transport.

Negotiations are still on-going, making this agreement the longest European bilateral trade talks to date. After a first halt in 1990, the GCC suspended EU FTA talks in 2008 and the FTA negotiations in 2010. Informal discussions have been on-going ever since, without any official outcome to date.

The EU's role

The EU's approach aims at building bridges with its GCC counterpart through declaratory and diplomatic ties as well as through direct financial support. By meeting annually with the GCC, the EU keeps discussions open on a vast array of topics. The very fact that regular meetings have been held 'is significant in its own right', demonstrating the importance of the relationship for both sides (Koch 2011). Furthermore, European pressure has had repercussions on intra-GCC relations. For example, it was essential to achieve a GCC common tariff, which in turn was a *sine qua non* condition for an FTA with the EU (Bower 2010).

Although FTA negotiations are on-going, several declarations have reiterated European political commitment to and interest in the region over the course of the past decade. The EU Strategic Partnership with the Mediterranean and the Middle East (SPMME) launched in 2004, for example, linked the Gulf to the wider European Middle East strategy, and symbolically the European Commission opened its first delegation in Riyadh (Aliboni 2006: 34). Most importantly, in 2010 a Joint Action Programme (JAP) was launched by the twentieth EU–GCC Joint Ministerial Council. It aimed to 'reinforce cooperation in a number of key strategic areas of mutual interest', ranking from economic cooperation to energy, investment and culture (Council of the European Union 2010: 2). The EU also opened an official delegation in Abu Dhabi in 2013. The JAP lapsed in 2013 and has not yet been renewed.

The EU's 'Industrialized Countries Instrument', dedicated to supporting European projects in industrialized and other high-income countries and territories, secured €6.3 million out of €77.6 million in the 2010–13 envelope for the Gulf. As of 2014, this financial instrument was replaced by the new Partnership Instrument (PI), which specifically aimed at supporting the EU's 2020 Strategy and allocated for 2014 €27 million out of €954.8 million to the Gulf.

EU motivations

The GCC accounts for 4.2 per cent of total EU trade and represents 5.5 per cent of total EU exports, the fifth biggest export market (European Commission 2014d). From a GCC perspective, the EU is 'the grouping's biggest trading partner, with trade flows totalling €152 billion, or 13 per cent of the GCC's global trade' (European External Action Service 2014a).[7] It is yet premature to establish whether the fact that the GCC countries no longer benefit from the EU's Generalized System of Preferences as of 2014 will significantly affect their trade flows or incentive to conclude an FTA.

Looking deeper into the nature of trade relations between the EU and the Gulf reveals that the former almost exclusively imports energy resources and derivatives: 78.5 per cent of the total EU imports in 2013 (European Commission 2014c). Energy has indeed been included in bilateral cooperation (art. 6 Cooperation Agreement) and reiterated in the fourth chapter of the JAP, which calls, for example, for an 'exchange of views on oil and gas market developments as well as the energy policies on both sides' (European External Action Service 2014a). As such, the core of the European interest in the region lies at the crossroads between economic interests and security objectives, in other words, in the securitization of energy supplies.

Stabilization of the region and tackling non-conventional threats also motivate the EU's involvement. In fact, one notes a discrepancy between the agreements signed between the EU and its Gulf counterparts and the issues covered during the Joint Council meetings. Whereas the first article of the Gulf's UEA clearly links economic development with 'contributing to peace and stability in the region' (European Community 1989: 2), the JAP does not. Yet security issues prevail in regular formal or informal meetings. The June 2013 Joint Council meeting held in Manama covered, for example, the Iranian nuclear issue, the Middle East peace process and the Syrian conflict (GCC–EU Joint Council 2013).

While European access to new markets is important, it does not appear to be crucial in these talks. For example, a 2004 Impact Assessment states that, were the most optimistic scenario to unfold – that is, an FTA with full respect of the

Most-Favoured Nation (MFN) clause[8] – the impact on the EU economy would be minimal but extremely beneficial for the GCC economies (Pricewaterhouse-Coopers 2004: 23).

Norm export has also been a peripheral element in the negotiations. In the early stage of EU–GCC cooperation, Europeans pushed for economic integration, akin to the European experience, and the 2010 JAP also clearly states that one objective is the 'exchange of expertise and information in all aspects of the GCC and EU experience in economic integration' (European External Action Service 2014a). However, the institutional spillover has been modest and fragile, both in security and economic terms, and the GCC project fundamentally remains a horizontal intergovernmental cooperation framework where power struggles are outplayed. For some, norm export is merely a reaction to the other competing project in the region, namely that of the US. For Aliboni (2006: 44), the 2004 SPMME was mainly a response to the Greater Middle East Initiative launched by the US for the G8.

The bridge, so far, is still only a half-built bridge as stumbling blocks still obstruct the path towards EU–GCC cooperation. First, internal divisions among the GCC members significantly slowed down the negotiation process. Inner Gulf difficulties hinder the establishment of a common position while negotiating with the EU; for example, GCC members crafted a mandate for the FTA negotiations only in 1997, and agreed on an external common custom tariff only in 2001 (Baabood and Edwards 2007: 541). Old rivalries and a suspicion on the part of the smaller states that any sub-regional integration would inevitably tip the power balance towards Saudi Arabia further increase the divide (Colombo and Committeri 2013: 11).

Second, European interest decreased due to strong opposition to the FTA led by several European industrial actors, such as petrochemical companies, the growing attention paid to the Central and Eastern European countries and the preparation of their accession to the European Union, and persistent difficulties encountered by European economic actors due the lack of liberalization in the Gulf's services industry (Baabood and Edwards 2007: 539, 541).

Finally, misunderstanding is evident in the actual procedure. For example, the Gulf has difficulty coming to terms with the EU imposing high tariffs on GCC exports, such as primary aluminium. Furthermore, political conditionality in trade talks causes recurrent Gulf ire (Issac 2008). Another main obstacle revolves around export duties, essentially a Saudi concern (Habboush 2010).

This relatively negative assessment of EU–Gulf economic cooperation has to be brought into the wider regional context and the desire of Gulf actors to tackle their internal and regional security concerns. In fact, the American project for the region offers both economic benefits and security insurance and successfully conveys the message that 'global trade liberalization was central to America's fight against terrorism' (Al Khouri 2008: 1). Each GCC member has secured bilateral agreements, for example in the form of FTAs, such as the 2004 UAE–USA FTA. Each member also has specific security and military cooperation with the United States, either in the form of providing US military bases as in Kuwait, through the provision of military equipment by the US defence industry to Saudi Arabia or by hosting US Navy ships in UAE ports (in fact, the UAE hold the largest presence of US military ships outside the United States) (US Department of State 2013a, 2013b, 2013c).

Conclusions on the GCC

EU initiatives towards the Gulf are primarily driven by security concerns and are essentially motivated by the securitization of access to energy supplies. Non-traditional security threats increasingly take importance on the agenda of the EU–GCC Joint Council, and will keep taking precedence as Iraqi, Syrian and Libyan turmoil unfolds. Economic interests, such as norm export or market access, rank lower on the European agenda. Consequently, in the Gulf, the EU is engaged in a bridging approach. Sub-regional integration with relevant third parties is not an objective *per se*, but tailored to the implementation of European security interests. The obstacles encountered reveal the difficulty of this approach and question the viability of a 'bridging' strategy to create a sustainable framework for EU–GCC relations.

Blocking regional integration: the Eurasian Economic Union

In this section our analytical framework will be applied to examine the motivations that explain the EU's attitude of suspicion and indisposition toward sub-regional integration processes in the post-Soviet space. The Eurasian integration process will serve as a case study.

Origins

The origins of the Eurasian integration process can be traced back to June 1994, when the President of Kazakhstan, Nursultan Nazarbaev, proposed the creation of supranational institutions responsible for the establishment of a common economic space and common security policy. According to him, this would lead to the elaboration of common policies in science, education, culture and ecology and, eventually, to the establishment of what he called a 'Eurasian Union' composed of a stable core of states and based on voluntary participation (Nazarbaev 1997: 44–50). This project lines up with a number of similar largely declaratory initiatives that emerged in the 1990s as a way to deepen economic integration between the members of the Commonwealth of Independent States (CIS) (see Table 9.1). The need for the newly independent states in the post-Soviet space to consolidate their statehood and to overcome the economic and social crises that hit their fragile transition economies made the pursuit of further sub-regional economic integration impossible in the 1990s. Nevertheless, as Cooper (2013) explains, 'Nazarbaev had sown seeds which were to bear fruit some 15 years later'.

On 10 October 2000, the forerunner of the Eurasian Economic Union – the Eurasian Economic Community (EurAsEC) – was established in Tashkent with the aim of fostering the development of the Eurasian Customs Union (ECU) and the Single Economic Space (SES) (see Table 9.1). The aim of the EurAsEC was to stimulate economic exchanges and trade and to increase coordination, thus allowing member states to better integrate into the world economy (EurAsEC 2000: art. 1). Although the numerous documents issued by the bodies of the EurAsEC 'remained at the intentions level, with little practical implementation' (Cooper 2013: 20), they paved the way to the creation of a customs union between the states of Belarus, Russia and Kazakhstan. On 1 July 2010, the ECU was formally declared as the three states eliminated all customs restrictions and adopted common customs clearance procedures for the goods exchanged between them and began to work on a uniform regime for trade toward non-member countries.

The undertaking of Eurasian economic integration, characterized by Dragneva and Wolczuk (2013:3) as a 'fast-moving and ambitious project', inherited both the existing legislation adopted by EurAsEC and the institutional structure of the organization. The institutional set-up was gradually adapted to the needs of the ECU and later to those of the SES. The Eurasian Economic Commission has been working on the alignment of the customs duties, non-tariff measures and technical regulations of the ECU and the SES with WTO requirements.[9] An Action Plan adopted by the Interstate Council of EurAsEC (2009) outlined the steps to be taken for the establishment of the SES. On 1 January 2012, 17 treaties, covering the areas of common economic policy, freedom of movement of capital and labour, common energy and transport policy, and sanitary, phytosanitary and veterinary measures, came into force, thus establishing the SES (EurAsEC 2011). On 1 July 2012, a year after the 'Customs Union Code' entered into force, customs control was transferred to the external borders of the ECU (Russian Ministry of Foreign Affairs 2014).

The ultimate objective of Eurasian economic integration, as stated in the 'Declaration on the Eurasian Economic Integration' signed in November 2011, was the creation of the Eurasian Economic Union (EEU) (EurAsEC 2011). The Treaty on the EEU was signed on 29 May 2014 in Astana, thus initiating the last stage of Balassa's classification of regional integration mechanisms. The EEU, whose treaty came into force on 1 January 2015, comprises a population of more than 170 million and seeks to be 'a reliable bridge between Europe and the developing Asia' (Nazarbaev 2014). The EEU embarked on a process of enlargement: the Treaty of Accession of Armenia to the EEU was signed on 10 October 2014 during the Minsk EurAsEC Interstate Council (Ria Novosti 2014a). On the same day, the Kyrgyz President, Almazbek Atambaev, confirmed the intention of Kyrgyzstan to become part of the EEU by the end of 2014 (Ria Novosti 2014b).

The EU's role

We argue that the overall approach that the EU has adopted toward the Eurasian economic integration process can be described as 'blocking'. The presidents of the ECU/SES member states, led by Russian President Putin, have been pushing for the recognition of the EEU as an equal negotiating partner, whereas the EU has so far refused to officially grant this status. For instance, at the meeting with the Presidents of the ECU/SES on the occasion of the Supreme Eurasian Economic Council in Minsk, High Representative/Vice-President Ashton did not mention the ECU/SES or the Eurasian integration process (European External Action Service 2014b; 2014c). As Haukkala (2013: 171) explains, in order to validate its position, the European Commission refers to the absence of a mandate to negotiate with the ECU as a whole and to the fact that not all ECU/SES member states are members of the WTO. What is more, the impression in Brussels is that 'Russia was pushing for direct dialogue between the Eurasian Union and the European Union just to legitimise the former, rather than to generate a meaningful trade liberalisation' (Popescu 2014: 41).

Nevertheless, the EU does indirectly cooperate on a practical level with the ECU/SES. The on-going negotiations on the implementation of the EU–Russia Common Spaces require such cooperation since certain trade competencies are transferred from Russia to the ECU/SES (European External Action Service 2013). EU–Russia economic and trade relations (and, in particular, the efforts to align technical regulations and standards) could indirectly influence the development of the Eurasian economic integration process. Moreover, the latter endeavours to make use of the best international practices and, in particular, of the experience of the EU. Indeed, one can find striking similarities between the Eurasian Economic Commission and the European Commission, between the Court of EurAsEC and the European Court of Justice, and between the Interstate Council of EurAsEC and the Council of the EU. Moreover, the Eurasian Economic Commission stresses that the EU 'is a strategic trading partner for the [ECU] and SES member states, generating about half of [ECU] and SES foreign trade' (Eurasian Economic Commission 2013: 36). There seem to be first signs of possible cooperation from the EU side as well. Indeed, on 11 April 2014, Commissioner Štefan Füle (2014) stated:

> The name of the game is a commitment to rules and norms and respect for international law backed by strong rule of law and democracy. The same logic could equally apply to the relationship with the future Eurasian Customs Union, which would allow a free trade zone to be created from Vladivostok to Lisbon.

The official stance of the EU toward the process does not allow it to financially support the Eurasian integration process. Indeed, since 1992, led by the endeavour to stabilize the region, the EU started delivering aid to individual countries through bilateral agreements rather than by using multilateral channels (Bachkatov 2012). This was perceived by Moscow as an attempt to decrease Russian influence in the post-Soviet space. Moreover, the annexation of Crimea in 2014, the subsequent sanctions that the EU imposed on Russia and the trade restrictions on EU products implemented by Russia have negatively impacted not only the economies of Russia and the EU but also the overall EU–Russian relationship.

EU motivations

This 'blocking' stance of the EU toward the Eurasian economic integration process can be explained by motivations that fall both under the economic and the political and security dimensions of the analytical framework. The major economic driver that predefines the other economic motivations is the competition with Russia as a norm exporter in the post-Soviet space. According to Popescu (2014: 35), the EU and Russia have incompatible visions of the power structures in their common neighbourhood. The EU has constructed an image of a Europe of concentric circles with the EU Member States in the centre and a 'friendly neighbourhood ... that would gradually adopt EU norms', while Russia sees Europe through a bipolar lens – with the EU being one pole and the EEU the other (ibid.: 35–36). Indeed, many countries in the post-Soviet space regard the EU as an attractive model of rule-based economic integration and of modernization. The EU launched the ENP in 2004 and the Eastern Partnership in 2008 to deepen the interaction with six countries of its eastern neighbourhood: Armenia, Azerbaijan, Belarus, Georgia, Moldova and Ukraine. However, the EU is no longer 'the only actor promoting deep economic integration premised on regulatory convergence in the post-Soviet space' (Delcour and Wolczuk 2013: 180). Delcour and Kostanyan (2014) argue that countries from the shared neighbourhood have now at least two choices – further integration with the EU or implication in the Eurasian integration project.[10] The EU's 'one size fits all' approach further weakens its offer: the 'massive legal approximation with EU *acquis*' (ibid.: 8) that the Eastern Partnership entails results in important short-term costs that are a major burden for these countries. The EU could strengthen the effectiveness of both the ENP and the Eastern Partnership by being more flexible, taking into account the needs and specificities of the countries, including the 'existing political, diplomatic, economic, energy and military ties between Russia and the countries in the common neighbourhood' (ibid.: 10).

When it comes to another important economic driver, convergence of policies and regulatory approximation to the EU, it should be underlined that most of the ex-Soviet countries continue to use the GOST technical standards which are less competitive than the EU standards; the implementation of the AA-Deep and Comprehensive Free Trade Area (DCFTA) supposes a gradual phasing out of GOST standards (Dreyer and Popescu 2014: 2). Moreover, membership in the ECU/SES is incompatible with the AA-DCFTAs. In the past, the EU implied that no alternative to the AA-DCFTA agreements would be given to the Eastern Partnership countries, and that accession to the EU was not an issue on the negotiation table. However, the crisis in Ukraine has brought some changes. First, the EU agreed to an EU–Ukraine–Russia trilateral negotiation process concerning the implementation of the EU–Ukraine AA-DCFTA signed on 27 June 2014, so as to 'address concerns raised by Russia' and allowed for a delay of the provisional application of the DCFTA until 1 January 2016 (European Commission 2014d). Second, a top official from the EU delegation to Armenia explained that the EU is ready to cooperate with Armenia in the spheres that do not hamper the accession of the country to the EEU and even hinted at the possibility of creating new legal instruments that would allow the strengthening of the bilateral relationship (Matevosyan 2014). Third, on 12 September 2014, the EU concluded an Enhanced Partnership and Cooperation Agreement with Kazakhstan covering, *inter alia*, trade, foreign and security policy and financial cooperation (European External Action Service 2014d). On this occasion, Commission President Barroso (2014) stated that the EU was 'open to build strong and solid relations with the members of Customs Union willing to do so'. In this respect, as suggested by Dreyer and Popescu (2014: 4), it 'would … be prudent for the EU to assess its own position regarding the economic impact of the Eurasian Union' and to arrange for a wider format to discuss the economic concerns, so as to 'avoid new trade barriers from being erected across the Eurasian landmass' (ibid.).

When it comes to political and security motivations, it is important to stress security as a driver, and in particular energy security. Closely linked to the economic interests of the EU, energy security is arguably a major EU interest related to the post-Soviet space. Indeed, the EU imports more than 30 per cent of its gas, 35 per cent of its crude oil and 26 per cent of its solid fuels from Russia (Neslen 2014). The ESS explicitly mentions the need to enter into dialogue with the neighbouring countries concerning energy security but at the same time specifies that cooperation would entail the 'implementation of relevant EU *acquis*' (European Commission 2014a: 17). Reading between the lines, this suggests both the necessity to take into account the Russian position (and increasingly that of the members of the Eurasian economic integration) and the impossibility, at least in the near future, to cooperate with the EEU.

Ensuring stability in the region is another important driver that could explain the EU's stance. In contrast to the two other regions examined above, the EU appears to perceive the Eurasian integration process more as a threat to regional security than as part of the solution to global challenges. The conflict in eastern Ukraine in 2014 and the ambiguous role of Russia confirmed these apprehensions, in the eyes of the EU institutions, the Member States and Western media.

The dynamic development of the Eurasian economic integration process makes it difficult to say whether or not it will suffer the fate of the other initiatives in the post-Soviet space. Although regional trade is increasing, major problems remain. According to Vinokurov (2014: 5–6), a new phenomenon of 'Eurasian scepticism' is emerging, due to four major effects of the ECU/SES: (1) the stronger position of Russian producers on the common market which causes discontent among small and medium-sized businesses in the other member states (and above all in Kazakhstan); (2) the abundance of non-tariff barriers that are still acting as protective mechanisms for the Russian economy; (3) the lack of tangible achievements of the ECU; and (4) the negative sentiment caused by the asymmetry between Russia and the other members. Indeed, more than 75 per cent of the population lives in Russia and the country accounts for more than 85 per cent of the GDP of the ECU/SES. Nevertheless, data from the Eurasian Development Bank (2014) show a considerable public support of the

ECU/SES: in Russia 84 per cent and in Kazakhstan 79 per cent of those surveyed said they supported participation in the ECU/SES, compared to 68 per cent in Belarus.

Some analysts suggest that both Russia and Ukraine need to be part of an economic sub-regional integration process in the post-Soviet space in order for such a process to be successful (Ziyadullaev 2014). Ukraine and its socioeconomic and political situation will continue to be a crucial factor impacting the interaction between the EU and the Eurasian economic integration process.

Conclusions on the EEU

'Russia and the EU have different visions of what is often called their "shared neighbourhood"' (Popescu 2014: 35). Bachkatov (2012: 324) talks about 'tensions between the desire to cooperate, the mutual distrust and conceptual disparity'. Even though the EU projects itself as a supporter of (sub-)regional integration, it is unwilling to show approval of most integration processes in the post-Soviet space and in particular of the ECU/SES. Being overly suspicious and avoiding contacts with the ECU/SES could soon prove to be a rather short-sighted strategy on the part of the EU, though, since these newly established organizations have gradually accumulated competency in a number of domains linked to trade. The fast development of the integration process combined with the crisis in Ukraine makes interaction with the Eurasian Economic Union necessary and even inevitable for the EU. The EU has to develop a strategy in relation to the Eurasian economic integration process. Ignoring its existence and expecting it to dissolve due to internal disagreement is unlikely to be a viable strategy. Moreover, as suggested earlier in this chapter, it is possible that greater interaction with the Eurasian sub-regional economic integration (in which Russia undoubtedly plays a major role but where other players participate as well) could help overcome the confrontation between the EU and Russia and contribute to unblocking the negotiation process between the two.

Conclusion

This chapter has sought to investigate why and how the EU is engaging with the sub-regional economic integration processes that have developed in its broader neighbourhood. A comparative model has been applied to three different sub-regional integration schemes: the Agadir Process for the Southern Mediterranean region, the Gulf Cooperation Council for the Arabic Peninsula and the Eurasian economic integration process for the post-Soviet space. The authors have argued that the EU has taken a different approach toward each sub-regional integration scheme, namely a 'building' approach in the case of the Agadir Process, a 'bridging' approach in relation to the GCC and a 'blocking' approach *vis-à-vis* the ECU/SES.

When pursuing inter-regionalism, the EU seeks to maximize both economic and political or security-driven interests. Elements of both of these motivations are present in the EU's approaches to the three regional schemes, but they are weighted differently. For instance, while the key driver for the Agadir Process lies with regulatory approximation, the Cooperation Agreement with the GCC essentially seeks norm promotion and market access. When it comes to the ECU/ SES, the EU's blocking stance is explained by norm promotion and the desire to ensure convergence of policies. In both the Eurasian and the Gulf cases, norm export meets a European interest in entrenching its normative system, usually in the face of other competing projects, be they American or Russian. Furthermore, whereas in the Agadir Process promoting sub-regional integration is a way for the EU to counter the influence of other norm exporters, in the case of the Eurasian economic integration process, the opposite strategy has been adopted to achieve the same goal.

Similarly, political and security motivations appear in all three processes, but each driver is of different importance for the EU. Unsurprisingly, relations with the GCC and the ECU/SES are essentially motivated by the European paucity of energy resources and the need to secure energy supplies. Similarly, both regions have recently faced security-related problems, increasing the strategic link between regional security and stability and European energy security. In the Agadir Process, ensuring stability in the region aims at preventing insecurity spill-over potentially having direct effects upon EU territory and interests.

The building, bridging and blocking approaches, motivated by different drivers, also produce dissimilar results. Within its broader neighbourhood, the EU's approach is shaped by the degree of compatibility between the European model and that of the other region. The Agadir Process offered the highest degree of compatibility, and has therefore placed regulatory approximation as the backbone of its relations. The GCC, an essentially intergovernmental framework, has been compatible only to the extent that the two projects openly adhered to the liberal aspirations of free trade and market openness. The Eurasian regional integration process, on the other hand, demonstrated how the incongruity of the projects initially led to a standstill, which is forcing the EU to reappraise its approach.

Although each regional bloc presents the EU with specific challenges and opportunities, the EU can draw several lessons from its broader neighbourhood experience. First, faced with crises, such as the consequences of the 'Arab Spring' or more recently the conflict in eastern Ukraine, the EU has the opportunity to adapt its approach to regional integration and, thus, pursue a more adequate policy. Second, sub-regional integration cannot take hold in the absence of political stability, a reality that permeates all three regions. In the case of the Agadir Process and the GCC, the EU was able to keep dialogue channels open, whereas it has only recently come to terms with the situation in its eastern neighborhood. European energy concerns also provide room for manoeuvre between the GCC and Eurasia.

We believe that the analytical framework presented in this chapter could be applied not only to the three regions studied but to others regions as well. It seems that the 'building' approach is the approach the EU would prefer if the following two conditions are met: that regulatory approximation is seen as crucial, even if there is no geographical contiguity; and that the partner countries need to be willing to actively engage with the EU. As for the 'bridging' strategy, the EU seems to pursue this strategy when the degree of engagement sought is essentially to agree on a set of common principles so as to ensure other foreign policy objectives, such as energy security. Finally, the EU would probably be more inclined to use a 'blocking' approach in order to counter other 'governance exporters' who the EU feels might endanger its objectives. Although the 'blocking' approach might seem useful in some cases, we argue that the EU should be wary of putting in place such a strategy. Instead, more cooperative ways should be considered, so as to avoid the standstills and security-related problems that are often triggered by adverse and unpropitious policies which we would argue are not in the interest of the Union. The positive approach of the EU toward the Black Sea Economic Cooperation initiative (see Table 9.1) proves that an alternative to the 'blocking' strategy toward sub-regional integration mechanisms in the post-Soviet space is conceivable.

To conclude, it is also important to acknowledge that the 'three-B' approach presented in this chapter is based on the EU's perceptions, which does not necessarily mean that members of the sub-regional integration initiatives in the EU's broader neighbourhood perceive it in the same way. It would be useful for further studies based on this framework to integrate the perceptions of these EU partner countries.

Table 9.1 Sub-regional integration schemes in the EU's broader neighbourhood, 2014

	Name	Year and instrument	Objectives	Members
SECURITY MENA/GCC	OSCE Mediterranean Contact Group (Mediterranean Partners for Cooperation)	1994: creation Budapest Summit, Budapest (Hungary)	• Facilitate the interchange of information and the generation of ideas	63 members 57 OSCE members Algeria Egypt	Israel Jordan Morocco Tunisia
	NATO Mediterranean Dialogue Initiated by North Atlantic Council as part of NATO strategy of adaptation to post-Cold War security environment	1994: creation	• Contribute to regional security and stability • Achieve better mutual understanding • Dispel misconceptions about NATO among Dialogue countries	35 members 28 NATO members Algeria Egypt	Israel Jordan Mauritania Morocco Tunisia
	5+5 Dialogue	1990: creation Rome Declaration, Rome (Italy)	• Provide an informal forum to discuss subjects of topical interest for the region and to identify new areas for practical cooperation • Complement other institutional frameworks of the region (e.g. UfM)	10 members Algeria France Italy Libya Malta	Mauritania Morocco Portugal Spain Tunisia
Post-Soviet space	Collective Security Treaty Organization (CSTO) Secretariat: Moscow (Russia)	1992: signature 1994: into force Collective Security Treaty, Tashkent (Uzbekistan) 2002: Charter signed, Chisinau (Moldova)	• Work for peace and ensure international and regional stability and security • Provide for collective protection of sovereignty and territorial integrity, non-interference in domestic matters • Promote fair and democratic world order based on the principles of international law • Ensure military and technological cooperation between members	6 members Armenia Belarus Kazakhstan Kyrgyzstan Russia Tajikistan	

continued

Name	Year and instrument	Objectives	Members	
Organization for Security and Cooperation in Europe (OSCE) Secretariat: Vienna (Austria) Founded as Conference for Security and Cooperation in Europe (CSCE); became OSCE in 1994	1975: signature Helsinki Final Act, Helsinki (Finland)	• Enhance arms control and border security • Combat human trafficking • Combat terrorism while protecting human rights • Prevent conflicts from arising and facilitate lasting comprehensive political settlements for existing conflicts • Build democratic institutions • Promote gender equality • Ensure respect for human rights, media freedom, minority rights and the rule of law • Promote tolerance and non-discrimination	57 members 28 EU members Albania Andorra Armenia Azerbaijan Belarus Bosnia and Herzegovina Canada Former Yugoslav Republic of Macedonia (FYROM) Georgia Holy See Iceland	Kazakhstan Kyrgyzstan Liechtenstein Moldova Monaco Mongolia Montenegro Norway Russia San Marino Serbia Switzerland Tajikistan Turkey Turkmenistan Ukraine United States Uzbekistan
South-Eastern Europe Defense Ministerial (SEDM) Secretariat: Bucharest (Romania)	1996: first meeting (Ministers of Defense), Tirana (Albania)	• Promote mutual understanding, confidence and security-building measures • Improve members' interoperability • Facilitate Euro-Atlantic integration of members • Implement and develop SEDM projects • Facilitate South-East European Brigades' (SEEBRIG) employment in peace support operations • Enlarge SEDM process • Cooperate with UN, EU, NATO and OSCE	14 members Albania Bosnia and Herzegovina Bulgaria Croatia FYROM Greece Italy	Montenegro Russia Serbia Slovenia Turkey Ukraine United States

ECONOMIC
MENA/GCC

Name	Year and instrument	Objectives	Members	
Council of Arab Economic Unity (CAEU) Secretariat: Cairo (Egypt) Established by resolution of Arab Economic and Social Council of League of Arab States (LAS)	1957: signature 1964: into force	• Achieve economic integration among Arab countries with the view of establishing an Arab Common Market • Serve as umbrella agreement to foster Arab economic unity, e.g. non-double taxation agreement, investment promotion agreements, dispute settlement	16 members Algeria Bahrain Egypt Iraq Jordan Kuwait Lebanon Libya Morocco Oman	Qatar Saudi Arabia Sudan Syria UAE Yemen 4 candidates Comoros Djibouti Mauritania Somalia

Organization	Dates	Objectives	Members
Arab Fund for Economic and Social Development (AFESD) Secretariat: Kuwait City (Kuwait) Established by Resolution 345 of Arab Economic and Social Council of LAS	1968: signature 1972: into force	• Achieve Arab integration and consolidating cooperation among member countries • Finance economic and social development projects in Arab States through loans • Encourage investment of public and private capital to promote economic growth • Provide technical expertise and assistance	21 members Algeria Bahrain Djibouti Egypt Iraq Jordan Kuwait Lebanon Libya Mauritania Morocco Oman Palestine Qatar Saudi Arabia Somalia Sudan Syria Tunisia UAE Yemen
Organization of Arab Petroleum Exporting Countries (OAPEC) Secretariat: Kuwait City (Kuwait)	1968: signature Kuwait City (Kuwait)	• Foster economic diversification between members to reduce petroleum dependency • Control oil prices	10 members Algeria Bahrain Egypt Iraq Kuwait Libya Qatar Saudi Arabia Syria UAE
Arab Organization for Agricultural Development (AOAD) Secretariat: Khartoum (Sudan)	1970: signature 1972: first meeting	• Identify and develop linkages between Arab countries • Develop and enhance agricultural sectors • Coordinate all agricultural and agriculture-related activities to achieve a fully integrated Arab economic union and food self-sufficiency	21 members Algeria Bahrain Djibouti Egypt Iraq Jordan Kuwait Lebanon Libya Mauritania Morocco Oman Palestine Qatar Saudi Arabia Somalia Sudan Syria Tunisia UAE Yemen
Arab Maghreb Union (AMU) Secretariat: Rabat (Morocco)	1989: signature Treaty of Marrakesh, Marrakesh (Morocco)	• Consolidate fraternal relations • Establish freedoms (progressive: free trade agreement, customs union, common market) • Adopt common policies in all spheres	5 members Algeria Libya Mauritania Morocco Tunisia

continued

Name	Year and instrument	Objectives	Members
Greater Arab Free Trade Area (GAFTA)/Pan-Arab Free Trade Area (PAFTA) Secretariat: Cairo (Egypt) Established by Economic and Social Council of LAS; GAFTA was to be an executive programme to activate the Trade Facilitation and Development Agreement, in force since 1 January 1998	1997: signature 1998: into force Amman Summit, Amman (Jordan)	• Remove tariffs and non-tariff barriers • Liberalize agriculture • Set out precise rules of origin (at least 40% of Arab components can access) • Encourage Arab countries to proceed quickly with bilateral/sub-regional agreements	18 members Algeria Bahrain Egypt Iraq Jordan Kuwait Lebanon Libya Morocco Oman Palestine Qatar Saudia Arabia Sudan Syria Tunisia UAE Yemen
Community of Sahel–Saharan States (CEN-SAD) Secretariat: Tripoli (Libya)	1998: signature Tripoli (Libya)	• Build a comprehensive economic union • Encourage investment in the agricultural, industrial, social, cultural and energy fields • Foster free movement of people and goods • Promote foreign trade through a policy of investment, growth and development of means of transport and communications by land, air and sea through joint projects	28 members Benin Burkina Faso Central African Republic Chad Comoros Djibouti Egypt Equatorial Guinea Eritrea Gambia Ghana Guinea Guinea-Bissau Ivory Coast Kenya Liberia Libya Mali Morocco Niger Nigeria Sao Tomé Senegal Sierra Leone Somalia Sudan Tunisia Togo
Agadir Agreement Secretariat: Amman (Jordan)	2004: signature 2006: into force Treaty of Agadir, Agadir (Morocco)	• Promote regional economic integration and cooperation • Support the creation of a Euro-Mediterranean FTA • Facilitate economic development and integration through Pan-Euro-Med rules of origin • Attract foreign direct investment • Reinforce South–South cooperation	4 members Egypt Jordan Morocco Tunisia
Danube Commission Secretariat: Budapest (Hungary)	1948: signature Convention Regarding the Regime of Navigation on the Danube, Belgrade (Serbia)	• Develop free navigation on the Danube for commercial vessels in accordance with interests and sovereign rights of members • Foster economic and cultural relations among members and with third countries • Promote creation of unified navigation system in Europe • Contribute to improvement of navigation conditions and safety of navigation	11 members Austria Bulgaria Croatia Germany Hungary Moldova Romania Russia Serbia Slovakia Ukraine

Post-Soviet space

Organization	Dates	Objectives	Members
Economic Cooperation Organization (ECO) Secretariat: Tehran (Iran) Successor of Regional Cooperation for Development (RCD), which existed 1964–79	1985: creation 1991: signature Treaty of Izmir, Izmir (Turkey)	• Promote economic, technical and cultural cooperation between members • Ensure sustainable development and integration of economies of members with world economy • Remove trade barriers, promote intra-regional trade, foster economic liberalization and privatization • Encourage regional cooperation in drug abuse control and ecological and environmental protection	10 members Afghanistan Azerbaijan Kazakhstan Kyrgyzstan Iran Pakistan Tajikistan Turkey Turkmenistan Uzbekistan
Eurasian Development Bank (EDB) Headquarters: Almaty (Kazakhstan)	2006: signature Agreement on the Establishment of the Bank, Astana (Kazakhstan)	• Foster sustainable economic development • Enhance trade and economic growth between members • Finance and implement projects that support Eurasian integration • Diversify the investment portfolios of members	6 members Armenia Belarus Kazakhstan Kyrgyzstan Russia Tajikistan
Eurasian Group on Combating Money Laundering and the Financing of Terrorism (EAG) An FATF (Financial Action Task Force)-style regional body.	2004: creation Moscow (Russia)	• Promote integration into international system of anti-money laundering and combat financing of terrorism • Exchange best practices of combating money laundering and terrorist financing while taking into account regional specificities	9 members Belarus China India Kazakhstan Kyrgyzstan Russia Tajikistan Turkmenistan Uzbekistan
Eurasian Economic Community (EurAsEC) Integration Committee Secretariat: Moscow (Russia)	2000: signature 2001: into force Treaty on the Establishment of the Eurasian Economic Community, Astana (Kazakhstan)	• Create fully-fledged free trade area and introduce unified procedure of currency regulation and control • Advance process of forming a Eurasian Customs Union and Common Economic Space • Form common external customs borders, develop common external economic policy, adopt common tariffs, prices etc. • Harmonize social policies to create community of welfare states based on common labour market, unified educational space, coordinated approaches in health issues, labour migration etc. • Create common programmes for socio-economic development • Establish common energy and transport markets	6 members Belarus Kazakhstan Kyrgyzstan Russia Tajikistan Uzbekistan (participation in governing bodies suspended 2008)

continued

Name	Year and instrument	Objectives	Members
Eurasian Customs Union (ECU) Secretariat of the Commission of the ECU: Moscow (Russia) Established within the framework of EurAsEC as a step toward establishment of Eurasian Economic Union	2007: signature 2007: into force 2010: Customs Code into force Treaty on the Creation of the Common Customs Territory and Establishment of the Customs Union, Dushanbe (Tajikistan)	• Eliminate tariff and non-tariff barriers in trade and ensure free movement of goods between members • Lift control at internal borders of customs union • Unify and simplify foreign trade procedures and ensure a common trade regime is applied in trade with third countries • Prepare creation of a Common Economic Space and ultimately of a Eurasian Economic Union	3 members Belarus Kazakhstan Russia
Eurasian Common Economic Space (CES) Secretariat: Moscow (Russia) Established within the framework of EurAsEC as a step toward establishment of Eurasian Economic Union	2010: signature 2012: into force	• Ensure effective functioning of a common market based on freedom of movement of goods, services, labour and capital • Create conditions for development of members to improve living standards • Provide for coordinated macroeconomic policies including common rules on competition and natural monopolies • Develop unified transport, energy and information systems • Ensure common approach to agriculture, industry, science and technology	3 members Belarus Kazakhstan Russia
Organization of the Black Sea Economic Cooperation (BSEC) Secretariat: Permanent International Secretariat (PERMIS), Istanbul (Turkey)	1992: signature Summit Declaration and the Bosphorus Statement, Istanbul (Turkey)	• Foster political and economic integration • Ensure peace, stability and prosperity in Black Sea region through cooperation in agriculture, banking and finance, combatting organized crime, customs matters, trade and economic development, energy, environment protection, education etc. • Promote relations with third parties concerning areas of mutual interest	12 members Albania Armenia Azerbaijan Bulgaria Georgia Greece Moldova Romania Russia Serbia Turkey Ukraine
POLITICAL MENA/GCC			
League of Arab States (LAS) Secretariat: Cairo (Egypt)	1945: signature Treaty of Cairo, Cairo (Egypt)	• Promote closer ties among Arab states to develop collective cooperation • Protect national security and maintain independence and sovereignty • Defend interests and national causes of the Arab world • Settle disputes between members by peaceful means • Promote economic, social and cultural activities among Arab countries	22 members Algeria Bahrain Comores Djibouti Egypt Iraq Jordan Kuwait Lebanon Libya Mauritania Morocco Oman Palestine Qatar Saudi Arabia Somalia Sudan Syria Tunisia UAE Yemen

| Organization of Islamic Cooperation (OIC) Secretariat: Jeddah (Saudi Arabia) Changed its name from Organization of the Islamic Conference in June 2011 | 1969: signature Rabat Summit, Rabat (Morocco) | • Consolidate bonds of fraternity/solidarity
• Safeguard common interests, unify and coordinate actions
• Respect right of self-determination and non-interference and territorial integrity of each member
• Ensure active participation of members in global political, economic and social decision-making processes
• Establish an Islamic Common Market
• Achieve sustainable and comprehensive human development and economic well-being
• Protect and defend the true image of Islam
• Encourage research and cooperation among members in these fields | 57 members
Afghanistan
Albania
Algeria
Azerbaijan
Bahrain
Bangladesh
Benin
Brunei
Burkina Faso
Cameroon
Chad
Comoros
Djibouti
Egypt
Gabon
Gambia
Guinea
Guinea-Bissau
Guyana
Indonesia
Iran
Iraq
Ivory Coast
Jordan
Kazakhstan
Kuwait
Kyrgyzstan
Lebanon | Libya
Malaysia
Maldives
Mali
Mauritania
Morocco
Mozambique
Niger
Nigeria
Oman
Pakistan
Palestine
Suriname
Qatar
Saudi Arabia
Senegal
Sierra Leona
Somalia
Sudan
Syria
Tajikistan
Togo
Tunisia
Turkey
Turkmenistan
UAE
Uganda
Uzbekistan
Yemen |

continued

Name	Year and instrument	Objectives	Members	
Euro-Mediterranean Partnership (Forum Euro-Méditerranéen)	1995: signature Barcelona Declaration, Barcelona (Spain)	• Promote emergence of a common area of peace and stability in the Mediterranean • Establish area of shared prosperity in the Mediterranean via FTA, aiming to create a Euro-Med FTA by 2010 • Develop human resources • Promote understanding between cultures and exchanges between civil societies	39 members (+1 observer*) 28 EU members Indonesia Iran Iraq Ivory Coast Jordan Kazakhstan Kuwait Kyrgyzstan Lebanon Libya Malaysia Maldives Mali Mauritania Morocco Mozambique Niger Nigeria Oman	Pakistan Palestine Qatar Saudia Arabia Senegal Sierra Leone Somalia Sudan Suriname Syria Tajikistan Togo Tunisia Turkey Turkmenistan UAE Uganda Uzbekistan Yemen
Union for the Mediterranean (UfM) Secretariat: Barcelona (Spain)	2008: signature Barcelona Process: the Union for the Mediterranean, Joint Declaration, Paris (France)	• Enhance regional cooperation and partnership between the two shores of the Mediterranean • Render relations more concrete and more visible with new regional and sub-regional projects	43 members 28 EU members Albania Algeria Bosnia and Herzegovina Egypt Israel Jordan	Lebanon Mauritania Monaco Montenegro Morocco Palestine Syria (suspended) Tunisia Turkey
Cooperation Council of the Arab States of the Gulf (CCASG), known as GCC Secretariat: Riyadh (Saudi Arabia); Name changed from Gulf Cooperation Council; Sub-organizations not listed here, see chapter text	1981: signature The GCC Charter, Abu Dhabi (UAE)	• Increase inter-member coordination and integration to achieve unity • Deepen inter-population relations • Encourage regulation convergence in economic, trade, customs, education, social, legislative and administrative issues • Stimulate scientific and technological progress in industry and agriculture	6 members Bahrain Kuwait Oman	Qatar Saudi Arabia UAE

	Signature/into force; place	Objectives	Members
Post-Soviet space			
Council of Europe (COE) Secretariat: Strasbourg (France)	1949: signature 1949: into force Statute of the Council of Europe, London (United Kingdom)	• Protect human rights, freedom of expression and of the media, freedom of assembly, and the protection of national minorities • Help members to fight corruption and terrorism • Promote the rule of law	47 members 28 EU members Albania Andorra Armenia Azerbaijan Bosnia and Herzegovina FYROM Georgia Iceland Liechtenstein Moldova Monaco Montenegro Norway Russia Switzerland San Marino Serbia Turkey Ukraine
Central European Initiative (CEI) Secretariat: Trieste (Italy)	1989 Budapest (Hungary)	• Enhance regional cooperation for European integration by increasing economic and technical cooperation, know-how transfer and exchange of experience • Promote intergovernmental, interparliamentary and business cooperation between members • Encourage development of a civil society in members	18 members Albania Austria Belarus Bosnia and Herzegovina Bulgaria Croatia Czech Republic FYROM Hungary Italy Moldova Montenegro Poland Romania Serbia Slovakia Slovenia Ukraine
Commonwealth of Independent States (CIS) Secretariat: (Executive Committee), Minsk (Belarus) Turkmenistan and Ukraine are not full members, not having signed CIS Charter; Georgia left in 2009; Ukraine started process of leaving in May 2014	1991: signature Almaty Protocol, Almaty (Kazakhstan)	• Strengthen political, economic, ecological, humanitarian and cultural cooperation between members • Promote comprehensive and sustainable economic and social development • Work for peace and security, encourage disarmament and elimination of nuclear and other weapons of mass destruction • Strengthen freedoms of speech and movement within CIS • Implement rule of law	9 members Azerbaijan Armenia Belarus Kazakhstan Kyrgyzstan Moldova Russia Tajikistan Uzbekistan

continued

Name	Year and instrument	Objectives	Members
GUUAM Group (Georgia, Ukraine, Uzbekistan, Azerbaijan and Moldova)	1997: statement Summit of the Council of Europe, Strasbourg (France)	• Work for peaceful settlement of regional conflicts while respecting sovereignty and territorial integrity • Enhance regional cooperation for integration to Euro-Atlantic and European structures of security and cooperation • Stimulate economic reforms aimed at developing democratic societies, free markets and integration into the global economy • Promote development of a Eurasian Europe–South Caucasus–Central Asia transport corridor	5 members Azerbaijan Georgia Moldova Ukraine Uzbekistan
Shanghai Cooperation Organization (SCO) Secretariat: Beijing (China)	2001: signature Shanghai Convention, Shanghai (China)	• Strengthen mutual confidence and good relations between members • Promote cooperation in politics, trade and economy, science and technology, culture and education, energy, transportation, tourism, environmental protection • Maintain and ensure peace, security and stability in the region • Work for establishment of a new political and economic international order	6 members China Kazakhstan Kyrgyzstan Russia Tajikistan Uzbekistan
Belarus–Russia Union State Secretariat (Permanent Committee): Moscow (Russia) Successor of Belarus–Russia Community established 1996	1999: signature 2000: in force Treaty on the Creation of a Union State, Moscow (Russia)	• Ensure peaceful and democratic development • Create a common economic space and customs area • Promote a single legal framework, equal rights of citizens and equal conditions for enterprises • Ensure sustainable economic development and introduce a single currency • Pursue agreed foreign, defence and social policies, ensure security and fight against crime	2 members Belarus Russia

Sources: The information in this table has been compiled by the authors from the official websites of the respective regional integration schemes which can be retrieved from SIPRI (2014), UNU-CRIS (2014) and WTO (2014).

Notes
The authors acknowledge that it is often difficult to make a clear-cut classification of the security, economic and political orientation of the different regional integration schemes.

* As a continuation of the EMP, the UfM was launched in 2008.

Notes

1 The post-Soviet space refers to the countries from the ex-USSR, except for the three Baltic states which joined the EU in 2004.
2 A distinct policy area known as 'inter-regionalism' has emerged to study the process of 'widening and deepening political, economic, and societal interactions between international regions' (Roloff 2006: 18).
3 See also Chapter 11 by Johannes Theiss in this volume.
4 See also Chapter 5 by Sieglinde Gstöhl in this volume.
5 In the Multi-Annual Financial Framework 2014–20, the ENPI has been replaced by the ENI, which no longer includes Russia.
6 See also Chapter 1 by Valeria Bonavita, Chapter 2 by Sarah Wolff and Chapter 4 by Gilles de Kerchove and Christiane Höhn in this volume.
7 See also Chapter 5 by Sieglinde Gstöhl in this volume.
8 MFN treatment is a core principle of WTO law. It avoids discrimination by ensuring that all WTO members benefit from the preferential conditions a country grants to another WTO member.
9 The Russian Federation, Kyrgyzstan and Armenia are members of the WTO since 2012, while Belarus and Kazakhstan are still observers. See also Chapter 5 by Sieglinde Gstöhl in this volume.
10 See also Chapter 5 by Sieglinde Gstöhl in this volume.

References

Agadir Agreement (2004) 'Agreement for the Establishment of a Free Trade Zone between the Arabic Mediterranean Nations', Rabat, 25 February, www.agadiragreement.org/CMS/UploadedFiles/10ac3206-5a49-4dd8-833e-0783d2ea4190.pdf (accessed March 2014).

Aggarwal, V. and E.A. Fogarty (2005) 'The Limits of Interregionalism: The EU and North America', *European Integration* 27(3), 327–346.

Akhtar, S. and M. Rouis (2010) *Economic Integration in MENA: The GCC, the Maghreb, and the Mashreq*, Washington, DC: World Bank.

Aliboni, R. (2006) 'Domestic Politics and External Challenges in the Middle East', *The International Spectator: Italian Journal of International Affairs* 41(2), 33–50.

Al Khouri, R. (2008) 'EU and US Free Trade Agreements in the Middle East and North Africa', *Carnegie Papers* 8, Beirut: Carnegie Middle East Center, http://carnegieendowment.org/files/cmec8_al_khouri_final.pdf (accessed August 2014).

Al-Sayed, K. (2013) *GCC and the Arab Spring*, Doha: Dar Al Sharq.

Antkiewicz, A. and B. Momani (2009) 'Pursuing Geopolitical Stability through Interregional Trade: The EU's Motives for Negotiating with the Gulf Cooperation Council', *Journal of European Integration* 31(2), 217–235.

Ayadi, R. and S. Gadi (2013) 'The Euro-Mediterranean Partnership and Development Assistance: Past Trends and Future Scenarios', *Medpro Technical Report* 32, Brussels, 1–49.

Baabood, A. and G. Edwards (2007) 'Reinforcing Ambivalence: The Interaction of Gulf States and the European Union', *European Foreign Affairs Review* 12(4), 537–554.

Bachkatov, N. (2012) 'L'Union européenne et la Russie: Entre convergeance et méfiance', in S. Santander (ed.) *Puissances émergentes: un défi pour l'Europe?* Paris: Editions Ellipses, 313–335.

Balassa, B. (1961) *The Theory of Economic Integration*, Homewood: Richard D. Irwin.

Barroso, J.M.D. (2014) 'Statement Following Meeting with Mr. Nursultan Nazarbaev,

240 *M. Fichet* et al.

President of Kazakhstan', Speech/14/675, 9 October, http://europa.eu/rapid/press-release_SPEECH-14-675_en.htm (accessed October 2014).

Bayar, A. (2006) 'An Evaluation of the Benefits and the Challenges of the South–South Integration among the Mediterranean Partner Countries', *FEMISE Research Network 2004–2005*, Marseille, 1–40.

Bicchi, F. (2006) '"Our Size Fits All": Normative Power Europe and the Mediterranean', *Journal of European Public Policy* 13(2), 286–303.

Börzel, T.A. and T. Risse (2009) 'Diffusing (Inter-) Regionalism: The EU as a Model of Regional Integration', *Working Paper* 7, Berlin: KFG The Transformative Power of Europe.

Boussetta, M. (2005) 'The Agadir Agreement, South–South Integration and the Euro-Mediterranian Partnership', in *IEMed Yearbook – Panorama*, Barcelona: IEMed, 174–177.

Bower, A. (2010) 'A Growing European Interest for EU–GCC Relations', *MEDEA Institute*, Brussels, www.medea.be/2010/10/a-growing-european-interest-for-eu-gcc-relations (accessed May 2014).

Bretherton, C. and J. Vogler (2006) *The European Union as a Global Actor*, London: Routledge.

Brunel, C. and G.C. Hufbauer (2008) *Maghreb Regional and Global Integration: A Dream to be Fulfilled*, Policy Analyses in International Economics 86, Washington, DC: Peterson Institute for International Economics.

Casero, P.A. and G. Seshan (2010) 'Economics Gain of Regional Agreements in the Maghreb: Deeper versus Wider Integration', in J.R. López-Cálix, P. Walkenhorst and N. Diop (eds) *Trade Competitiveness of the Middle East and North Africa: Policies for Export Diversification*, Washington, DC: World Bank, 299–330.

Colombo, S. and C. Committeri (2013) 'Need to Rethink the EU–GCC Strategic Relation', *Shakara Research Papers* 1, 1–26, www.iai.it/pdf/sharaka/sharaka_rp_01.pdf (accessed July 2014).

Cooper, J. (2013) 'The Development of Eurasian Economic Integration', in R. Dragneva and K. Wolczuk (eds) *Eurasian Economic Integration: Law, Policy and Politics*, Cheltenham: Edward Elgar, 15–34.

Cottey, A. (2009) 'Sub-regional Cooperation in Europe: An Assessment', *Bruges Regional Integration and Global Governance Papers* 3, Bruges: UNU-CRIS/College of Europe.

Council of the European Union (2010) 'Joint Communiqué – 20th EU–GCC Joint Council and Ministerial Meeting', Brussels, www.consilium.europa.eu/uedocs/cms_Data/docs/pressdata/en/er/115186.pdf (accessed August 2014).

Council of the European Union (2013) 'Follow-up to the European Council of 22 May 2013: Review of Developments on the External Dimension of the EU Energy Policy', Council Report 17756/13, Brussels, 12 December.

Damro, C. (2012) 'Market Power Europe', *Journal of European Public Policy* 19(5), 682–699.

Delcour, L. and H. Kostanyan (2014) 'Towards a Fragmented Neighbourhood: Policies of the EU and Russia and their Consequences for the Area that Lies in Between', *CEPS Essay* 17, Brussels: CEPS.

Delcour, L. and K. Wolczuk (2013) 'Eurasian Economic Integration: Implications for the EU Eastern Policy', in R. Dragneva and K. Wolczuk (eds) *Eurasian Economic Integration: Law, Policy and Politics*, Cheltenham: Edward Elgar, 179–204.

De Ville, F. and V. Reynaert (2010) 'The Euro-Mediterranean Free Trade Area: An Evaluation on the Eve of the (Missed) Deadline', in *L'Europe en Formation: Journal of Studies on European Integration and Federalism* 356, 193–206.

Dragneva, R. and K. Wolczuk (2012) 'Russia, the Eurasian Customs Union and the EU: Cooperation, Stagnation or Rivalry?', *Russia and Eurasia Programme Briefing Paper* 1, London: Chatham House, www.chathamhouse.org/sites/files/chathamhouse/public/Research/Russia%20and%20Eurasia/0812bp_dragnevawolczuk.pdf (accessed November 2014).

Dragneva, R. and K. Wolczuk (2013) 'The Eurasian Customs Union: Framing the Analysis', in R. Dragneva and K. Wolczuk (eds) *Eurasian Economic Integration: Law, Policy and Politics*, Cheltenham: Edward Elgar, 1–15.

Dreyer, I. and N. Popescu (2014) 'Trading with Moscow: The Law, the Politics and the Economics', *Brief Issue* 31, Paris: EUISS, www.iss.europa.eu/uploads/media/Brief_31_Russia-Ukraine.pdf (accessed November 2014).

EurAsEC (2000) *Treaty on the Establishment of the Eurasian Economic Community*, Astana, 10 October, www.wipo.int/wipolex/en/regeco_treaties/text.jsp?file_id=234738 (accessed October 2014).

EurAsEC (2011) *Declaration on the Eurasian Economic Integration*, 18 November, http://sudevrazes.org/en/main.aspx?guid=19471 (accessed May 2014).

Eurasian Development Bank (2014) *Eurasian Integration Barometer 2014*, http://eabr.org/e/research/centreCIS/projectsandreportsCIS/integration_barometer/index.php?id_16=42460 (accessed October 2014).

Eurasian Economic Commission (2013) 'Eurasian Economic Integration: Facts and Figures', Moscow, http://eurasiancommission.org/ru/Documents/broshura26Body_ENGL_final2013_2.pdf (accessed August 2014).

Euro-Mediterranean Conference (1995) 'Barcelona Declaration', adopted at the first Euro-Mediterranean Conference, Barcelona, 27–28 November, www.eeas.europa.eu/euromed/docs/bd_en.pdf (accessed February 2014).

Euro-Mediterranean Conference (2000) 'Presidency Formal Conclusions', Fourth Euro-Mediterranean Conference of Foreign Affairs Ministers, Marseilles, 15–16 November, www.consilium.europa.eu/ueDocs/cms_Data/docs/pressData/en/er/00006.en0.html (accessed May 2014).

European Commission (2003) Communication from the Commission to the Council and the European Parliament, *Wider Europe – Neighbourhood: A New Framework for Relations with our Eastern and Southern Neighbours*, COM(2003) 104 final, Brussels, 11 March.

European Commission (2004) 'Commissioner Patten Attends Signature of Agadir Agreement', Press Release, IP/04/256, Brussels, http://europa.eu/rapid/press-release_IP-04-256_en.htm (accessed February 2014).

European Commission (2006) *Communication from the Commission to the Council and the European Parliament – On Strengthening The European Neighbourhood Policy*, COM(2006) 726 final, Brussels, 4 December.

European Commission (2010) 'Our Neighbours: Panorama of Regional Programmes and Projects in the Mediterranean Countries', *ENPI – Working Together*, Brussels: EuropeAid Cooperation Office, http://ec.europa.eu/europeaid/where/neighbourhood/documents/infonotes_south_2010_en.pdf (accessed May 2014).

European Commission (2013) 'New Support to Boost Cooperation in the Southern Mediterranean', Press Release, Brussels, 15 July, http://ec.europa.eu/europeaid/documents/aap/2013/pr_aap_2013_enpi-s.pdf (accessed October 2014).

European Commission (2014a) *Communication from the Commission to the European Parliament and the Council, European Energy Security Strategy*, COM(2014) 330 final, Brussels, 28 May.

European Commission (2014b) 'The Instrument for Cooperation with Industrialized Countries', http://ec.europa.eu/dgs/fpi/what-we-do/ici_en.htm (accessed June 2013).

European Commission (2014c) 'Trade in Goods with the GCC (6)', Brussels: DG Trade, http://trade.ec.europa.eu/doclib/docs/2006/september/tradoc_113482.pdf (accessed August 2014).

European Commission (2014d) 'Trade in the Gulf region', Brussels: DG Trade, http://ec.europa.eu/trade/policy/countries-and-regions/regions/gulf-region (accessed August 2014).

European Community (1989) 'Council Decision 89/147/EEC of 20 February 1989 Concerning the Conclusion of a Cooperation Agreement between the European Economic Community, of the one part, and the Countries Parties to the Charter of the Cooperation Council for the Arab States of the Gulf (the State of the United Arab Emirates, the State of Bahrain, the Kingdom of Saudi Arabia, the Sultanate of Oman, the State of Qatar and the State of Kuwait) of the other part', *Official Journal of the European Union*, L 54, 25 February, 1–15.

European Council (2003) *A Secure Europe in a Better World: European Security Strategy*, Brussels, www.consilium.europa.eu/uedocs/cmsUpload/78367.pdf (accessed May 2014).

European External Action Service (2013) 'EU–Russia Common Spaces', *Progress Report*, March, http://eeas.europa.eu/russia/docs/commonspaces_prog_report_2012_en.pdf (accessed October 2014).

European External Action Service (2014a) 'European Relations with the Gulf Cooperation Council', http://eeas.europa.eu/gulf_cooperation/index_en.htm (accessed July 2014).

European External Action Service (2014b) 'Press Remarks of the EU Representatives at Minsk Meetings', Brussels, 26 August, http://eeas.europa.eu/statements/docs/2014/140826_02_en.pdf (accessed October 2014).

European External Action Service (2014c) 'Opening Remark by EU High Representative Catherine Ashton at the Meeting of Heads of States of the Republic of Belarus, Republic of Kazakhstan, Russian Federation, Ukraine and Representatives of the European Union', Brussels, 26 August, http://eeas.europa.eu/statements/docs/2014/140826_01_en.pdf (accessed October 2014).

European External Action Service (2014d) 'EU-Kazakhstan Enhanced Partnership and Cooperation Agreement', *Factsheet*, 9 October, www.eeas.europa.eu/statements/docs/2014/141009_01_en.pdf (accessed October 2014).

Füle, Š. (2014) 'New Europe and Enlargement in a New Political Context', speech at conference on 10 years of Czech membership in the EU: 'The Czech Republic and Europe through Each Other's Eyes', Prague, 11 April, http://europa.eu/rapid/press-release_SPEECH-14-323_en.htm (accessed October 2014).

Galal, A. and J.-L. Reiffers (eds) (2012) *Femise Report on the Euro-Mediterranean Partnership: The Season of Choices*, Marseilles: Femise.

GCC-EU Joint Council (2013) 'Co-Chairs' Statement 23rd GCC-EU Joint Council and Ministerial Meeting Manama', 30 June, www.consilium.europa.eu/uedocs/cms_Data/docs/pressdata/EN/foraff/137671.pdf (accessed July 2014).

Ghoneim, A.F. (2013) 'Trade and Investment Dynamics in the Mediterranean Region: No Real Change After the Arab Spring', in S. Colombo *et al.* (eds) *Regional Dynamics in the Mediterranean and Prospects for Transatlantic Cooperation, Mediterranean Paper Series*, The German Marshall Fund of the United States, 1–12.

Habboush, M. (2010) 'GCC's Free Trade Deal with the EU Sticks over Saudi Export Tariff', *The National*, 25 June, www.thenational.ae/news/uae-news/gccs-free-trade-deal-with-eu-sticks-over-saudi-export-tariff (accessed September 2014).

Handoussa, H. and J.-L. Reiffers (2002) *Rapport Femise 2002 sur Le Partenariat Euro-Mediterraneen*, Marseilles: Femise.

Haukkala, H. (2013) 'The Impact of the Eurasian Customs Union on EU–Russia Relations', in R. Dragneva and K. Wolczuk (eds) *Eurasian Economic Integration: Law, Policy and Politics*, Cheltenham: Edward Elgar, 163–179.

Holden, P. (2011) 'A New Beginning? Does the Union for the Mediterranean Herald a New Functionalist Approach to Cooperation in the Region?', *Mediterranean Politics* 16(1), 155–169.

Interstate Council of EurAsEC (2009) *Decision Nr 35, Action Plan on the Formation of the Single Economic Space between the Republic of Belarus, the Republic of Kazakhstan and the Russian Federation for 2010–2011*, 19 December, http://evrazes.com/i/data/item7220-2.pdf (accessed May 2014).

Issac, J. (2008) 'GCC Suspends FTA Talks with EU', *Khaleej Times Online*, 24 December, www.bilaterals.org/?gcc-suspends-fta-talks-with-eu&lang=en#sthash.iHQXnxWO.dpuf (accessed June 2014).

Kadhim, A. (ed.) (2013) *Governance in the Middle East and North Africa*, Abingdon: Routledge.

Koch, C. (2011) 'Strengthening an Enduring EU–GCC Partnership', *GRC Commentary*, Gulf Research Center, 20 April, www.grc.net/index.php?frm_action=view_newsletter_web&sec_code=grccommentary&frm_module=contents&show_web_list_link=1&int_content_id=73520 (accessed May 2014).

Lannon, E. and I. Martín (2009) 'Report on the Euro-Mediterranean Partnership Status and Progress 2009', *Documents IEMed*, Barcelona: IEMed.

Lavenex, S. (2004) 'EU External Governance in "Wider Europe"', *Journal of European Public Policy* 11(4), 680–700.

Lawson, F. (2012) 'Transformations of Regional Economic Governance in the Gulf Cooperation Council', *Occasional Paper* 10, Center for International and Regional Studies, Georgetown University School of Foreign Service in Qatar, https://repository.library.georgetown.edu/bitstream/handle/10822/558217/CIRSOccasionalPaper10FredLawson2012.pdf?sequence=5 (accessed July 2014).

Liargovas, P. (2013) 'EU Trade Policies towards Neighboring Countries', *Search Working Paper* 2/01, www.ub.edu/searchproject/wp-content/uploads/2013/01/WP-2.1.pdf (accessed May 2014).

Mandelson, P. (2008) 'Agadir and After: Prospects for a Free Trade Area of the Mediterranean', speech delivered at the First Agadir Investment Forum, Brussels, http://europa.eu/rapid/press-release_SPEECH-08-179_en.htm (accessed May 2014).

Manners, I. (2002) 'Normative Power Europe: A Contradiction in Terms?', *Journal of Common Market Studies* 40(2), 235–258.

Matevosyan, G. (2014) 'ЕС готов сотрудничать с Арменией и после ее вступления в ЕАЭС' ['The EU is Ready to Cooperate with Armenia after the Accession to the Eurasian Economic Union (EEU)'], *Ria Novosti*, 7 October, http://ria.ru/economy/20141007/1027319868.html (accessed October 2014).

Mattli, W. (1999) *The Logic of Regional Integration: Europe and Beyond*, Cambridge: Cambridge University Press.

Momani, B. (2007) 'The EU, the Middle East, and Regional Integration', *World Economics* 8(1), 1–10.

Nazarbaev, N. (1997) *Евразийский союз: идеи,практика, перспективы 1994–1997* [*The Eurasian Union: Ideas, Practice and Perspectives 1994–1997*], Moscow: Fund for the Development of Social and Political studies.

Nazarbaev, N. (2014) 'Press Statement Following the Supreme Eurasian Economic Council Meeting', President of Russia, 10 October, http://eng.kremlin.ru/transcripts/22404 (accessed October 2014).

Neslen, A. (2014) 'Europe's Dependency on Russian Gas may be Cut amid Energy Efficiency Focus', *Guardian*, 9 September.

Partrick, P. (2011) 'The GCC: Gulf State Integration or Leadership Cooperation?', Research Paper 19, Kuwait Programme on Development, Governance and Globalisation in the Gulf States, www.lse.ac.uk/middleEastCentre/kuwait/documents/Partrick%202%20paper.pdf (accessed February 2014).

Patten, C. (2001) 'The EU and Morocco – Close Partners in Regional Leadership', speech/01/296, Rabat.

Popescu, N. (2014) 'Eurasian Union: The Real, the Imaginary and the Likely', *Chaillot Paper* 132, Paris: EUISS, September, www.iss.europa.eu/uploads/media/CP_132.pdf (accessed October 2014).

PricewaterhouseCoopers (2004) 'Sustainability Impact Assessment (SIA) of the Negotiations of the Trade Agreement between the European Community and the Countries of the Cooperation Council for the Arab States of the Gulf (GCC) – Final Report', report in cooperation with the Centre for European Policy Studies (CEPS), with the financial cooperation of the European Commission, 30 May, http://trade.ec.europa.eu/doclib/docs/2005/january/tradoc_121208.pdf (accessed October 2014).

Ria Novosti (2014a) 'Все вопросы вступления Армении в ЕАЭС согласованы, заявил Назарбаев'['All Issues around the Accession of Armenia to the EEU were Coordinated, states Nazarbaev'], 10 October, http://ria.ru/world/20141010/1027808495.html (accessed October 2014).

Ria Novosti (2014b) 'Глава Киргизии просит подготовить проект договора о вступлении в ЕАЭС'['Kyrgyz Head of State Demands the Draft of the EEU Accession Treaty'], 10 October, http://ria.ru/world/20141010/1027808495.html (accessed October 2014).

Roloff, R. (2006) 'Interregionalism in Theoretical Perspective: State of the Art', in H. Hänggi *et al.* (eds) *Interregionalism and International Relations: A Stepping Stone to Global Governance*, New York: Routledge, 17–30.

Russian Ministry of Foreign Affairs (2014) 'Eurasian Economic Integration'. www.mid.ru/bdomp/ns-rsng.nsf/559a6afd63b0fb02432569ee0048fe70/229a0f397bf687fc44257a52004a3889!OpenDocument (accessed May 2014).

Shui, L. and P. Walkenhorst (2010) 'Regional Integration: Status, Developments, and Challenges', in J.R. López-Cálix, P. Walkenhorst and N. Diop (eds) *Trade Competitiveness of the Middle East and North Africa: Policies for Export Diversification*, Washington, DC: The World Bank, 267–298.

SIPRI (2014) 'Facts of International Relations and Security Trends (FIRST)', database, Stockholm: Stockholm International Peace and Research Institute, http://first.sipri.org (accessed October 2014).

Söderbaum, F. and A. Sbragia (2010) 'EU Studies Meets the New Regionalism: What can be Gained from Dialogue?', *Journal of European Integration* 32(6), 563–582.

Strange, S. (1988) *States and Markets*, London: Pinter.

UNU-CRIS (2014) 'Regional Integration Knowledge System (RIKS)', database, Bruges: United Nations University-Centre for Regional Integration Studies www.cris.unu.edu/riks/web/arrangement (accessed October 2014).

US Department of State (2013a) 'US Relations with Saudi Arabia Fact Sheet', www.state.gov/r/pa/ei/bgn/3584.htm (accessed June 2014).

US Department of State (2013b) 'US Relations with U.A.E Fact Sheet', www.state.gov/r/pa/ei/bgn/5444.htm (accessed June 2014).

US Department of State (2013c) 'US Relations with Kuwait Fact Sheet', www.state.gov/r/pa/ei/bgn/26414.htm (accessed June 2014).

Vinokurov, E. (2014) 'Зарождение евразоскептицизма' ['The Birth of Eurasian Scepticism'], *Eurasian Economic Integration* 1(22).

Wippel, S. (2005) 'The Agadir Agreement and Open Regionalism: The New Forum for Integration on the Southern Shore of the Mediterranean in the Context of Multiple Regional Orientations', *EuroMesco Paper* 45, Lisbon.

WTO (2014) 'Regional Trade Agreements Information System (RTA-IS)', database, Geneva: World Trade Organization, http://rtais.wto.org/UI/PublicMaintainRTAHome.aspx (accessed October 2014).

Ziyadullaev, N. (2014) 'Евразийский экономический союз: история успеха или мыльный пузырь' ['The Eurasian Economic Union: A Success Story or a Soap Bubble'], 15 September, www.ng.ru/courier/2014-09-15/11_soyuz.html (accessed October 2014).

10 Financing investments connecting the neighbours of the EU's neighbours[1]

Alessandro Carano

Introduction

The European Union (EU) acts as a global player through policies in areas such as enlargement, the European Neighbourhood Policy (ENP), development, trade and climate action. These policies are of direct relevance to the EU's eastern neighbourhood region, Russia and Central Asia, as well as to the EU's southern neighbourhood region and sub-Saharan Africa. EU policies have both a regional and a country-specific dimension, and in broad geographical terms the EU's focus has traditionally been on its own Member States, followed by the candidate and potential candidate countries (currently Turkey, Iceland and the Western Balkans), the ENP countries and partners worldwide.

The EU has progressively developed an integrated policy approach towards its neighbours to the east and to the south. Recent policy developments include the 'Partnership for Democracy and Shared Prosperity with the Southern Mediterranean' (European Commission and High Representative 2011a) in the context of the 'Arab Spring' and the revision of the ENP (European Commission and High Representative 2011b). The partnership includes investment in socio-economic sectors and trade as key areas of cooperation. Moreover, the EU Member States have long-standing cooperation, including on investments, with the African, Caribbean and Pacific (ACP) countries, currently in the framework of the Cotonou Agreement.

At the same time, the EU has several sectoral policies, notably in the transport, energy and environmental sectors, which all have an important dimension beyond the EU's borders. In an increasingly globalized world, policy and economic developments in more distant regions become more and more relevant for Europe, and thus the links and connections with regions beyond its immediate neighbourhood are gaining in importance for the EU, both in terms of opportunities and challenges. The traditional pattern of development cooperation based on aid assistance from countries of the Organization for Economic Cooperation and Development (OECD) towards developing countries is also evolving with the perspective of the post-2015 Development Agenda, the emergence of the BRICS countries (Brazil, Russia, India, China, South Africa) and other global actors, and the increased emphasis on inclusive economic growth, climate action and an integrated approach to sustainable development.

This chapter outlines the key challenges and opportunities that the EU faces in financing investments connecting the 'neighbours of its neighbours' to the east and to the south. The key factors which influence these investments are (1) strategic elements including geopolitical factors; (2) policy and regulatory frameworks; (3) project aspects; (4) financing sources and ownership; and (5) risks.

This chapter focuses on connections between North African countries (Morocco, Algeria, Tunisia, Libya, Egypt) and sub-Saharan Africa, and between Eastern Partnership countries (Armenia, Azerbaijan, Georgia, Belarus, Moldova, Ukraine), Russia and Central Asia (Kazakhstan, Kyrgyz Republic, Tajikistan, Turkmenistan, Uzbekistan). All the countries concerned, except Russia, are classified as 'developing countries' according to the OECD definition (OECD 2014). The connections are either physical – notably transport, energy, water or information and communication technology (ICT) infrastructure – or more broadly related to flows of capital, goods or services, for instance through foreign direct investment (FDI) and trade.

EU policy context

With the entry into force of the Lisbon Treaty in late 2009, EU external action has been reinforced with the ambition to act as global player in a coherent way. For this purpose, the post of High Representative of the Union for Foreign Affairs and Security Policy and the European External Action Service (EEAS) have been created. As indicated in art. 21 TEU, the EU defines and pursues common policies and actions in order to, *inter alia*, foster the sustainable economic, social and environmental development of developing countries, with the primary aim of eradicating poverty, and encourage the integration of all countries into the world economy, including through the progressive abolition of restrictions on international trade. The EU aims to foster closer relations with its neighbours to the east and south, promoting prosperity, security and stability, as described in the ENP (European Commission and High Representative 2011b). The EU closely cooperates with the ACP countries through the Cotonou Agreement. At the same time, the EU is promoting increased cooperation with the Central Asian countries. As part of these policies, the EU and partner countries aim also to promote socio-economic cooperation and regional integration, and investments in infrastructure, private sector and trade are a key component in fostering cooperation.[2] Furthermore, EU development policy for the period 2014–20 recognizes the importance of growth and investment in developing countries, as well as food security and access to electricity, as key drivers to reduce poverty and support the global development agenda (European Commission 2011a).[3]

Several initiatives are being undertaken by the EU at the sector level to promote extended connections with neighbouring countries, most notably in the transport and energy sectors. For instance, in the transport sector, the Council of the European Union (2011) emphasized the importance of better transport connections in achieving 'deeper economic integration' and closer 'political association' with the neighbouring regions. The European Commission (2011b) adopted a renewed policy framework promoting transport infrastructure and market development in the countries covered by the European Neighbourhood Policy and by the enlargement policy. The EU has been taking forward transport cooperation with its neighbours to the east within the Eastern Partnership Transport Panel (European Commission 2012), while it cooperates within the EuroMed Transport Project with neighbours to the south (ENPI-Info 2014). The Commission has also financed the launch of a website, EU Neighbourhood Info, which provides information about the cooperation and partnership programmes, including projects, between the EU and countries covered by the European Neighbourhood Policy.[4]

Several instruments exist to finance investments connecting the various regions. However, there is no single overarching EU policy framework nor instrument which encompasses the connections in all relevant sectors between the eastern neighbours and Russia as well as Central Asia, and between the southern neighbours and sub-Saharan Africa.

Financing cross-regional investments

Cross-border investments between countries within a certain region are very common and exist in all regions, particularly within the more economically integrated regions, such as within the EU or within Central Asia. A relatively limited level of cross-border investment can be observed between countries within the North African region and within sub-Saharan Africa. Investments connecting countries within regions may have broader cross-regional implications. This is typically the case for investments having impacts on global public goods such as water or climate stability.[5] Less common or widespread are the investments connecting bordering regions, such as between the eastern partners and Central Asia or between the Southern Mediterranean countries and sub-Saharan Africa. However, the inward investment flows in these regions are increasing, particularly in the eastern neighbours and in Central Asia (UNCTAD 2013).

Infrastructure investments

Infrastructure is essential to ensure basic services for any society, for example access to clean and safe water and sanitation, mobility of people and goods, access to energy for private and public purposes, or access to means of communication. Additionally, an efficient infrastructure is crucial for generating economic growth, promoting competitiveness and decreasing poverty. In developing countries the development of infrastructure and improvement of the associated basic services positively affect long-term economic growth (Calderon 2009). On the other hand, inefficient infrastructure can hold back economic and social development and have negative impact on the environment. In transition economies, the impact of infrastructure has large positive effects through higher productive efficiency and is estimated to be high if institutional reforms are in place (Sugolov *et al.* 2003).

Examples of initiatives promoting cross-regional connections in key infrastructure sectors are provided here below within the transport, energy and ICT sectors.

Transport

First, the extension of the transport Trans-European Networks (TEN) from the EU to neighbourhood countries is a key priority for the EU in the region. Faster, cheaper and more efficient transport connections between the EU and the neighbourhood countries are essential for the sustainable economic development of the region and for its integration with EU markets. The completion of an integrated, technology-led and user-friendly transport system in the immediate and broader neighbourhood countries is considered to be a key factor in the competitiveness of the European Union. Specific transport corridors have been identified since 2007 (European Commission 2007): Motorways of the Seas to link the Baltic, Barents, Atlantic, Mediterranean, Black and the Caspian Sea areas; the northern axis to connect the northern EU with Norway to the north and with Belarus and Russia to the east; the central axis to link the centre of the EU to Ukraine and the Black Sea and through an inland waterway connection to the Caspian Sea; the south-eastern axis to link the EU with the Balkans and Turkey and further with the Southern Caucasus and the Caspian Sea as well as with the Middle East up to Egypt and the Red Sea; and the south-western axis to connect the south-western EU with Switzerland and Morocco.

The EU has established new guidelines for the development of the trans-European transport network, which underline that cooperation with neighbouring countries is necessary in order to ensure connection and interoperability between the respective infrastructure networks (European Union 2013). The EU should promote projects of common interest in order to connect the trans-European transport network with the infrastructure networks of neighbouring countries. The guidelines include indicative maps of the trans-European transport network extended to specific neighbouring countries, mainly the Western Balkans and Turkey.

Second, cooperation on transport in the Mediterranean region has developed within the Euromed transport framework under the auspices of the Union for the Mediterranean (UfM), with the aim of promoting the Trans-Mediterranean Transport Network to be connected with the Trans-European Transport Network (TEN-T).[6] The transport ministers of the 43 countries of the Euro-Mediterranean area have been meeting regularly since 2005 to discuss strategic priorities. Cooperation was initiated within the 'Barcelona Process' with a regional transport action plan applied over 2007–13, succeeded by a new plan for 2014–20 approved by the Ministerial Conference of November 2013 (Union for the Mediterranean 2013). The Euro-Mediterranean Transport Forum, a permanent joint structure of experts, focuses on specific aspects to step up regional integration, especially the regulatory plan, and complementarity between strategies in each of the member states.

Third, the development of a modern, compatible and inter-operable infrastructure network between Europe, the Caucasus and Asia is promoted by TRACECA (Transport Corridor Europe–Caucasus–Asia), a transport cooperation programme among 12 countries in the Black Sea, Eastern Partnership and Central Asian regions.[7] With a permanent secretariat in Azerbaijan, it covers the areas of maritime transport, aviation, road and rail, transport security, and transport infrastructure. Initially started in 1993 as a programme funded by the EU, TRACECA aims at the creation of a sustainable infrastructure chain ensuring multi-modal transport with step-by-step integration of the corridor into the TEN-T, thus strengthening economic relations, trade and transport links between the countries. In this regard, cross-border transport projects are of a high priority. The rationale behind creating transport corridors is to ensure quality improvements along the corridor with regard to safety, reliability, cost and transit time of shipment. TRACECA has developed a methodology for measuring corridor attractiveness for the transport industry, allowing for comparison of the attractiveness of the TRACECA routes through the Caucasus, through Turkey and Iran and the alternative route through the Russian Federation (TRACECA 2011). Up to 2013, the EU has supported this cooperation through technical assistance with a total of €180 million for 80 projects, which since 2004 have mostly focused on transport safety and security, legal harmonization initiatives, trade facilitation and institutional support (European Commission 2013).

Fourth, the Central Asia Regional Economic Cooperation (CAREC) programme is a partnership of 10 countries (Afghanistan, Azerbaijan, Kazakhstan, Kyrgyz Republic, Mongolia, Pakistan, China, Tajikistan, Turkmenistan and Uzbekistan), supported by six multilateral institutions (including the World Bank and Asian Development Bank), working together to promote development through cooperation, leading to accelerated growth and poverty reduction.[8] The CAREC programme has highlighted a number of trade and transport corridors that are instrumental in creating land-linked economies (CAREC 2013). They incorporate, for example, the aspirations of a number of land-locked countries to become pivotal land bridges between regions, such as Central Asia to Iran and Pakistan via Afghanistan or China to Europe via Central Asia and Kazakhstan – the so-called 'New Silk Road' (ADB-CAREC 2011).

Fifth, the Euro-Asian Transport Links (EATL) project was started in 2002 as a joint undertaking between the United Nations Economic Commission for Europe (UNECE) and the United Nations Economic and Social Commission for Asia and the Pacific (UNESCAP).[9] In close cooperation with designated national focal points in the Euro-Asian region, the EATL project has identified the main Euro-Asian road and rail routes for priority development and cooperation (UNECE 2012). An expert group established under the project proved to be a useful cooperation platform for the coordinated development of coherent Euro-Asian inland transport links. The expert group identified nine rail and nine road corridors that link the two continents, and administrative impediments to transport and trade have been identified. UNECE also created and made freely available these corridors in the Geographical Information System (GIS) application. The EATL Ministerial meeting in February 2013 endorsed the Phase II (2008–13) final report including the priority projects and support for the next phase of the project (2013–17).

Sixth, the Organization for Security and Cooperation in Europe (OSCE) has a specific mandate in the area of transport. The Ministerial Council Decision on Future Transport Dialogue in the OSCE (2006) focuses on building partnerships between countries and relevant organizations; assisting landlocked developing countries in addressing their unique transit transportation challenges; supporting relevant international legal instruments; promoting good governance and public private partnerships; disseminating best practices and standards; and supporting on-going coordination mechanisms such as the EATL. The 'Handbook on Best Practices at Border Crossings: A Trade and Transport Facilitation Perspective' (OSCE-UNECE 2012) provides useful support to OSCE countries in their efforts to make their border crossing practices more efficient, taking into account trade and transport facilitation as well as security aspects.

Seventh, trans-African networks are developed under the framework of the African Union and the 'EU–Africa Partnership on Infrastructure' (European Commission 2007). The Trans-African Highways network comprises 10 transcontinental road projects in Africa as coordinated within the framework of the Programme for Infrastructure Development in Africa (PIDA). The total length of the 10 highways in the network is about 62,000 km (African Union 2014a). The aim is to promote trade and alleviate poverty in Africa through highway infrastructure development and the management of road-based trade corridors. An intergovernmental agreement is being negotiated by the African Union Commission, the United Nations Economic Commission for Africa (UNECA), the African Development Bank and African institutions and agencies with the objective of contributing to the integration and cohesion of Africa, to the facilitation of safe movement of goods and persons and reduction of transport cost, and to the setting up of common minimum norms and standards for design and maintenance of the network (African Union 2014b).

Energy

Significant benefits are possible through the financing of investments in the energy sector between Central Asia, the Eastern partners and the EU. INOGATE is the extension of the EU's Trans-European Energy Network (TEN-E) to the eastern neighbourhood and Central Asia.[10] These regions share with the EU a strong interest in enhancing energy security and in diversifying export routes, demand and supply structures and energy sources. Specific examples of cross-regional projects include the following. First, the Mediterranean electricity grid increases electricity interconnection capacities between Mediterranean Member States and Morocco, Algeria, Tunisia, Libya, Egypt, the Near Eastern countries and Turkey.[11] Six interconnections are in development or under construction, and eight are the subject of feasibility studies. Second, the Nord Stream project, which was inaugurated in late 2012, transports natural gas from Russia to Germany through the Baltic Sea.[12] Third, new natural gas pipeline networks are envisaged, such as the Trans Anatolian Gas Pipeline (TANAP) and the Trans Adriatic Pipeline (TAP), to supply natural gas to the European Union from the Caspian Sea and Azerbaijan through Turkey to Europe.[13] Fourth, the West African Power Pool (WAPP) aims to integrate the national power systems of the Economic Community of West African States (ECOWAS) into a regional electricity market in West Africa through the development of infrastructure projects.[14] The plan foresees the development of interconnection transmission lines and hydropower and renewable energy projects. Fifth, Cameroon's gas infrastructure connects the country to neighbouring African countries and enables the export of liquefied natural gas to Europe.

Information and communication technology

ICT investments provide significant opportunity for cross-regional connections in information technology, with the advantage of lower geographical barriers than other infrastructure investments. For example, the Eastern Africa Submarine Cable System (EASSy) is an undersea fibre-optic network connecting countries in Eastern Africa to the rest of the world via a specific cable connection between Sudan and South Africa.[15] EASSy has landing points in nine countries and is connected to 10 landlocked countries, enabling onward connectivity with Europe, the Middle East and Asia, and North America. The project started operation in 2010. Another example is broadband satellite for North Africa and some countries in sub-Saharan Africa. There are unique challenges in bringing communication and connectivity to Africa's vast wide-open spaces. Because the cost of installing cable for people living in such a rural landscape is expensive and time-consuming, satellite broadband stands out as an efficient solution to connecting Africa's previously disconnected regions to the internet.

Infrastructure in Africa

The EU–Africa Infrastructure Trust Fund is an example of a financial instrument covering sub-Saharan Africa and South Africa. It aims to increase investment in regional infrastructure in Africa by blending long-term loan financing from public financial institutions with grant resources from the European Development Fund (EDF) and EU Member States. Eligible sectors include energy, transport, water and sanitation, and information and communication. Projects must have a cross-border focus and/or be able to demonstrate a regional impact. The fund also recently opened a window to support investment under the UN 'Sustainable Energy for All Initiative' (United Nations 2013).

Foreign Direct Investment

In 2012 – for the first time ever – developing economies absorbed more FDI than developed countries, accounting for 52 per cent of global FDI flows. This is partly because the biggest fall in FDI inflows occurred in developed countries, which now account for only 42 per cent of global flows (UNCTAD 2013). Developing economies also generated almost one-third of global FDI outflows, continuing a steady upward trend. Over two decades between 1992 and 2012, the inward FDI globally and for the G20 countries has increased by about seven times, the inward FDI into the eastern partners, Russia and Central Asia by about 54 times, the inward FDI into sub-Saharan Africa by about 16 times, and the inward FDI into North Africa by almost five times (ibid.).

Global FDI fell by 32 per cent between 2007 and 2012 to US$1.35 trillion, and even more significantly in the EU, decreasing by 70 per cent, and in North Africa, decreasing by 58 per cent. A different trend can be noticed in sub-Saharan Africa, where FDI increased by 38 per cent (mainly driven by Asian or South African investors), and in the eastern partners, Russia and Central Asia, where FDI increased by 5 per cent (mainly driven by Russian investors) (UNCTAD 2013).

FDI inflows to the Central Asian region have been rising in recent years, reaching US$23 billion in 2012, driven largely by FDI into Kazakhstan and Turkmenistan (UNCTAD 2013). The main investors are from China, Russia and Turkey. Abundant natural resources, such as oil and gas, and expanding intraregional and interregional linkages are contributing to attract growing attention from investors. Across the individual economies, there is diversity in sector opportunities, but there are also extensive prospects for combining factors of production across these economies for regional investment opportunities in selected sectors. The region's rich natural resources have helped attract a significant level of extraction and processing activities. Light industries (mostly related to processing), trade and retail, energy and real estate have also brought in foreign investors.

Further regional integration and cooperation is seen as key to addressing the structural disadvantages of land-locked developing countries in sub-Saharan Africa and Central Asia. In countries that are not rich in mineral resources, these challenges are a major obstacle for investors and largely determine the low rates of FDI. Regional integration and cooperation efforts, such as the 'New Silk Road' (ADB-CAREC 2011) to enhance regional infrastructure connections and trade facilitation in Central Asia, should therefore be at the heart of strategies to overcome these problems and boost trade and investment.

Trade

Today's global economy is characterized by global value chains, in which intermediate goods and services are traded in fragmented and internationally dispersed production processes. Global value chains are typically coordinated by trans-national corporations, with cross-border trade of inputs and outputs taking place within their networks of affiliates, contractual partners and arm's-length suppliers. According to the UNCTAD World Investment Report 2013, global value chains coordinated by trans-national corporations account for some 80 per cent of global trade (UNCTAD 2013).

The total merchandise trade between the EU Member States, the neighbours, and the neighbours of the neighbours shows an increase in exports to the EU over the period 2000–12, both in absolute and relative terms.[16] As indicated in Table 10.1, exports from selected ENP countries and neighbours of the neighbours to the EU increased from about US$120 billion in 2000 to US$520 billion in 2012. In particular, over the period 2000–12, merchandise exports from the Eastern Partnership countries, Russia and Central Asia to the EU increased from 8.5 per cent to 14.6 per cent of total exports into the EU. Merchandise exports from the southern neighbourhood, sub-Saharan Africa and South Africa to the EU increased from 6.5 per cent to 8.3 per cent of total exports into the EU. Merchandise exports from the neighbours of the EU's neighbours (Russia, Central Asia, sub-Saharan Africa and South Africa) to the EU reached 17.3 per cent of total exports to the EU in 2012, rising from 10.7 per cent in 2000.

As indicated in Table 10.2, exports from the EU to the ENP countries and the neighbours of its neighbours increased from about US$71 billion in 2000 to US$306 billion in 2012. In particular, over the period 2000–12, merchandise exports from the EU to the Eastern Partnership countries, Russia and Central Asia increased from 2.8 per cent to 7.3 per cent of total exports from the EU. Merchandise exports from the southern neighbourhood, sub-Saharan Africa and South Africa to the EU increased marginally from 6.3 per cent to 6.8 per cent of total exports from the EU. Merchandise exports from the EU to the neighbours of its neighbours (Russia, Central Asia, sub-Saharan Africa and South Africa) reached 8.1 per cent of total exports from the EU in 2012, rising from 4.9 per cent in 2000.

Opportunities and challenges – key factors

Investments connecting the 'neighbours of the EU's neighbours' have the potential to develop further, particularly in light of the increasingly interconnected and globalized economies, which drive trade and investment between Europe, Russia, Asia and Africa, and the potential political and economic development in the EU's immediate neighbourhood. The experience with EU enlargement shows the benefit of regional integration for sustainable and inclusive growth, and the benefit of convergence towards EU standards, particularly in terms of environmental and social standards, public procurement and governance. There are both challenges and risks for investments connecting different regions, which are to a large extent similar to those related to cross-border investments.

It is argued that the following five broad factors can be considered as guidance to analyse both the opportunities and challenges of investments connecting different regions beyond EU's neighbourhood (see Table 10.3): (1) strategic

Table 10.1 Merchandise exports from selected countries to the EU and worldwide (in US$ million) 2000 and 2012

from	2000 to EU27		to world	2012 to EU27		to world
All countries	2,462,210		6,495,000	5,908,103		18,401,000
EU27	1,667,800		2,452,620	3,636,530		5,803,285
All countries excluding EU27	794,410	100.0%		2,271,573	100.0%	
Russian Federation	55,983	7.0%	105,565	236,758	10.4%	529,255
Ukraine	4,826		14,573	17,081		68,530
Belarus	2,085	0.9%	7,326	17,471	1.6%	45,991
Moldova	166		472	1,013		2,162
Azerbaijan	1,112		1,745	11,199		32,634
Armenia	110	0.2%	294	560	0.5%	1,428
Georgia	79		323	353		2,377
Kazakhstan	2,224		8,812	46,338		92,286
Uzbekistan	—		2,817	—		10,836
Turkmenistan	485	0.4%	2,506	—	2.0%	16,500
Kyrgyz Republic	189		505	189		1,894
Tajikistan	245		785	—		1,358
Morocco	5,625		7,432	12,171		21,417
Algeria	13,912		22,031	39,767		71,866
Tunisia	4,695	3.3%	5,850	13,634	4.5%	17,007
Libya	—		13,380	29,799		62,216
Egypt	1,919		5,276	7,875		29,385
Sub-Saharan Africa	16,952	2.1%	68,680	68,649	3.0%	344,704
South Africa	8,700	1.1%	29,983	17,377	0.8%	87,256

Source: based on World Trade Organization (2013).

Table 10.2 Merchandise exports from the EU27 to the neighbours (in US$ million) and the neighbours of the neighbours, 2000 and 2012

from EU27 to	2000		2012	
All countries	2,452,620		5,803,285	
EU27	1,667,800		3,636,530	
All countries excluding EU27	784,820	100.0%	2,166,755	100.0%
Russian Federation	13,474	1.7%	107,170	4.9%
Ukraine	4,185		26,159	
Belarus	1,844	0.8%	9,260	1.7%
Moldova	412		2,319	
Azerbaijan	276		2,667	
Armenia	320	0.1%	1,013	0.3%
Georgia	216		2,425	
Kazakhstan	1,200		7,476	
Uzbekistan	—		—	
Turkmenistan	238	0.2%	—	0.4%
Kyrgyz Republic	77		553	
Tajikistan	82		—	
Morocco	6,814		21,221	
Algeria	5,408		26,332	
Libya	2,572	3.3%	5,557	4.0%
Tunisia	6,144		13,770	
Egypt	5,239		20,376	
Sub-Saharan Africa	12,262	1.6%	30,366	1.4%
South Africa	10,736	1.4%	29,173	1.3%

Source: based on World Trade Organization (2013).

factors; (2) policy and regulatory frameworks; (3) financing sources; (4) project aspects; and (5) risks. Both challenges and opportunities exist at the strategic and policy level, depending on the vision and choices of policy-makers, while several challenges need to be addressed at the level of financing, project issues and risks.

Strategic factors

The establishment of connections between countries across regions is driven by the 'needs' and by the 'willingness' of the countries concerned, based on various political, economic and social elements. The connections between regions are influenced by major global trends such as global economic developments, increased competition for access to markets, technological progress and the digitalization of information. For example, global gross domestic product by 2050 is projected to return to a broadly similar regional composition as in the long-term trend before the industrial revolution, most notably characterized by a share of global output by China and India close to 50 per cent. According to PricewaterhouseCoopers (2013), China is

Table 10.3 Key opportunities and challenges in financing cross-regional investments

Opportunities	Challenges
Strategic factors • Global stability and security • Protection of global public goods (environment, climate, water) • Mobility of people, goods or services • Better access to energy • Economic growth through trade and investment, including foreign direct investment (FDI) • Technology transfer	• Political, geographical and cultural barriers between countries • Potential conflicts on the use of natural resources (e.g. fossil fuels, water, commodities) • Environmental impact on neighbouring countries • Trade protectionist measures
Policy and regulatory frameworks • Incentives to connect with other countries • Policy incentives to trade and investment including FDI • Ease of doing business	• Differing rules and procedures between countries • Differing cross-border standards • Barriers to trade and investment, in particular across borders
Financing sources and ownership • Leverage between public and private financing, with adequate risk-sharing • Leverage budget funds with loans and other type of financing • Attraction of foreign capital and FDI	• Balancing financial returns with sustainable development • Finding appropriate public/private financing • Funds for long-term sustainability over the project life-cycle
Project aspects • Economic and financial benefits • Environmental and social benefits • Technological advances • Technical assistance to improve quality	• Project preparation with adequate feasibility studies • Identification of routes and corridors • Capacity of connections • Project implementation (time/cost) • Project sustainability including operation and maintenance
Risk identification	• Political risks • Project risks • Reputational risks

Source: author's compilation.

projected to overtake the US as the largest economy by 2017 in purchasing power parity terms and by 2027 at market exchange rates. Russia could overtake Germany to become the largest European economy before 2020 in purchasing power parity terms and by around 2035 at market exchange rates (ibid.).

Investment, particularly involving public funds, is increasingly influenced by the concern for impact, sustainability and involvement of broader sets of stakeholders. The future Development Agenda, as illustrated by the EU 'Agenda for Change' (European Commission 2011a) and the report of the UN 'High-Level Panel of Eminent Persons on the Post-2015 Development Agenda', is likely to focus much more extensively than in the past on economic growth, based on investment, including from the private sector. The parallel policy focus on investment and on development seems to converge into a single set of integrated issues.

These trends influence the connections between the neighbours of the EU's neighbours, given their geographical position linking the EU towards Russia, Asia and Africa, and the rich resources available in these regions. As a matter of fact, among the economic factors, access to resources such as water, raw materials and energy is a key concern that can foster or hinder connections between countries. For example, Kazakhstan has some of the world's largest oil reserves; and Kyrgyzstan and Tajikistan have vast hydropower potential that has barely been tapped.[17]

Support for increased physical and financial connections between neighbouring regions beyond the EU's borders has benefits in terms of increased economic growth and trade which can yield important benefits to the European economy and increase the stability and security of the neighbourhood. The mobility of goods, services and people which can be fostered by good connections between regions provides opportunities for economic and social development. Moreover, increased connections with resource-rich economies in Africa, the Eastern Partnership region and Central Asia contribute to the EU economy, notably in the energy sector. Finally, these investments can positively contribute to global sustainability and combating climate change.

Opportunities for increased connectivity in the transport sectors are significant, as shown by the regional corridors identified between Europe and Asia. In addition to rails and roads, there are opportunities to develop the aviation sector, particularly in connections across Africa where geographical barriers (for example the Sahara) limit the possibilities to develop land transport. Opportunities in more technologically advanced sectors, including ICT, research, development and innovation, are also significant, as they require relatively limited capital investment and produce relatively high benefits, provided that the policy and regulatory frameworks are supportive.

Policy and regulatory frameworks

Policy measures and the applicable regulatory frameworks can promote or limit cross-border connections between regions. First, trade facilitation measures and the removal of trade barriers are key to unlocking the potential of FDI and cross-border trade. Examples include the compatibility or recognition of standards, the regulatory requirements to establish a subsidiary of a foreign company, or limits on foreign ownership of companies (this is the case for certain Central Asian countries). Kazakhstan approved a law that establishes the priority right of the state to take part in any new trunk pipeline built in the country, with at least a 51 per cent share (UNCTAD 2013).

Second, the legal framework of a country is a key factor in enabling cross-border investments. This includes adequate legal protection in case of disputes, or the efficiency and transparency of the legal system.

Third, cross-border regulations and standards have great influence on both infrastructure interconnections and trade in goods. For example, often one of the biggest problems that transport corridors seek to address is the time and money lost in the transshipment of goods between borders or modes of transport. Transshipment problems also occur between the same modes of transport: for example, due to differences in gauges of rail track in Asia. The solution to the issue requires a move towards standardization and greater cooperation between countries.

Fourth, transport plays a key role in trade flows between neighbouring countries. However, cumbersome administrative procedures at border crossings remain an obstacle to the efficient flow of goods between the EU and its neighbours in the East. On average, 40 per cent of total transportation time is lost at the borders due to divergences in administrative procedures (European Commission 2011b). Over time, economic development efforts will need to shift from transport corridors to more integrated economic corridors that incorporate new trade and settlement patterns, including corridor town development and corridor value chains.

Fifth, policy framework and infrastructure can strongly influence the ability to attract investments and to generate business opportunities. The ranking of selected EU neighbourhood countries and Central Asian countries in terms of 'ease of doing business' as assessed by the World Bank is shown in Table 10.4.

Table 10.4 Ease of doing business in selected countries, 2012

	Ranking among 189 countries
Georgia	8
Armenia	37
South Africa	41
Kazakhstan	50
Belarus	63
Turkey	69
Azerbaijan	70
Moldova	78
Russian Federation	92
Ukraine	112
Tajikistan	143
Uzbekistan	146

Source: based on World Bank Group (2013).

The countries' economies are assessed in 10 areas of business regulation, such as starting a business, resolving insolvency and trading across borders. A high ranking on the 'ease of doing business' index means the regulatory environment is more conducive to the starting and operation of a local firm.

Of the 20 economies narrowing the gap with the regulatory frontier the most since 2009, nine are in sub-Saharan Africa, while eight are in Europe and Central Asia (World Bank Group 2013).

Financing sources and ownership

According to the OECD (2012) and the International Energy Agency (IEA 2012), global financing needs for infrastructure between 2011 and 2030 are estimated to be about US$100 trillion, that is, about US$5 trillion annually, under a business-as-usual scenario. Moreover, the additional investment to keep the global temperature rise below 2°C would require about US$14 trillion over the same period.

The mitigation and adaptation of the effects of climate change over the next 40 years would cost around US$1 trillion per year (IEA 2012). Such levels of investments are estimated to be hard to achieve by public finance alone. There is a widespread recognition that the infrastructure gap is impossible to cover without attracting private capital. However, the financial crisis also reduced the capacity of the traditional sources of private capital such as banks, as they are facing capital and liquidity constraints. Multilateral lending institutions have increased their support to the infrastructure sector during the crisis but do not provide the ultimate solution to the infrastructure gap (OECD 2011). Possible financing sources include public financing, private financing and public–private partnerships (PPPs). Financing can be provided in various types: equity/risk capital, lending (with various levels of seniority, and potentially concessionality, where appropriate), grants, and various forms of risk sharing/guarantees.

Public financing can be provided by the beneficiary sovereign entities, by a third country or by their public institutions, and/or by multilateral public institutions such as the international financial institutions (IFIs). Private financing can be provided by the investment promoter's own funds, by private sponsors on a co-financing basis, or by private financial institutions such as banks. PPPs are schemes involving a contract between a public authority and a private entity, in which the latter is responsible for providing a public service or a project and assumes financial, technical and operational risks in the project. The public authority typically provides a concession to build and/or operate a public service, such as transport or water supply, and may provide a financial contribution.

Given the limits of public financing (budget constraints, debt sustainability) as well as of private financing (typically more focused on financial profitability and less on long-term economic, environmental and social sustainability), it is crucial to define the strategic priorities on which the investments should focus, and the criteria they should comply with, taking into account all relevant socio-economic factors and externalities. For this purpose, the countries concerned, based on a common understanding, need to define the priority sectors and specific investments (for instance transport corridors) which are of strategic importance. To facilitate this dialogue, multinational fora and international organizations, including IFIs, can play a very important role, also in enabling discussions focused on common standards and fact-based analysis.

However, investment financing in developing countries is hampered by fragmentation of aid and other financing sources. Many developing countries receive funding from too many donors (OECD 2011). The OECD estimates that in 2009 the average donor was present in 71 partner countries, and partner countries had to cope with an average of 21 donors, though there are major differences between regions, with many countries in Africa experiencing the highest incidences of fragmentation. There are three possible methods for reducing fragmentation and addressing the growing number of donors (Mackie 2013): first, pooling of resources through one donor mechanism, while also making sure not to multiply the number of such mechanisms; second, concentration through which donors could reduce the number of partner countries or sectors in which they work; and third, coordination and complementarity of donor support in any one partner country to make it easier for partner governments to manage the support as one package. The same approach could be extended to all sources of financing beyond donor aid.

The European Commission has sought to provide evidence on the benefits of a more integrated EU approach to aid effectiveness, highlighting the estimated savings to be made by reducing aid fragmentation from EU actors (Carlsson *et al.* 2009; Bigsten *et al.* 2011). It is estimated that the EU could potentially make savings between €340 million (Carlsson *et al.* 2009) and €744 million per year (Bigsten *et al.* 2011) through various measures such as reducing the number of partner countries which the EU and its Member States support; changing aid modalities, moving from projects to programmes and using more budget support avoiding duplication of country strategy processes; reducing duplication of country offices; and avoiding duplication of missions and studies.

In conclusion, these factors (financing needs, sources and fragmentation) indicate that there is a need to, first, define a strategy and allocate funding to priority investments, ensuring country ownership and governance provisions; second, combine financing means from public and private sources; and third, reduce fragmentation of financing sources.

The experience of EU blending facilities combining grants with loans for investment projects in partner countries offers an opportunity to address some of these issues. Since 2009, the European Commission, the European Investment Bank (EIB) and other IFIs, together with the EU Member States, have created a single Western Balkans Investment Framework (WBIF) focusing on regional integration, reducing fragmentation of financial instruments, maximizing country ownership and fostering the impact and synergies among all investors.[18] Between 2009 and 2013 the WBIF mobilized €300 million in grants and €2.7 billion in loans in favour of 144 priority projects worth €13 billion in socio-economic sectors promoting regional integration of Western Balkans and supporting the enlargement process (European Commission 2014a). Through the Neighbourhood Investment Facility (NIF), in the period 2008–13, nearly €750 million in grants from the EU and the EU Member States have been combined with loans from European financial institutions in favour of projects in socio-economic sectors worth about €20 billion in the southern and eastern neighbourhood (European Commission 2014b). Through the EU–Africa Infrastructure Trust Fund, in the period 2007–13, almost €500 million in grants have been combined with loans from the EIB and other European financial institutions to finance infrastructure projects with regional impact in sub-Saharan Africa, for a value of investments of about 14 times the value of the grant (European Investment Bank 2014).[19]

Project aspects

The feasibility, design, implementation and operation of an investment project represent both an opportunity and a challenge to ensure adequate delivery of the expected outcomes and impact. In particular for infrastructure projects, the upstream planning phase requires close interaction with public authorities and relevant stakeholders to identify the appropriate project feasibility and design. Technical assistance is often necessary to finance the necessary upstream studies and project preparation, to ensure quality and the timely delivery of the project, and to strengthen the promoter's implementation and operational capacities.

With respect to cross-border projects, an additional difficulty is represented by the diversity between country standards, rules and procedures which the project has to comply with. Technical measures help speed up border crossing procedures, improving safety, security and efficiency in all transport modes. Examples of such measures include the compatibility and interoperability of systems with those in the neighbouring countries, or new technologies such as traffic management and information systems.

In line with international best practices, several project-related aspects have to be addressed: the environmental impact, including a plan to mitigate environmental risks; the social aspects, including human rights, safety, security and conflict prevention; open and transparent procurement processes, to promote 'value for money' and fair competition; and compliance with international standards of anti-fraud, anti-corruption, anti-money laundering and transparency requirements.

Risk identification

A series of risks have to be identified as early as possible in the process of investment preparation, during project implementation and during a project's economic life. The investment promoters and the relevant public authorities have to identify the risks and related probability and impact, so that a risk reduction or mitigation plan can be defined and implemented. The typical risks associated with investments across regions and countries include first of all political risks such as safety and security risks, such as border management, risks of expropriation of assets or breach of contract affecting foreign investors. Second, project risks comprise, *inter alia*, the financial and economic sustainability risk of the investment and risks of harmful environmental and social impact. In addition, there may be risks for intellectual property, particularly relevant for technology and innovation investments in ICT/energy infrastructure and in FDI. Third, there are reputational risks for the investors, the promoter and the companies involved, and the countries or regions affected by the project, typically deriving from one of the above risks materializing and negatively affecting the reputation of the stakeholders involved in the investment.

Conclusions and way forward

The investments connecting the 'neighbours of the EU's neighbours' are of strategic political and economic relevance to the EU, the world's largest economy, as a global player. In order to match this ambition in a globalized world, the EU has an interest in promoting economic development and trade with developing economies, a large number of which are located in Africa and in Asia.

This chapter has examined the opportunities and challenges that the EU faces when connecting the 'neighbours of its neighbours' through investments. It has been argued that there are challenges and risks for investments connecting different regions, which are similar to those related to cross-border investments. The following broad factors can be considered as guidance in analysing the opportunities and challenges in financing investments connecting the 'neighbours of the EU's neighbours', in particular to the east and to the south of the EU: strategic elements, including geopolitical factors; policy and regulatory framework; project aspects; financing sources and ownership; and risks. Both challenges and opportunities exist at the strategic and policy level, depending on the vision and choices of policy-makers, while several key challenges need to be addressed at the level of financing, project issues and risks.

The EU policies and instruments are largely organized by region, for instance in the ENP. The EU also engages in partnership and cooperation with the 'neighbours of its neighbours', with sub-Saharan countries to the south (as part of cooperation with ACP states), and Russia and Central Asian countries to the east. The interconnections between these countries and the EU's neighbours, and thus the EU, are becoming increasingly relevant for the EU's own interests in terms of security, stability, access to energy, economic growth, trade and investment.

The recent establishment of platforms focusing on investments in socio-economic sectors (such as the Transport Panel in the Eastern Partnership or the UfM initiatives in the Mediterranean) are important policy initiatives which strengthen the cooperation and the connections between the countries within these regions and with the EU. In addition, there is an opportunity to take a broader strategic approach in promoting investments connecting the 'neighbours of the EU's neighbours' on the basis of mutual interest. This should include a focus on sectoral studies, reforms underpinning gradual economic integration, the planning of networks and the preparation of a pipeline of projects.

There is an opportunity to pool resources and reduce the fragmentation of fora, task forces and financial instruments. At present, several cooperation mechanisms and financing instruments exist, each within a specific region, with various eligibility criteria, participants and methods. An integrated investment framework to finance priority investments in socio-economic sectors could be considered, based on the principles of country ownership, pooling of financial resources and technical expertise, prioritization of investments based on best practices of due diligence, and a robust impact assessment and monitoring system to ensure delivery of expected results.

A pan-African strategy would help to foster a strategic approach to the connections and cooperation among all the countries of the continent. As part of the EU's 2014–20 financial instruments, in particular under the Development Cooperation Instrument, the European Union approved the development of a Pan-African Programme with a budget of €845 million to complement existing instruments in both North and sub-Saharan Africa to overcome fragmentation on the continent (European Union 2014). The programme will notably support activities on trans-regional, continental and global levels. This partnership has the potential to foster cooperation in the sectors of energy, regional economic integration and trade and infrastructure and this could be further developed in future. Areas include, for instance, the diversification of energy sources across the continent and the improvement of transport links.

The progressive extension of the Trans-European Transport Network (TEN-T) beyond the EU's borders facilitates the flow of goods and passengers and increases economic activity with neighbouring regions. Closer transport integration will also offer new market opportunities for companies, both in the EU and neighbouring countries. Having common standards on both sides of the border ensures a level playing field for all operators and companies. The extension of the Trans-European Energy Network (TEN-E) beyond the EU's borders and the energy interconnections support the security of energy supply to the EU and diversify the sources of energy. They also help to improve the efficiency of energy networks utilization across countries.

The EU, acting as a global player, has an interest to further seize the opportunities offered by enhancing connections between its neighbours to the east, Russia, and Central Asia, and between its neighbours to the south and sub-Saharan Africa. These connections are particularly relevant in the transport, energy and trade-related sectors.

The experience with EU enlargement shows the benefit of regional integration for sustainable and inclusive growth, stability and security, trade and convergence towards EU standards, particularly in terms of environmental and social standards, policy and legal frameworks, and governance. Investments connecting the EU, the ENP countries and the 'neighbours of the EU's neighbours' have the potential to develop further, particularly in light of the increasingly interconnecttion and globalization of economies, which drive trade and investment between

Europe, Russia, Asia and Africa, and the potential political and economic development in the EU's immediate neighbourhood.

Notes

1 The views presented in this chapter are those of the author and do not necessarily represent the views of the European Investment Bank nor of the European Commission.
2 See also Chapter 9 by Maud Fichet, Enrique Ibáñez and Veronika Orbetsova in this volume.
3 See also Chapter 6 by Tressia Hobeika in this volume.
4 See www.enpi-info.eu.
5 See also Chapter 12 by Anders Jägerskog in this volume.
6 See www.euromedtransport.eu.
7 See www.traceca-org.org.
8 See www.carecprogram.org.
9 See www.unece.org/trans/main/eatl.html.
10 See www.inogate.org.
11 See www.medgrid-psm.com.
12 See www.nord-stream.com.
13 See www.tanap.com and www.tap-ag.com.
14 See www.ecowapp.org.
15 See www.eassy.org.
16 See also Chapter 5 by Sieglinde Gstöhl in this volume.
17 See also Chapter 11 by Johannes Theiss in this volume.
18 See www.wbif.eu.
19 See www.eu-africa-infrastructure-tf.net.

References

ADB-CAREC (Asian Development Bank – Central Asia Regional Economic Cooperation Program) (2011) *The New Silk Road: Ten Years of the Central Asia Regional Economic Cooperation Program*, Manila: Asian Development Bank, Central Asia Regional Economic Cooperation Program.

African Union (2014a) *Trans-African Highways Network routes*, http://ie.au.int/en/sites/default/files/E%20-%20TAH%20Annex%20I%20TAH%20Network.pdf (accessed July 2014).

African Union (2014b) *Third Session of the African Union Conference of African Ministers of Transport (CAMT)*, Malabo, 7–11 April, http://ie.au.int/en/content/third-session-african-union-conference-african-ministers-transport-camt-malabo-equatorial-gu (accessed July 2014).

Bigsten A., J.-P. Platteau and S. Tengstam (2011) *The Aid Effectiveness Agenda: The Benefits of Going Ahead*, Brussels: SOGES for the European Commission.

Calderon, C. (2009) *Infrastructure and Growth in Africa*, World Bank Policy Research Working Paper 4914, http://elibrary.worldbank.org/doi/book/10.1596/1813-9450-4914 (accessed November 2013).

CAREC (2013) *Transport and Trade Facilitation Strategy 2020*, endorsed at the 12th Ministerial Conference on Central Asia Regional Economic Cooperation, Astana, 23–24 October.

Carlsson, B., C. Schubert and S. Robinson (2009) *The Aid Effectiveness Agenda: Benefits of a European Approach*, Hemel Hempstead: HTSPE for the European Commission.

Council of the European Union (2011) *Council Conclusions on Transport Cooperation with the EU's Neighbouring Regions*, 3116th Transport, Telecommunications and Energy Council meeting, 6 October.

ENPI-Info (2014) *EuroMed Transport Project*, http://enpi-info.eu/mainmed.php?id= 306&id_type=10 (accessed July 2014).

European Commission (2007) Communication from the Commission to the Council and the European Parliament, *Interconnecting Africa: The EU–Africa Partnership on Infrastructure*, COM(2006) 376 final, Brussels, 13 July.

European Commission (2011a) Communication from the Commission, *Increasing the Impact of EU Development Policy: An Agenda for Change*, COM(2011) 637 final, Brussels, 13 October.

European Commission (2011b) Communication from the Commission to the Council and the European Parliament, *The EU and its Neighbouring Regions: A Renewed Approach to Transport Cooperation*, COM(2011) 415 final, Brussels, 7 July.

European Commission (2012) *Eastern Partnership Transport Panel*, Brussels, http://ec. europa.eu/transport/themes/international/regional_cooperation/doc/2012-eap-transport-panel-terms-of-reference.pdf (accessed July 2014).

European Commission (2013) *Development Cooperation with Central Asia – Transport*, Brussels, https://ec.europa.eu/europeaid/regions/central-asia/eu-support-transport-development-central-asia_en (accessed July 2014).

European Commission (2014a) *Western Balkans Investment Framework: Annual Report 2013*, Brussels, www.wbif.eu/uploads/lib_document/attachment/373/WBIF_Annual_Report_2013_-_17_March_2014.pdf (accessed July 2014).

European Commission (2014b) *Neighbourhood Investment Facility: Operational Annual Report 2013*, Brussels, http://ec.europa.eu/europeaid/sites/devco/files/nif-operational-annual-report-2013_web_en.pdf (accessed July 2014).

European Commission and High Representative (2011a) Joint Communication of the Commission and High Representative to the European Parliament, *A Partnership for Democracy and Shared Prosperity with the Southern Mediterranean*, COM(2011) 200 final, Brussels, 8 March.

European Commission and High Representative (2011b) *Joint Communication to the European Parliament on a New Response to a Changing Neighbourhood*, COM(2011) 303, Brussels, 25 May.

European Investment Bank (2014) *EU–Africa Infrastructure Trust Fund: Annual Report 2013*, www.eu-africa-infrastructure-tf.net/attachments/Annual%20Reports/eu_africa_infrastructure_trust_fund_annual_report_2013_en.pdf (accessed July 2014).

European Union (2013) 'Regulation (EU) No 1315/2013 of the European Parliament and the Council on Union Guidelinees for the Development of the Trans-European Transport Network and Repealing Decision No 661/2010/EU', *Official Journal of the European Union*, L 348, 20 December, 1–128.

European Union (2014) 'Regulation (EU) of the European Parliament and of the Council of 11 March 2014 Establishing a Financing Instrument for Development Cooperation for the Period 2014–2020', *Official Journal of the European Union*, L 77, 15 March, 44–76.

IEA (2012) *Energy Technology Perspectives: Pathways to a Clean Energy System*, Paris: International Energy Agency.

Mackie, J. (2013) *How Serious is the EU about Reducing Fragmentation?* Paper for DIE Conference 10–11 October 2013, 'Fragmentation or Pluralism?', Maastricht: European Centre for Development Policy Management.

OECD (2011) *Report on the Division of Labour: Addressing Cross-Country Fragmentation of Aid*, Report for the Busan 4th HLF on Aid Effectiveness, Paris: OECD Publishing.

OECD (2012) *Strategic Transport Infrastructure Needs to 2030*, Paris: OECD Publishing.

OECD (2014) 'DAC List of ODA Recipients', www.oecd.org/dac/stats/daclistofoda-recipients.htm (accessed January 2014).

OSCE-UNECE (2012) *Handbook of Best Practices at Border Crossings – A Trade and Transport Facilitation Perspective*, Vienna: OSCE, Geneva: UNECE, www.unece.org/fileadmin/DAM/trans/bcf/publications/OSCE-UNECE_Handbook.pdf (accessed July 2014).

PricewaterhouseCoopers (2013) *World in 2050: The BRICs and Beyond – Prospects, Challenges and Opportunities*, PricewaterhouseCoopers Economics.

Sugolov, P., B. Dodonov and C. von Hirschhausen (2003) *Infrastructure Policies and Economic Development in East European Transition Countries: First Evidence*, Dresden: Institute for Economic Research, Working Paper, http://tudresden.de/die_tu_dresden/fakultaeten/fakultaet_wirtschaftswissenschaften/bwl/ee2/lehrstuhlseiten/ordner_publikationen/publications/wp_psm_02_sogulov_dodonov_hirschhausen_infrastructure_growth_transition.pdf (accessed November 2013).

TRACECA (2011) 'Maps of Rail and Road Routes between Europe, Caucasus and Asia', www.traceca-org.org/en/routes/gis-database-maps-downloads (accessed November 2013).

UNCTAD (2013) *World Investment Report 2013 – Global Value-Chains: Investment and Trade for Development*, Geneva: UNCTAD.

UNECE (2012) *Euro-Asian Transport Linkages: Paving the Way for a More Efficient Euro-Asian Transport*, Phase II – Expert Group Report, New York and Geneva: United Nations Economic Commission for Europe.

Union for the Mediterranean (2013) *Ministerial Declaration of the Ministerial Conference on Transport*, Brussels, 14 November.

United Nations (2013) 'Sustainable Energy for All Initiative', www.se4all.org.

World Bank Group (2013) *Doing Business 2014 – Understanding Regulations for Small and Medium-Size Enterprises*, Washington, DC: World Bank, 29 October.

World Trade Organization (2013) 'International Trade and Market Access Data', 2000–2012, www.wto.org/english/res_e/statis_e/trade_data_e.htm (accessed December 2013).

11 Geopolitics vs. governance in the European Union's energy cooperation with its broader neighbourhood

Johannes Theiss

Introduction: geopolitics or governance?[1]

While energy issues have been at the heart of European integration since the establishment of the European Coal and Steel Community (ECSC) in 1952 and the European Atomic Energy Community (EAEC or Euratom) in 1958, the European Union (EU) has only recently created a genuine energy policy; however, a coherent and consistent external EU energy policy is still pending. Energy had not found its way into the Single European Act (SEA) but was considered relevant in the internal market programme in 1988 (Egenhofer and Behrens 2011: 241). Differences between Member States that produce and consume energy as well as the variety of national approaches, for instance regarding network industries or the energy mix, had prevented the EU from gaining legal competence in this field (ibid.).

Apart from pursuing overarching objectives, such as reducing the dependency on oil imports or promoting efficient energy use, the EU was in the 1990s nonetheless able to exert influence through policies in which it had the right to act, notably related to the internal market, competition policy, and the environment. Already in its White Paper, the European Commission (1995) argued in favour of a European approach to energy policy. While the White Paper identified a triangle of objectives – overall competitiveness, security of energy supply, and environmental protection – 'as being most relevant to the energy sector' (ibid.: 14), the debate in the new millennium was driven by concerns about secure energy supplies, starting with the 2000 Green Paper 'Towards a European Strategy for the Security of Energy Supply' (European Commission 2000). This debate was fuelled by the changing energy landscape throughout the previous decade. Among the risks threatening the security of European energy supply were a rising energy demand, especially in China; an increasing political destabilization of the Middle East, where 65 per cent of the global oil reserves are located; several gas disputes between Russia and Ukraine; and natural disasters as possible outcomes of climate change (Natorski and Herranz Surrallés 2008: 71–72).[2] The various documents following the 2000 Green Paper paved the way towards a more integrated internal approach in order to tackle these challenges, acknowledging also the need for more external coherence (ibid.: 72).

After the 2006 Green Paper 'A European Strategy for Sustainable, Competitive and Secure Energy' had reiterated the triangle of energy objectives (European Commission 2006a), several packages of legislation were agreed on. The 2007 'EU Climate and Energy Package' focused on EU-wide binding targets to reduce greenhouse gas emissions by 20 per cent compared to 1990 and to raise the share of renewable energy sources in energy consumption to 20 per cent (including 10 per cent in transport) by 2020 (European Commission 2007a). Thus Member States' sovereignty over the energy mix was somewhat constrained (Egenhofer and Behrens 2011: 242). Also in 2007, a 'Third Package of Legislative Proposals for Electricity and Gas Markets' (known as the 'Third Energy Package') was adopted, mainly in order to increase competition in these markets (see, for instance, European Union 2007). The 'Second Strategic Energy Review' of 2008 re-emphasized in particular the security of energy supplies, also accounting for the external dimension of energy policy (European Commission 2008b). Eventually, with the entry into force of the Treaty of Lisbon in 2009, energy policy became a shared competence according to art. 4(2)(i) TFEU and a chapter was dedicated to it. The latter restates the aims of EU energy policy but also provides some sovereignty guarantees for Member States, for instance regarding their energy mix (art. 194(2) TFEU). While an EU energy policy seems to be taking shape internally, its external dimension is still at a formulation stage, as demonstrated by the Commission's 2011 Communication on 'Security of Energy Supply and International Cooperation' and the Council Conclusions on 'Strengthening the External Dimension of the EU Energy Policy' (European Commission 2011; Council of the European Union 2011b). The EU institutions viewed external energy policy through the prism of the internal market and enlargement. Since the Russian annexation of Crimea in 2014, the destabilization of eastern Ukraine and the cooling of relations between the EU and Russia, security of supply has been reemphasized, most notably in the 2014 'European Energy Security Strategy' (European Commission 2014).

Events such as the crisis in Ukraine have meant that the focus of energy relations between the EU and third countries has often been reduced to concerns about security of supply and, more specifically, the geopolitical risks related to it. In this sense, the analysis of energy cooperation often appears to be all about resource-rich developed autocracies. This chapter suggests an alternative but complementary view on energy cooperation. It is based on the idea of governance, defined as 'a system of rules that exceeds the voluntarism implicit in the term cooperation and refers to recurrent forms of coordinated action that aim at the production of collectively binding agreements' (Lavenex 2011: 374). Specifically, this chapter asks to what extent the governance perspective can explain EU energy cooperation with the 'neighbours of its neighbours' in the Sahel, the Middle East and Central Asia, compared to geopolitical considerations on security of supply.

The chapter starts with a closer look at the governance concept and uses it to provide a typological overview of the various EU frameworks of energy cooperation. It then assesses the energy sector relations between the EU and its broader neighbourhood, focusing on the 'neighbours of the EU's neighbours' (European Commission 2006b: 11), that is, the three regions that border countries participating in the European Neighbourhood Policy (ENP). In the Sahel, the immediate neighbours to ENP members are Mauritania, Mali, Niger, Chad, and Sudan.[3] In the Middle East, this is the case for Saudi Arabia, Iraq and Iran. In Central Asia, Turkmenistan and Kazakhstan are neighbours of the ENP countries in Eastern Europe and South Caucasus. The regional assessment will be complemented by individual country examples. The chapter concludes with a comparative overview of the findings.

Frameworks of EU energy cooperation

As stated above, governance is understood as a binding rule system that guides recurrent coordinated action. Scholars using this conceptualization in the context of the EU's external relations have identified two dimensions characterizing the quality of governance: legalization and institutionalization (Lavenex 2004; 2011; Lavenex *et al.* 2009). Legalization determines third countries' compliance with the EU's rules, the *acquis*. The quality range is defined by the degree of legal approximation, the scope of covered rules, and the procedures of enforcement. The European Economic Area (EEA) can be found at the upper end of the continuum and the ENP framework in the middle (ibid.). Most 'neighbours of the EU's neighbours' could be located at the lower end, which is characterized by the exchange of information and communication (low legal approximation), references to principles rather than specific rules of the *acquis* (narrow scope) and political supervision, if any (weak enforcement).

Institutionalization, the second governance dimension, focuses on third countries' inclusion in bodies and structures that shape the EU's approach towards them. Here, the quality range is defined by the degree of participation in EU structures, the level of dependence in structures parallel to the EU, and the depth of interactions between EU and third country officials. Again, the EEA marks the upper end of the continuum and the ENP takes a medium position, whereas the broader neighbourhood could be placed at the lower end, that is, being excluded from EU internal structures (no participation), organized in parallel regional or multilateral structures (low dependence), and interacting with the EU on an *ad hoc* basis and limited to the political level (low depth) (ibid.).

Using the examples of the EEA, the ENP and the 'neighbours of the neighbours' means putting the emphasis on governance circles of territorial proximity, in which energy is one among many aspects.[4] With the Energy Community (ENC) and the Energy Charter Treaty (ECT),[5] there are also tiers of influence specific to cooperation in the energy sector, which are not congruent with these territorial circles. The analysis of these sector-specific frameworks does not, however, constitute a focus of this chapter (see Theiss 2013).

Of the 10 'neighbours of the EU's neighbours' covered in this analysis, none is affiliated with the ENC, and only Turkmenistan and Kazakhstan have ratified the ECT. The latter are even provisionally applying its 1998 Trade Amendment (in force since 2010) and therefore complying with the entire ECT rule book (Energy Charter Secretariat 2012). The Trade Amendment is regarded as an 'important stepping stone' towards membership in the World Trade Organization (WTO) (Energy Charter 2013a). Moreover, Iran and Saudi Arabia hold observer status (Energy Charter 2013b).

Besides using other international fora of energy cooperation, such as the International Renewable Energy Agency (IRENA) or the International Energy Forum (IEF) (Lesage *et al.* 2010: 68–69, 61–63), the EU engages with its broader neighbourhood in a number of regional and bilateral agreements. The following puts forward some hypotheses and initial empirical data, which will be assessed subsequently.

Hypotheses and data

In order to assess the extent to which governance can explain EU energy cooperation with the 'neighbours of its neighbours' compared to geopolitics, three hypotheses guide the analysis for each perspective. First, from a geopolitical perspective on security of supply, the availability of resources in a third country should catalyse energy cooperation with the EU, as there is a mutual interest to diversify supply (EU) and demand (third country) respectively. Second, a high level of economic development, measured by the Human Development Index (HDI), provides an attractive investment environment, which should foster energy cooperation. Third, autocratic regimes, as gauged by the Freedom House Index, would be reliable energy partners, as they often use the income from energy sales to consolidate power.

Expectations from a governance perspective are the opposite. First, a third country's resources could constitute a power source, which would allow it to resist the EU's attempts to export its model, thus impeding *acquis*-based energy cooperation. Fossil fuel reserves could be even used as a trump card to influence cooperation in other areas, such as human rights. Second, it could be argued that a certain lack of development provides room for leverage, for instance in allowing the EU to implement its energy model through development aid. Third, the governance view would expect that autocratic arbitrariness impedes continuous cooperation and a consistent adaption to the EU's model. The data in Table 11.1 is hence open to different interpretations.

Looking at the resources, the geopolitical perspective would expect that the EU's energy cooperation with the Middle East would be most advanced, followed by that with Central Asia, while energy cooperation with the Sahel countries would be least advanced. With regard to development, partners in the Middle East and Central Asia would constitute a more attractive investment environment compared to partners in the Sahel. Formulating expectations concerning the political system seems to be difficult at the regional level, due to variation within rather than between the three regions.

Interpretations from the governance perspective reverse the picture. With regard to resources, the Sahel partners would be more open to cooperate on

Table 11.1 Resources, development and political systems in the Sahel, the Middle East and Central Asia, 2012–13

	Oil		Gas		Human Development Index (rank)	Freedom House Index
	% of proven reserves	% of EU imports	% of proven reserves	% of EU imports		
Chad	0.1	—	***	—	184 (low)	6.5 (not free)
Mali	***	—	***	—	182 (low)	6 (not free)
Mauritania	***	—	***	—	155 (low)	5.5 (not free)
Niger	***	—	***	—	186 (low)	3.5 (partly free)*
Sudan	0.4	**	***	—	171 (low)	7 (not free)
Iran	9.1	—	15.9	—	76 (high)	6 (not free)
Iraq	8.7	3.4	1.7	—	131 (medium)	6 (not free)
Saudi Arabia	16.1	9.1	3.9	—	57 (high)	7 (not free)
Kazakhstan	1.8	5.9	0.9	—	69 (high)	5.5 (not free)
Turkmenistan	***	—	11.7	—	102 (medium)	7 (not free)

Sources: British Petrol (2012); European Commission (2013c); own calculations based on Eurostat (2013); Freedom House (2013); United Nations Development Programme (2013).

Notes

* Electoral democracy according to Freedom House (2013).

** 6.0% of EU oil imports in 2011, 1.3% in 2012, oil embargo between 2012 and 2013.

*** Share smaller than 0.05% according to British Petrol (2012).

Human Development Index ranking categories: very high (1–47), high (48–94), medium (95–141), low (142–186); Freedom House categories (mean between political rights and civil liberties): free (1.0–2.5), partly free (3.0–5.0), not free (5.5–7.0).

energy issues with the EU than the partners in Central Asia, let alone the Middle East. There also appears to be more leverage for development aid in the Sahel, compared to the other two regions.[6] Table 11.2 shows the disbursements in energy projects under the EU budget from 2007 to 2012.

The biggest investments have been conducted under the European Development Fund (EDF) in the Sahel, notably in the renewables sector, followed by funding under the Nuclear Safety Instrument (NSI) and the Development Cooperation Instrument (DCI) in Central Asia. Thus there appears to be governance potential for the EU in these two regions. Table 11.3 shows disbursements on the regional level under the European Neighbourhood and Partnership Instrument (ENPI), which was oriented towards ENP countries and Russia but was also open to the broader neighbourhood under certain conditions (see the next section, which discusses the Sahel).

As the Commission does not encode the data on the country level, the disbursements shown in these tables do not distinguish between ENP and non-ENP countries. The low outcome for Central Asia is not to be underestimated, as these countries may also be included in projects under the labels 'CEEC/NIS Unallocated' and 'Europe'. In comparison, Middle Eastern energy disbursements are lower than in the northern Sahara (potentially including Sahel neighbours). These figures again point towards EU governance potential with the Sahel countries and Central Asia. The following sections explore this data in greater detail.[7]

EU energy cooperation with the Sahel countries

This section analyses the EU's energy cooperation with the Sahel countries, covering the political and legal framework as well as financial instruments, first at the regional and then on the country level. From a geopolitical view on security of supply, the first two hypotheses take a pessimistic stance on the EU's energy cooperation with the 'neighbours of its neighbours' in the Sahel (Mauritania, Mali, Niger, Chad, Sudan). First, none of the countries in this region holds significant gas reserves, while the oil reserves of Sudan and Chad account for only around 0.5 per cent of the world's total (see Table 11.1). Compared to the Middle East or Central Asia, these oil stocks are negligible and, in addition, do not play any role for the EU's oil imports at the time of writing. The reserves do not therefore suffice to create a diversification incentive, either for the supplier or the consumer. Second, the Sahel neighbours are among the least developed countries in the world. Ranked 186 out of 186, Niger marks the bottom of the HDI (United Nations Development Programme 2013: 147). Concerns may thus be raised regarding these countries' attractiveness for investments. This being said, foreign direct investment (FDI) is higher for less developed countries with energy resources (Youngs 2009: 127). Regarding the third geopolitical hypothesis, EU governments have been accused of accepting autocratic structures in Africa, as these focus 'all their competences on managing energy relationships with the outside world, through decisions taken by an ever-decreasing circle of political elites' (ibid.: 136). The governance perspective reverses this picture, expecting an optimistic outlook

Table 11.2 EU disbursements to energy projects by country, instrument and energy subsector, 2007–12

Country	Instrument	Energy subsector	€1,000	Energy share of total
Chad	EDF	Electrical transmission/distribution	92	
		Energy policy and administrative management	1,156	
		Hydro-electric power plants	129	
		Power generation/renewable sources	427	
		Solar energy*	2,352	
		Total energy disbursement	**4,156**	1.5%
Mali	EDF	Power generation/renewable sources	126	
		Solar energy*	7,620	
		Total energy disbursement	**7,746**	1.6%
Mauritania	EDF	Biomass	356	
		Energy policy and administrative management*	3908	
		Power generation/non-renewable sources	29	
		Power generation/renewable sources	1,450	
		Total energy disbursement	**5,743**	2.9%
Niger	EDF	Power generation/renewable sources*	1,121	
		Solar energy	804	
		Total energy disbursement	**1,925**	0.4%
Iraq	DCI – Geo	Energy research*	110	
		Total energy disbursement	**110**	0.1%
Kazakhstan	DCI – Geo	Coal-fired power plants	23	
	NSI	Nuclear power plants*	1,639	
		Total energy disbursement	**1,662**	3.5%
Turkmenistan	DCI – Geo	Energy policy and administrative management*	240	
		Gas distribution	148	
		Total energy disbursement	**389**	
All countries		**Total energy disbursement**	**21,731**	1.3%

Sources: compiled by the author based on data provided by the European Commission upon the author's request in September 2013.

Notes
Rounded figures; country not listed = no energy-related disbursements; * = dominant energy subsector; EDF = European Development Fund; DCI – Geo = Development Cooperation Instrument – Geographic Programme; NSI = Nuclear Safety Instrument; Total energy disbursement = sum across subsectors; Energy share of total = energy share of the total sum disbursed in a country across all mentioned instruments.

Table 11.3 EU disbursements to energy projects under the ENPI by region and energy subsector, 2007–12

Region	Energy subsectors	€1,000	Energy share of total
North of Sahara	Energy policy and administrative management*	14,948	2.5%
	Total energy disbursement	**14,948**	
Middle East	Energy policy and administrative management	1,114	
	Solar energy*	2,298	
	Total energy disbursement	**3,411**	5.1%
Central Asia	Energy policy and administrative management	502	
	Gas distribution*	2,043	
	Total energy disbursement	**2,544**	21.7%
CEEC/NIS unallocated	Energy policy and administrative management*	128	
	Total energy disbursement	**128**	0.1%
Europe	Energy policy and administrative management*	32,662	
	Energy research	76	
	Gas distribution	1,359	
	Energy education/training	1,082	
	Total energy disbursement	**35,178**	8.5%
All regions	**Total energy disbursement**	**56,210**	4.7%

Sources: compiled by the author based on data provided by the European Commission upon the author's request in September 2013.

Notes
Rounded figures; only regional level = ENP and non-ENP countries covered; * = dominant energy subsector; ENPI = European Neighbourhood and Partnership Instrument; CEEC/NIS = Central Eastern European countries/newly independent states; Total energy disbursement = sum across subsectors; Energy share of total = energy share of the total sum disbursed in a region under the ENPI.

for energy cooperation due to the lack of resources and economic development, clouded only by potentially unreliable autocratic regimes.

Political and legal framework

On the regional level, there is indeed evidence for energy relations between the EU and the Sahel being linked to the notion of governance (Youngs 2009: 126). This idea is embedded in the European Union's general approach towards Africa, politically defined by the 2007 Joint Africa–EU Strategy (JAES) and the Cotonou Agreement with the African, Caribbean, and Pacific (ACP) group of states (African Union and European Union 2007; European Commission 2012c).

As the most tangible part of EU–Sahel cooperation, the Cotonou Agreement has, however, a comparably poor governance quality. Convergence towards the *acquis* is not envisaged (low legal approximation), only general principles instead of specific rules are covered (narrow scope), and, while supervision takes place, sanctions are hardly applied (weak to modest enforcement). On the institutional side, the Cotonou Agreement does not foresee inclusion into EU structures (no participation) and features a parallel institutional setup (modest dependence), including a council of ministers, a committee of ambassadors, and a joint parliamentary assembly (art. 14–17 Cotonou Agreement). Interactions within these 'joint institutions' take place (bi)annually under rotating presidencies and cover only political staff (low depth).

With regard to the energy sector, the JAES takes a development-oriented stance, aiming at 'sustainable management of ... energy resources ... access to energy, ... investments for energy infrastructure ... [and] sustainable energy sector development' (African Union and European Union 2007: 18). More specifically, the Second Action Plan in the framework of this Strategy highlights the promotion of renewable energy and energy efficiency but also the development of Africa's gas sector with possible export increases to Europe (African Union and European Union 2010: 5). While the latter aspect reflects a geopolitical consideration, this line of argument puts energy development mainly in a climate change perspective, following the EU's internal model. This is also legally reflected in the Cotonou Agreement;[8] however, the Agreement's (albeit not energy-specific) sanction mechanism under art. 96 was hardly used (Youngs 2009: 137–138). Where it was used, it targeted countries with limited importance for oil and gas extraction, such as Niger, hence backing the hypothesis that a lack of resource wealth means less leverage for resisting the EU's governance attempts. None of the Sahel partners is affiliated with the energy-specific cooperation frameworks of the ENC or the ECT.

Financial instruments

The main financial tool for funding cooperation under the Cotonou Agreement is the European Development Fund, which in its tenth round, 2008–13, devoted €22.7 billion to EU–ACP cooperation on the bilateral, regional, and ACP-wide level (European Commission 2012a). The EDF also provides the budget for the

ACP–EU Energy Facility, an instrument created in the wake of the 2002 World Summit on Sustainable Development (European Commission 2012d). After €220 million financed through the ninth EDF in the first budget term of the Energy Facility 2006–09, the 2009–13 term foresaw €200 million, entirely focusing on access to renewable energy services (ibid.; European Community and ACP Group of States 2009: 42). Besides this limitation in terms of content, the EU's main instrument for energy cooperation under the EDF represents not even one per cent of the whole EDF budget. Moreover, of the €1.4 billion invested in the Sahel countries under the EDF between 2007 and 2012, €19.6 million has been disbursed in the energy sector, accounting for 1.4 per cent (see also Table 11.2).

In addition to the EDF, energy cooperation with Sahel neighbours may have profited from the Development Cooperation Instrument, but only under very specific conditions, such as projects under the Thematic Programme for Environment and Sustainable Management of Natural Resources (ENRTP) or projects and programmes targeting cross-border, regional or global cooperation (European Parliament and Council of the European Union 2006b: art. 31(1), 36). From 2007 to 2012, €11 million out of €152 million under the ENRTP has been disbursed for energy projects, but none of this was in the regions and countries of interest in this chapter.

Financing was also available under the ENPI, an instrument mainly oriented at ENP countries and Russia. Specifically, the ENPI Regulation foresaw participation in cross-border, regional and global endeavours and, 'in duly substantiated cases', of entities in countries 'having traditional economic, trade or geographical links with neighbouring [ENP] countries', which would apply to the 'neighbours of the neighbours' (European Parliament and Council of the European Union 2006a: art. 27, 21(2)). In this sense, the Sahel countries may have profited together with North African ENP countries from the €14.9 million invested between 2007 and 2012 under the ENPI in the northern Sahara region (see Table 11.3). The projects, related to energy policy and administrative management, account for 2.5 per cent of the ENPI disbursements in this region, without distinguishing between ENP and non-ENP countries.

While these are attempts to connect the EU's immediate and broader neighbourhood under the EU's governance model, the respective DCI and ENPI clauses constitute the exception rather than the rule. The EU's 2011 Sahel Strategy does not even mention energy issues (Council of the European Union 2011a). Nevertheless, of the 139 projects between 2006 and 2012 under the abovementioned ACP–EU Energy Facility, 28 have been carried out in the Sahel (European Union 2012b: 10).[9] In addition to this regional assessment, there are several particularities on the country level.

EU energy cooperation with the Sahel on the country level

Moving from west to east, Mauritania is the first potential partner in the EU's broader neighbourhood. With neither significant oil nor gas resources, its energy is more than 80 per cent derived from traditional biomass fuels, such as firewood and charcoal, whose sustainable management is therefore one of the key energy challenges for the country (European Community and Mauritania 2008: 132). Mauritania is the only country in the Sahel which is specifically foreseen to profit from funding under the ENPI, as it is part of the Union for the Mediterranean (UfM) (European Commission 2008a: 9). One-third of the Sahel projects under the ACP–EU Energy Facility have been executed in Mauritania (European Union 2012b: 10; see also Table 11.2).

With a Freedom House score of 5.5, Mauritania is at the border of being partly free (see Table 11.1). Indeed, after long-term authoritarian rule and military *coups d'état*, democratic elections were held in 2006–07 and 2009 (European External Action Service 2013c). There is evidence that business with the authoritarian regime impeded energy cooperation rather than promoting it. An example is Woodside Petroleum's struggle over exploitation rights for Mauritania's minor oil reserves, as a deal struck in 2004 with autocratic ruler Maaouya Ould Sid'Ahmed Taya was questioned after his regime had been toppled in 2005 (Embassy of the United States in Mauritania 2011).

On Mauritania's eastern border, Mali shows a similar energy balance, relying up to more than 90 per cent on firewood and charcoal (European Community and Mali 2007: 21, 87). It has not even minor oil or gas reserves; its electricity sector is predominantly based on renewables (80 per cent hydro), which accounts, however, only for 1.2 per cent of the total energy balance (ibid.: 14, 89). Still, there is potential for energy transition as a means to attain sustainable development objectives. This is also demonstrated by the number of projects carried out under the ACP–EU Energy Facility (8 out of 28 in the Sahel, see European Union 2012b: 10) and the energy-related disbursements under the EDF, which are higher than for any other Sahel country analysed (see Table 11.2). Mali had been a democracy until the rebellion and the *coup d'état* in the beginning of 2012. After the military intervention by France and the deployment of the Multidimensional Integrated Stabilization Mission in Mali (MINUSMA) by the United Nations (UN) in April 2013, democratic elections were held (Paolo and Derryck 2013). The fall-back into autocratic patterns had impeded the EU's relations with Mali, as it had led to the suspension of cooperation until 'progress towards a return to constitutional order' had been accomplished (European External Action Service 2013b).

Like Mauritania, Niger has negligible oil reserves, but it relies up to 90 per cent on firewood (European Community and Niger 2008: Annex 4: 1). However, coal may soon represent an alternative and there is potential for solar energy (ibid.: 3). Energy transition might be a path for Niger, as demonstrated by five projects under the ACP–EU Energy Facility and energy-related disbursements under the EDF (see Table 11.2; European Union 2012b: 10). With a Freedom House score of 3.5, Niger is freer than any other 'neighbour of the EU's neighbours' analysed in this chapter, but the least developed at the same time (see Table 11.1). Having suffered a military *coup d'état* in 2010, Niger 'restored democracy in an exemplary transition process' (European External Action Service 2013d). Given the country's exceptionally low economic development, the suspension of cooperation following art. 96 of the Cotonou Agreement may have been instrumental for bringing Niger back in line (ibid.).

Chad has since 2003 been recovering oil from the 0.1 per cent of the global reserves it owns (see Table 11.1). As this production is entirely destined for exports, wood remains the country's main source of energy (Youngs 2009: 127; European Community and Republic of Chad 2007: Annex 6). Five projects have been implemented under the ACP–EU Energy Facility and funding focused again on energy transition and notably renewables (see Table 11.2; European Union 2012b: 10). The case of Chad further shows that relying on autocrats can be a double-edged sword. One example are the struggles of Total and the French government with the rule of long-term president Idriss Déby (Youngs 2009: 149).

Sudan and its recently independent southern part are the EU's easternmost 'neighbour of the neighbours' in the Sahel and, at the same time, the most resource-rich and autocratic (see Table 11.1). Since Sudan did not ratify the 2005 revision of the Cotonou Agreement, it did not receive funding under the tenth EDF; it did, however, receive special funds under former EDFs (European External Action Service 2013e). In Sudan's Country Strategy Paper and National Indicative Programme, energy was the sector with the least priority for cooperation with the EU (European Community and Republic of the Sudan 2005: Annex: 43–44). The fact that none of the projects executed under the ACP–EU Energy Facility was located in Sudan points in a similar direction (European Union 2012b: 10). Rather than renewables and energy efficiency, the distribution of Sudan's fossil resources between the north and the south has been the key issue, relevant not only for the 2005 peace agreement after years of civil war but also a main reason for various conflicts in the aftermath (Youngs 2009: 146–148). More generally speaking, the security situation has so far undermined continuous cooperation with Sudan.

Whereas geopolitics would have largely ignored EU energy cooperation with the Sahel countries due to the lack of resources and economic development, energy relations are being implemented, albeit rather as governance. For the most part, the countries analysed are receptive to the EU's model, which is implemented through development aid. However, autocratic regimes represent obstacles for cooperation. Although there is a case for governance, energy issues are not a priority for the EU in the region and the governance quality of the frameworks in place remains poor.

EU energy cooperation with the Middle East

The Middle East constitutes the classical case for regarding energy cooperation through the lens of geopolitical considerations on security of supply. Together, these 'neighbours of the EU's neighbours' (Saudi Arabia, Iraq, Iran) own more than one-third of the world's proven oil reserves and more than one-fifth of the globally known gas reserves (see Table 11.1). While the latter are not important for EU imports at the time of writing, the former represented 12.5 per cent in 2013 (ibid.). Thus there appears to be an incentive to maintain and improve cooperation in the oil sector and potentially further diversify in gas. Moreover, the three Middle Eastern countries analysed here are also more developed than partners in the Sahel, implying positive prospects for investment. Finally, the Gulf states and their largest representative Saudi Arabia have been regarded as reliable partners, whose autocratic rule would be preferred to less predictable Islamist governments potentially emerging from democratic elections (Youngs 2009: 54, 68). EU leverage through governance is to be questioned, as the Middle Eastern partners can afford not to follow the EU's model owing to their resource wealth and are less dependent on development aid. According to the governance view, autocratic regimes would present another obstacle to continuous cooperation.

Political and legal framework

At a first glance, the European Union's approach towards the Middle East is much more fragmented compared to its approach to Africa and in particular the Sahel. It lacks an encompassing legal framework, such as the Cotonou Agreement (European External Action Service 2013i). Politically, the 2004 EU Strategic Partnership with the Mediterranean and the Middle East (SPMME) sought, *inter alia*, to foster energy interconnections between the EU, its immediate and its broader neighbourhood (European Union 2004: 13). Developed on a proposal by Germany and France for an EU response to the United States' Greater Middle East Initiative, the partnership has, however, not had any significant practical impact (Echagüe 2007: 3–4).

Another political setting which seeks to unite relations with Saudi Arabia, Iraq and Iran is explicitly focused on the energy sector: the Energy Dialogue between the EU and the Organization of the Petroleum Exporting Countries (OPEC). Set up in 2004, the dialogue is a purely political framework without legal basis or commitments. A look at the 2012 ministerial meeting shows that the Energy Dialogue is, far from a fully-fledged strategy, a platform to exchange information and views between high-level officials, aiming at smooth producer–consumer relations within a functioning market environment (European Commission 2012b). The EU's interest in the dialogue can be summarized as 'more stable international oil markets and prices, an attractive investment climate, a more transparent market, a better market analysis and forecasts as well as technological and international cooperation' (European Commission 2013b). Needless to say, the Energy Dialogue scores low on all criteria of governance, both on the legislative and the institutional dimensions (poor governance quality). Likewise, the Middle Eastern partners are bound by neither of the energy-specific frameworks of governance, namely the ENC and the ECT. Saudi Arabia's and Iran's observer status at the Energy Charter Conference reflects at least some interest in the latter (Energy Charter 2013b).

Financial instruments

On the financial side, none of the countries have profited individually from energy investments under the EU budget, with the small exception of Iraq, which received €110,000 for energy research projects under the Middle East geographical programme of the DCI between 2007 and 2012 (see Table 11.2). Middle Eastern 'neighbours of the EU's neighbours' may have been included in cross-border, regional or global endeavours financed under the ENPI (see Table 11.3). Here, energy projects were related mainly to solar energy but also to energy policy and administrative management (emphasizing, however, predominantly ENP countries). With a total of €3.4 million between 2007 and 2012, these energy investments were much lower than the €14.9 million in North Africa (potentially including the Sahel neighbourhood) but accounted for a somewhat higher share of the respective total ENPI disbursements in the two regions (5.1 per cent vs. 2.5 per cent).

In a nutshell, compared to the EU's approach towards the 'neighbours of its neighbours' in the Sahel, energy cooperation in the Middle East is not embedded in an overarching development framework but in fact constitutes the main focus of the regions' relations. However, it remains at the declaratory level, is largely decoupled from any governance attempts and is hardly accompanied financially. At the regional level, the evidence therefore hints at a rejection of the governance view on energy cooperation. However, this general assessment becomes more nuanced when examining the different country cases.

Energy cooperation with the Middle East on the country level

Crossing the Red Sea in the north-east of Sudan, Saudi Arabia is the first neighbour in the Middle East bordering ENP countries. It owns substantial hydrocarbon reserves and is with 9.1 per cent the EU's most important oil supplier in the broader neighbourhood (see Table 11.1). At the same time, it is the highest-developed country analysed here, while being one of the least free. This points towards favouring geopolitics over governance.

The EU's relations with Saudi Arabia are mainly conducted under the 1988 Cooperation Agreement between the European Economic Community (EEC) and the Gulf Cooperation Council (GCC).[10] Therein, energy cooperation is understood as improving trade in the oil and gas sector, exchanging views and information, training of personnel and conducting studies (European Economic Community and Gulf Cooperation Council 1988: art. 6). These objectives are implemented through joint action programmes. On the institutional side, the agreement has set up a joint council, which meets annually in the configuration of foreign ministers and is supported by senior officials in a joint cooperation committee and assisting committees (ibid.: art. 12–15; European External Action Service 2013f). While this hints at an overall poor governance quality, relations could be upgraded through a free trade agreement (FTA), which had already been envisaged under art. 2 of the EEC–GCC Cooperation Agreement but whose negotiations were suspended by the GCC in 2010 (European External Action Service 2013f). Among other things, the GCC criticized the EU for protectionism in petrochemicals and opposed a human rights clause, whereas the EU complained about the low domestic energy prices in the Gulf (Youngs 2009: 64, 68).

A memorandum of understanding (MoU) on energy cooperation was regarded as second-best option by the GCC and rejected (ibid.: 65). In general, energy relations were impeded by the conflicting approaches of the two partners, with the EU focusing on energy matters only and the GCC looking for a broader strategic cooperation (ibid.: 65–66). In addition, the EU's emphasis on interregional cooperation enabled Saudi Arabia to play the role of a gatekeeper,[11] shaping relations with the smaller Gulf states, while competition between EU Member States undermined a coherent Union approach (ibid.: 66–67). Considering finally the high level of economic development of the GCC countries, the 'EU lacked the degree of leverage it gained in other regions through the combination of development aid and technical cooperation on energy infrastructure links – neither of these policy instruments of strong relevance to the Gulf' (ibid.: 66).

This is also reflected in the financial commitment. The relevant tool to finance cooperation between the EU and the GCC, *inter alia* in the energy sector, has been the Financing Instrument for Cooperation with Industrialized and Other High-income Countries and Territories (ICI). From its planned €172 million for the budget cycle 2007–13 (Council of the European Union 2006: art. 16), €1.9 million to establish an EU–GCC Clean Energy Network has been the most notable output (European Commission 2008c: 8–9). Of the approximately €400,000 disbursed in Saudi Arabia under the ICI in this period, none has been in the energy sector. Limited financial leverage combined with resource dependency may be some of the underlying reasons for the EU shying away from attempts to apply political conditionality in the GCC and Saudi Arabia in particular, while energy cooperation remained 'rudimentary' (Youngs 2009: 66–68).[12]

In the wake of the 9/11 terrorist attacks and the 2003 US invasion of Iraq, the management of oil prices by the Saudi rulers characterized them as reliable partners. However, the idiosyncrasies of patronage within the royal family and its reluctance to open up the Saudi energy sector introduce several elements of unpredictability. These issues challenge to some extent the notion of the autocratic Saudi regime being beneficial for energy cooperation (ibid.: 54–56).

The assessment is different for Iraq. The country owns significant hydrocarbon reserves and is a relevant exporter of oil to the EU, but even after the regime change it is considered as not free according to Freedom House (see Table 11.1). The situation may even deteriorate with the jihadist organization of the 'Islamic State of Iraq and the Levant' (ISIL) proclaiming a caliphate in parts of Iraq's territory since June 2014.[13] Iraq's development had already been marked by the war in 2003 and its aftermath, as the comparably low HDI score suggests (ibid.). The intervention had a significant impact on EU–Iraq energy relations, as 'deepening and tragic turmoil left little space for the development of a European energy policy in Iraq' (Youngs 2009: 75). However, the lack of development seems to constitute an entry point for EU governance. In 2010, an MoU on a Strategic Partnership in Energy was signed, which highlighted, *inter alia*, Iraq's potential as gas supplier for the EU, the necessity to put in place technical and environmental standards as well as general market reform following the EU's blueprint, and even a certain potential for energy transition, that is, renewables and energy efficiency (European Union and Government of Iraq 2010). The MoU was followed by a Partnership and Cooperation Agreement (PCA) signed in 2012, which put the development of an Iraqi energy policy 'on principles of environmental sustainability, sound management of energy resources and on free, competitive and open market', while specifying the points raised under the MoU (European Union 2012a: art. 91). Violations of the PCA's provisions may lead to the initiation of a dispute settlement procedure (ibid.: art. 61–80). On the institutional level, the PCA features a cooperation council, annual meetings at ministerial level, a cooperation committee and specialized sub-committees, as well a parliamentary cooperation committee (ibid.: art. 111–113). The council and the parliamentary committee may voice recommendations. This setup is reminiscent of the Cotonou Agreement, although the PCA's dispute settlement mechanism is certainly weaker than the sanction mechanism under Cotonou. While the overall governance quality therefore remains poor, the EU–Iraq PCA is more advanced than any other framework in the Middle Eastern broader neighbourhood. Although the EU has supported Iraq with almost €1 billion since 2003 (European External Action Service 2013a), the figures for energy investment have been rather modest (see Table 11.2). However, with a share of 17 per cent, energy was the largest sector financed under worldwide bilateral grants in 2009, including from the EU Member States (European Union and Iraq 2010: 23).

Potential issues for FDI related to the lack of development are reflected, for instance, in the quarrels over the legitimate development of resources. In the absence of a national hydrocarbon law, the Kurdish region has issued its own contracts, which risk to be revoked by the central government (Youngs 2009: 76–77). Moreover, in the fight against ISIL, Kurdish forces have seized oil fields abandoned by the Iraqi army. Given the specific situation of turmoil at the time of writing, assessing the impact of different regime types on energy cooperation would be pure speculation and therefore not advisable.

Instead, the focus shifts to Iran, the last potential partner for energy cooperation in the broader neighbourhood of the Middle East. The country owns significant hydrocarbon reserves (9.1 and 15.9 per cent of global proven oil and gas reserves respectively) and provided six per cent of the EU's oil supplies in 2011 before an oil embargo was introduced between 2012 and 2013 (see Table 11.1). Together with Iran's comparably high level of economic development under an autocratic regime, this hints at a rejection of the governance hypotheses. However, there has been significant potential for energy cooperation with Iran. A working group in charge of this task took office in 1999 (Youngs 2009: 69). Iran could become a member of the Interstate Oil and Gas Transportation to Europe (INOGATE) Programme, which connects the littoral states of the Black and Caspian Seas and their neighbours under the EU's model (see below on Central Asia; European Commission 2001: 6). Negotiations for a trade and cooperation agreement (TCA) were begun in 2002 (European Union Presidency and Commission 2002). However, Iran's way of dealing with its uranium enrichment programme had a negative impact on energy relations, resulting in the 2012 oil embargo among other sanctions (European External Action Service 2013g). The Iranian example shows how decisions of an autocratic regime may backfire on energy cooperation.

Despite expectations pointing to a clear rejection of the governance hypotheses, there is no uniform conclusion for the Middle East. While evidence was weak for Saudi Arabia and the Gulf, there is a case for governance in Iraq and potentially Iran. Energy issues are a clear priority for the EU in the Middle East, but it is not in a position to set the agenda and on the whole the governance quality of the frameworks in place remains poor. At the time of writing, further assessment is prevented in Iran and Iraq, as the negotiations with Iran regarding uranium enrichment are on-going and Iraq finds itself between a quarrelling central government, an increasingly self-confident Kurdish region, and an Islamist organization terrorizing the civilian population.

EU energy cooperation with Central Asia

At first glance, the Central Asian case is similar to that of the Middle East. Kazakhstan and Turkmenistan own more resources than the partners in the Sahel and are (potentially) relevant suppliers for the EU (see Table 11.1). Like the Middle Eastern countries, they are economically rather developed and authoritarian at the same time. Resource-rich developed autocracies provide an overall optimistic outlook for energy cooperation viewed from a geopolitical perspective on security of supply. The outlook is less optimistic when taking the governance angle: resources can be used to counterbalance the EU's approach, there is less need for development aid, and autocratic rulers may act in an unpredictable manner.

Political and legal framework

The two 'neighbours of the EU's neighbours' in the east, Turkmenistan and Kazakhstan, are politically covered by the EU Central Asia Strategy, which also includes Kyrgyzstan, Tajikistan and Uzbekistan. Adopted by the European Council in 2007, the Strategy identifies energy and transport as one of seven priority areas (Council of the European Union 2007). The Strategy builds on previous initiatives in the region, notably the PCAs[14] and Strategy Papers as well as Indicative Programmes (European External Action Service 2012; 2013h; European Commission 2002). The treaties with the two countries include references to the ECT, as both Turkmenistan and Kazakhstan are members of the Energy Charter Conference and provisionally apply the 1998 Trade Amendment (European Community 1999; European Union 2011; Energy Charter Secretariat 2012). As regards energy, the PCA with Kazakhstan is similar to the one with Iraq, except for the lack of references to energy transition, linked to the promotion of renewables and energy efficiency,[15] and including a conciliation procedure that is weaker than a dispute settlement mechanism (art. 87 EC-Kazakhstan PCA). These two agreements also share the same institutional setup. The Interim Trade Agreement with Turkmenistan is much more provisional, as it is limited to the trade-related aspects of a PCA, whose ratification is still pending. This points, once again, towards an overall poor governance quality. The adoption of the EU Central Asia Strategy, which was flanked by bilateral Memoranda of Understanding on Energy Cooperation, updated existing roadmaps for policy implementation and changed the main financial basis from the Technical Assistance to the Commonwealth of Independent States (TACIS) to the DCI (European Union and Kazakhstan 2006; European Union and Turkmenistan 2008; European Community 2007; European Commission 2007b; European Commission 2010a).

Financial instruments

Under a total budget of €61.8 million for the two countries from 2007 to 2012 within the DCI's geographical programme for Central Asia, around €412,000 has been disbursed in the energy sector, accounting for 0.7 per cent (see also Table 11.2). An analysis of the two National Indicative Programmes under the DCI budget 2007–13 reveals two things. First, energy cooperation is not mentioned at the bilateral level, as poverty reduction, higher living standards, good governance and economic reform constitute the priorities. This, second, leaves energy issues for the regional level, representing the smaller budget line (European Commission 2007b: 4–5; European Commission 2010a: 13–16). Here, the most notable output has been the Investment Facility for Central Asia (IFCA), created in 2010 and modelled after the Neighbourhood Investment Facility (NIF) of the ENP (European Commission 2013a: 1; European Commission 2010b). The IFCA aims at promoting investments, *inter alia*, in energy infrastructures focusing on transit connections, safety and security, energy efficiency and renewable energy (European Commission 2013a: 4). It therefore channels non-refundable financial contributions and loans from a number of sources, such as the EU Member States' development finance bodies, the European Investment Bank (EIB) and the European Bank for Reconstruction and Development (EBRD) (ibid.: 2).

However, Central Asian partners also benefit from the INOGATE Programme for Energy Cooperation between the EU, the littoral States of the Black and Caspian Seas and their neighbours. Besides objectives and functions similar to the IFCA, this programme centres on the convergence of energy markets following the EU's model (INOGATE 2013b). This approach to energy cooperation is underlined by INOGATE's funding. The approximately €51 million to €61 million include funding from the DCI, but also, and more importantly, from the ENPI (INOGATE 2010: 4; INOGATE 2012: 170).[16] In this sense, INOGATE can be understood as a concrete application of the ENPI clause aiming at connecting the immediate and broader neighbours (see above on the Sahel). The accompanying rhetoric matches the facts, as the Regional Strategy Paper for Central Asia 2007–13 points out:

> To help achieve this wider objective, it is important to anchor the Central Asian countries in broader EU policies promoted through ENPI, to enhance

regional cooperation and integration.... Indeed, these countries are already fully associated with a number of regional initiatives involving Eastern Europe ENP countries and Russia designed to enhance cooperation in key sectors such as transport, energy, higher education and the environment.

(European Community 2007: 7)

More generally, Turkmenistan and Kazakhstan may be included together with ENP countries in ENPI-funded energy projects not only encoded with the regional label 'Central Asia' but also 'CEEC/NIS Unallocated', and even 'Europe' (see Table 11.3). Besides investments in energy policy and administrative management, the emphasis lies on gas distribution. While it is not possible to distinguish between disbursements in ENP and non-ENP countries, the overall sum of €37.9 million is larger than for the other two regions in the EU's broader neighbourhood taken together. Energy projects also enjoy a higher relative importance.

Together with the Central Asian Investment Facility modelled after its ENP equivalent, the EU's cooperation with Central Asian partners appears on the whole much more determined to extend energy governance to the broader neighbourhood than in the Sahel or the Middle East. This is also displayed on the country level, although more for the Kazakh than for the Turkmen case.

Energy cooperation with Central Asia on the country level

Turkmenistan's potential importance mainly derives from its gas reserves, representing roughly 12 per cent of the world's total reserves (see Table 11.1). The EU had signed a PCA with the country in 1998, but it is still not ratified by a number of Member States and so far lacks the consent of the European Parliament, which criticizes the situation of human rights and democracy in Turkmenistan (European Parliament 2009). Indeed, the country's score according to Freedom House is among the lowest of all countries analysed in this chapter (see Table 11.1). The 2008 MoU on Energy Cooperation and the 2010 Interim Trade Agreement eschewed the conditionality question in circumventing the European Parliament. Both, however, had only become possible at all after the death of long-term dictator Saparmurat Niyazov in 2006 (Youngs 2009: 123–124). His rule was marked by constant replacements within public administration, the lack of an investment framework, and opacity, for instance with regard to available reserves, only to mention some factors impeding cooperation (ibid.: 122–123). EU energy investments in Turkmenistan are lower than, for instance, in the Sahel countries, but still higher than in the Middle East, and focus mainly on energy policy and administrative management (see Table 11.2).

Sharing the border with Russia, Kazakhstan is the last country in this analysis covering the 'neighbours of the EU's neighbours'. Providing 5.9 per cent of the EU's oil imports, Kazakhstan is the second most important energy supplier in the broader neighbourhood after Saudi Arabia (see Table 11.1). Following the HDI, it is also economically highly developed and, according to Freedom House, at the border of being partly free. In spite of its hydrocarbon reserves, Kazakhstan surprisingly benefited between 2007 and 2012 mainly from EU funds under the Nuclear Safety Instrument (see Table 11.2). These figures do not, however, cover regional projects such as INOGATE.

Energy relations are covered by the PCA, in force since 1999, which places them 'against a background of the progressive integration of the energy markets in Europe' (art. 53 EC–Kazakhstan PCA). This albeit very general approximation objective has been somewhat specified for the energy sector under the 2006 MoU, its governance quality still falling far behind the MoU with the ENP country Azerbaijan (Youngs 2009: 116). However, there is potential, as the EU and Kazakhstan are planning to conclude an enhanced PCA, agreeing that 'a stronger convergence of Kazakhstan toward the EU standards and regulatory system would be beneficial for further increasing trade flows and investments' (Council of the European Union 2009: 2). While this reflects the governance view, the Kazakh regime under president Nursultan Nazarbaev could be regarded as a 'benign form of autocracy' and therefore reliable from the perspective of European energy supply concerns (Youngs 2009: 116–117). This is, however, questioned by corruption, the reopening of already concluded contracts, and a foreign policy 'attempting to drive wedges between [EU] member states' (ibid.: 119–120).

In contrast to the expectations for Central Asia, the governance perspective complements – or even prevails over – a purely geopolitical reasoning driven by concerns over energy supplies, although the case is less clear-cut when the country level is taken into account. While the overall quality of governance remains poor, the (planned) agreements are more advanced than in the Middle East, follow the EU's internal logic and are backed with financial means otherwise reserved for the ENP. In addition, both countries present evidence for autocratic regimes impeding rather than promoting energy cooperation. There are several potential explanations for the partly different outcome in Central Asia, compared to the Middle East. Certainly, Turkmenistan and Kazakhstan do not own as many reserves as their Middle Eastern counterparts and are currently less important suppliers for the EU, making them more open for its approach to energy policy (see Table 11.1). However, cooperation under European governance frameworks could also be interpreted as an attempt to counterbalance traditionally strong Russian influence, derived from a common Soviet past.

Conclusion: EU energy cooperation beyond geopolitics

This chapter has sought to explain the EU's cooperation with the 'neighbours of its neighbours' in the field of energy by taking a governance perspective, as compared to geopolitical considerations on secure energy supplies. Table 11.4 provides an overview of the various frameworks under which energy relations between the EU and the countries in the broader neighbourhood are conducted.

Hypotheses following a geopolitical narrative expect energy relations to focus on countries with resources, representing (potential) suppliers, whose economic

Table 11.4 EU frameworks of cooperation with the 'neighbours of its neighbours'

Country	Legal framework		Political framework	
	Territorial	Energy-specific	Territorial	Energy-specific
Chad	Cotonou 2010	—	JAES	—
Mali	Cotonou 2010	—	JAES	—
			Sahel Strategy	
Mauritania	Cotonou 2010	—	UfM	—
			JAES	
			Sahel Strategy	
			SPMME	
Niger	Cotonou 2010	—	JAES	—
			Sahel Strategy	
Sudan	Cotonou 2000	—	JAES	
Iran	TCA (planned)	ECT observer	SPMME	EU-OPEC Energy Dialogue
				Energy Dialogue (planned)
				INOGATE (planned by EU)
Iraq	PCA	—	SPMME	MoU on Strategic Partnership
				EU-OPEC Energy Dialogue
Saudi Arabia	ECC-GCC Cooperation Agreement	ECT observer	SPMME	EU-OPEC Energy Dialogue
	FTA (planned)			MoU (rejected by GCC)
Kazakhstan	PCA (enhanced PCA planned)	ECT TA applied provisionally	CAS	MoU
				INOGATE
Turkmenistan	Interim Trade Agreement	ECT TA applied provisionally	CAS	MoU
	PCA (planned)			INOGATE

Source: compiled by the author.

Notes
CAS = EU Central Asia Strategy; Cotonou 2000 = 2000 version of the Cotonou Partnership Agreement; Cotonou 2010 = 2010 revised version of the Cotonou Partnership Agreement; ECC = European Economic Community; ECT TA = Energy Charter Treaty Trade Amendment (highest ratification stage); FTA = free trade agreement; GCC = Gulf Cooperation Council; INOGATE = Interstate Oil and Gas Transportation to Europe Programme; JAES = Joint Africa-EU Strategy; MoU = memorandum of understanding; OPEC = Organization of the Petroleum Exporting Countries; PCA = partnership and cooperation agreement; SPMME = EU Strategic Partnership with the Mediterranean and the Middle East; TCA = trade and cooperation agreement.

development would attract investment, and in which the self-interest of autocratic regimes would play a beneficial role. With the governance perspective, an alternative but complementary view is suggested, which expects energy cooperation to take place when partners lack resources and economic development and hence would be more open to the EU's model. In this view, autocratic regimes would be a factor of uncertainty at best.

Evidence suggests that there is a case for governance complementing the picture of EU energy cooperation with the broader neighbourhood, although its governance quality remains much lower than for the EU's immediate neighbours. In contrast to geopolitical expectations, energy issues play a role within EU–Sahel relations and point towards a confirmation of the governance hypotheses. However, they are embedded in a larger framework of sustainable development. Governance is executed under the Cotonou Agreement, although conditionality has not been rigorously applied so far. With the JAES, political emphasis lies on energy transition as a means for sustainable development and especially the promotion of renewables. Moreover, the financial backup under the EDF has been stronger than in the other regions, keeping in mind that this framework does not particularly focus on the Sahel but on all ACP countries.

Energy relations with the Middle East are more visible but also more fragmented. In line with the geopolitical narrative, the regional level has not provided evidence for the governance argument, as there is no encompassing legal framework in place and both the SPMME and the EU–OPEC Energy Dialogue constitute weak fora to exert any form of governance. Moreover, financial engagement under the EU budget has been limited. At the country level, this picture was confirmed for Saudi Arabia under the umbrella of the EEC–GCC Cooperation Agreement. While the future direction of Iraq remains unclear at the time of writing, there appears to be a case for EU governance in the country. This is highlighted by the PCA and an MoU on Strategic Partnership in Energy, although energy investments have mainly been conducted outside the EU budget. Iran may follow the trajectory of the partners in Central Asia, provided that the nuclear issue is solved.

In Central Asia, energy issues are of paramount importance, with evidence supporting the governance perspective, despite resource wealth and economic development. Governance frameworks exist and there are plans for them to be enhanced, following the EU's internal approach. The EU Central Asian Strategy prioritizes energy and transport, a PCA for Kazakhstan is in place and one is under way for Turkmenistan, MoUs on energy cooperation have been concluded, countries apply the rule book of the ECT, and connections with the ENP are being promoted, *inter alia*, through financing under the ENPI. In all three regions autocratic regimes did not present an obstacle to energy cooperation *prima facie*; however, a closer look revealed significant issues, leaving relations behind their potential. The most prominent example in this regard is certainly Iran.

An analysis covering such a broad geographical scope can naturally only be partial. While the focus here has been on countries geographically bordering the

ENP, an approach including, for instance, countries in the Horn of Africa (Eritrea, Ethiopia, Somalia), in the broader Gulf (the smaller Gulf states and Yemen in particular) and all of Central Asia (Kyrgyzstan, Tajikistan, Uzbekistan) could be fruitful. As for the present analysis, there is a great deal of untapped potential for energy cooperation between the EU and its broader neighbourhood beyond geopolitics. Europe is therefore well advised to continue making use of the rules and institutions of the *acquis* – probably the greatest governance achievement in its own history.

Notes

1 The author would like to thank Christian Egenhofer for his helpful comments and suggestions on earlier drafts of this chapter.
2 For a sector-specific supply risk analysis see Checchi *et al.* (2009). See also Chapter 3 by Alyson J.K. Bailes and Pál Dunay and Chapter 4 by Gilles de Kerchove and Christiane Höhn in this volume.
3 While only Sudan represents a direct neighbour, the available data also include South Sudan, as the latter has only gained independence from the north since 2011.
4 Relations between the EU and Switzerland and between the EU and the (potential) candidates for accession also fall into this category.
5 The Energy Community is an energy cooperation framework between the EU and (potential) accession candidates in southern Eastern Europe as well as the eastern ENP countries. The Energy Charter Treaty is an international agreement on energy market rules originating from the declaration of the 1991 European Energy Charter.
6 See also Chapter 6 by Tressia Hobeika in this volume.
7 If not indicated otherwise, references to figures in the text which cannot be calculated from the tables and are not explicitly listed there were provided by the Commission upon the author's request in September 2013.
8 See art. 29(3)(a), 32(c)(iii), 32A(d)(vii) and 43(4) of the Cotonou Agreement.
9 Mauritania (10), Mali (8), Niger (5), Chad (5), Sudan (0).
10 Besides Saudi Arabia, the GCC comprises Bahrain, Kuwait, Oman, Qatar and the United Arab Emirates. See also Chapter 5 by Sieglinde Gstöhl in this volume.
11 It is symptomatic that the EU delegation in Riyadh is accredited to all GCC countries.
12 See also Chapter 8 by Alexander Warkotsch and Richard Youngs in this volume.
13 See Chapter 4 by Gilles de Kerchove and Christiane Höhn in this volume.
14 While the PCA with Kazakhstan entered into force in 1999, an Interim Agreement with Turkmenistan on trade matters has been in force since 2010, as the ratification of the PCA signed in 1998 is still pending.
15 This idea had not yet existed EU internally by the time the PCA with Kazakhstan entered into force (1999) and did not find its way into the Interim Agreement with Turkmenistan, which focuses on trade only.
16 The INOGATE website even mentions the ENPI as the only source of funding for INOGATE (INOGATE 2013a).

References

African Union and European Union (2007) *The Africa–EU Strategic Partnership: A Joint Africa–EU Strategy*, www.africa-eu-partnership.org/sites/default/files/eas2007_joint_strategy_en.pdf (accessed February 2013).

African Union and European Union (2010) *Joint Africa EU Strategy: Action Plan 2011–2013*, www.africa-eu-partnership.org/sites/default/files/doc_jaes_action_plan_2011_13_en.pdf (accessed February 2013).

British Petrol (2012) *BP Statistical Review of World Energy June 2012*, London: British Petrol.

Checchi, A., A. Behrens and C. Egenhofer (2009) 'Long-Term Energy Security Risks for Europe: A Sector-Specific Approach', *CEPS Working Paper* 309, Brussels: Centre for European Policy Studies, 29 January.

Council of the European Union (2006) 'Council Regulation (EC) No 1934/2006 of 21 December 2006 Establishing a Financing Instrument for Cooperation with Industrialised and Other High-income Countries and Territories', *Official Journal of the European Union*, L 405, 30 December.

Council of the European Union (2007) *European Union and Central Asia: Strategy for a New Partnership*, Brussels, October.

Council of the European Union (2009) *11th Cooperation Council EU–Kazakhstan 17 November 2009 Joint Statement*, 16175/09 (Presse 338), Brussels, 17 November.

Council of the European Union (2011a) *Strategy for Security and Development in the Sahel*, Annex to the Council Conclusions on a European Union Strategy for Security and Development in the Sahel, Brussels, 21 March.

Council of the European Union (2011b) *Council Conclusions on Strengthening the External Dimension of the EU Energy Policy*, 3127th Transport, Telecommunications and Energy Council Meeting (Energy Items), Brussels, 24 November.

Echagüe, A. (2007) 'The European Union and the Gulf Cooperation Council', *FRIDE Working Paper* 39, Madrid: FRIDE, May.

Egenhofer, C. and A. Behrens (2011) 'Resource Politics: The Rapidly Shifting EU Energy Policy Agenda', in P. Heywood, E. Jones, M. Rhodes and U. Sedelmeier (eds) *Developments in European Politics*, Houndmills, Palgrave Macmillan, 2nd edn, 241–261.

Embassy of the United States in Mauritania (2011) *Mauritania: 2011 Investment Climate Statement*, January, http://mauritania.usembassy.gov/media/pdf/investment-climate-january-2011.pdf (accessed October 2013).

Energy Charter (2013a) *1998 Trade Amendment*, www.encharter.org/index.php?id=26&L (accessed January 2013).

Energy Charter (2013b) *Members and Observers*, www.encharter.org/index.php?id=61&L (accessed January 2013).

Energy Charter Secretariat (2012) *Status of Ratification of the Trade Amendment to the Energy Charter Treaty as of August 2012*, www.encharter.org/fileadmin/user_upload/document/Trade_Amendment_ratification_status.pdf (accessed January 2013).

European Commission (1995) *White Paper: An Energy Policy for the European Union*, COM(95) 682 final, Brussels, 13 December.

European Commission (2000) *Green Paper: Towards a European Strategy for the Security of Energy Supply*, COM(2000) 769 final, Brussels, 29 November.

European Commission (2001) Communication from the Commission to the European Parliament and the Council, *EU Relations with the Islamic Republic of Iran*, COM(2001) 71 final, Brussels, 7 February.

European Commission (2002) *Strategy Paper 2002–2006 and Indicative Programme 2002–2004 for Central Asia*, Brussels, 30 October.

European Commission (2006a) *A European Strategy for Sustainable, Competitive and Secure Energy*, COM(2006) 105 final, Brussels, 8 March.

European Commission (2006b) *Communication from the Commission to the Council and the European Parliament on Strengthening the European Neighbourhood Policy*, COM(2006) 726 final, Brussels, 4 December.

European Commission (2007a) Communication from the Commission to the European Council and the European Parliament, *An Energy Policy For Europe*, COM(2007) 1 final, Brussels, 10 January.

European Commission (2007b) *Central Asia Indicative Programme (2007–2010)*, Brussels, www.eeas.europa.eu/central_asia/rsp/nip_07_10_en.pdf (accessed March 2013).

European Commission (2008a) Communication from the Commission to the European Parliament and the Council, *Barcelona Process: Union for the Mediterranean*, COM(2008) 319 final, Brussels, 20 May.

European Commission (2008b) Communication from the Commission to the European Parliament, the Council, the European Economic and Social Committee and the Committee of the Regions, *Second Strategic Energy Review: An EU Energy Security and Solidarity Action Plan*, COM(2008) 781 final, Brussels, 13 November.

European Commission (2008c) *Annual Work Programme for Grants for Cooperation with Industrialised Countries and other High-income Countries and Territories in 2008*, Brussels, 3 April.

European Commission (2010a) *Central Asia DCI Indicative Programme 2011–2013*, Brussels, www.eeas.europa.eu/central_asia/docs/2010_ca_mtr_en.pdf (accessed March 2013).

European Commission (2010b) *Commission Decision of 23/04/2010 on the Annual Action Programme 2010 Part 1 in Favour of Central Asia to be Financed under Article 19.10.02 of the General Budget of the European Union*, C(2010)2314 – PE/2010/1937, Brussels, 23 April.

European Commission (2011) Communication from the Commission to the European Parliament, the Council, the European Economic and Social Committee and the Committee of the Regions, *On Security of Energy Supply and International Cooperation: The EU Energy Policy: Engaging with Partners beyond Our Borders*, COM(2011) 539 final, Brussels, 7 September.

European Commission (2012a) *Development and Cooperation: Europeaid: European Development Fund (EDF)*, 17 February, Brussels, http://ec.europa.eu/europeaid/how/finance/edf_en.htm (accessed March 2013).

European Commission (2012b) *EU–OPEC Energy Dialogue, Ninth Meeting: Joint Conclusion*, MEMO/12/506, Brussels, 28 June.

European Commission (2012c) *The Cotonou Agreement: Signed in Cotonou on 23 June 2000, Revised in Luxembourg on 25 June 2005, Revised in Ouagadougou on 22 June 2010*, 16 August, http://ec.europa.eu/europeaid/where/acp/overview/documents/devco-cotonou-consol-europe-aid-2012_en.pdf (accessed February 2013).

European Commission (2012d) *Development and Cooperation: Europeaid: ACP–EU Energy Facility*, Brussels, 21 November, http://ec.europa.eu/europeaid/where/acp/regional-cooperation/energy/index_en.htm (accessed February 2013).

European Commission (2013a) *Annual Action Programme for Central Asia 2010 Part 1: Action Fiche for Central Asia*, Brussels, http://ec.europa.eu/europeaid/documents/aap/2010/af_aap_2010_central-asia.pdf (accessed March 2013).

European Commission (2013b) *Energy from Abroad: EU–OPEC Energy Dialogue*, Brussels, http://ec.europa.eu/energy/international/organisations/opec_en.htm (accessed March 2013).

European Commission (2013c) *Monthly and Cumulated Crude Oil Imports (Volumes and Prices) by EU and Non EU Country: Registration of Crude Oil Imports and Deliveries* in the European Union (EU27): Extra EU, Brussels, http://ec.europa.eu/energy/observatory/oil/import_export_en.htm (accessed August 2014).

European Commission (2014) Communication from the Commission to the European Parliament and the Council, *European Energy Security Strategy*, COM(2014) 330 final, Brussels, 28 May.

European Community (1999) 'Partnership and Cooperation Agreement Between the European Communities and their Member States and the Republic of Kazakhstan', *Official Journal of the European Union* L 196, Brussels, 28 July.

European Community (2007) *Regional Strategy Paper for Assistance to Central Asia for the Period 2007–2013*, Brussels, www.eeas.europa.eu/central_asia/rsp/07_13_en.pdf (accessed March 2013).

European Community and ACP Group of States (2009) *Intra-ACP Cooperation: 10th EDF: Strategy Paper and Multiannual Indicative Programme 2008–2013*, Brussels, 13 March.

European Community and Mali (2007) *Country Strategy Paper and National Indicative Programme for the Period 2008–2013*, Lisbon, 9 December [original in French].

European Community and Mauritania (2008) *Country Strategy Paper and National Indicative Programme for the Period 2008–2013* [original in French].

European Community and Niger (2008) *Country Strategy Paper and National Indicative Programme for the Period 2008–2013*, 4 July [original in French].

European Community and Republic of Chad (2007) *Country Strategy Paper and National Indicative Programme for the Period 2008–2013*, Lisbon, 9 December [original in French].

European Community and Republic of the Sudan (2005) *Country Strategy Paper and National Indicative Programme for the Period 2005–2007*, 25 January.

European Economic Community and Gulf Cooperation Council (1988) 'Cooperation Agreement between the European Economic Community, of the one part, and the Countries Parties to the Charter of the Cooperation Council for the Arab States of the Gulf (the State of the United Arab Emirates, the State of Bahrain, the Kingdom of Saudi Arabia, the Sultanate of Oman, the State of Qatar and the State of Kuwait) of the other part – Joint Declarations – Declaration by the European Economic Community – Exchange of Letters', *Official Journal of the European Union*, L 054, 25 February 1989, 3–15.

European External Action Service (2012) *Treaties Office Database*, Brussels, 12 July, http://ec.europa.eu/world/agreements/prepareCreateTreatiesWorkspace/treatiesGeneral-Data.do?step=0&redirect=true&treatyId=7222 (accessed March 2013).

European External Action Service (2013a) *EU Assistance to Iraq*, www.eeas.europa.eu/iraq/assistance_en.htm (accessed September 2013).

European External Action Service (2013b) *EU Relations with Mali*, http://eeas.europa.eu/mali/index_en.htm (accessed September 2013).

European External Action Service (2013c) *EU Relations with Mauritania*, www.eeas.europa.eu/mauritania/index_en.htm (accessed September 2013).

European External Action Service (2013d) *EU Relations with Niger*, http://eeas.europa.eu/niger/index_en.htm (accessed September 2013).

European External Action Service (2013e) *EU Relations with Sudan*, www.eeas.europa.eu/sudan/index_en.htm (accessed September 2013).

European External Action Service (2013f) *EU Relations with the Gulf Cooperation Council (GCC)*, http://eeas.europa.eu/gulf_cooperation/index_en.htm (accessed September 2013).

European External Action Service (2013g) *Iran*, www.eeas.europa.eu/iran/index_en.htm (accessed September 2013).

European External Action Service (2013h) *Kazakhstan*, www.eeas.europa.eu/kazakhstan/index_en.htm (accessed March 2013).

European External Action Service (2013i) *The EU and the Mediterranean, Middle-East and the Gulf*, www.eeas.europa.eu/mideast/index_en.htm (accessed March 2013).

European Parliament (2009) *Resolution on the Interim Trade Agreement with Turkmenistan, Text Adopted by Parliament, Single Reading*, 2009/2513(RSP), Brussels, 22 April.

European Parliament and Council of the European Union (2006a) 'Regulation (EC) No 1638/2006 of the European Parliament and of the Council of 24 October 2006 Laying Down General Provisions Establishing a European Neighbourhood and Partnership Instrument', *Official Journal of the European Union*, L 310, 9 November, 164–177.

European Parliament and Council of the European Union (2006b) 'Regulation (EC) No 1905/2006 of the European Parliament and of the Council of 18 December 2006 Establishing a Financing Instrument for Development Cooperation', *Official Journal of the European Union*, L 378, 27 December, 41–71.

European Union (2004) *Final Report (Approved by the European Council in June 2004) on an EU Strategic Partnership with the Mediterranean and the Middle East*, June.

European Union (2007) *Energising Europe: A Real Market with Secure Supply*, IP/07/1361, Brussels, 19 September.

European Union (2011) 'Interim Agreement on Trade and Trade-related Matters Between the European Community, the European Coal and Steel Community and the European Atomic Energy Community, of the one part, and Turkmenistan of the other part', *Official Journal of the European Union*, L 80, 26 March, 1.

European Union (2012a) 'Partnership and Cooperation Agreement Between the European Union and its Member States, of the one part, and the Republic of Iraq, of the other part', *Official Journal of the European Union*, L 204, 31 July, 18–130.

European Union (2012b) *The ACP–EU Energy Facility: Improving Access to Energy Services for the Poor in Rural and Peri-urban Areas*, http://ec.europa.eu/europeaid/where/acp/regional-cooperation/energy/documents/brochure_print_en.pdf (accessed March 2013).

European Union and Government of Iraq (2010) *Memorandum of Understanding Between the Government of Iraq and the European Union on Strategic Partnership in Energy*, Baghdad, 18 January.

European Union and Iraq (2010) *Cooperation between the European Union and Iraq: Joint Strategy Paper 2011–2013*, www.eeas.europa.eu/iraq/docs/2011_2013_jsp_nip_en.pdf (accessed September 2013).

European Union and Kazakhstan (2006) *Memorandum of Understanding on Cooperation in the Field of Energy between the European Union and the Republic of Kazakhstan*, 4 December.

European Union and Turkmenistan (2008) *Memorandum of Understanding on Cooperation in the Field of Energy between the European Union and Turkmenistan*, 26 May.

European Union Presidency and Commission (2002) *Joint Press Release on the Opening of the Negotiations with Iran*, 12 December.

Eurostat (2013) *Imports (by Country of Origin): Gas: Annual Data*, dataset nrg_124a (accessed January 2013).

Freedom House (2013) *Freedom in the World 2013: Democratic Breakthroughs in the Balance: Selected Data from Freedom House's Annual Survey of Political Rights and*

Civil Liberties, www.freedomhouse.org/sites/default/files/FIW%202013%20Booklet%20 -%20for%20Web_0.pdf (accessed March 2013).

INOGATE (2010) *INOGATE Programme Annual Report 2009: A Review of the INOGATE Programme's Activities in 2009*, June, www.inogate.org/attachments/article/ 46/Inogate_AR_2009_en_PRINT.pdf (accessed March 2013).

INOGATE (2012) *INOGATE Programme Status Report 2011: An Energy Review of the INOGATE Partner Countries*, October, www.inogate.org/media/documents/INOGATE%20 Status%20Report%20EN.pdf (accessed March 2013).

INOGATE (2013a) *About INOGATE: Funding*, www.inogate.org/index.php?option=com_ content&view=article&id=46&Itemid=72&lang=en (accessed March 2013).

INOGATE (2013b) *About INOGATE: Objectives*, www.inogate.org/index.php?option=com_c ontent&view=article&id=46&Itemid=72&lang=en (accessed March 2013).

Lavenex, S. (2004) 'EU External Governance in "Wider Europe"', *Journal of European Public Policy* 11(4), 680–700.

Lavenex, S. (2011) 'Concentric Circles of Flexible "EUropean" Integration: A Typology of EU External Governance Relations', *Comparative European Politics* 9(4/5), 372–393.

Lavenex, S., D. Lehmkuhl and N. Wichmann (2009) 'Modes of External Governance: A Cross-national and Cross-sectoral Comparison', *Journal of European Public Policy* 16(6), 813–833.

Lesage, D., T. van de Graaf and K. Westphal (eds) (2010) *Global Energy Governance in a Multipolar World*, Farnham: Ashgate.

Natorski, M. and A. Herranz Surrallés (2008) 'Securitizing Moves to Nowhere? The Framing of the European Union's Energy Policy', *Journal of Contemporary European Research* 4(2), 71–89.

Paolo, B. and V.L. Derryck (2013) '2 Successful Elections: Democracy Grows in Mali', *New York Times*, www.nytimes.com/2013/08/17/opinion/2-successful-elections- democracy-grows-in-mali.html (accessed September 2013).

Theiss, J. (2013) 'EU External Energy Governance: An Internal Remedy?', in B. Delvaux, M. Hunt and K. Talus (eds) *EU Energy Law and Policy Issues*, vol. 4, Cambridge: Intersentia, 269–292.

United Nations Development Programme (2013) *Human Development Report 2013: The Rise of the South: Human Progress in a Diverse World*, New York: UNDP.

Youngs, R. (2009) *Energy Security: Europe's New Foreign Policy Challenge*, London: Routledge.

12 Challenges and opportunities related to transboundary waters in the EU's broader neighbourhood

Anders Jägerskog

Introduction[1]

Concern over water is gaining increasing attention on the international scene. This trend can be identified in the practices of the European Union (EU) through the stronger focus on 'water security' at national, regional and global levels. During the 2012 UN General Assembly the High Representative of the Union for Foreign Affairs and Security Policy Catherine Ashton (2012) joined forces with US Secretary of State Hillary Clinton to discuss the challenges threatening water security. On 22 July 2013, the Council of the European Union (2013) adopted the conclusions on 'EU Water Diplomacy' and outlined the need for the EU and its Member States to work towards strengthening water cooperation. In the regions surrounding the EU, such as the countries of the European Neighbourhood Policy (ENP) and beyond in Africa, the Middle East and Central Asia, water security is a key challenge for their present and future development (World Water Assessment Programme 2012).

This chapter investigates the challenges that the EU is facing with regard to transboundary water management in its broader neighbourhood. It provides an overview of 'state of the art' transboundary water management and of the emerging challenges that affect it. It presents an analysis of cases in Africa, Central Asia and the Middle East, including a more in-depth case study of Jordanian–Israeli water cooperation.

Water is a resource used to energize all sectors of society, ranging from basic food production to advanced industrial technologies. The rising demand for water can be attributed to a variety of factors, such as population growth and urbanization. The sustainable management of water resources is of extreme importance in the developing world, which often faces major challenges to improve its water management due to shortages of adequate financial resources, infrastructure and capacity.

Water is one of the most 'shared' resources on earth. About two billion people worldwide depend on groundwater, a resource which includes approximately 300 transboundary aquifer systems (Puri and Struckmeier 2010). At the same time, more than 263 transboundary rivers account for approximately 60 per cent of all global freshwater flows (Wolf *et al.* 2005). Naturally, as the demand for shared resources escalates, water that crosses boundaries is increasingly a focal point for debate, research and international engagement. The management of these transboundary water resources takes centre stage in the world's development debate.The 2006 UNDP Human Development Report noted that managing hydrological interdependence is 'one of the great human development challenges facing the international community' (UNDP 2006).

Unfortunately, water management initiatives are often planned at national level, inevitably from a national perspective, even if they are transboundary in nature. This is still the case despite wide recognition that management of transboundary water bodies is better addressed in multinational settings. Failure to cooperate on transboundary waters can carry a high price. Tensions can hurt regional integration, trade and stability, and can limit the potential for sustainable development. When the management of shared water is handled with the appropriate tools and implemented with cooperative tolerance and mutual respect, it can pave the way toward sustainable and peaceful development. In this mode, political, social, economic, cultural and ecological benefits can all be achieved.

This may explain why cooperation over water, not conflict, has been the norm during the past century. Since 1948, records show that only 37 incidents of acute multi-country conflict over water have occurred, whereas during the same period approximately 295 international water agreements were negotiated and signed (Transboundary Freshwater Dispute Database 2013). While large-scale open conflict over water remains rare, increasing populations alongside economic and climate change pressures will likely intensify tensions over shared water resources around the globe. Multi-country cooperation on a wide range of issues pertaining to water and its use will prove essential as these pressures advance and strain water security realities.

However, pressure can also present opportunities. The need to identify mutually acceptable solutions to shared water issues can prompt and facilitate multi-country dialogue, governance reform, stakeholder participation, transparency, regional economic integration and coordinated investment (Jägerskog 2012). Instead of being a source of conflict, shared waters can be an effective vehicle for the promotion of multi-country dialogue and cooperation. This is even true in water-deprived and politically tense regions, such as the Middle East and North Africa region (MENA). Each year, more and more countries as well as international organizations take an interest in transboundary water management. The UN General Assembly designated 2013 as the International Year of Water Cooperation.

The chapter starts with an overview of the benefits of cooperation on transboundary waters as well as costs of non-cooperation. It moves on to discuss the new challenges to well-functioning cooperation (such as the impact of climate change and the effects of increasing land acquisitions) before moving on to a discussion of the 'neighbours of EU's neighbours' with a special focus on the Jordan basin.

Benefits of cooperation and costs of non-cooperation

Cooperation over transboundary waters presents actors with a host of potential benefits. Subramanian *et al.* (2012) outlined three fundamental benefits that may be attained. First, hydropower infrastructure situated on a transboundary water source can be more effectively planned and built in locations which minimize evaporation and have the best possible climatic conditions. This can promote increased trade between countries since goods (power, agricultural produce, etc.) need to be moved to the site of consumption. In turn, increased trade promotes regional integration and in some cases can contribute to improved overall relations between countries. Second, cooperation can also make it easier to reuse water more effectively. For example, it is possible to return water into a river system after it has been used to produce hydropower. This water can then be repurposed and sent further downstream to be used for industrial, domestic or agricultural purposes. Third, cooperative management can help stakeholders to better respond to risks such as droughts and floods. These risks are easier to address when joint systems for the management of the transboundary water system are in place.

This list of benefits is far from exhaustive. Improved prospects for peace, stability and development can also result from cooperation over water. But what are the costs of non-cooperation?[2] Unpredictability poses a large potential impact on transboundary water management. Technical cooperation mechanisms such as the sharing of data on stream flows, precipitation and water quality measurements or setting up a joint research institution to scientifically assess the basin can do much to mitigate these impacts. Without developing technical cooperation each country has to prepare and respond to floods and droughts independently and without crucial information on the whole basin. With cooperation that functions, on the other hand, economic costs, environmental damages and human suffering can be avoided, or at least reduced.

Another cost of non-cooperation is the potential negative impact of growing political tensions. As water becomes scarce relative to demand, transboundary competition for shared rivers will grow. If water issues are not addressed and taken seriously, negative effects on trade between the nations, economic growth and human security are likely. If states cooperate, it is possible to develop mechanisms for addressing conflicting demands for water. The resulting higher levels of predictability and controlled use of water resources could encourage investments and economic growth.

While national institutions and legislative bodies provide mechanisms for addressing conflicting demands within a country, there are no equivalent institutional mechanisms to respond to transboundary problems. Without such mechanisms, competition for water, which also has shown the potential to function as a catalyst for deeper cooperation, might lead to disruptive conflicts. Managing shared water can be a force for peace or for conflict. Without proper attention it may lead to conflicts and parties becoming increasingly entrenched in opposing positions, which hinders international relations, overall development and efforts to reduce poverty.

New and emerging challenges

While the sharing and allocation of water is already a challenge within nations, the level of complexity is compounded at international level. Transboundary rivers, lakes and aquifer systems often cross the boundaries of many states, making relations and discussions highly complicated and delicate. Sometimes well above 10 states share the same resource, leading to highly challenging politics and logistics with transboundary management. Furthermore, dependency on naturally provided water (that is, water that travels through the ground, above ground or in the atmosphere) is of crucial importance for most countries in the world since – unlike, for instance, some of the Gulf states – the majority do not have the financial means to opt for alternative solutions such as desalination to produce 'new' water (Earle *et al.* 2010).

A number of new challenges in relation to transboundary water cooperation have surfaced during recent years. First, countries have to adjust to increased climate variability and change, which affects water availability across time and space. This is likely to bring about increased tensions and challenges. Second, surges in land acquisitions will likely increase water use as new land is developed for agriculture. This creates another source of pressure on transboundary water systems. Currently, these potential impacts are not yet fully understood. Third, increasing 'competition' over water, particularly to produce more energy and food, is another challenge which can undermine the levels of sustainable management and cooperation over transboundary waters.

An investment in land is an investment in water

National, regional and global demand for water is increasing constantly. As populations grow, a greater amount of water is needed to produce food, energy and consumer goods. Historically, economic development has led to an increased consumption of water. Prosperity increases generally lead to shifts in habits: individuals consume more water in general and also consume larger quantities of water-intensive products. Shifts to diets which include more meat tend to follow from economic development and significantly increase an individual's water footprint (Jägerskog and Jønch Clausen 2012).

Furthermore, climate change is impacting water. Climate change means increased variability in water supply with more water concentrated in certain locations and during certain times and much less water in other locations and at other times. Droughts and floods are bound to increase and the world may have to get used to them. Global food production is already affected by their increased occurrences and when harvests are destroyed by drought, food prices respond by increasing. This has pushed many water-scarce countries to buy or lease (often for a period up to 100 years) land for food production in countries that have (at least in relative terms) more water. This trend increased significantly after the 2008 food price crises (World Bank 2011). The economic incentives behind the sharp rise in interest in land acquisitions (internationally and domestic) in recent years are arguably shaped to an extent by various political decisions. These are in turn affected by broader socio-political factors, such as the search for water, food and energy security through other mechanisms than pure market exchange. When international food prices soared in 2008 the governments of both food-exporting and -importing countries implemented trade restrictions, further exacerbating the price hikes. Another factor behind the price increases was the policy-induced increase in demand for bio-fuels, mainly seen in the EU and the US. The trend of increasing land acquisitions is at least partly characterized by a disbelief in markets providing long-term solutions to national challenges in food and energy security (Smaller and Mann 2009; HighQuest Partners 2010).

To complicate matters further, land acquisitions are being used as a means to cater for improved food security but often do not acknowledge water in their contracts. It seems that water is taken for granted. The foreign investments, which are performed by a range of actors including companies and actors from India, China, North America, the Middle East and the EU, are primarily made in Africa but are also occurring in Latin America and Asia. Table 12.1 presents a range of examples of investments from the African continent.

A 2012 report from the Stockholm International Water Institute (SIWI) concluded that there are inter-linkages between local, national, regional and global levels in land investments, which are having clear impacts on the water situation (Jägerskog *et al.* 2012). Water used to irrigate acquired lands in a region will inevitably come from a transboundary water resource. That in itself can be a reason for heightened political tensions and increased pressure on the cooperation between transboundary states. Countries and companies investing in the land become, in a sense, hydro-political actors with a stake in how transboundary resources are used. This can presumably be positive or negative for the likelihood of cooperation. While in certain cases it may lead to increased pressure to divert more water at the expense of other users and the environment, in other situations it could be a feature which spurs cooperation. It is also worth noting that in almost all cases regional actors working with transboundary waters are often not involved in land investment discussions since the agreements and contracts generally are between the investor and the national governments (or in some cases are made at the provincial level). As countries sign individual agreements with investors, there is a risk that the implications for water and land resources may not be in line with national development plans or may affect water relations and cooperation with their neighbours. The reasons for this are primarily twofold. First, since the agreements take place at national level, basin-level impacts are generally not considered. Second, provisions for water are often lacking in the agreements and access to water on the land seems to be taken for granted (Jägerskog *et al.* 2012).

Water, food and energy

The relationship between water, food and energy is attracting attention. In times of increasing competition for scarce water resources, many actors have highlighted the importance of understanding how inter-related demands for water,

Table 12.1 Large-scale land investment in selected countries, 2004–09

Country	Transboundary waters	World Bank (2011) (ha)	Cotula et al. (2009) (ha)	Share of total agricultural land (%)	Total agricultural land (ha)
Ethiopia	Gosh, Juba-Shibeli, Nile	1,190,000	602,760	1.7–3.4	34,985,000
Nigeria	Lake Chad, Niger	793,000		1.1	74,500,000
Mali	Niger, Senegal, Volta		162,850	0.4	41,101,000
Sudan	Gosh, Lake Chad, Nile	3,965,000		2.9	136,731,000
Liberia	—	1,602,000		61.4	2,610,000
Ghana	Volta		452,000	2.9	15,500,000
Madagascar	—		803,414	2.0	40,845,000
Mozambique	Zambezi, Maputo, Incomati, Limpopo, Ruvuma, Umbeluzi	2,670,000		5.4	49,300,000

Source: Jägerskog et al. (2012).

Note
World Bank (2011) data for Nigeria covers 1990–2006 and the figure for Liberia includes earlier concessions. The World Bank (2011) includes only data for projects above 500ha for Ethiopia, Liberia, Nigeria and Sudan and 1,000ha for Mozambique. Cotula et al. (2009) include data only for projects above 1,000ha.

food and energy affect each other. If the current increase in demand continues, much more water will be needed to grow food and produce energy. Water requirements for energy generation are growing fast, including for hydropower; for biofuel production; for cooling of nuclear and coal power plants; and for shale gas fractioning ('fracking') (Hoff 2011). This increasing competition puts additional weight on decision-makers to exert more pressure on their neighbours when it comes to negotiations over transboundary waters.

Flexibility needed to respond to climate change

As outlined above, climate change will affect the flows of rivers as well as the availability of water in lakes and aquifer systems. These effects will manifest themselves as increased variability in rainfall and thereby reduce the predictability of volumes of available transboundary water. This will put an additional burden on many agreements that exist today, as they are often based on multi-year averages and fixed volumetric allocations. As the actual availability of water resources will not always match the stipulations in the agreements, these figures will become less and less relevant. This could lead to increased tension and potential conflict. The adoption of a more flexible approach in the agreements could mitigate these risks (Falkenmark and Jägerskog 2010).

Water cooperation between the 'neighbours of the EU's neighbours'

Water connects the EU and its neighbours to countries beyond its immediate borders. It is clear that hydrological interdependence creates bonds which extend beyond water and into politics, trade, energy, security and other sectors. The EU is very active in the neighbours of its neighbours. Support to regional actors, such as the Nile Basin Initiative, UNECE programmes in Central Asia plus regional cooperation in the MENA region as well as in West Africa (such as support to the Volta basin),[3] are among the most extensive cooperation projects.

Eastern Africa, namely the Horn of Africa, is a key region of interest in close proximity to the EU. Historical ties intersect with interests related to trade, security and development cooperation. In the Lake Victoria region cooperation over shared waters is a main feature of the cooperation activities within the East African Community (EAC). One of the EAC's key institutions is the Lake Victoria Basin Commission (LVBC) with responsibility for the management of the shared lake basin between Burundi, Kenya, Rwanda and Tanzania. The LVBC is setup under the shared protocol for the sustainable development of the Lake Victoria basin (Earle *et al.* 2010). The Lake Victoria basin is also part of the White Nile river in which Sudan connects to the Blue Nile river, with its roots in Ethiopia, before reaching Egypt. Cooperation in the Nile basin has progressed significantly during the past decade, although the cooperation is presently experiencing some challenges. On the margins of the Lake Victoria basin and the Nile basin other transboundary water resources also exist, such as Lake Turkana (Africa's fourth largest lake), located between Ethiopia and Kenya, as well as shared rivers between Somalia and Ethiopia. These transboundary water resources have hitherto been neglected as the political situation has not allowed for cooperation on these water resources. Yet as development on the river progresses, primarily through the building of dams and irrigation systems upstream in Ethiopia, these issues will increasingly come into focus. If Somalia continues to take positive steps towards some kind of normalization, this could also contribute to increased attention to the river. Taken together, the national plans of the respective countries sharing the Shabelle and Juba river basins (Somalia, Kenya and Ethiopia) are impossible to fulfil at the same time. There are no agreements at present, nor are there platforms to meet and discuss their shared waters. As Somalia further stabilizes and Ethiopia and Kenya press on with their respective plans, the potential for conflict over shared waters will increase. However, enhanced regional integration through the trading of hydropower and foodstuffs (and the water embedded within) is also possible and is a topic that should be studied further (Elmi Mohamed 2013). Trade-offs between water for energy (hydropower), water for food production (irrigation) and water in the environment (for instance, keeping enough water to maintain the health and essential functions of the ecosystem in the Lake Turkana) are issues that need to be addressed (Avery 2010).

Transboundary water management is also an important area of concern in Central Asia, where there has been a shift away from a more regional approach to the joint management of the rivers. The draining of the Aral Sea carried out during the Soviet era is a clear example of this. Following the independence of states in the region, unilateral action has become the norm. This shift is not a surprising development. The existence of a central authority during the Soviet period made it possible for centralized planning to take place, albeit primarily with negative consequences in particularly for the Aral Sea. With the formation of newly sovereign states, many governments embody a strong motivation to assert themselves in regional settings and cater primarily for national interests. Most often this results in diminished cooperation over transboundary water (Granit *et al.* 2012). While historically the regime in place helped the management of transboundary waters, an increased contemporary focus on security by independent nations has decreased overall support for it. In a sense, the water issue has become 'securitized', to use the terminology of Buzan *et al.* (1998). Granit *et al.* (2012) suggest that while increased cooperation may not be easy to achieve, there is scope to spur collective action between actors by applying a 'nexus perspective' to the demand for and use of water, food and energy.[4] While a number of somewhat embryonic institutional structures with a 'nexus perspective' exist at regional level, there may be potential to strengthen and enable them to work more closely with transboundary water cooperation. Cooperative management of the transboundary water resources is key to overcoming many national challenges. Still, joint management – for which clear benefits exist – is not easily achieved since the distrust between the states is too strong.

Transboundary waters are a critical issue in the MENA region, which is the most water-scarce region in the world. The challenges posed by scarcity are compounded by a political environment that includes many conflicts between and within states. The following section analyses in more detail the relations between Israel and Jordan, focusing on their shared waters contextualized within their political relations. Both countries are included in the EU's European Neighbourhood Policy. This regional case is a good example of how water is central to a political conflict but also how water can be used to maintain a basic level of coordination despite challenging political circumstances. As such it offers lessons that go beyond the scope of the specific case.

Case study: the Jordan basin

The Arab–Israeli conflict is one with a history of war, political dispute and clashing ideology. Water scarcity in the MENA region (which holds roughly 1 per cent of globally available freshwater resources, but more than 5 per cent of global population) adds another set of significant challenges (Jägerskog 2003). Twenty years ago, both researchers and politicians predicted that water would be the next reason for war in the MENA region (Allan 2001; Shapland 1997). While there have been wars and conflicts in the region, water has not been yet the key factor in them. Still, water has been (and remains) an issue of contention and conflict (Jägerskog 2008), not least in the case of Israel and Palestine where Selby (2003; 2013) has shown that the 'cooperation' which is sometimes claimed to exist in essence represents Israeli dominance over the Palestinians.

To put the October 1994 'Treaty of Peace between the Hashemite Kingdom of Jordan and the State of Israel' into its regional context, it is important to link it to the Israeli–Palestinian peace track. While Israel and Jordan had to some degree enjoyed a relative and tacit understanding on the key areas relating to their shared water in the Jordan basin, it was not politically possible for Jordan to enter into an agreement on water (or other issues) before Israel and the Palestine Liberation Organization (PLO) reached an agreement.

Thus, the Israeli–Palestinian agreement which resulted from negotiations following the signing of the 'Declaration of Principles' (DoP) in September 1993 paved the way for an Israeli–Jordanian peace treaty (Israel and PLO 1993). Like the Interim Agreement between Israel and the Palestinians, the peace treaty between Israel and Jordan stipulates that a Joint Water Committee (JWC) should be established (Jägerskog 2003). The JWC was required to consist of three members from each side and to be able to call in experts whenever deemed necessary (Jordan 1994: art. 6, annex II). The JWC was established in 1994 and is responsible for the implementation of the water clauses of the peace treaty. Thus, in order to be able to assess the pace and quality of the implementation of the treaty, it is relevant to study the work of the JWC. As noted, the Israeli–Jordanian peace treaty was a natural next step after the Israeli–Palestinian DoP. Israel and Jordan had for a relatively long time viewed a peace agreement to be in their long-term interests. However, King Hussein of Jordan could not politically be seen to go further in rapprochement towards Israel than the Palestinian leadership. It was only when the DoP had been agreed that Jordan was able to negotiate with Israel. Water is dealt with rather extensively in the agreement, which outlines that both countries are entitled to water allocations from the Jordan river, including its tributary Yarmouk, and the shared groundwater in Wadi Araba/Arava (Jordan 1994). One very interesting item in the agreement is that the parties agreed to allow the storing of Jordanian 'winter water' in Lake Tiberias, located in Israel, when they do have a relative surplus of water flow. Israel subsequently releases the water in the dry summer period when Jordan needs it in its urban centres such as Amman (Jägerskog 2003).

Evolution of cooperation

Israel and Jordan have enjoyed basic coordination of some joint actions pertaining to the Jordan basin since the 1950s. In the so-called 'Picnic Table Talks' that began in the 1950s, the parties met and discussed issues of common concern. In that sense, the role of the UN Truce Supervision Organization (UNTSO), which worked as an 'umbrella' for discussions on water coordination, was important notwithstanding the absence of a peace treaty. The activities involved many meetings between Israelis and Jordanians and started as early as the 1950s, continuing up until the peace treaty was signed in 1994 (Wolf 1995). As in this case, the process of developing a water regime is often a long one and it meets setbacks on occasions. It must be remembered that the institutionalization of cooperation requires time and not just a signed agreement.

The Israeli–Jordanian peace treaty was to a certain extent an agreement that codified some of the existing practices. This regarded issues such as coordination over water issues of common concern under the auspices of UNTSO, while allowing parties to develop them further at a later time. In spite of being formally in conflict, Israel and Jordan regularly unofficially met to discuss and coordinate action on the Jordan river. The advantage in the case of the Israeli–Jordanian peace treaty was that there was a code of practice and the issues were understood by the two sides, which provided for easier negotiations. The ambition was also to try to solve most of the water issues directly in the treaty. Admittedly some ambiguity is present, particularly in relation to water allocations in times of lower availability in the Jordan river system. This is not unheard of in a region which usually experiences a drought every seventh year, but most issues are dealt with in detail.

To understand the negotiations it is important to have an overview of how water issues are framed in the national discourses, as policies pursued at the international level are often a reflection of national-level discussion.

Water discourse in Israel

The national discourse on water in Israel has been largely influenced by Zionism, where the focus was on agriculture as a means to build the state. From the 1940s to the 1970s, irrigation to support traditional farming communities was the normative perspective (Feitelson 2002). Later, and even more so today, there has been a shift towards wider economic reasoning being applied to national water allocations. The preference for farming in Israel continues to some degree, as it enjoys disproportionate political power relative to its economic influence and input (Jägerskog 2003). Previously, there was also a strategic argument in relation to water and irrigation, which meant that it was important to keep buffer zones in remote areas of the country as a resource against potential enemies. Today, as wars are not waged to the same degree on the ground but through missiles and in other ways, this argument has lost some of its appeal despite previous strong currency. Hajer (1995) notes that a military–farming discourse coalition had similar interests in maintaining high water allocation to agriculture. This was also, in a sense, in line with the interests in negotiations since having a high allocation of water for agriculture would mean that the 'entry point' into the negotiations would be higher than it would be if less water had been allocated to begin with (Jägerskog 2003).

The water discourse in Jordan

In Jordan there is a sense that the water problems are partly man-made. This sense comes from the fact that on various occasions, Jordan has had to absorb many refugees – and even today this situation continues with the refugees coming from Syria as a result of the civil war there. After the Second World War Jordan accepted around 450,000 Palestinians. Irrigation was a key feature in providing livelihoods for the Palestinian refugees and placed additional pressure on Jordan's already scarce water resources. Some Jordanians argue that Israel is partly responsible for the water shortage in Jordan (Jägerskog 2003). Within the elite in Jordan, many felt that a peace agreement with Israel would be beneficial to Jordan as it would attract military and financial assistance, not least from the US. Another important feature in Jordan is the strong tradition of farming. Even though, in economic terms, the value of agricultural input to the gross domestic product of Jordan is declining, there are many people still employed either directly in the agricultural sector or in the sectors dependent upon it (ibid.).

Analysis of the cooperation[5]

Historically, water in the Jordan basin has been seen as a potential source of conflict and even war (Starr 1991). However, authors who focus on the potential for war, apart from ignoring the ameliorating factor of virtual water (that is, water being imported in its 'virtual' form through the import of water-intensive foodstuffs), have also tended to neglect the water-regulating systems in place between Israel and Jordan since the early 1950s. These systems could even be described as an international water regime. Krasner (1983: 2) defines an international regime as 'sets of principles, norms, rules, and decision-making procedures around which actors' expectations converge in a given issue-area'. The common understanding that started in the 1950s was reached in UN-led talks and concentrated on the use of the disputed waters of the Jordan river basin between Israel and Jordan during a period when they were *de jure* in a state of war. This is a good example of a water regime greatly reducing the tensions between two adversaries (Wolf 1995). Dinar (2000) argues that the US viewed cooperation on water issues in the Jordan basin as a tool for the creation of peace in the region.

Already in 1955 the so-called Johnston Plan for water management in the Jordan river basin can be seen as part of a water regime between the parties, even though it was not formally recognized by the states (Wolf 1995). The Plan has been used as a sort of baseline for water relations in the basin. The peace treaty between Israel and Jordan has enhanced and formalized the cooperation between the two states. However, post-agreement practices and the implementation of the water clauses of the peace treaty should not be viewed as separate from the history of water cooperation and coordination. Even before the actual treaty, principles and norms for water relations between the parties existed (Jägerskog 2003). Principles involve goal orientation and beliefs at a general level in areas such as the environment and security. Norms describe general rights and obligations, which operate mainly on the level of issue areas but are still very general. Hence, the basics of the regime were in place before peace negotiations started. In a fully-fledged regime there are also rules which are specific prescriptions and proscriptions for action that are often stated in a formal agreement such as the water clauses in the Israeli–Jordanian Peace Treaty. In addition, there are decision-making procedures in a regime, which are prevailing practices for making and implementing collective choices. These can be seen in the JWC and its procedures for taking decisions.

The JWC has not been without its challenges. Haddadin (2001) maintains that there has been a 'slippage of dates' on the part of Israel in the implementation of its commitments to Jordan. For example, according to the agreement, Jordan and Israel shall be entitled to equal amounts of water from the lower Jordan river. However, in order to decide the exact amount, a survey of existing Israeli use had to be conducted. An agreement on how to conduct this survey has not yet been reached. Thus, the Jordanian argument is that Israel is deliberately delaying action that is required as background for the implementation of the water clauses of the treaty. Dureid Mahasneh (2002), who was the Jordanian head of the JWC from 1996 to 1999, even went so far as to argue that the Israelis were obstructing the implementation of the treaty. One of the heads of the JWC from Israel, Meir Ben-Meir (2001), also maintained that there were problems in the implementation of the agreement and the work of the JWC, although both parties recognized that it was still imperative for the committee to stay in place. Haddadin (2001) also attributes the implementation problems to ineffectiveness on the Jordanian side, thus recognizing that Israel was not the only problematic actor.

Politics also affects the working of the JWC. The changes in the political scene in Israel, which brought Likud to power in 1996, also affected Jordan's water relations with Israel (Mahadin 2002). According to Haddadin (2001), although some studies were implemented, the meetings became intermittent and less productive. On technical matters, however, the working relations between Israel and Jordan still functioned reasonably well (Alem 2002). Having noted the problematic areas of the implementation process, it is also important to discuss the positive aspects. For example, the canal for storage of Yarmuk water from Jordan in Lake Tiberias was built quickly and was inaugurated by King Hussein in July 1995. However, there are no provisions for how to respond to drought. This is a serious issue for the parties. Apart from the problems of 1999, when Israel did not want to supply Jordan with the stipulated amounts of water (although it eventually did), there has been no problem in the transfer of water from Israel to Jordan (Alem 2002; El-Nazer 2002; Mahadin 2002). There is a fear on the Jordanian side that the quality of water that Israel releases to it in the summer is of much worse quality than the water Israel receives from Jordan in the winter from the Yarmuk river (Trottier 1999). However, the Jordanians involved in the JWC who are responsible for the water coming from Israel claim that the water released has been of the agreed quality (Alem 2002; el-Nazer 2002).

The professional relations within the JWC can be seen as functioning rather well (Mahadin 2002; Ben-Meir 2001). This stems from a joint professional understanding of the importance of having functions in place which enable cooperation over the shared waters. At the same time, the institutionalization of the JWC as an arena for discussion, coordination and cooperation can be seen as an enabling structure for a professional understanding to grow among those participating in the discussions. However, there are also 'external' structures that can effectively constrain or enable the work in the JWC and, consequently, the implementation of the agreement as well. As mentioned above, the change in government in Israel from Labour to Likud affected the work of the JWC and was perceived by the Jordanian side as delaying implementation. While the actors within the JWC (from both parties) had a wider range of avenues for action available to them under a Labour government in Israel, room for manoeuvre decreased during the Likud period. Thus the surrounding political environment effectively sets boundaries for what is feasible in the water sector.

Tools and effectiveness of the arrangements

The workings of the JWC between Israel and Jordan can be described as relatively well developed, in particular if one compares it to Israeli–Palestinian water relations. Professionals on both sides testify that cooperation functions rather well and has been maintained since 1994 despite some challenges (Jägerskog 2007) – not least in relation to the fact that there are no provisions on how to address the issue of drought in the agreement (Jägerskog 2003).

As noted above, the Israeli–Jordanian agreement has also been effective. In a region plagued by conflict, the fact that the peace treaty has been honoured is significant. The storage arrangements of 'Jordanian' water in Lake Tiberias in Israel and Israel's subsequent release of the water have functioned. That in itself has been a trust-building feature of the arrangements. There has been disagreement on how to share the deficiency in drought years, but the matter has been solved through the JWC. This testifies to the relative robustness of the agreement and the cooperation between the countries. It is clear that they are mutually dependent on each other for somewhat different reasons: Israel has a strong interest in maintaining peace with Jordan, and Jordan has various incentives to keep the cooperation going both in relation to the water and environmental aspects but also from a more political perspective as this secures international support from outside (Jägerskog 2003). In addition, the level of cooperation between the professionals engaging from each side is also an important feature in the further institutionalization of cooperation. In this respect, the environmental group Friends of the Earth Middle East (FoEME) has encouraged and managed to activate a cooperation between Israelis, Jordanians and Palestinians at the local and transboundary levels – often between cities and their mayors in areas physically close to each other but separated by political borders (ibid.). The cooperation that FoEME engaged in has been made possible by the existence of the peace agreement between Israel and Jordan as well as an interim agreement between Israel and the Palestinian Authority.

The Israeli–Jordanian agreement has proved to be durable. Despite some challenges during the past two decades, the agreement is still in force and honoured by both sides. Studying the processes that helped to achieve and sustain this cooperation can provide illustrative insights. Three key lessons are presented below. These lessons also have general value beyond the scope of the specific case, not least in the EU context since challenging contexts for transboundary cooperation exists in the regions bordering the EU's neighbours.

First, support geared at low-intensity cooperation, when politics does not allow for more, is important. Process financing is often what is needed to secure, deepen and improve water-related collaboration in transboundary basins where the parties have a low degree of other forms of cooperation. The long-term support prior to the agreement of the UNTSO in facilitating low-level cooperation is key in this respect. Thus, for a donor or organization to engage in building cooperative structures in a shared river basin requires courage and a vision that goes beyond the lifetime of a single project. Thinking should be process-oriented. The financial support that international donor institutions could provide to bring about water cooperation is seldom rewarding to the donor in the beginning and can be seen as a high-risk investment. In this respect the UNDP 'Shared Waters Partnership' (SWP) provides a mechanism for sustained support of 'risky' political processes in basins.[6]

Second, the institutionalization of cooperation is critical to build trust and to provide solutions for the challenges in the shared waters area. Jordan's storage of its 'winter water' inside of Israel is important. It creates the possibility to build trust. This trust has, by and large, been present and has provided Jordan with the possibility to store water until it is needed in Amman and other densely populated areas during its dry periods. The institutionalization of the JWC also ensured regular meetings and coordination between both sides, an essential ingredient to making a cooperative agreement function.

Third, water (and water cooperation) is intimately linked to politics. For those who come from a political science background this may sound like an obvious statement, but from a water practitioner's perspective it is seldom well understood.

While donor agencies and international organizations sometimes see water as separate from other fields, this research suggests that such an approach will lead to misunderstandings and disappointments, for example, with regard to why support activities do not accomplish expected results in the estimated time.

Conclusions

This chapter has focused on the challenges that the EU is facing with regard to transboundary water management in its broader neighbourhood. The challenges that have been discussed and that are relevant for the EU range from being able to 'incentivize' cooperation over shared waters by clearly outlining the benefits of cooperation to being able to view the achievement of improved cooperation over transboundary waters as a process that often takes time. It is clear that notwithstanding models showing that it is rational to cooperate over shared water resources, it takes a long time to build robust cooperation. Even if most activities relating to transboundary waters are cooperative in nature, around 166 of the 276 basins of the world still lack agreements on how to cooperatively manage their transboundary water (Jägerskog 2012).

Why are we not seeing more cooperation? What drives cooperation? Subramanian *et al.* (2012) identified the three main factors which drive cooperation. First, internal drivers are seen as a key ingredient. Countries make national development plans and often cooperate in areas needed to obtain goals set in these national strategies. The World Bank (2010) concluded that regional markets for energy in Africa, for example the East African Power Pool, will lower annual costs for electricity by around US\$ two billion. This is because hydropower can provide cheap energy and also make it possible to connect markets by sending energy to where it is most needed at any given time. Improved cooperation on transboundary waters is critical for developing energy markets in many places.

Second, external drivers are important factors. For example, the Southern African Development Community (SADC) devised a protocol on shared watercourses which subsequently became a major inspiration in the development of frameworks for other basins. Furthermore, encouragement or support from outside actors can also spur cooperation. When the Global Environmental Facility, UNDP, the World Bank or the EU support and provide resources for countries to work together this generates further cooperation. Still, support for transboundary water cooperation is largely underdeveloped in the sense that in recent decades inadequate financing has been provided for political processes dealing with transboundary waters (Nicol *et al.* 2001; Earle *et al.* 2010). For a donor to engage in building cooperative structures in a shared river basin, courage and a vision that must transcend the lifetime of a single project are required because these processes are bound to be challenging and often rather messy. Process financing is often what is needed to secure, deepen and improve water-related collaboration in transboundary basins where parties have a low degree of other forms of cooperation. There are some emerging initiatives such as the

UNDP 'Shared Waters Partnership' programme, geared solely to support and encourage dialogue, but such initiatives should be increased and strengthened.

Third, global trends are encouraging change and can advance cooperation. For example, the EU Water Framework Directive has expanded cooperation in Europe and can also provide a basis for cooperation beyond the EU Member States (European Union 2000). Climate change is another global trend that shines a spotlight on the often unsustainable setting up of transboundary water agreements (Falkenmark and Jägerskog 2010).

Another key aspect not addressed in detail in this chapter but which needs to be taken into account in the political analysis of transboundary waters is the study of the quality of the cooperation (see, for instance, Zeitoun and Mirumachi 2008). Often, the fact that cooperation is happening at some level is taken as a positive sign and further analysis is neglected. However, a deconstruction of the cooperative activities will often reveal another picture. This raises important questions to consider in future research. On whose terms is the cooperation happening? Is there power asymmetry between the riparians? Is there scope for activities that would be geared towards 'levelling the playing field' in this respect? Research seems to suggest that if parties can engage on more equal terms, the prospects for equitable and lasting cooperative processes increase.

In conclusion, transboundary water cooperation is often entangled in messy political processes that go beyond water, and actors working to facilitate cooperation require continued support to navigate them. Furthermore, it is critical to connect water with other key areas such as energy, security, food markets, regional integration and trade.

Notes

1 The views expressed in this chapter are those of the author and do not necessarily represent the views of the Swedish International Development Cooperation Agency (SIDA) or the Swedish Government.
2 This section is based on Jägerskog (2012).
3 For more information on EU activities, see for instance the EU Water Initiative website: www.euwi.net.
4 See also Chapter 6 by Tressia Hobeika in this volume on the 'security–politics–development nexus'.
5 This section is based on Jägerskog (2007), reproduced with permission of Springer Science+Business Media.
6 See www.watergovernance.org/sa/node.asp?node=1467 (accessed June 2014).

References

Alem, Z. (2002) Interview, Director General, Jordan Valley Authority, member of the Water Negotiation team and member of Joint Water Committee, Amman, 10 March.
Allan, J.A. (2001) *The Middle East Water Question: Hydropolitics and the Global Economy*, London: I.B. Tauris.
Ashton, C. (2012) 'Remarks by European Union High Representative for Foreign Affairs and Security Policy Catherine Ashton at the High Level Roundtable Discussion on

Water, Peace and Security at the United Nations', New York, 25 September, www.eu-un.europa.eu/articles/en/article_12626_en.htm (accessed June 2014).

Avery, S. (2010) 'Hydrological Impacts of Ethiopia's Omo Basin on Kenya's Lake Turkana Water Levels and Fisheries', Report prepared for the African Development Bank, Tunis, November.

Ben-Meir, M. (2001) Interview, Water Commissioner in Israel 1977–81 and 1996–2001, Israeli Head of the Joint Water Committees with the Palestinians and Jordan, Kfar Masorik, 29 April.

Buzan, B., O. Waever and J. de Wilde (eds) (1998) *Security: A New Framework for Analysis*, Boulder: Lynne Rienner.

Cotula, L., S. Vermeulen, R. Leonard and J. Keeley (2009) *Land Grab or Development Opportunity? Agricultural Investment and International Land Deals in Africa*, Rome: FAO and IFAD, London: IIED.

Council of the European Union (2013) 'Council Conclusions on EU Water Diplomacy', Foreign Affairs Council meeting, Brussels, 22 July, www.consilium.europa.eu/uedocs/cms_data/docs/pressdata/EN/foraff/138253.pdf (accessed June 2014).

Dinar, S. (2000) 'Negotiations and International Relations: A Framework for Hydropolitics', *International Negotiation* 5(2), 375–407.

Earle, A., A. Jägerskog and J. Öjendal (eds) (2010) *Transboundary Water Management: Principles and Practice*, London: Earthscan.

Elmi Mohamed, A. (2013) Interview, Royal Institute of Technology in Stockholm, Stockholm, 11 February.

El-Nazer, H. (2002) Interview, Minister of Water and Irrigation, member of the Water Negotiation team, Amman, Jordan, 11 March.

European Union (2000) 'Directive 2000/60/EC of the European Parliament and of the Council of 23 October 2000 Establishing a Framework for Community Action in the Field of Water Policy', *Official Journal of the European Union*, L 327, 22 December, 1–73.

Falkenmark, M. and A. Jägerskog (2010) 'Sustainability of Transnational Water Agreements in the Face of Socio-economic and Environmental Change', in A. Earle, A. Jägerskog and J. Öjendal (eds) *Transboundary Water Management: Principles and Practice*, London: Earthscan, 157–170.

Feitelson, E. (2002) 'Implications of Shifts in the Israeli Water Discourse for Israel–Palestinian Water Negotiations', *Political Geography* 21(3), 293–318.

Granit, J., A. Jägerskog, G. Björklund, A. Bullock, R. Löfgren, G. de Goijeer, A. Lindström and S. Pettigrew (2012) 'Regional Options for Addressing the Water, Energy and Food Nexus in Central Asia and Aral Sea Basin', *International Journal of Water Resources Development* 28(3), 419–432.

Haddadin, M. (2001) *Diplomacy on the Jordan: International Conflict and Negotiated Solution*, Boston: Kluwer Academic.

Hajer, M. (1995) *The Politics of Environmental Discourse: Ecological Modernization and the Policy Process*, Oxford: Clarendon Press.

HighQuest Partners (2010) 'Private Financial Sector Investment in Farmland and Agricultural Infrastructure', OECD Food, Agriculture and Fishing Working Papers 33, Paris: OECD.

Hoff, H. (2011) *Understanding the Nexus*, Background Paper for the Bonn 2011 Conference: 'The Water, Energy and Food Security Nexus', Stockholm: Stockholm Environment Institute, www.water-energy-food.org/documents/understanding_the_nexus.pdf (accessed August 2013).

Israel and PLO (1993) 'Declaration of Principles on Interim Self-Governance Arrangements between the Government of the State of Israel and the P.L.O.', 13 September, www.unsco.org/Documents/Key/Declaration%20of%20Principles%20on%20Interim%20Self-Government%20Arrangements.pdf (accessed August 2014).

Jägerskog, A. (2003) *Why States Cooperate over Shared Water: The Water Negotiations in the Jordan River Basin*, Linköping University, PhD Dissertation, Linköping Studies in Arts and Science, www.ep.liu.se/diss/arts_science/2003/281/digest.pdf (accessed June 2014).

Jägerskog, A. (2007) 'Why States Cooperate over Shared Water: Water Negotiations in the Jordan River Basin', in H. Shuval and H. Dweik (eds) *Water Resources in the Middle East: Israel-Palestinian Water Issues – from Conflict to Cooperation*, Berlin: Springer Verlag, 194–202.

Jägerskog, A. (2008) 'Functional Water Cooperation in the Jordan River Basin: Spillover or Spillback for Political Security', in H.G. Brauch, U. Oswald Spring, J. Grin, C. Mesjasz, P. Kameri-Mbote, N. Chadha Behera, B. Chourou and H. Krummenacher (eds) *Facing Global Environmental Change: Environmental, Human, Energy, Food, Health and Water Security Concepts*, Berlin: Springer-Verlag, 633–640.

Jägerskog, A. (2012) 'Background Document for Ministerial Roundtable on Transboundary Waters', Marseille: World Water Forum 2012.

Jägerskog, A., A. Cascao, M. Hårsmar and K. Kim (2012) *Land Acquisitions: How Will They Impact Transboundary Waters?*, Report 30, Stockholm: SIWI.

Jägerskog, A. and T. Jønch Clausen (eds) (2012) *Feeding a Thirsty World: Challenges and Opportunities for a Water and Food Secure Future*, Report 31, Stockholm: SIWI.

Jordan (1994) *Treaty of Peace between the Hashemite Kingdom of Jordan and the State of Israel, 26 October 1994*, www.kinghussein.gov.jo/peacetreaty.html (accessed June 2014).

Krasner, S.D. (1983) *International Regimes*, Ithaca: Cornell University Press.

Mahadin, K. (2002) Interview, former Minister of Water and Irrigation, Amman, 9 March.

Mahasneh, D. (2002) Interview, Water and Environment negotiator, member of the Joint Water Committee, Amman, 9 March.

Nicol, A., F. van Steenbergen, H. Sunman, A. Turton, T. Slaymaker, J.A. Allan, M. de Graaf and M. van Harten (2001) *Transboundary Water Management as an International Public Good*, Development Financing 2000 Study 2001:1, Stockholm.

Puri, S. and W. Struckmeier (2010) 'Aquifer Resources in a Transboundary Context: A Hidden Resource? Enabling the Practitioner to "See It and Bank It" for Good Use', in A. Earle, A. Jägerskog and Ojendal (eds) *Transboundary Water Management: Principles and Practice*, London: Earthscan, 74–90.

Selby, J. (2003) 'Dressing up Domination as "Cooperation": The Case of Israeli–Palestinian Water Relations', *Review of International Studies* 29 (1), 121–138.

Selby, J. (2013) 'Cooperation, Domination and Colonisation: The Israeli–Palestinian Joint Water Committee', *Water Alternatives* 6(1), 1–24.

Shapland, G. (1997) *Rivers of Discord: International Water Disputes in the Middle East*, London: Hurst and Co.

Smaller, C. and H. Mann (2009) 'A Thirst for Distant Lands: Foreign Investment in Agricultural Land and Water', Winnipeg: IISD.

Starr, J.R. (1991) 'Water Wars', *Foreign Policy* 82, 17–36.

Subramanian, A., B. Brown and A. Wolf (2012) *Reaching Across the Waters: Facing the Risks of Cooperation in International Waters*, Washington, DC: World Bank.

Transboundary Freshwater Dispute Database (TFDD) http://transboundarywater.geo.orst. edu/index.html (accessed March 2013).

Trottier, J. (1999) *Hydropolitics in the West Bank and Gaza Strip*, Jerusalem: PASSIA.

UNDP (2006) *Beyond Scarcity: Power, Poverty and the Global Water Crisis*, New York: United Nations Development Programme, Human Development Report Office.

Wolf, A. (1995) *Hydropolitics along the Jordan River: Scarce Water and its Impact on the Arab–Israeli Conflict*, Tokyo: United Nations University Press.

Wolf, A., A. Kramer, A. Carius and G.D. Dabelko (2005) 'Managing Water Conflict and Cooperation', in *State Of the World: Redefining Global Security*, Washington, DC: World Watch Institute, 80–95.

World Bank (2010) 'Deepening Regional Integration', in V. Foster and C. Briceno-Garmendia (eds) *Africa's Infrastructure: A Time for Transformation*, Washington, DC: World Bank, 143–162.

World Bank (2011) *Rising Global Interest in Farmland*, Washington, DC: World Bank.

World Water Assessment Programme (2012) *Managing Water under Uncertainty and Risk*, The United Nations World Water Development Report 4, vol. 1, Paris: UNESCO.

Zeitoun, M. and N. Mirumachi (2008) 'Transboundary Water Interaction I: Reconsidering Conflict and Cooperation', *International Environmental Agreements* 8(4), 297–316.

Conclusion

Lessons and policy proposals

Erwan Lannon

Introduction: the 'defragmentation challenge'

The aim of this conclusion is to put forward the main lessons and policy proposals identified in the different chapters of this volume. Also some of the good practices identified by the contributors will be highlighted. This is not an easy task given the great variety of topics, countries and regions addressed and the sectoral approach followed in this volume. However, the general diagnosis is clear: the European Union (EU) still suffers from a lack of global strategic vision in its broader neighbourhood, and its policies and strategies *vis-à-vis* the three regions (Saharan Africa, the Arabian Gulf and Central Asia) are still very fragmented.

A 'defragmentation process' is therefore needed, so that the EU can act in a more comprehensive and flexible way *across* its traditional policy and development cooperation frameworks, progressively building new bridges while developing synergies and complementarities between and among the existing frameworks at regional, sub-regional and local (notably cross-border) levels.

On the other hand, there is a great convergence of views to assert that a simple extension of the European Neighbourhood Policy (ENP) to its broader neighbourhood is not appropriate, at least for the foreseeable future. It is quite clear, for instance, that Central Asia remains far away from the EU compared to the Sahel, the Horn of Africa or even the Arabian Gulf. On the other hand, the potential for connecting the Central Asia Strategy to the Eastern Partnership and the Black Sea Synergy is relatively important.

Another convergence is that the EU's approach cannot be limited to a narrow or short-term security approach. On the contrary, the EU should develop a more comprehensive approach based on a long-term strategic vision, keeping in mind its limited influence in certain regions. There is obviously a challenge to be overcome by the EU and its Member States: to find the right balance between the EU's supranational and the Member States' national strategic interests on the one hand, and the values on which the EU is based on the other hand.

Political, legal and security challenges

The first part of this volume addresses some major political, legal and security challenges. It starts with two chapters addressing, mainly from a legal and political point of view, issues that are high on the EU's current political agenda: migration and border controls. Then the two following chapters are devoted to security challenges such as the fight against terrorism and the strategic roles played by the European Union, notably in the framework of the Common Security and Defence Policy (CSDP).

Migration and border controls: values vs. security interests

The Mediterranean Sea is turning into a mass grave while the eastern borders of the enlarged European Union are also facing increasing migratory pressures. According to the International Organization for Migration, in 2014 'up to 3,072 migrants are believed to have died in the Mediterranean, compared with an estimate of 700 in 2013. Globally, IOM estimates that at least 4,077 migrants died in 2014, and at least 40,000 since the year 2000' (Brian and Laczko 2014: 11). Migratory issues being, by nature, transnational, their management implies the conclusion of numerous agreements with all actors concerned in the countries of origin, transit and final destination. Thus, addressing these topics in the framework of an analysis devoted to the 'neighbours of the EU's neighbours' is of particular interest and relevance. Refugees, asylum-seekers and irregular migrants are a major issue not only for the EU but also for its neighbours, which sometimes become the final destination of a long and perilous journey. Cooperation in the management of migratory flows is therefore essential both from a political and also from a human point of view.

Sarah Wolff stresses in her chapter that the 'externalization of EU return and readmission practices raises some concerns about fundamental rights' and that the EU has underestimated the need to address migration challenges comprehensively and cross-regionally. Moreover, 'security-oriented and national approaches to migration remain huge obstacles to a comprehensive global and regional governance of migration'. In the same vein, Valeria Bonavita, addressing the externalization of border controls towards the EU's broader neighbourhood, notes that 'FRONTEX operational arrangements with countries such as Mauritania and EU-financed border-control capacity-building in sub-Saharan Africa' entail the 'risk of sacrificing migrants' fundamental rights'. The conclusion is that '[t]his jeopardizes in several ways the consistency between the internal and external dimensions of EU fundamental rights protection, particularly in relation to matters of transparency, accountability and access to justice'.

The lessons are very clear: a one-sided security approach to migration may generate the perception of a double standard. The balance between values and interests is still very difficult to achieve, especially in highly sensitive political areas such as migration and border controls. A more comprehensive policy based on a real co-ownership and co-development approach is therefore urgently needed. This can only be achieved by including all actors involved: the EU, its neighbours and their neighbours.

The EU's strategic roles in the broader neighbourhood and the fight against terrorism

For Alyson J.K. Bailes and Pál Dunay the diagnosis is that 'in all three regions under study, the EU operates from a relatively weak strategic starting-point shaped by geography, resources, limited historical engagement and the absence of strong institutional partners'. Moreover,

> The three more specific security roles that it can play in spaces situated at such a remove – CSDP missions, weapons-related measures and efforts for broader security governance – apply differentially across the regions, with CSDP action very limited outside the African zones and with both CSDP and weapons policies largely undeveloped in Central Asia.

What is striking, as one of the lessons, is that 'the EU's choices seem to be shaped more by local conditions and other actors' agendas than by a single, creative European will'. It is also difficult to 'imagine a case where some of the power-set Russia, China, India and Iran would not remain doughty rivals in Central Asia, or where all the powers of the greater Middle East would happily choose the EU as arbiter'. The conclusion is that

> the only other way the EU's relative strategic role might grow is if its more immediate neighbours participating in the European Neighbourhood Policy became part of a new enlargement zone, a contingency that seems remote in the Eastern Mediterranean and only a little less so in outer Eastern Europe.

However, it 'might be worth putting a small bet on the possibility that the Sahel and/or Horn of Africa might one day be discussed not as a "neighbour of the EU's neighbours" but as a direct neighbourhood zone for the EU'.

One proposal is thus – if the EUs wants to play an increasing strategic role in Central Asia or the greater Middle East – to continue to enlarge, if not the EU, at least the ENP. However, for the next five years, the President of the European Commission, Jean-Claude Juncker (2014: 11), has clearly limited the prospects. On the other hand, the conclusion of three new Association Agreements including Deep and Comprehensive Free Trade Areas (AA-DCFTA) with Georgia, Moldova and Ukraine (Van der Loo *et al.* 2014) and the negotiations going on with Morocco (Lannon 2014) imply, in the medium term, an enlargement of the internal market through normative convergence and legislation approximation. Nevertheless, enlargement certainly remains a key factor not only at EU but also NATO level.

For Gilles de Kerchove and Christiane Höhn, the fight against terrorism in the EU's broader neighbourhood, and more specifically in the Sahel region, is a challenge requiring a 'comprehensive development and security approach'. Due to the 'increased links of the threat between North and West African countries', the answer must include 'both the EU's neighbours and their neighbours, as appropriate'. In this regard an important lesson is that the

> Maghreb countries have interesting projects of their own in the Sahel, such as the training of justice officials, training on terrorist financing and projects related to prevention of radicalization, so that the EU Member States and the Maghreb countries could cooperate in the Sahel not only politically, but also through projects.

In fact, it is important 'not to think in silos depending on the EU financial or other instrument, but rather have a vision of what needs to be done and find the means to do so'. Another lesson is that the

> challenge for the EU will now be to learn the development assistance lessons from the past – Mali imploded despite decades of considerable amounts of development assistance – and together with the partners from the region design a security and development approach which will provide viable alternatives to the EU's neighbours and their neighbours, and in particular their youth populations, who will shape the future of these countries.

As a concrete proposal 'security experts in EU delegations can help to create relationships, establish trust and work with the security and justice authorities of the partner countries, as well as helping to design security and justice projects'.

Economic and societal challenges

The second part of this volume is devoted to some important economic and societal challenges. It starts with a trade analysis centred on the possibility of extending, in one way or another, the foreseen Neighbourhood Economic Community (NEC) to the broader neighbourhood. Then a second chapter addresses the 'security–politics–development nexus' in the fragile states of the Sahel, the Horn of Africa and the Arabian Peninsula. The third chapter concentrates on gender issues in Saharan Africa and Central Asia, while the fourth deals with the limits of EU democracy support in Central Asia and the Gulf.

Trade and development: variable geometry and strategic policy-making

Sieglinde Gstöhl, addressing EU trade relations 'beyond the Neighbourhood Economic Community', argues that an 'inclusion of the neighbours of the EU's neighbours in the ENP does not appear to be a future option' as 'developing an NEC constitutes already a big challenge for the ENP countries'. This is certainly one of the major lessons to keep in mind. One the other hand, 'the systematic development of linkages between the European Union, the ENP countries and the neighbours of the EU's neighbours is feasible and desirable'. Moreover, the 'different EU initiatives should generally reinforce pan-regional dynamics instead of cross-cutting them and should open the possibility to build bridges across policy frameworks'. It is important to note that two cross-regional programmes already connect 'the EU, its immediate and more distant neighbours, and are funded by more than one EU financial instrument': INOGATE (Interstate Oil and Gas Transport to Europe for EU-riparian states of the Black and Caspian Seas and their neighbours) and the TRACECA programme (Transport Corridor Europe–Caucasus–Asia linking EU–Asia across the Black Sea, South Caucasus and the Caspian Sea and Central Asia). The obvious conclusion is that with a 'functional approach to the extended neighbourhood which allows for "variable geometry", the EU could engage subsets of its partners in function of both sides' interests'. In fact, such an approach 'could be embedded in an overarching strategy for the neighbours of the EU's neighbours that draws as well on the already existing regional strategies for parts of the broader neighbourhood'.

For Tressia Hobeika, development cooperation in the Sahel, the Horn of Africa and the Arabian Peninsula 'requires strategic policy-making' as one of the main lessons. The challenges remain considerable as 'strategic considerations have not yet found their way into ... [the EU's] development assistance in the fragile states'. In fact, 'beyond aid, non-financial development instruments are not widely used and, where they are used, less strategically. Pro-development political dialogue, although increasing, leaves regional pivotal states aside'. Moreover, the 'CFSP toolbox, such as the appointment of EUSRs [EU Special Representatives], is not particularly employed to promote pro-development policies'. On the other hand, 'Political thinking in connection with fragility ... is progressively finding fertile ground in the EU institutions'; however, 'acting politically ... which entails the use of smart tools and producing evidence, has not found particular resonance in Brussels yet'. These are certainly important lessons that need to be addressed by the European Union.

The human factor: gender issues in Saharan Africa and Central Asia

According to Zuhal Yeşilyurt Gündüz, 'security should go way beyond state security as for women security incorporates the lack of *all* types of violence and security from discrimination, oppression, poverty and domestic as well as state violence'. The diagnosis is evident: 'women in Saharan Africa and in Central Asia ... face patriarchy, discrimination, inequality, subordination and domination'. In fact, under the influence of colonialism, 'in the case of Saharan Africa women's status deteriorated whereas in the Central Asian case it improved'. By contrast, 'women's representation is more limited now than in the past in Central Asia, whereas in Saharan Africa their political representation is on the rise'.

One of the major lessons of this chapter on gender issues is that there is a 'huge gap between the many policy declarations and high rhetoric regarding gender equality and women's empowerment, and the practice in reality'. In this regard, it is proposed that the EU concentrates on 'the realization of human security, with which survival, basic human needs and human dignity can be achieved and oppressive structures at local, national and global levels can be eliminated'. In this respect, Zuhal Yeşilyurt Gündüz underlines that '[r]eal security incorporates security from domestic, physical, military, economic, sexual, ecological and structural violence' and that it can only be achieved 'when gender relations of dominance and oppression as well as poverty are eradicated'. Priority should therefore be given to 'a basic needs approach' so that 'material needs for survival and the need for political contribution and involvement of women are being promoted'. What is needed are 'more resources, better training, greater awareness', the conclusion being that 'feminism itself provides the key to the solution'.

The limits of EU democracy support in Central Asia and in the Arabian Gulf

Alexander Warkotsch and Richard Youngs deal, in their chapter, with the limits of democracy support in Central Asia and in the Gulf – a real challenge for the EU. They find that in 'both regions geopolitical interests continue to militate against more ambitious democracy support policies'. For them, the 'kind of policy instruments that the EU has developed in the ENP have not been easily extended into these two crucial "neighbours of the neighbours" regions', an observation which 'does caution against any easy optimism that the ENP can simply be extended outward without taking into account the set of very different strategic and political factors encountered in more distant regions'.

A lesson to be drawn is that Central Asia and the Gulf are regions 'where geopolitical and geo-economic calculations still compromise the EU's focus on democracy promotion'. In fact, after the so-called 'Arab Spring', 'political trends in ENP countries have not necessarily spread outwards to the broader "neighbours of the neighbours" band of states'. The challenges are huge as some of the 'basic principles' of the ENP 'have little traction in these two regions; this is the case in particular with the uploading of EU rules and proposed integrative initiatives'. In fact, 'even if the EU's commitment was stronger', the Central Asian and Gulf 'political regimes do not seem propitious to pro-reform influences'.

Concrete opportunities for connecting the neighbours of the EU's neighbours

The third part of this volume is about more concrete opportunities for connecting the neighbours of the EU's neighbours. The first chapter focuses on the EU's approach towards sub-regional economic integration in its broader neighbourhood and the second on financing investments connecting the neighbours of the EU's neighbours. The two last chapters are devoted to sectoral issues where there is an important potential for transnational cooperation: energy and transboundary water management.

Rethinking the EU's support to sub-regional economic integration

Maud Fichet, Enrique Ibáñez and Veronika Orbetsova investigate 'why and how the EU is engaging with the sub-regional economic integration processes that have developed in its broader neighbourhood'. The chosen case studies are the Agadir Process, the Gulf Cooperation Council (GCC) and the Eurasian economic integration process. The authors argue that the EU has taken a 'building' approach in the case of the Agadir Process, a 'bridging' approach in relation to the GCC and a 'blocking' approach *vis-à-vis* the Eurasian Customs Union. As the EU's approach is 'shaped by the degree of compatibility between the European model and that of the other region', the Agadir Process offers 'the highest degree of compatibility', whereas the GCC has been 'compatible only to the extent that the two projects openly adhered to the liberal aspirations of free-trade and market openness'. The Eurasian regional integration process, however, 'demonstrated how the incongruity of the projects initially led to a standstill, which is forcing the EU to reappraise its approach'.

Two major lessons have been identified. First, given the current crisis context, 'the EU has the opportunity to adapt its approach to regional integration and, thus, pursue a more adequate policy'. Second, 'sub-regional integration cannot take hold in the absence of political stability, a reality that permeates all three regions'. The EU would prefer to pursue the 'building' approach if two conditions are met: the first one is that 'regulatory approximation is seen as crucial, even if there is no geographical contiguity'; and the second one is that the 'partner countries need to be willing to actively engage with the EU'. Moreover, the 'positive approach of the EU toward the Black Sea Economic Cooperation initiative proves that an alternative to the "blocking" strategy toward sub-regional integration mechanisms in the post-Soviet space is conceivable'.

Promoting investments connecting the neighbours of the EU's neighbours

For Alessandro Carano 'the investments connecting the "neighbours of the EU's neighbours" are of strategic political and economic relevance to the EU, the world's largest economy, as a global player' and the EU 'needs to promote economic development and trade with developing economies, a large number of which are located in Africa and in Asia'. For him, the 'interconnections between these countries and the EU's neighbours, and thus the EU, are becoming increasingly relevant for the EU's own interests in terms of security, stability, access to energy, economic growth, trade and investment'. One of the proposals is to take a 'broader strategic approach in promoting investments connecting the "neighbours of the EU's neighbours" on the basis of mutual interest' and to 'include a focus on sectoral studies, reforms underpinning gradual economic integration, the planning of networks and the preparation of a pipeline of projects'. Moreover, there is 'an opportunity to pool resources and reduce the fragmentation of fora, taskforces and financial instruments' and an 'integrated investment framework to finance priority investments in socio-economic sectors could be considered'.

Several good practices were also identified, such as the development, in the framework of the EU's Development Cooperation Instrument, of a Pan-African Programme to 'complement existing instruments in both North and sub-Saharan Africa to overcome fragmentation on the continent'; the extension of the Trans-European Transport Network (TEN-T) beyond the EU to 'facilitate the flow of goods and passengers and increase economic activity with neighbouring regions'; and the extension of the Trans-European Energy Network (TEN-E) beyond the EU to 'support the security of energy supply to the EU and diversify the sources of energy'.

Using the potential for energy cooperation in the EU's broader neighbourhood

Johannes Theiss compares the geopolitical and governance perspectives on EU energy cooperation with the broader neighbourhood. He finds that 'energy issues play a role within EU–Sahel relations'. Further east, 'energy relations with the Middle East are more visible but also more fragmented', while the EU–OPEC energy dialogues 'constitute weak fora to exert any form of governance' and 'financial engagement under the EU budget has been limited'. At the bilateral level, the 'future direction of Iraq remains unclear', but 'there appears to be a case for EU governance in the country' with the Partnership and Cooperation Agreement and the Memorandum of Understanding (MoU) on Strategic Partnership in Energy. Iran 'may follow the trajectory of the partners in Central Asia, provided that the nuclear issue is solved'. Obviously, energy issues are of 'paramount importance' in Central Asia, and 'governance frameworks exist and there are plans for them to be enhanced' as the

> EU Central Asian Strategy prioritizes energy and transport, a PCA for Kazakhstan is in place and one is under way for Turkmenistan, MoUs on Energy Cooperation have been concluded, countries apply the rule book of the ECT, and connections with the ENP are being promoted, *inter alia*, through financing under the ENPI.

Theiss concludes that 'there is a great deal of untapped potential for energy cooperation between the EU and its broader neighbourhood beyond geopolitics'.

Developing transboundary water management

Anders Jägerskog's chapter concentrates on the 'challenges that the EU is facing with regard to transboundary water management in its broader neighbourhood' and how the EU can promote 'cooperation over shared waters by clearly outlining the benefits of cooperation'. Among the lessons identified is, first of all, the need to understand what drives cooperation in this sector. In this regard, various drivers have to be taken into consideration. For example, at the internal level, 'improved cooperation on transboundary waters is critical for developing energy markets in many places'. The external drivers such as 'support from outside actors' (United Nations, World Bank, EU) are also important 'resources for countries to work together' as this 'generates further cooperation'. However, 'for a donor to engage in building cooperative structures in a shared river basin, courage and a vision that must transcend the lifetime of a single project are required'. In this respect, the good practice of the UNDP 'Shared Waters Partnership' programme, 'geared solely to support and encourage dialogue' has been identified and the recommendation is that 'such initiatives should be increased and strengthened'.

Another crucial aspect to be taken into account in the 'political analysis of transboundary waters' is the 'study of the quality of the cooperation'. In this regard, three important questions must be taken into consideration: 'On whose terms is the cooperation happening? Is there power asymmetry between the riparians? Is there scope for activities that would be geared towards "levelling the playing field" in this respect?' These questions are crucial as 'research seems to suggest that if parties can engage on more equal terms the prospects for equitable and lasting cooperative processes increase'. The general conclusion is also of relevance in terms of lessons: it is 'critical to connect water with other key areas such as energy, security, food markets, regional integration and trade'.

Conclusion

In sum, there is considerable contrast among the results of the various analyses. The first series of political, legal and security issues are key challenges for the EU itself, as they affect directly its own prosperity, stability and security. These challenges are also very sensitive and, in most cases, a long-term approach will be necessary to develop fruitful cooperation in the broader neighbourhood. The second series of economic and societal issues is also to be addressed in terms of challenges, but there is perhaps, compared to the first category, a better potential for developing new proposals in the short to medium term. The last series of issues is where the EU can act more quickly and develop a series of concrete measures in order to better connect the EU, its neighbours and their neighbours.

First, there are a number of key challenges that need to be carefully handled by the European Union. At the level of migration and border controls, the challenges are not new (Khader and de Wenden 2010). Despite the 'communitization' of migration management, the EU is still confronted with the lack of a comprehensive strategic vision that is mainly due to the political instrumentalization of this issue by some political parties in the EU Member States. What is crucial is to avoid considering the EU's neighbours as being a kind of 'buffer zone' to stop illegal migration originating from their own neighbours and beyond. However, as stated by Sarah Wolff, the 'Sahara–Sahel region has become the "new frontier" for security issues and controlling the EU's borders and irregular migration'. The externalization of border controls entails serious risks in terms of fundamental rights protection. Of course, differentiation is also to be taken into account. For example, and as stressed by Valeria Bonavita, 'while cooperation in border management seems to be migration-oriented with countries in the Sahel and the Horn of Africa, a trade facilitation and anti-trafficking approach seems to inspire the EU's cooperation in border control with the Central Asian republics'. Nevertheless, what is key for the EU is to develop a consistent long-term approach towards its broader neighbourhood in this respect.

In terms of security issues, the picture also shows contrasts. As far as the CSDP is concerned, as underlined by Alyson J.K. Bailes and Pál Dunay, there is again a strong differentiation between the three regions as outside Africa the leverage of the EU is very limited. There is thus an obvious need to update again the European Security Strategy (European Union 2003; 2008) so as to define more clearly the limits and the ambitions of the EU in this area. Terrorism is certainly a threat that also needs to be addressed, as shown by Gilles de Kerchove and Christiane Höhn, in a 'comprehensive fashion based on the rule of law and human rights'. The lesson of the military operations against the 'Islamic State of Iraq and the Levant' (ISIL) is that this will take much time and financial and military efforts.

Second, there are opportunities to create bridges at the level of trade and development cooperation. But this should be carefully handled. As shown by Sieglinde Gstöhl, in terms of trade, it is crucial to take into consideration 'the "hub-and-spoke" pattern of the relationship between the EU and its partners which militates against regional cooperation'. Indeed, the trade relations among the EU's neighbours and with their neighbours should be prioritized from a 'win–win' perspective.

The specificities of some neighbours of the EU's neighbours must also be taken into consideration when devising development strategies. For instance, Tressia Hobeika stressed that 'all the Sahelian states figure in the bottom 30 of the United Nations Development Programme's ... Human Development Index'. For development in the Sahel, the Horn of Africa and Central Asia more attention should be paid to women's empowerment. It is essential that women take part at 'all levels of economic planning', as put forward by Zuhal Yeşilyurt Gündüz. At the level of democracy promotion, Alexander Warkotsch and Richard Youngs stress that, for the time being, the potential for the EU to promote democracy is quite limited in the neighbours of its neighbours. Nevertheless, the EU cannot take the risk of applying a 'double standard' approach *vis-à-vis* its neighbours and their neighbours. Therefore, it is absolutely essential for the EU to implement a consistent approach in promoting democracy and human rights in its broader neighbourhood.

Third, there is an important short-term potential for broadening the investments connecting the neighbours of the EU's neighbours in a wide perspective, as highlighted by Alessandro Carano. The energy and water sectors, studied in this volume by Johannes Theiss and Anders Jägerskog, are two strategic areas of major importance for the EU's partners and could generate important gains for populations often deprived of basic resources and access to education. Moreover, there is an opportunity for the EU to rethink its support to sub-regional economic integration, notably in Eurasia, as recommended by Maud Fichet, Enrique Ibáñez and Veronika Orbetsova.

Two broader EU policy frameworks can be used to promote a more consistent approach *vis-à-vis* the broader neighbourhood. The Strategic Partnership with the Mediterranean and the Middle East (SPMME), which encompasses not only most of the members of the Arab League but also Iran, Israel and Turkey, could be reactivated, as all issues addressed in this volume have been identified as potential areas for cooperation under this peculiar framework. The development of the opportunities offered by the Joint Africa–EU Strategy (JAES) is also not to be neglected for the broader neighbourhood, given that many potential areas for cooperation identified in this volume are considered as priorities for the JAES (such as security, human rights, regional economic integration, trade and infrastructure, energy, and migration and mobility). Further east, the Central Asia Strategy could also be better connected to the Eastern Partnership and the Black Sea Synergy, notably in terms of infrastructures and networks.

As far as the methodology is concerned, it is also obvious that the use of the 'Jean Monnet method', which inspired the 9 May 1950 declaration of Robert Schuman, is, to a certain extent, of relevance as any broader neighbourhood strategy should be *progressively* built through concrete achievements which first create a *de facto* solidarity. Also the human factor is to be kept in mind, women and youth being of particular importance as clearly demonstrated by Zuhal Yeşilyurt Gündüz.

Despite the heterogeneity of the neighbours of the EU's neighbours and the manifold challenges that have to be faced, there is a potential for reinforced cooperation. The EU needs, however, to increase the funding devoted to inter-regional cooperation (under the framework of the new 'Neighbourhood Wide' programme for example)[1] and to extend, when possible, actions and good practices to its broader neighbourhood. The EU needs also to improve synergies among different financial instruments and to carry out a 'defragmentation' of its current approach to its broader neighbourhood. In this regard, the potential of the new horizontal financial regulation 'laying down common rules and procedures for the implementation of the Union's instruments for financing external action' should be fully exploited (European Parliament and Council of the European Union 2014). In order to do so, dialogue and training, associating partners from the EU and the three regions, has to be promoted and rapidly developed on a large-scale basis. In terms of co-ownership it could be useful to think about new frameworks for developing informal political dialogues in a spirit of partnership, associating the civil society at large and in particular local actors with regard to some of the key challenges identified in this volume. It is a matter of political will and strategic thinking.

Note

1 See   http://ec.europa.eu/enlargement/neighbourhood/neighbourhood-wide/index_en.htm (accessed October 2014).

References

Brian, T. and F. Laczko (eds) (2014) *Fatal Journeys: Tracking Lives Lost during Migration*, Geneva: International Organization for Migration.

European Parliament and Council of the European Union (2014) 'Regulation (EU) No 236/2014 of 11 March 2014 Laying Down Common Rules and Procedures for the Implementation of the Union's Instruments for Financing External Action', *Official Journal of the European Union*, L77/95, 15 March, 77–84.

European Union (2003) '*A Secure Europe in a Better World*', *European Security Strategy*, Brussels, 12 December, www.consilium.europa.eu/uedocs/cmsUpload/78367.pdf (accessed October 2014).

European Union (2008) *Report on the Implementation of the European Security Strategy – Providing Security in a Changing World*, Brussels, 11 December, S407/08, www.consilium.europa.eu/ueDocs/cms_Data/docs/pressdata/EN/reports/104630.pdf (accessed October 2014).

Juncker, J.-C. (2014) 'A New Start for Europe: My Agenda for Jobs, Growth, Fairness and Democratic Change', Strasbourg, 15 July, http://ec.europa.eu/priorities/docs/pg_en.pdf (accessed October 2014).

Khader, B. and C. de Wenden (2010) 'Les dynamiques de mouvement de personnes', 10 papers for Barcelona 2010, Institut Européen de la Méditerranée and Institut d'Etudes de Sécurité de l'UE, mai, www.iss.europa.eu/uploads/media/10papers_07_Les-dynamiques-de-mouvement-de-personnes.pdf (accessed October 2014).

Lannon, E. (2014) 'An Economic Response to the Crisis: Towards a New Generation of Deep and Comprehensive Free Trade Areas with the Mediterranean Partners Countries', in *The Euromed Region after the Arab Spring and the New Generation of DCFTAs*, Brussels: European Parliament Committee on International Trade (INTA), 37–63.

Van der Loo, G., P. Van Elsuwege and R. Petrov (2014) 'The EU–Ukraine Association Agreement: Assessment of an Innovative Legal Instrument', *EUI Working Papers*, LAW 2014/09, Florence: European University Institute.

Index

Page numbers in *italics* denote tables.

For Product Safety Concerns and Information please contact our EU
representative GPSR@taylorandfrancis.com
Taylor & Francis Verlag GmbH, Kaufingerstraße 24, 80331 München, Germany

www.ingramcontent.com/pod-product-compliance
Lightning Source LLC
Chambersburg PA
CBHW060138280326
41932CB00012B/1552